I WISH I COULD SLEEP IN MY FUTON...

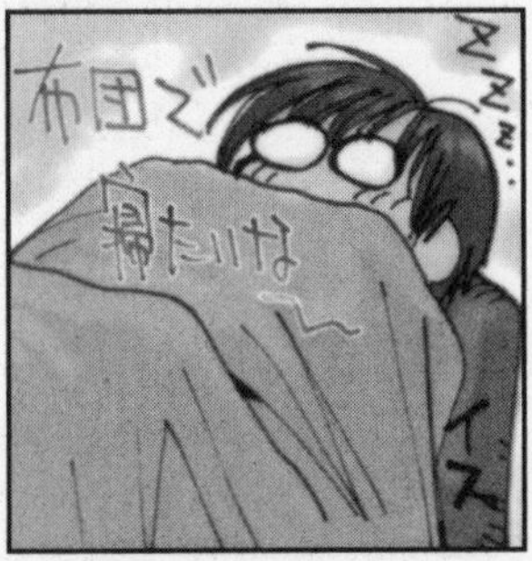
布団で寝たいな～
イス

叶 恭弘

I don't believe in anything as unscientific as fortune telling, gods or ghosts. I'm often told that there are things in the world that can't be explained by science, but that's only because there isn't enough data or man's ability to understand hasn't progressed that far yet. Even so, I love manga and movies about psychic powers and ghosts. In fact, those are pretty much the only themes I'm interested in. I suppose somewhere in my heart I long for the existence of those unexplained mysteries.

—Yasuhiro Kano, 2003

Yasuhiro Kano made his manga debut in 1992 with *Black City*, which won *Weekly Shonen Jump*'s Hop★Step Award for new artists. From 1993 to 2001, he illustrated Mugen's serialized novels *Midnight Magic* in *Jump Novel* magazine, and also produced a manga adaptation. *Pretty Face* appeared in *Weekly Shonen Jump* from 2002 to 2003. Kano's newest series, *M x O*, began running in *Weekly Shonen Jump* in 2006.

PRETTY FACE
VOL. 4

The SHONEN JUMP ADVANCED Manga Edition

STORY AND ART BY
YASUHIRO KANO

Translation & English Adaptation/Anita Sengupta
Touch-up Art & Lettering/Eric Erbes
Design/Hidemi Dunn
Editor/Jason Thompson

Editor in Chief, Books/Alvin Lu
Editor in Chief, Magazines/Marc Weidenbaum
VP of Publishing Licensing/Rika Inouye
VP of Sales/Gonzalo Ferreyra
Sr. VP of Marketing/Liza Coppola
Publisher/Hyoe Narita

PRETTY FACE © 2002 by Yasuhiro Kano. All rights reserved. First published in Japan in 2002 by SHUEISHA Inc., Tokyo. English translation rights in the United States of America and Canada arranged by SHUEISHA Inc. The stories, characters and incidents mentioned in this publication are entirely fictional.

Printed in the U.S.A.

Published by VIZ Media, LLC
P.O. Box 77010
San Francisco, CA 94107

SHONEN JUMP ADVANCED Manga Edition
10 9 8 7 6 5 4 3 2 1
First printing, February 2008

www.viz.com

www.shonenjump.com

Pretty Face

Vol. 4

STORY & ART BY
YASUHIRO KANO

CHARACTERS

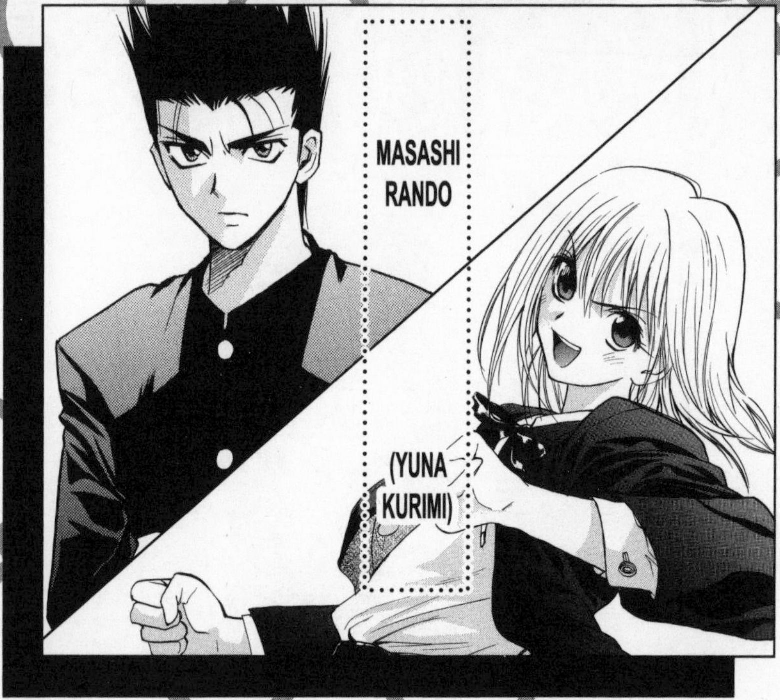
MASASHI RANDO
(YUNA KURIMI)

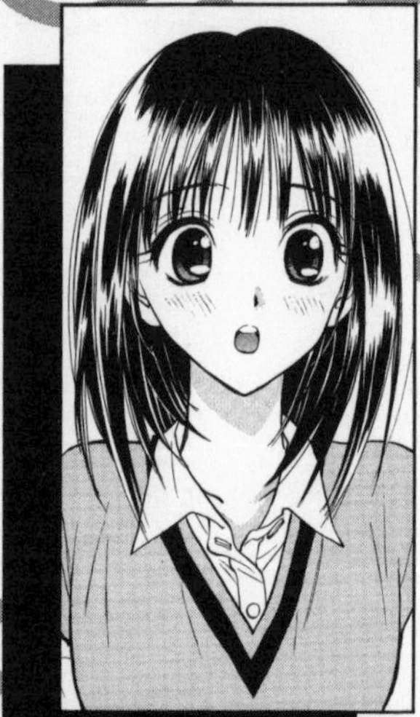

RINA KURIMI

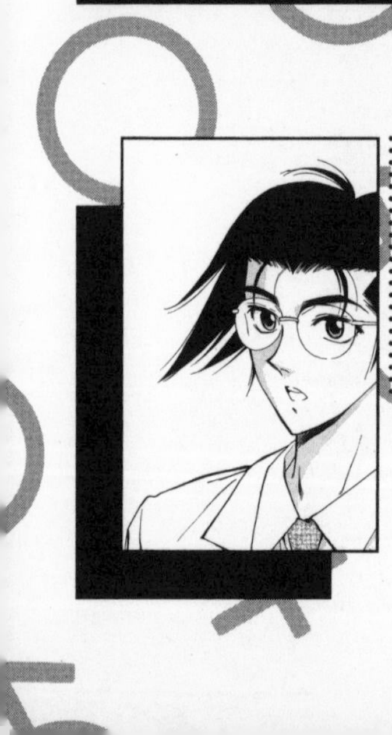

DR. MANABE

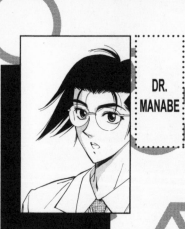

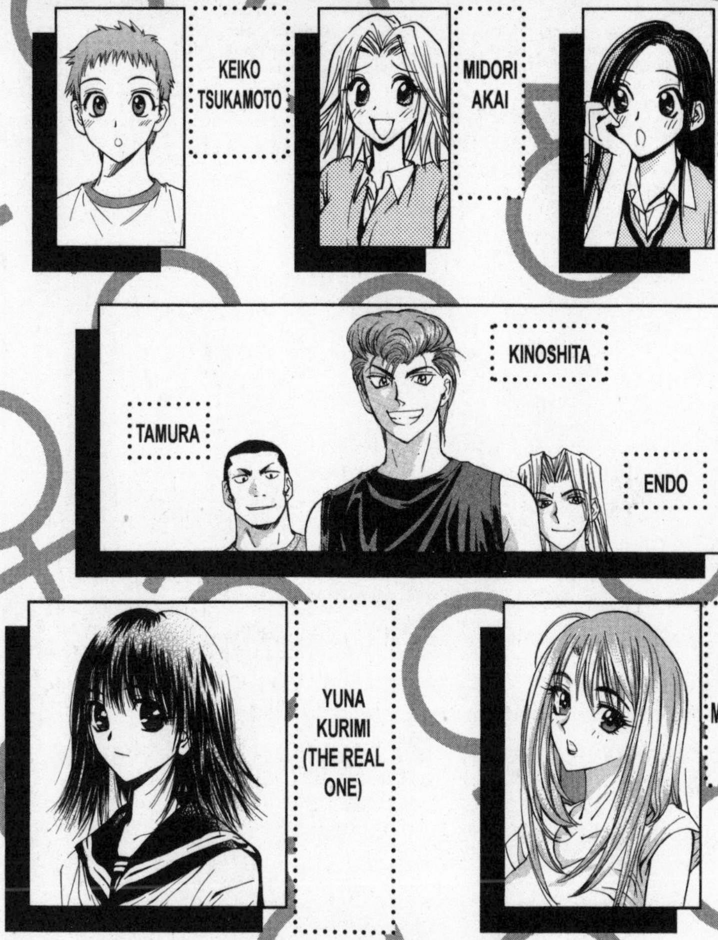
YUKIE SANO
MIDORI AKAI
KEIKO TSUKAMOTO
ENDO
KINOSHITA
TAMURA
MIWA MASUKO
YUNA KURIMI (THE REAL ONE)

STORY

On the way home from a karate tournament, teenage badass Masashi Rando is caught in a horrible bus accident. When he wakes up from his coma a year later, his disfigured face has been reconstructed into the image of *Rina Kurimi, the girl he has a crush on!* Not knowing what Rando originally looked like, the mad plastic surgeon Dr. Manabe used a photo in Rando's wallet as the model for his reconstruction. Abandoned by his friends and parents, Rando is mistaken for Rina's long-lost twin sister and adopted into her family. So far, Rando has managed to pass as a girl during clothes shopping, sleepovers and even swim class. But what about his noble goal of finding Rina's real twin sister...?

PRETTY FACE
Vol. 4
CONTENTS

Chapter 28: The Real One Found?!

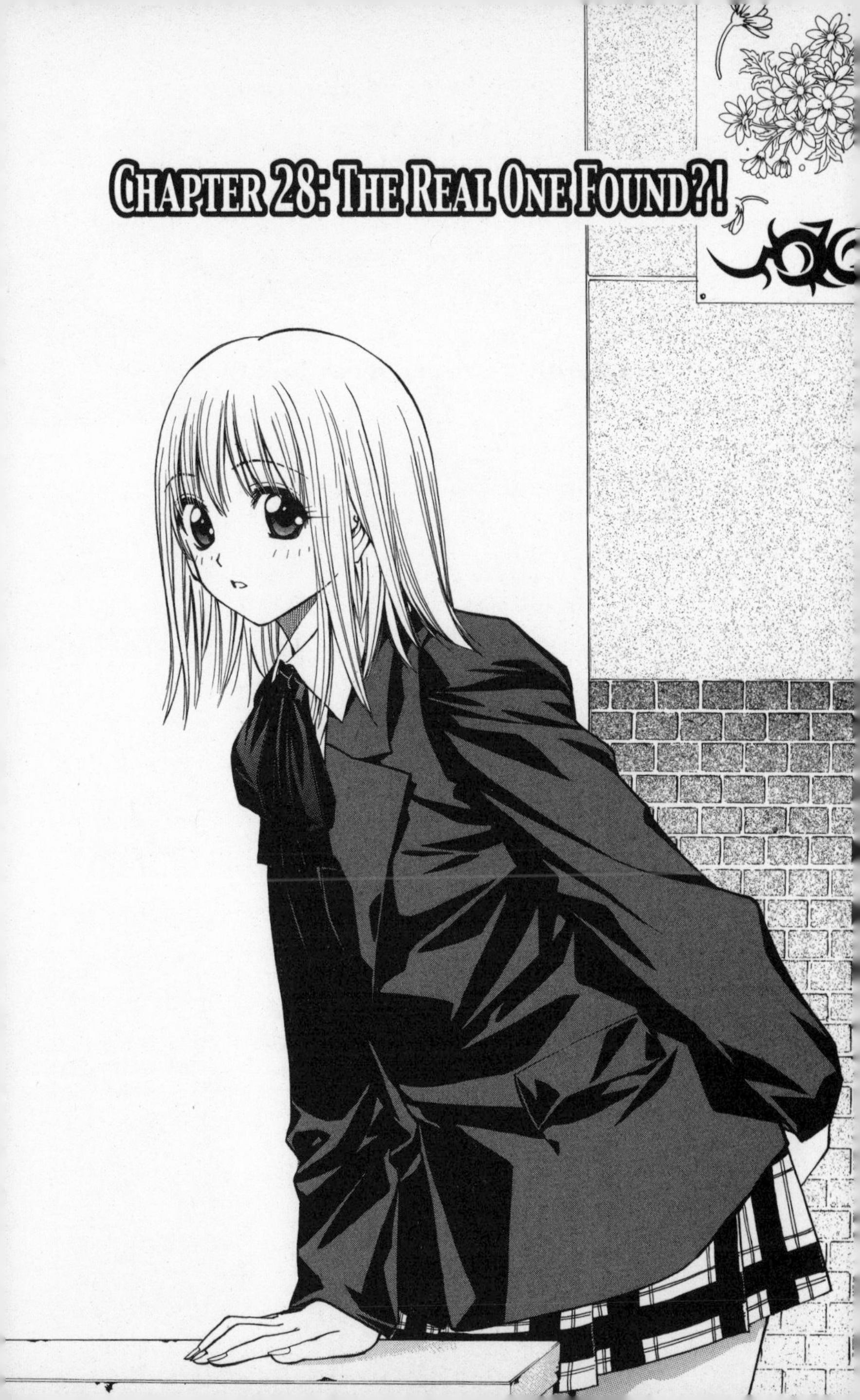

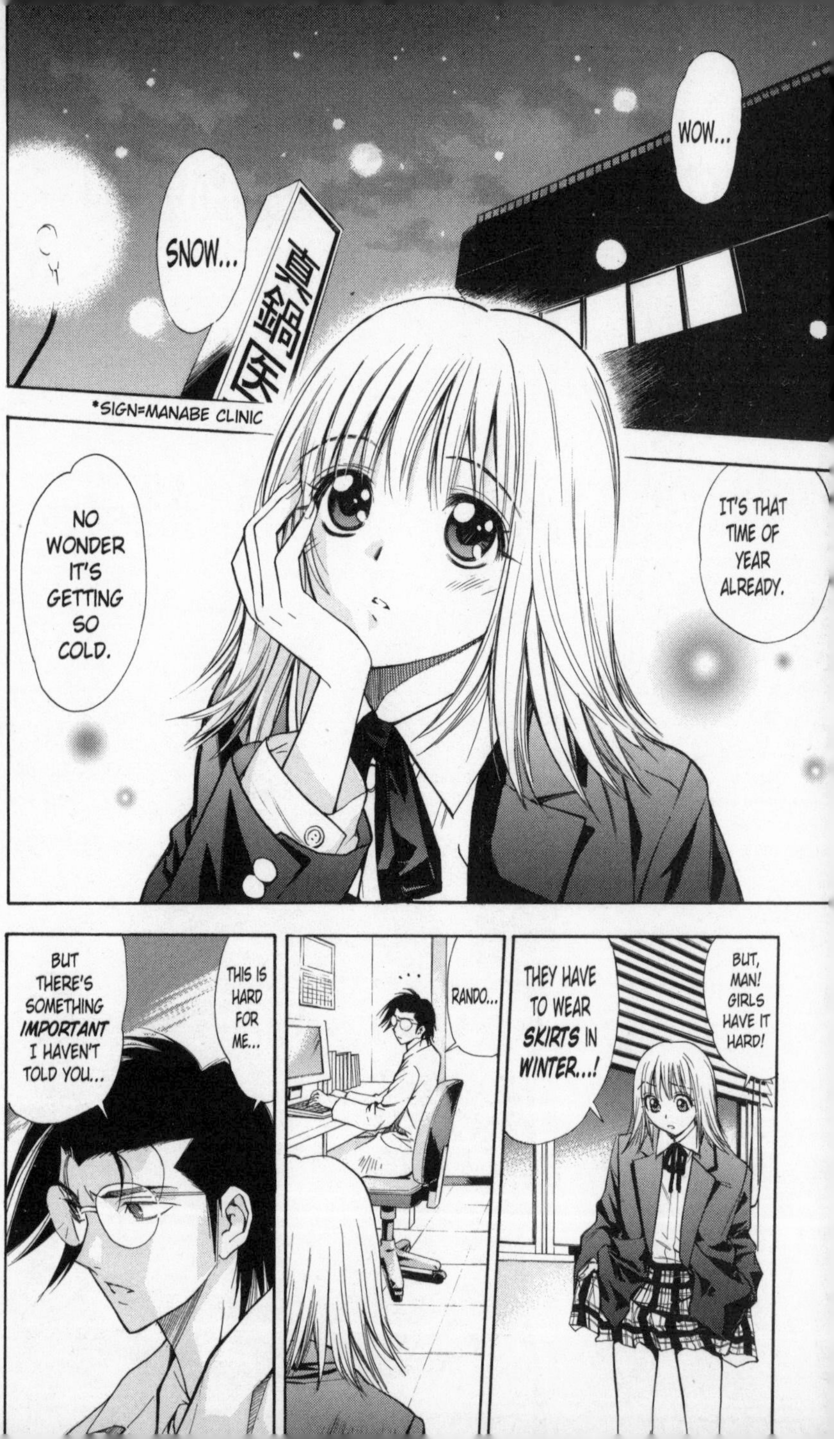
WOW...
SNOW...
*SIGN=MANABE CLINIC
IT'S THAT TIME OF YEAR ALREADY.
NO WONDER IT'S GETTING SO COLD.
BUT, MAN! GIRLS HAVE IT HARD!
THEY HAVE TO WEAR **SKIRTS** IN **WINTER...!**
RANDO...
. . .
THIS IS HARD FOR ME...
BUT THERE'S SOMETHING ***IMPORTANT*** I HAVEN'T TOLD YOU...

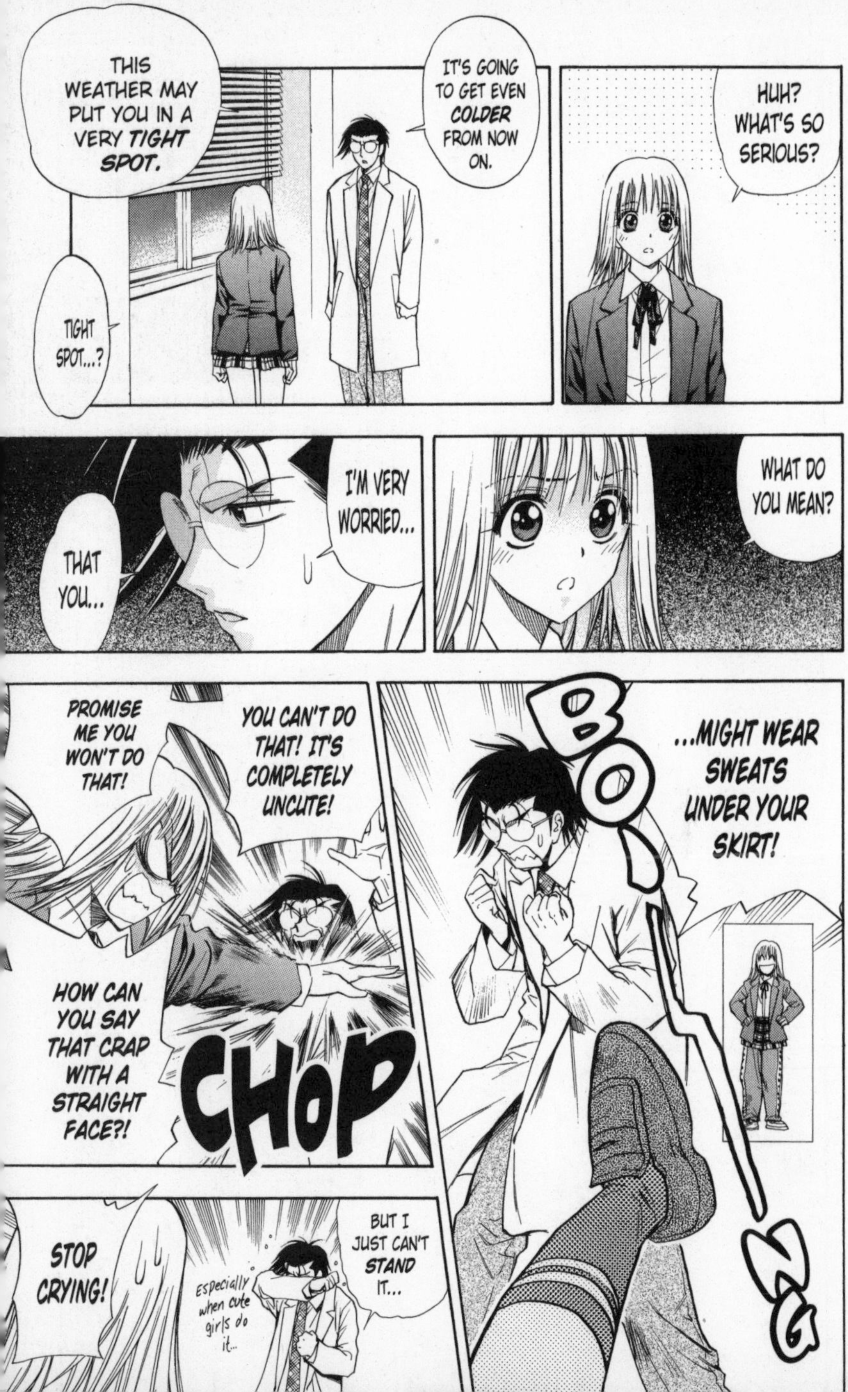
HUH? WHAT'S SO SERIOUS?
IT'S GOING TO GET EVEN COLDER FROM NOW ON.
THIS WEATHER MAY PUT YOU IN A VERY TIGHT SPOT.
TIGHT SPOT...?
WHAT DO YOU MEAN?
I'M VERY WORRIED...
THAT YOU...
BOING
...MIGHT WEAR SWEATS UNDER YOUR SKIRT!
YOU CAN'T DO THAT! IT'S COMPLETELY UNCUTE!
PROMISE ME YOU WON'T DO THAT!
CHOP
HOW CAN YOU SAY THAT CRAP WITH A STRAIGHT FACE?!
BUT I JUST CAN'T STAND IT...
Especially when cute girls do it...
STOP CRYING!

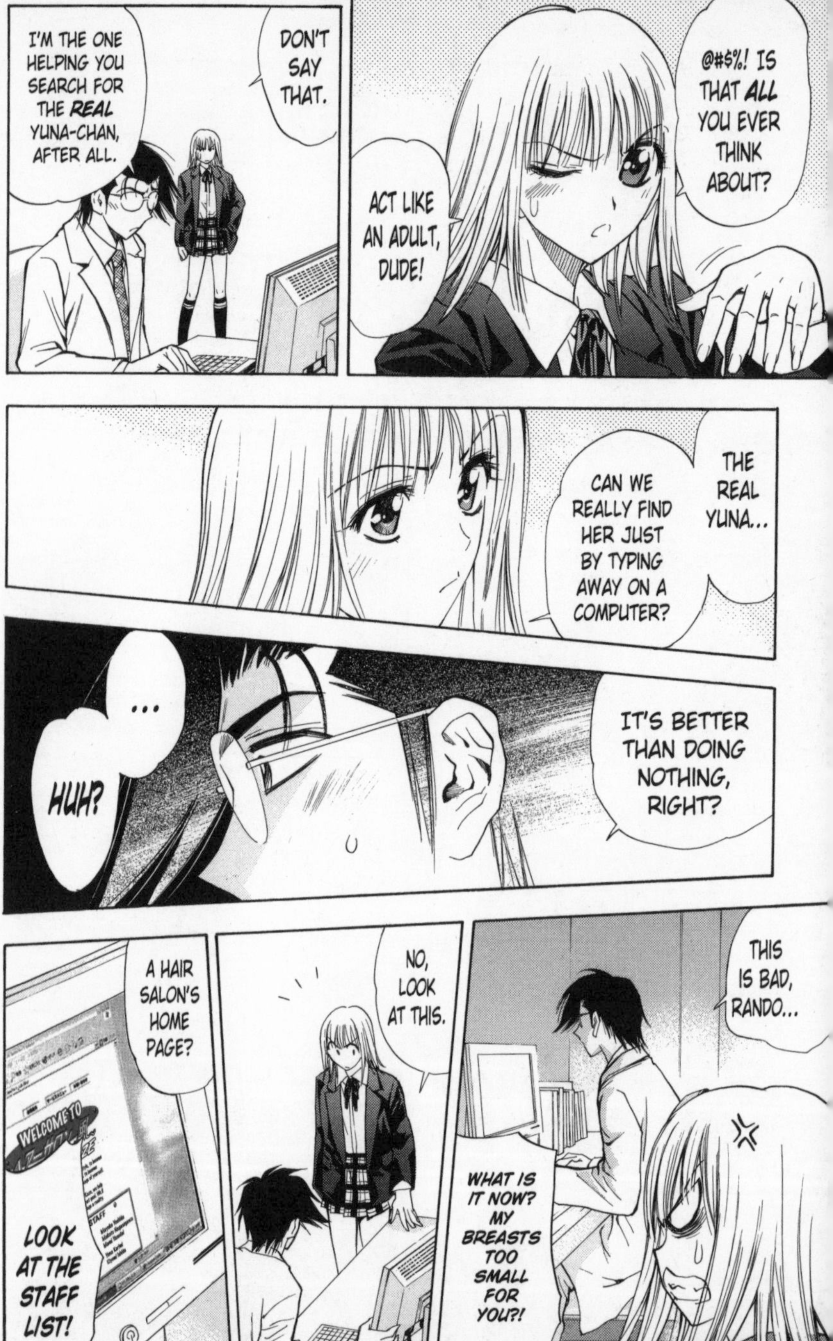
@#$%! IS THAT ALL YOU EVER THINK ABOUT?
ACT LIKE AN ADULT, DUDE!
DON'T SAY THAT.
I'M THE ONE HELPING YOU SEARCH FOR THE REAL YUNA-CHAN, AFTER ALL.
THE REAL YUNA...
CAN WE REALLY FIND HER JUST BY TYPING AWAY ON A COMPUTER?
IT'S BETTER THAN DOING NOTHING, RIGHT?
...
HUH?
THIS IS BAD, RANDO...
WHAT IS IT NOW? MY BREASTS TOO SMALL FOR YOU?!
NO, LOOK AT THIS.
A HAIR SALON'S HOME PAGE?
WELCOME TO
STAFF
LOOK AT THE STAFF LIST!

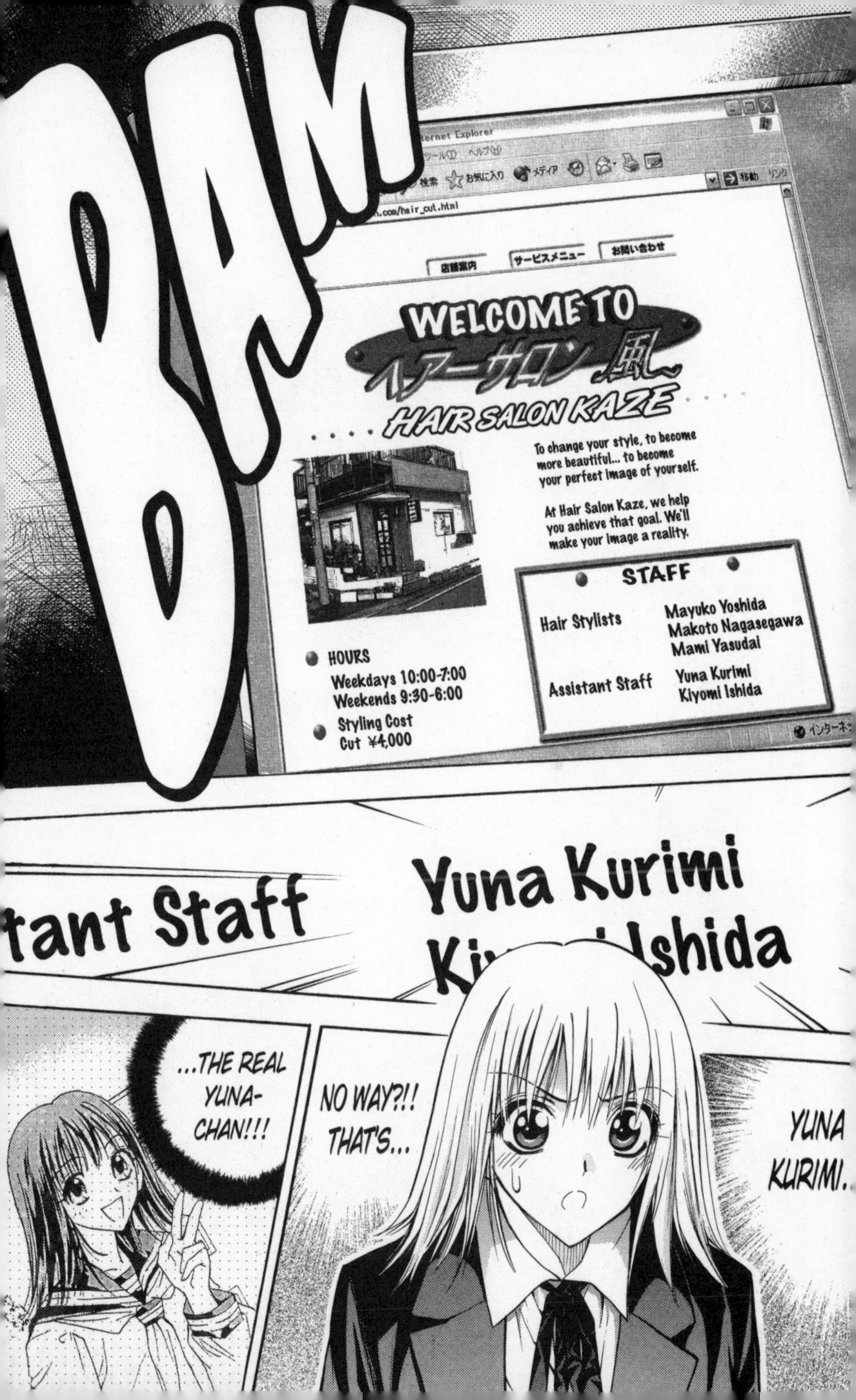
BAM
店舗案内
サービスメニュー
お問い合わせ
WELCOME TO
HAIR SALON KAZE
To change your style, to become more beautiful... to become your perfect image of yourself.
At Hair Salon Kaze, we help you achieve that goal. We'll make your image a reality.
STAFF
Hair Stylists
Mayuko Yoshida
Makoto Nagasegawa
Mami Yasudai
Assistant Staff
Yuna Kurimi
Kiyomi Ishida
HOURS
Weekdays 10:00-7:00
Weekends 9:30-6:00
Styling Cost
Cut ¥4,000
tant Staff
Yuna Kurimi
Ishida
YUNA KURIMI..
NO WAY?!! THAT'S...
...THE REAL YUNA-CHAN!!!

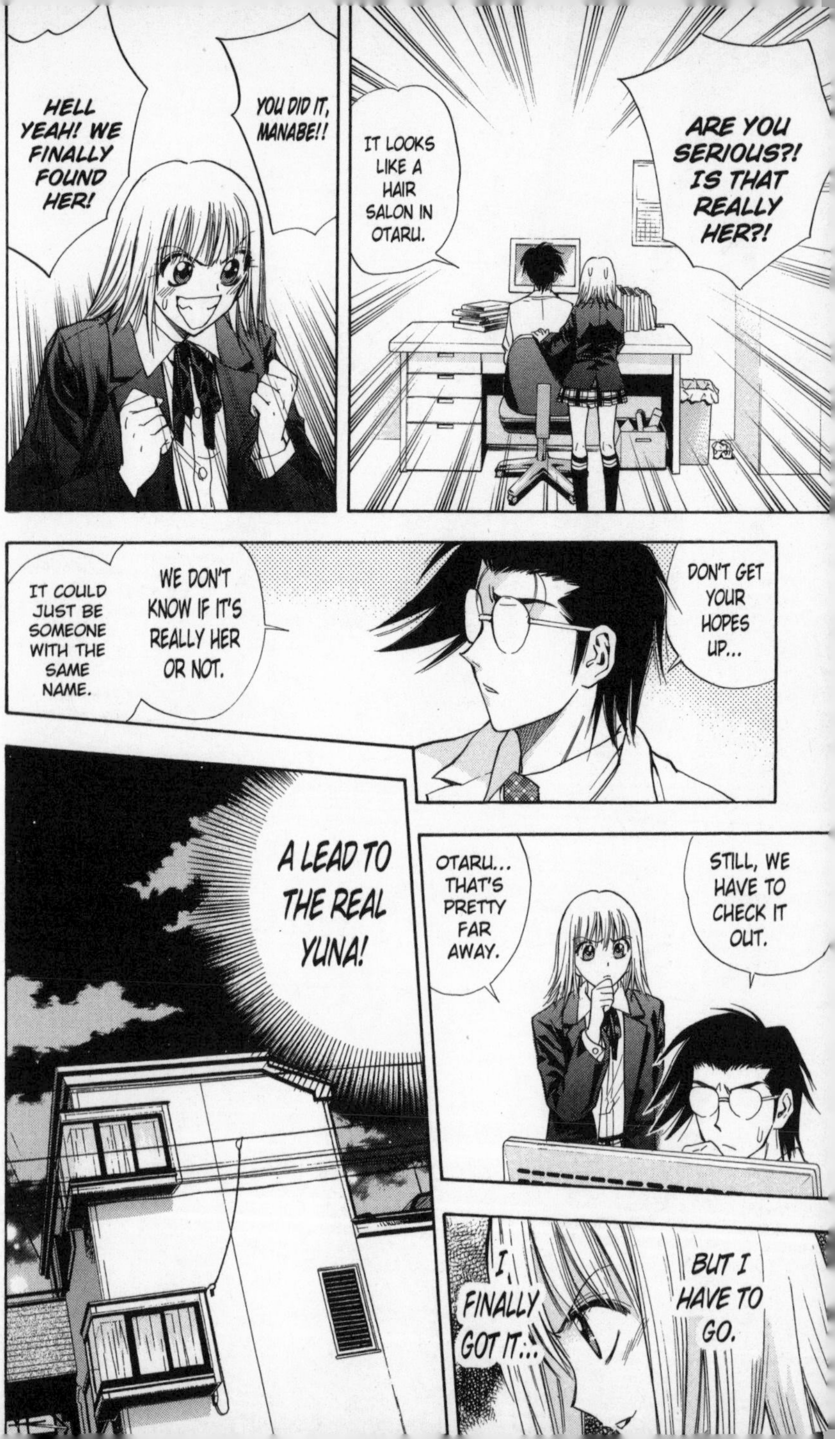
ARE YOU SERIOUS?! IS THAT REALLY HER?!
IT LOOKS LIKE A HAIR SALON IN OTARU.
YOU DID IT, MANABE!!
HELL YEAH! WE FINALLY FOUND HER!
DON'T GET YOUR HOPES UP...
WE DON'T KNOW IF IT'S REALLY HER OR NOT.
IT COULD JUST BE SOMEONE WITH THE SAME NAME.
STILL, WE HAVE TO CHECK IT OUT.
OTARU... THAT'S PRETTY FAR AWAY.
BUT I HAVE TO GO.
I FINALLY GOT IT...
A LEAD TO THE REAL YUNA!

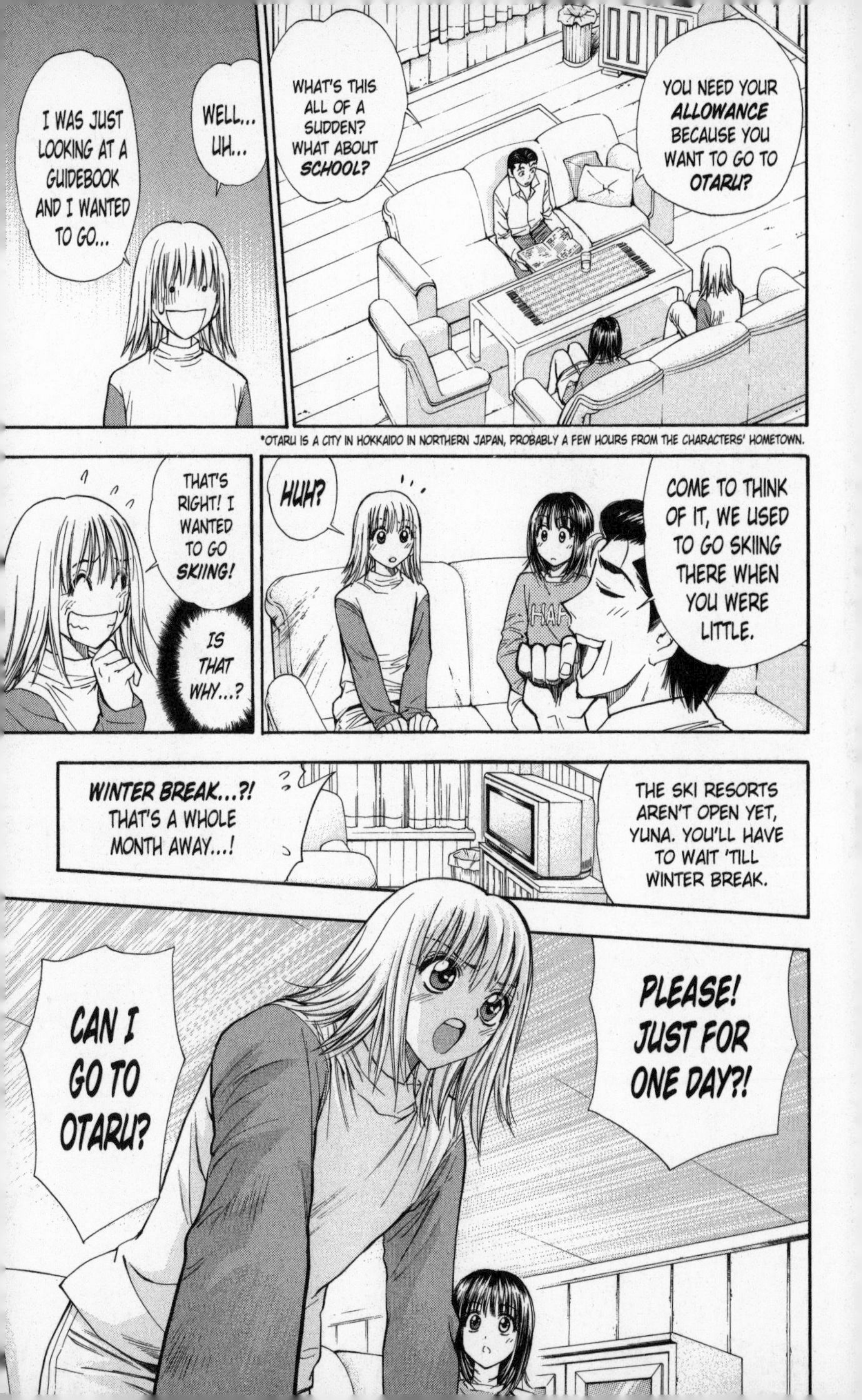
YOU NEED YOUR ALLOWANCE BECAUSE YOU WANT TO GO TO OTARU?
WHAT'S THIS ALL OF A SUDDEN? WHAT ABOUT SCHOOL?
WELL... UH...
I WAS JUST LOOKING AT A GUIDEBOOK AND I WANTED TO GO...
*OTARU IS A CITY IN HOKKAIDO IN NORTHERN JAPAN, PROBABLY A FEW HOURS FROM THE CHARACTERS' HOMETOWN.
COME TO THINK OF IT, WE USED TO GO SKIING THERE WHEN YOU WERE LITTLE.
HUH?
THAT'S RIGHT! I WANTED TO GO SKIING!
IS THAT WHY...?
THE SKI RESORTS AREN'T OPEN YET, YUNA. YOU'LL HAVE TO WAIT 'TILL WINTER BREAK.
WINTER BREAK...?! THAT'S A WHOLE MONTH AWAY...!
PLEASE! JUST FOR ONE DAY?!
CAN I GO TO OTARU?

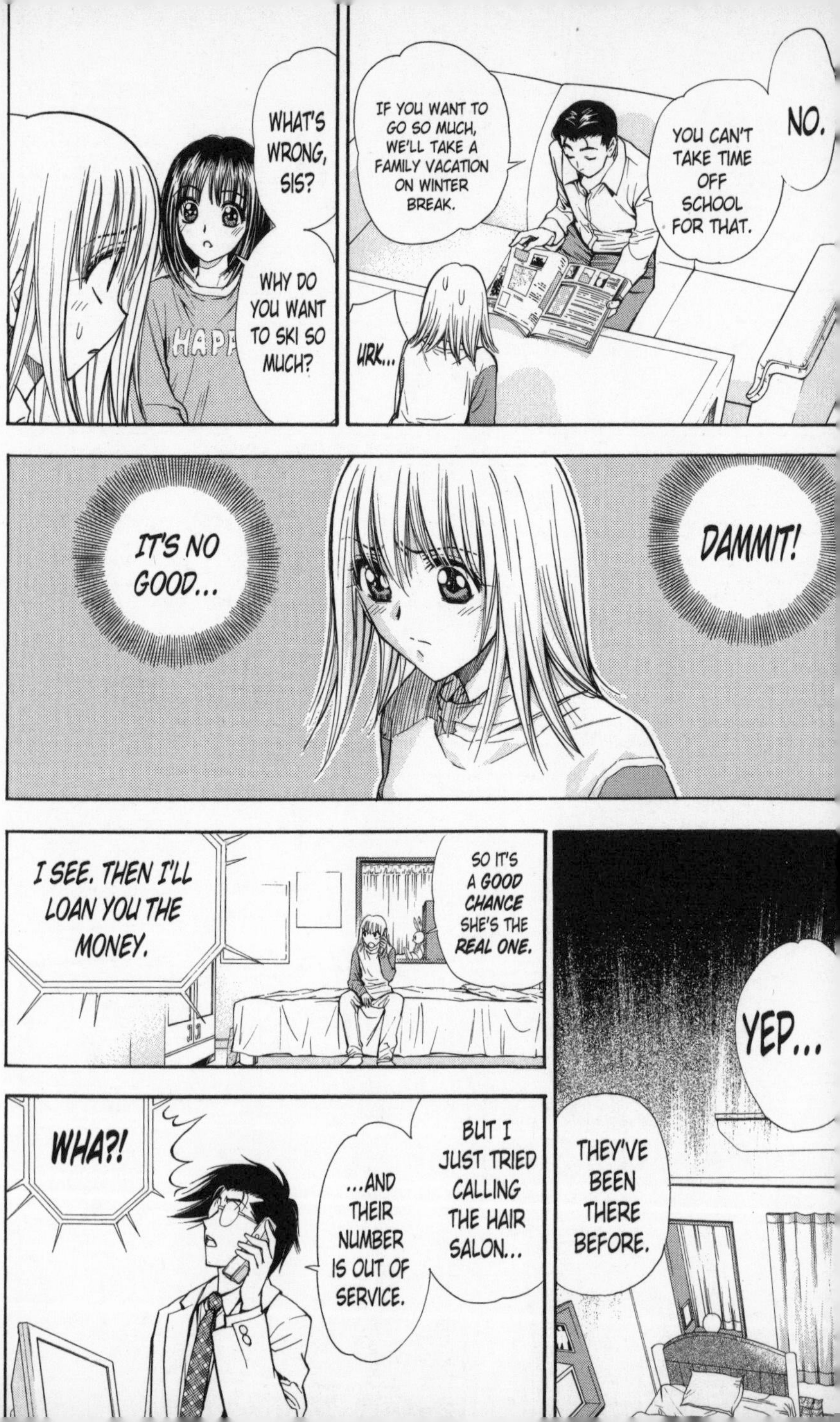

NO.
YOU CAN'T TAKE TIME OFF SCHOOL FOR THAT.
IF YOU WANT TO GO SO MUCH, WE'LL TAKE A FAMILY VACATION ON WINTER BREAK.
URK...
WHAT'S WRONG, SIS?
WHY DO YOU WANT TO SKI SO MUCH?
HAPP
DAMMIT!
IT'S NO GOOD...
YEP...
THEY'VE BEEN THERE BEFORE.
SO IT'S A GOOD CHANCE SHE'S THE REAL ONE.
I SEE. THEN I'LL LOAN YOU THE MONEY.
BUT I JUST TRIED CALLING THE HAIR SALON...
...AND THEIR NUMBER IS OUT OF SERVICE.
WHA?!

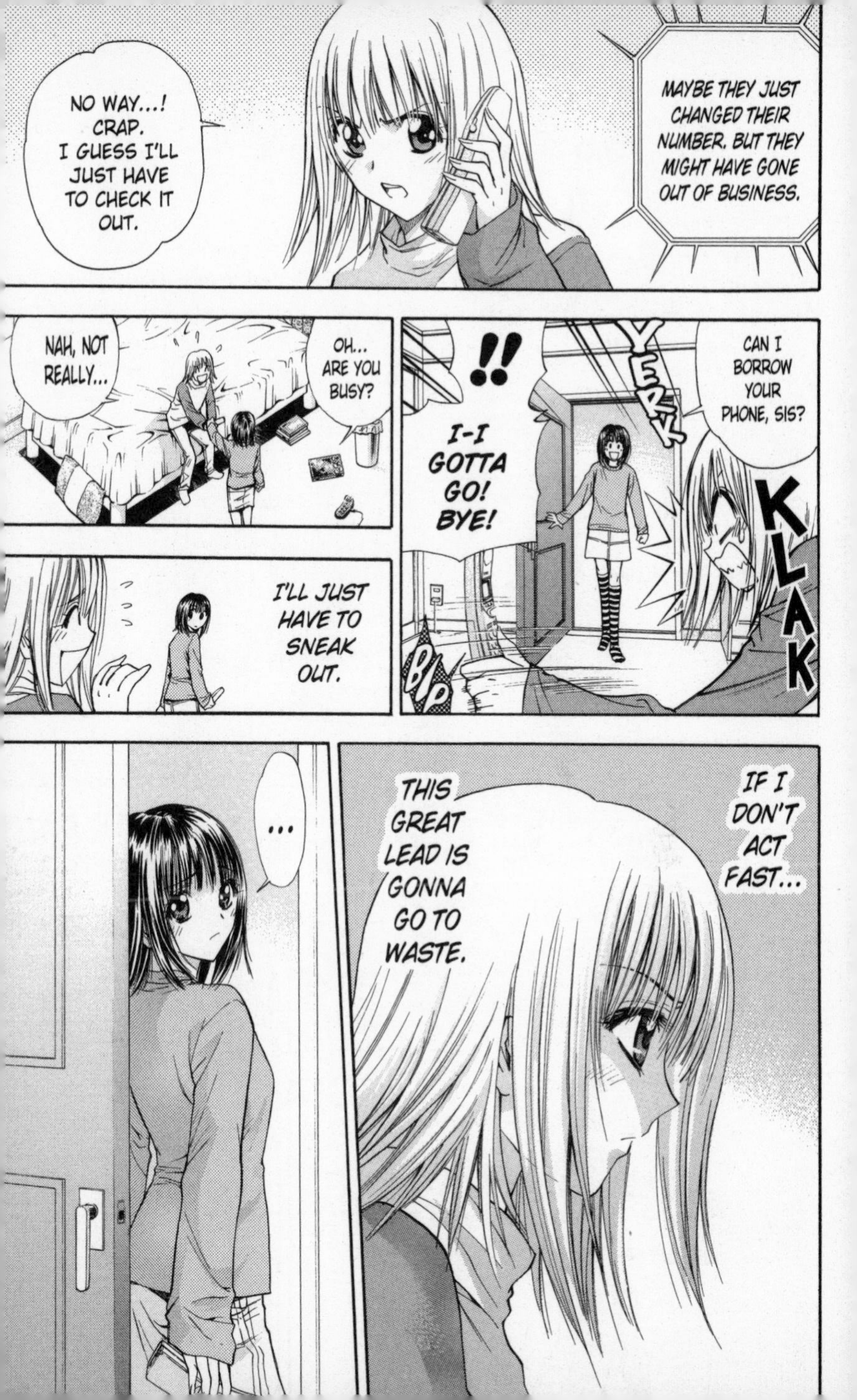
MAYBE THEY JUST CHANGED THEIR NUMBER. BUT THEY MIGHT HAVE GONE OUT OF BUSINESS.
NO WAY...! CRAP. I GUESS I'LL JUST HAVE TO CHECK IT OUT.
CAN I BORROW YOUR PHONE, SIS?
YERK
!!
KLAK
I-I GOTTA GO! BYE!
BIP
OH... ARE YOU BUSY?
NAH, NOT REALLY...
I'LL JUST HAVE TO SNEAK OUT.
IF I DON'T ACT FAST...
THIS GREAT LEAD IS GONNA GO TO WASTE.
...

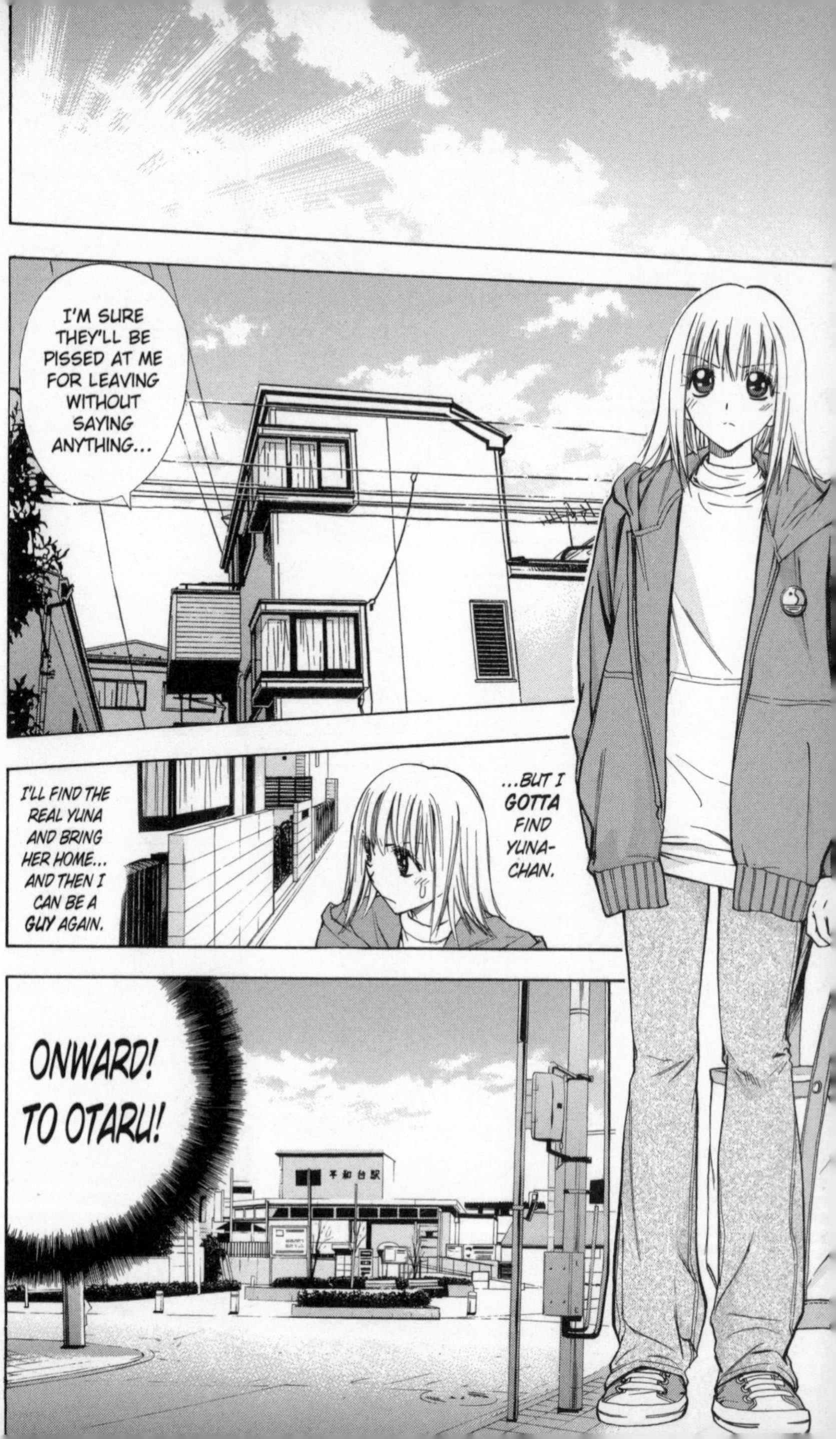
I'M SURE THEY'LL BE PISSED AT ME FOR LEAVING WITHOUT SAYING ANYTHING...
...BUT I GOTTA FIND YUNA-CHAN.
I'LL FIND THE REAL YUNA AND BRING HER HOME... AND THEN I CAN BE A GUY AGAIN.
ONWARD! TO OTARU!

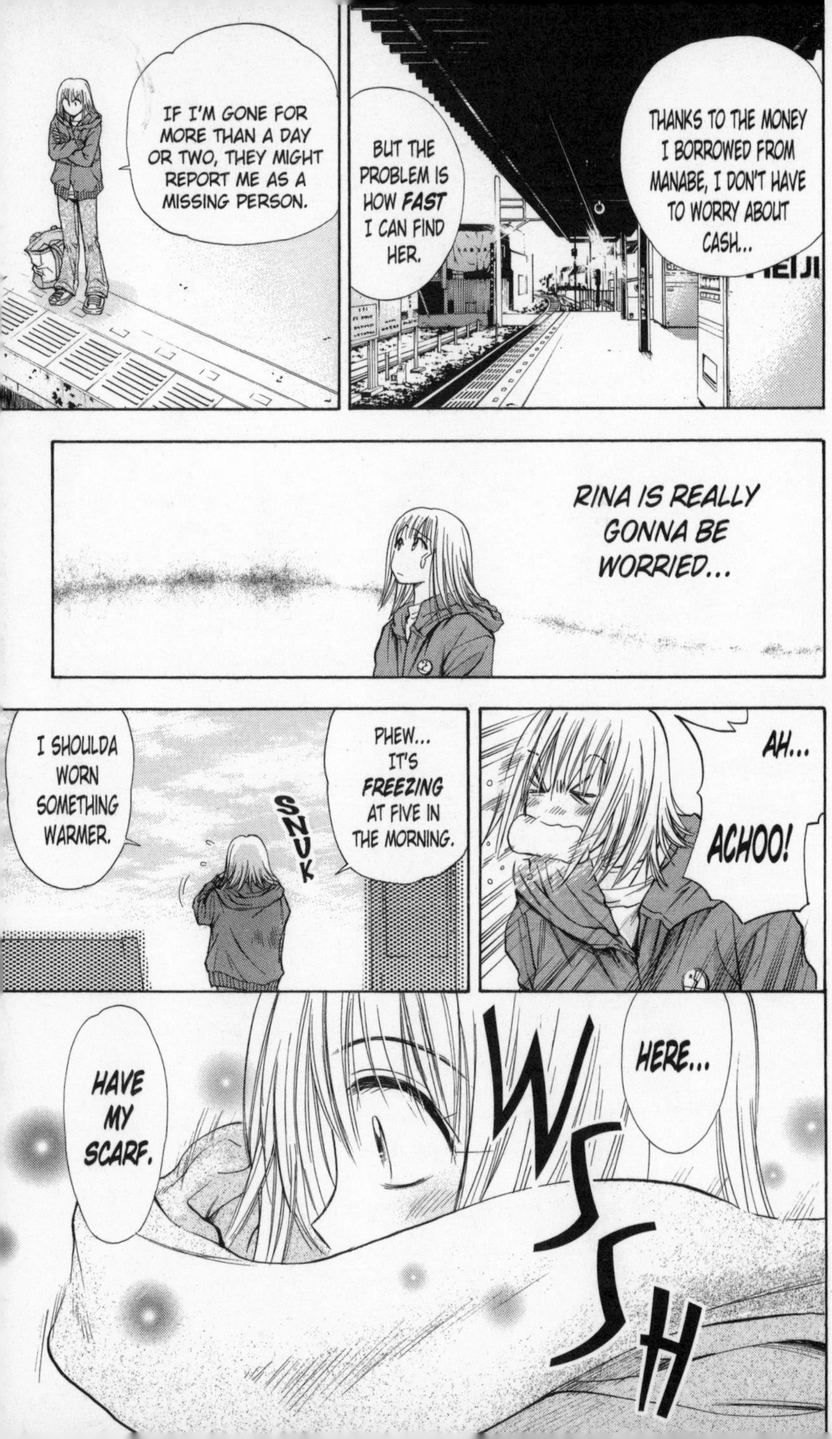
THANKS TO THE MONEY I BORROWED FROM MANABE, I DON'T HAVE TO WORRY ABOUT CASH...
BUT THE PROBLEM IS HOW FAST I CAN FIND HER.
IF I'M GONE FOR MORE THAN A DAY OR TWO, THEY MIGHT REPORT ME AS A MISSING PERSON.
RINA IS REALLY GONNA BE WORRIED...
AH...
ACHOO!
PHEW... IT'S FREEZING AT FIVE IN THE MORNING.
SNUK
I SHOULDA WORN SOMETHING WARMER.
HERE...
WSSH
HAVE MY SCARF.

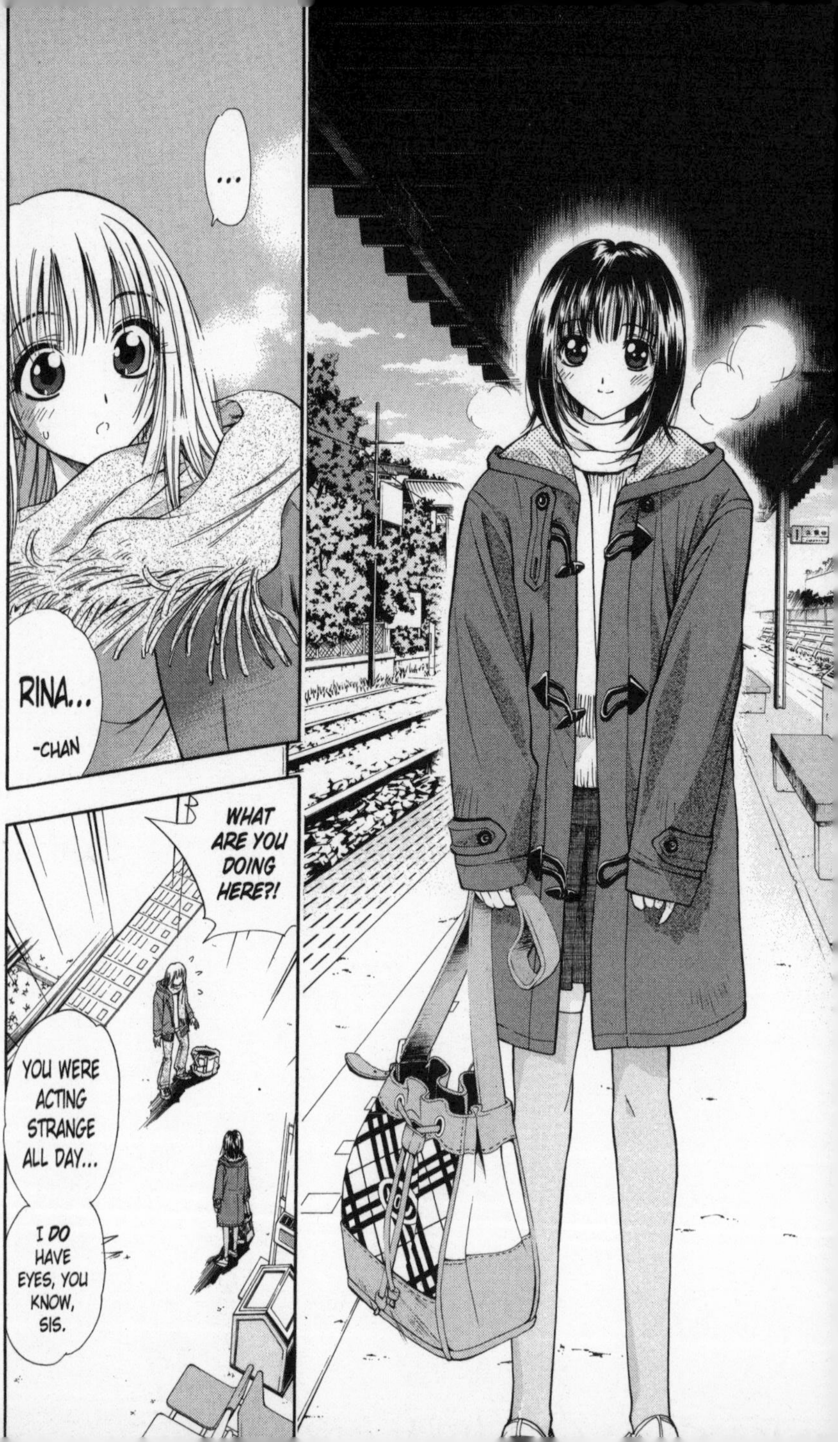
...
RINA... -CHAN
WHAT ARE YOU DOING HERE?!
YOU WERE ACTING STRANGE ALL DAY...
I DO HAVE EYES, YOU KNOW, SIS.

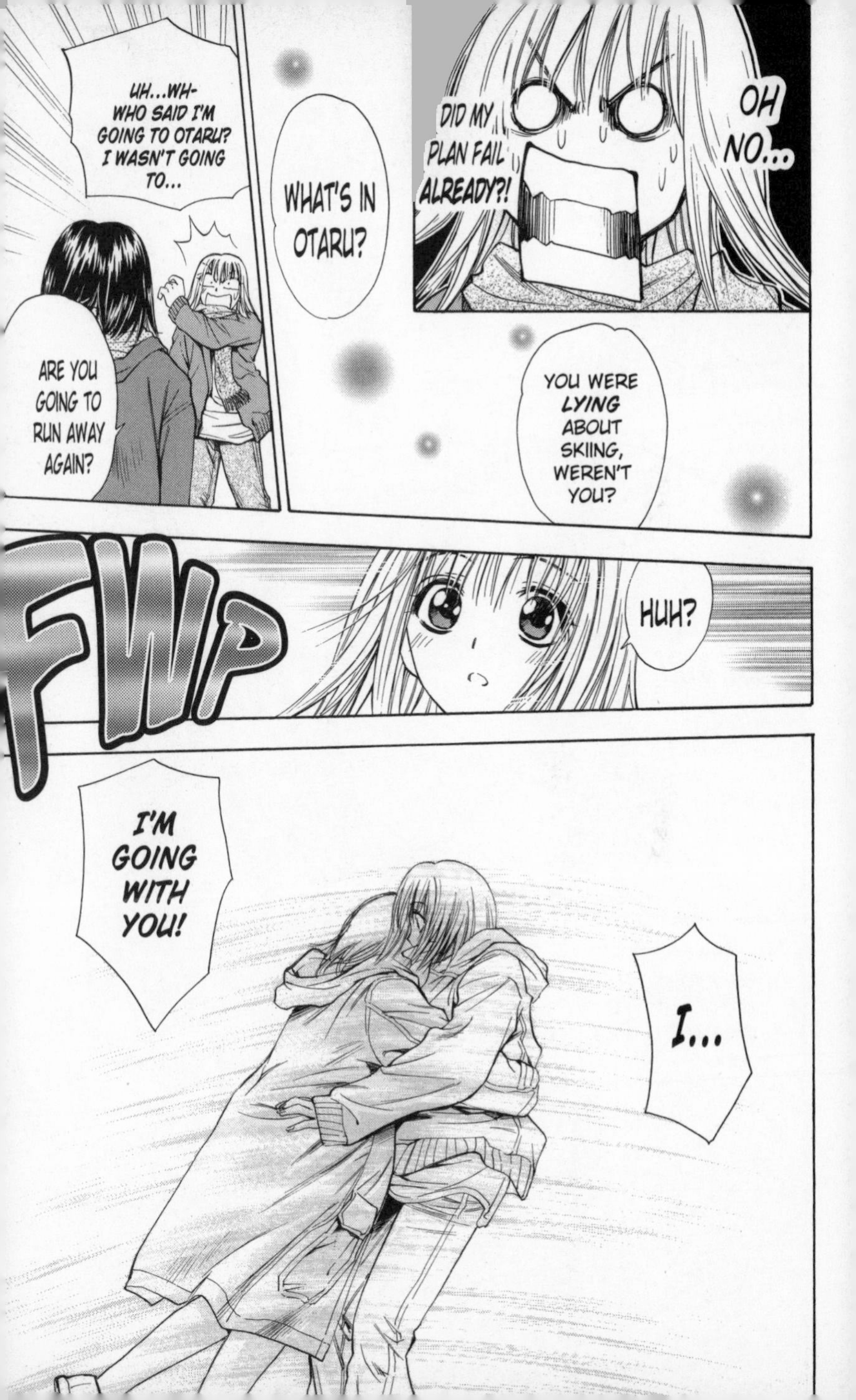
OH NO...
DID MY PLAN FAIL ALREADY?!
WHAT'S IN OTARU?
YOU WERE *LYING* ABOUT SKIING, WEREN'T YOU?
UH...WH-WHO SAID I'M GOING TO OTARU? I WASN'T GOING TO...
ARE YOU GOING TO RUN AWAY AGAIN?
HUH?
FWIP
I...
I'M GOING WITH YOU!

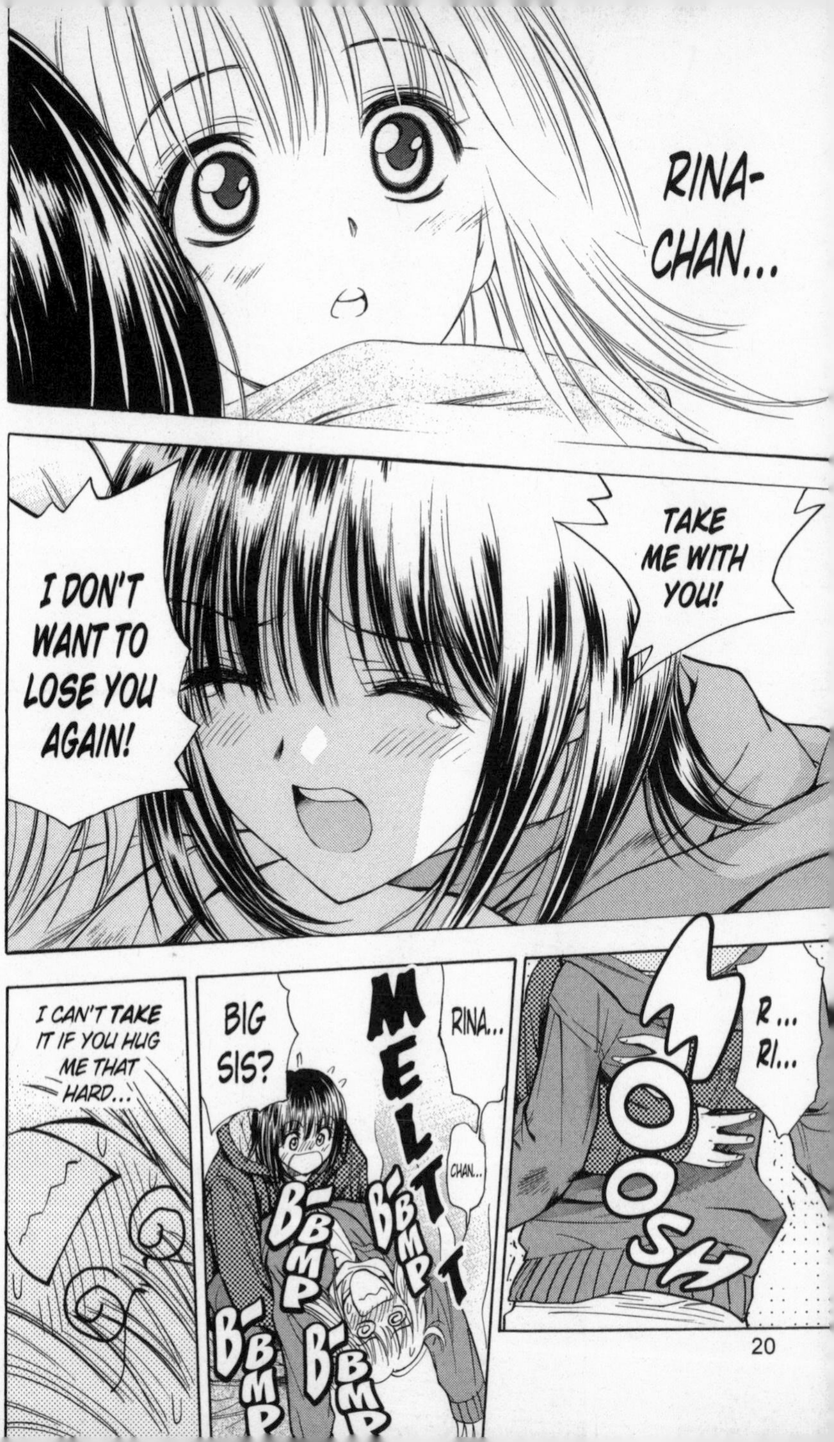
RINA-CHAN...
TAKE ME WITH YOU!
I DON'T WANT TO LOSE YOU AGAIN!
R... RI...
WOOSH
RINA...
CHAN...
MELT
BIG SIS?
B-BMP
B-BMP
B-BMP
B-BMP
I CAN'T TAKE IT IF YOU HUG ME THAT HARD...

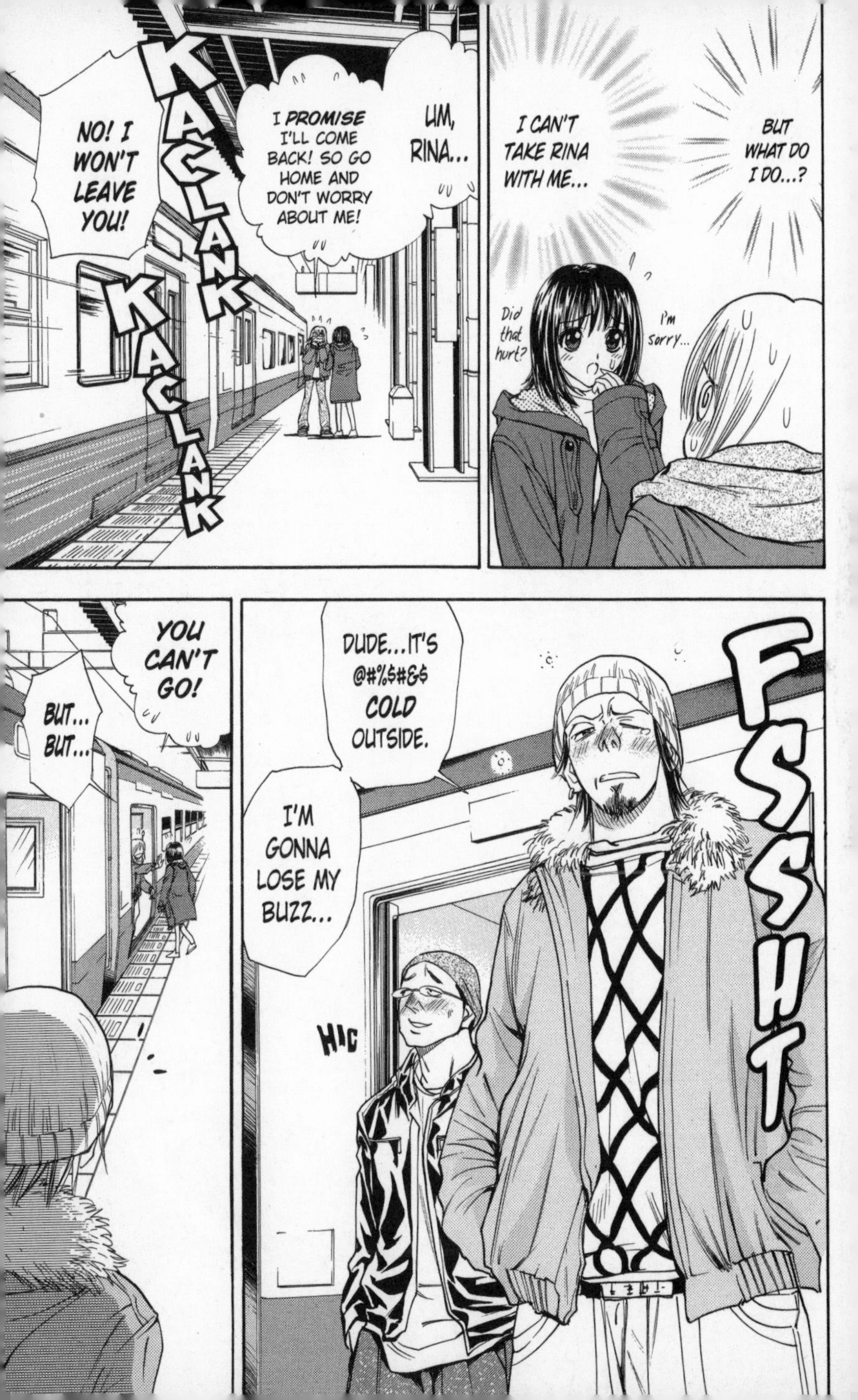

I CAN'T TAKE RINA WITH ME...
BUT WHAT DO I DO...?
I'm sorry...
Did that hurt?
UM, RINA...
I PROMISE I'LL COME BACK! SO GO HOME AND DON'T WORRY ABOUT ME!
NO! I WON'T LEAVE YOU!
KACLANK
KACLANK
FSSHT
DUDE...IT'S @#%$#&$ COLD OUTSIDE.
I'M GONNA LOSE MY BUZZ...
HIC
YOU CAN'T GO!
BUT... BUT...

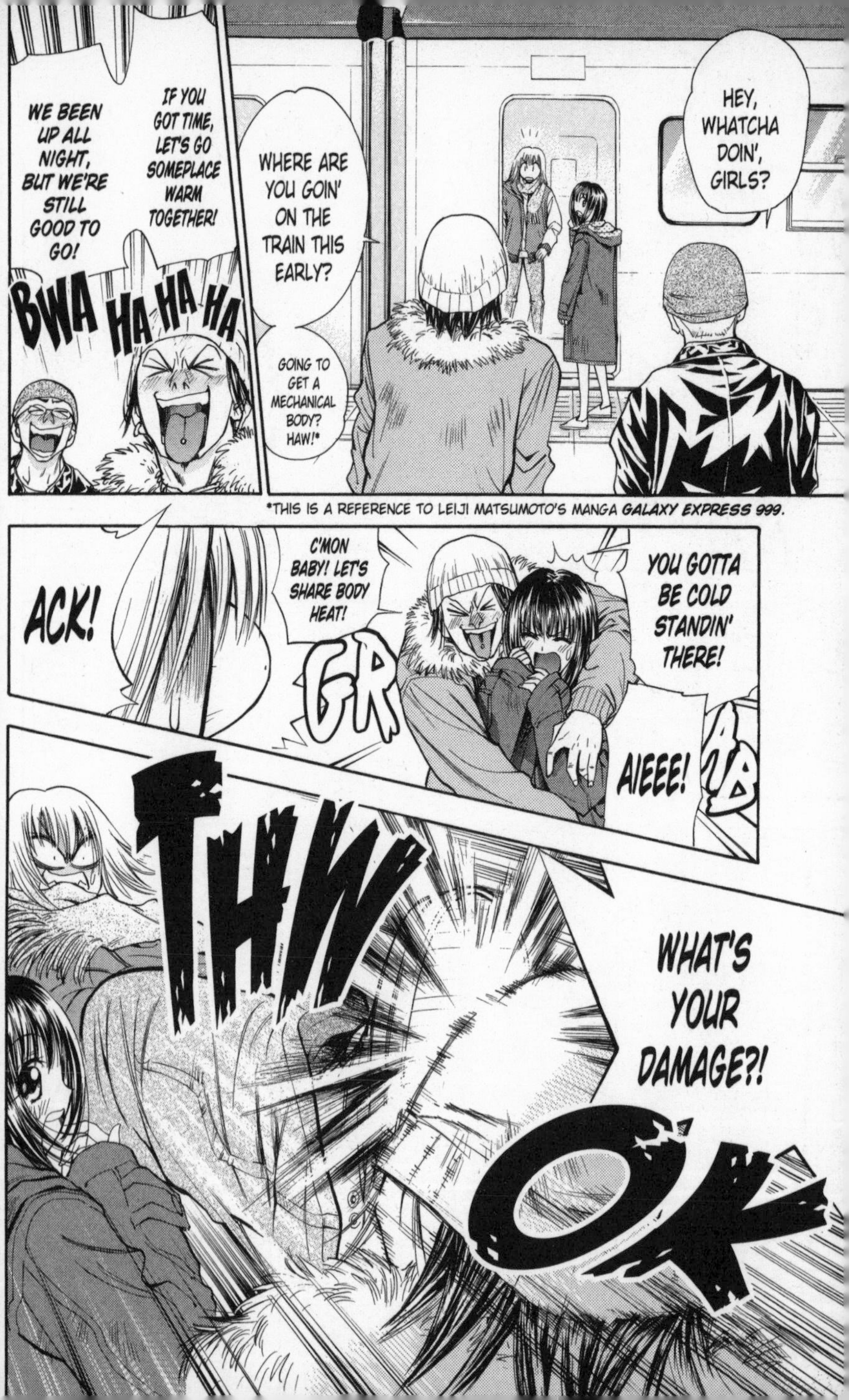
HEY, WHATCHA DOIN', GIRLS?
WHERE ARE YOU GOIN' ON THE TRAIN THIS EARLY?
GOING TO GET A MECHANICAL BODY? HAW!*
IF YOU GOT TIME, LET'S GO SOMEPLACE WARM TOGETHER!
WE BEEN UP ALL NIGHT, BUT WE'RE STILL GOOD TO GO!
BWA HA HA HA
YOU GOTTA BE COLD STANDIN' THERE!
C'MON BABY! LET'S SHARE BODY HEAT!
GR
AIEEE!
ACK!
THWOK
WHAT'S YOUR DAMAGE?!

*THIS IS A REFERENCE TO LEIJI MATSUMOTO'S MANGA *GALAXY EXPRESS 999*.

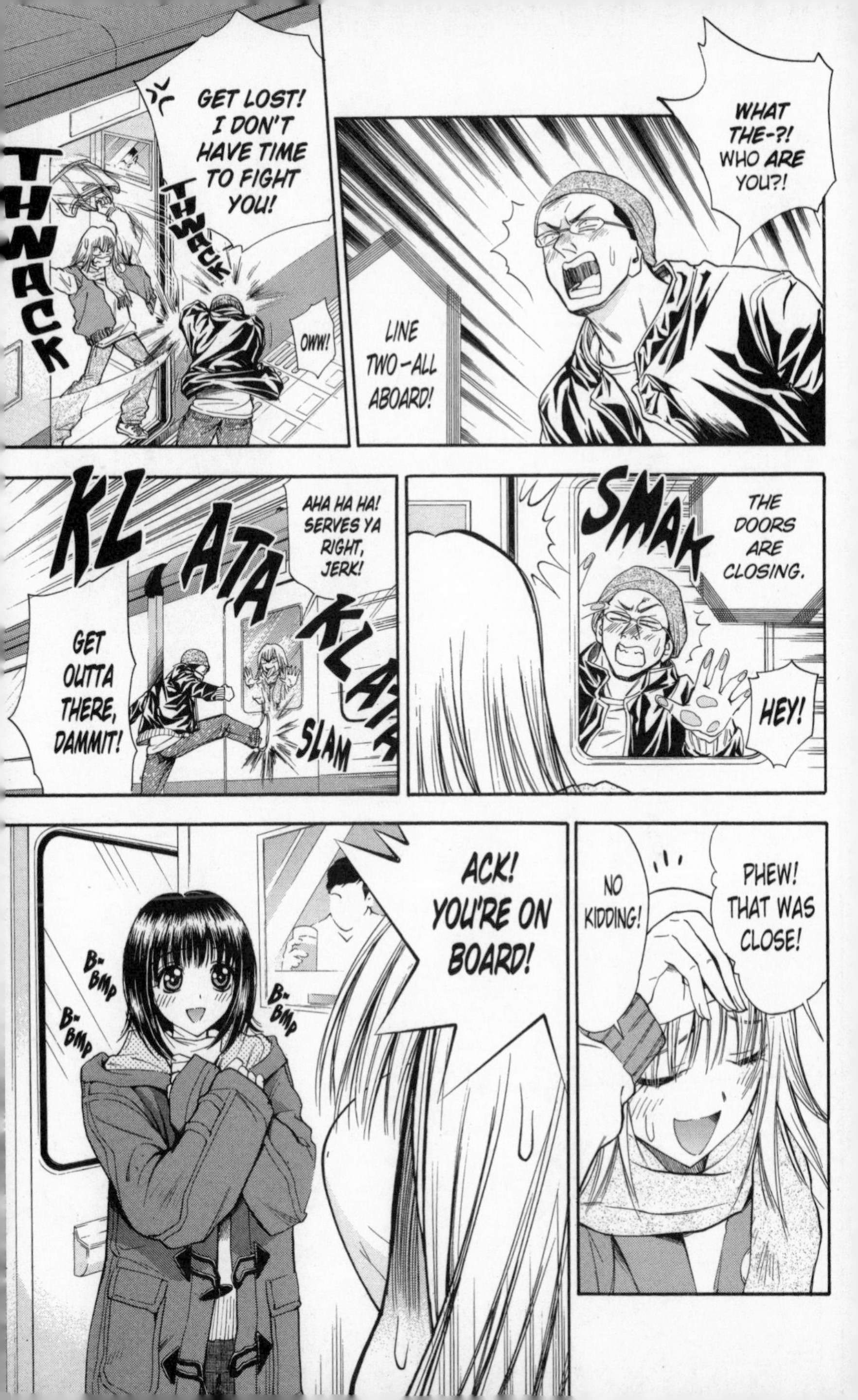
WHAT THE-?! WHO ARE YOU?!
LINE TWO–ALL ABOARD!
GET LOST! I DON'T HAVE TIME TO FIGHT YOU!
THWACK
THWACK
OWW!
SMAK
THE DOORS ARE CLOSING.
HEY!
AHA HA HA! SERVES YA RIGHT, JERK!
KLATA KLATA
GET OUTTA THERE, DAMMIT!
SLAM
PHEW! THAT WAS CLOSE!
NO KIDDING!
ACK! YOU'RE ON BOARD!
B-BMP
B-BMP
B-BMP

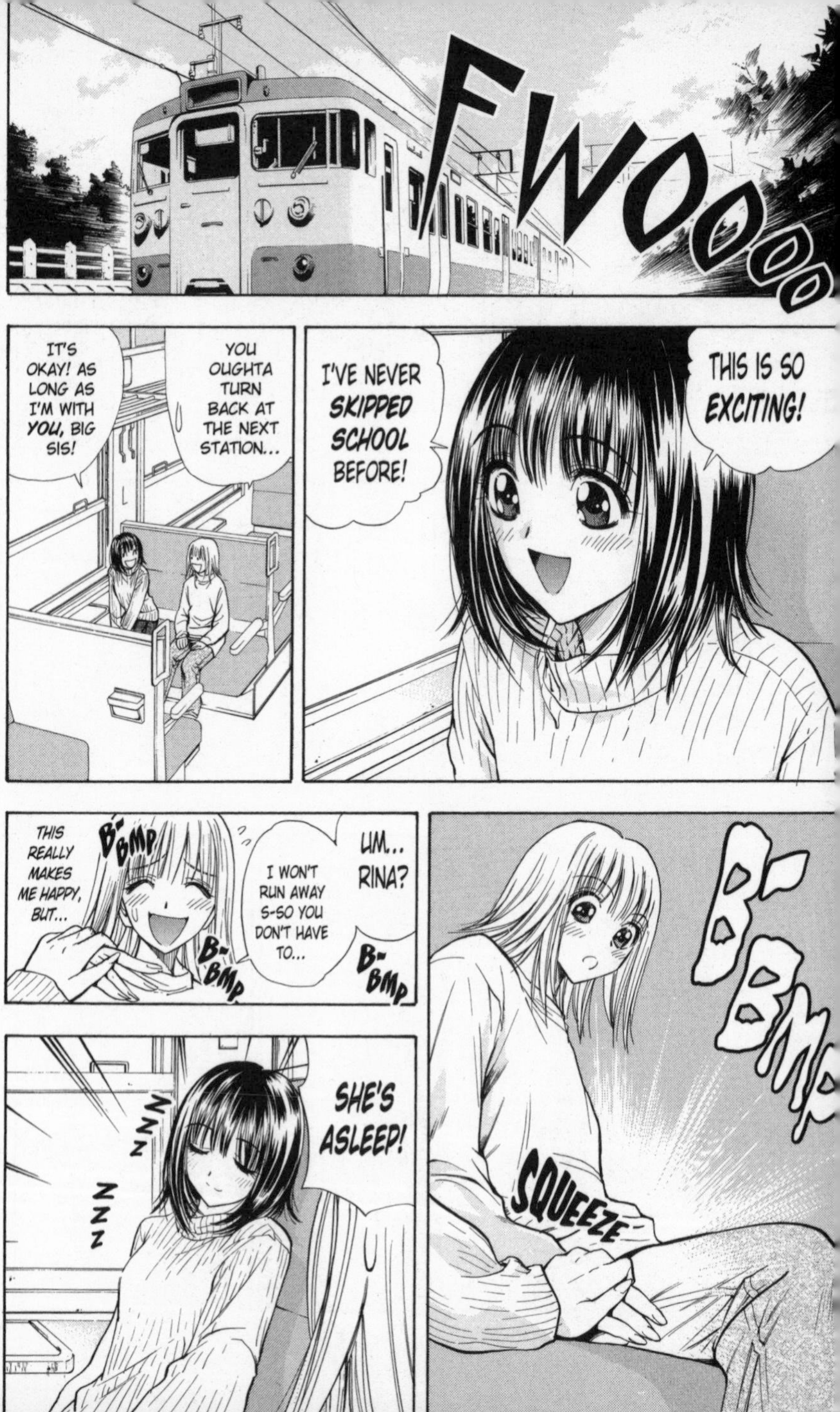
FWOOOO
THIS IS SO EXCITING!
I'VE NEVER SKIPPED SCHOOL BEFORE!
YOU OUGHTA TURN BACK AT THE NEXT STATION...
IT'S OKAY! AS LONG AS I'M WITH YOU, BIG SIS!
B-BMP
SQUEEZE
UM... RINA?
I WON'T RUN AWAY S-SO YOU DON'T HAVE TO...
B-BMP
B-BMP
THIS REALLY MAKES ME HAPPY, BUT...
B-BMP
SHE'S ASLEEP!
ZZZ
ZZZ

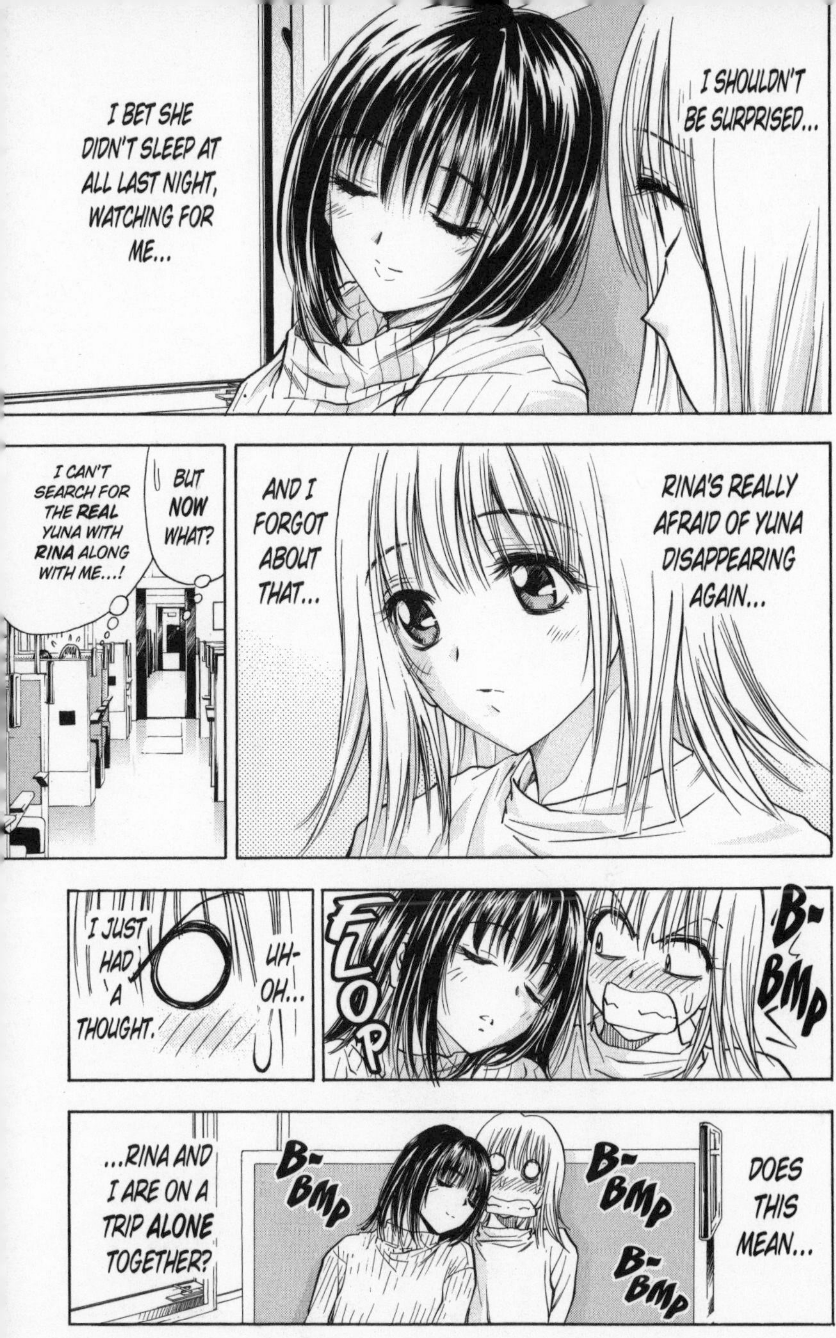
I SHOULDN'T BE SURPRISED...
I BET SHE DIDN'T SLEEP AT ALL LAST NIGHT, WATCHING FOR ME...
RINA'S REALLY AFRAID OF YUNA DISAPPEARING AGAIN...
AND I FORGOT ABOUT THAT...
BUT NOW WHAT?
I CAN'T SEARCH FOR THE REAL YUNA WITH RINA ALONG WITH ME...!
B-BMP
FLOP
UH-OH...
I JUST HAD A THOUGHT.
DOES THIS MEAN...
B-BMP
B-BMP
B-BMP
B-BMP
...RINA AND I ARE ON A TRIP ALONE TOGETHER?

Pretty Face

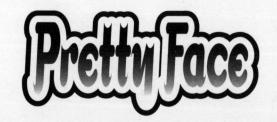

Chapter 29:

The Great Otaru Expedition: Part 1

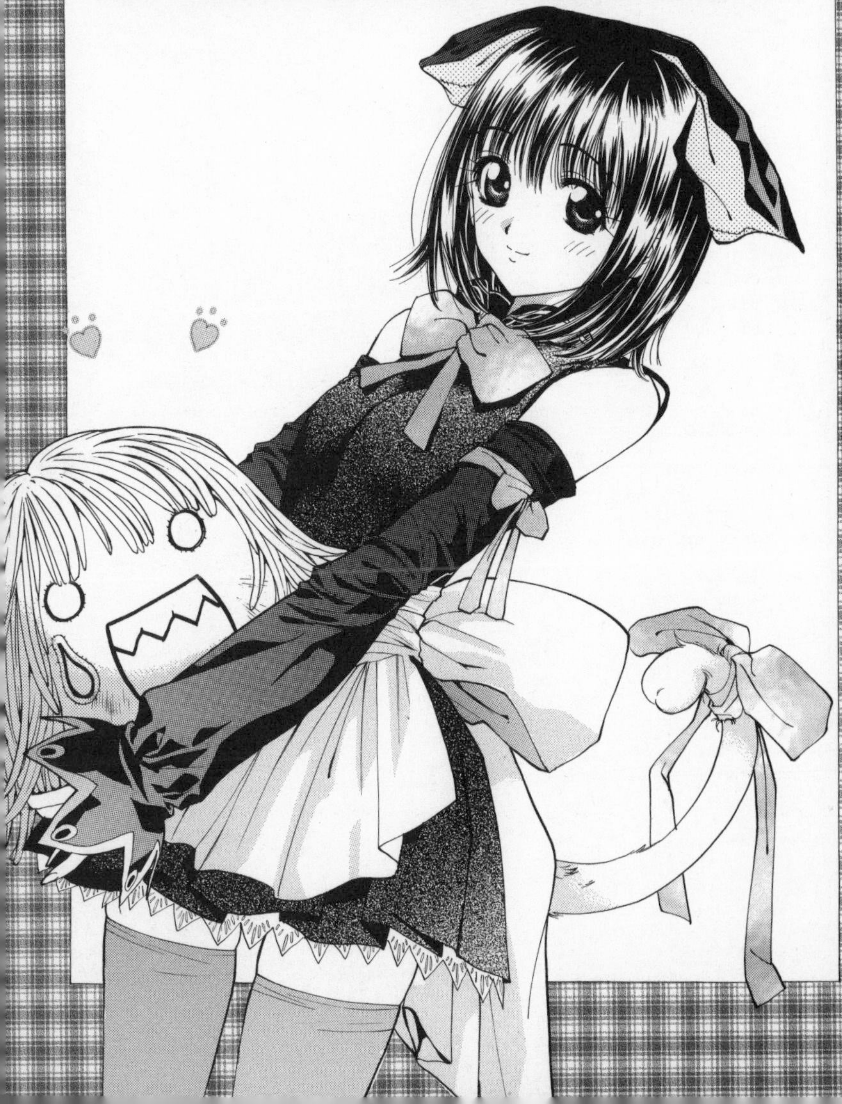

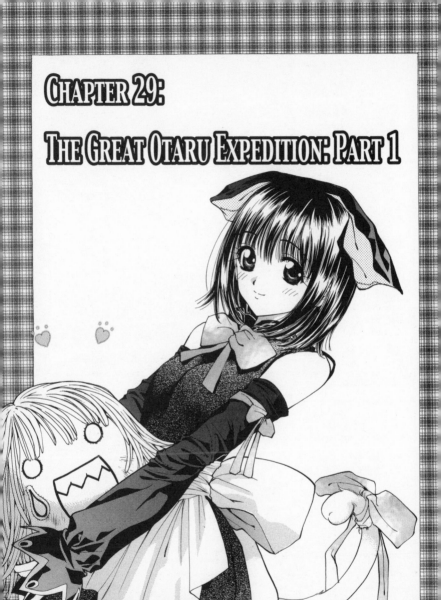

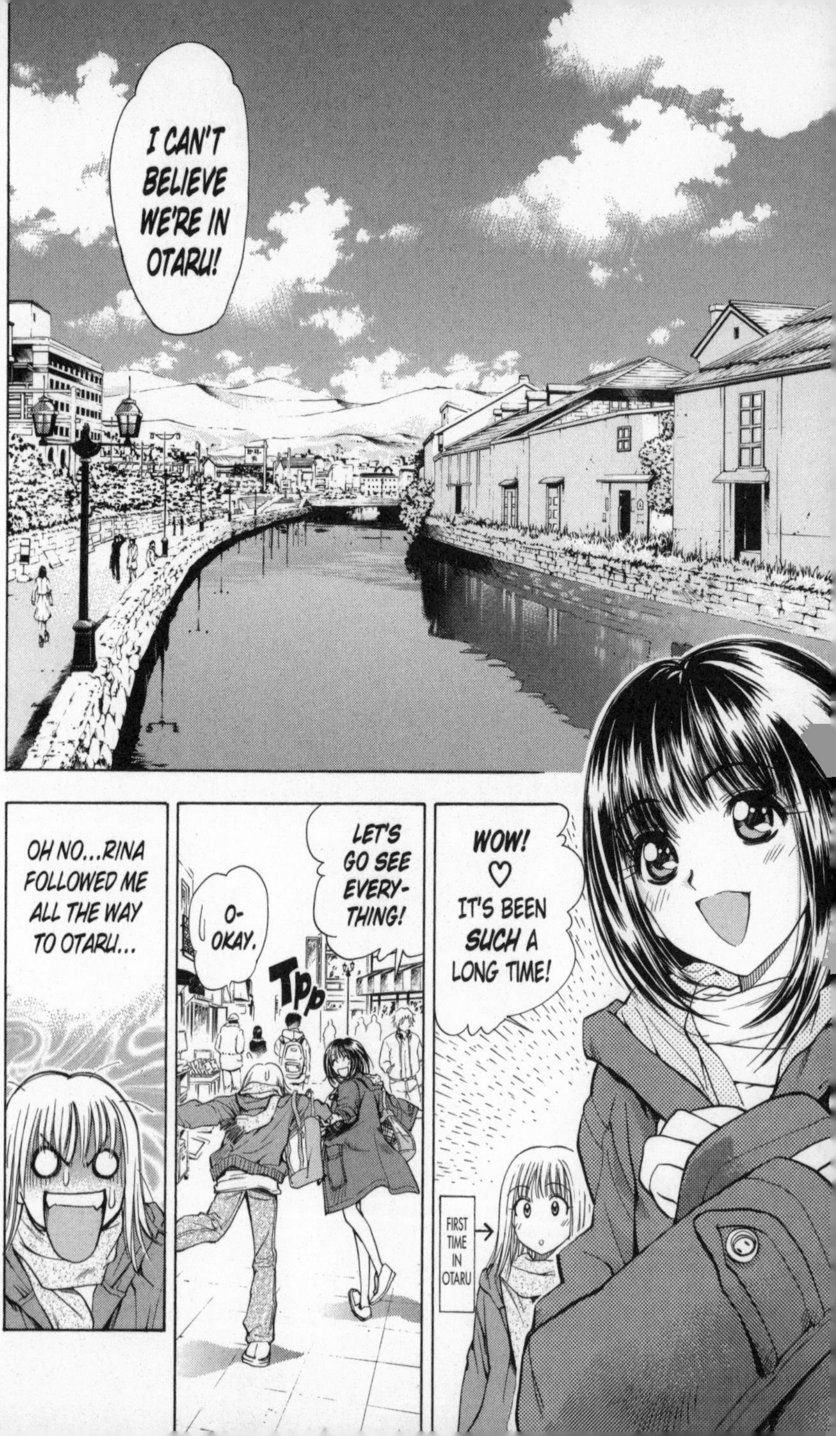
I CAN'T BELIEVE WE'RE IN OTARU!
WOW! ♡ IT'S BEEN SUCH A LONG TIME!
FIRST TIME IN OTARU
LET'S GO SEE EVERY-THING!
O-OKAY.
Tpp
OH NO...RINA FOLLOWED ME ALL THE WAY TO OTARU...

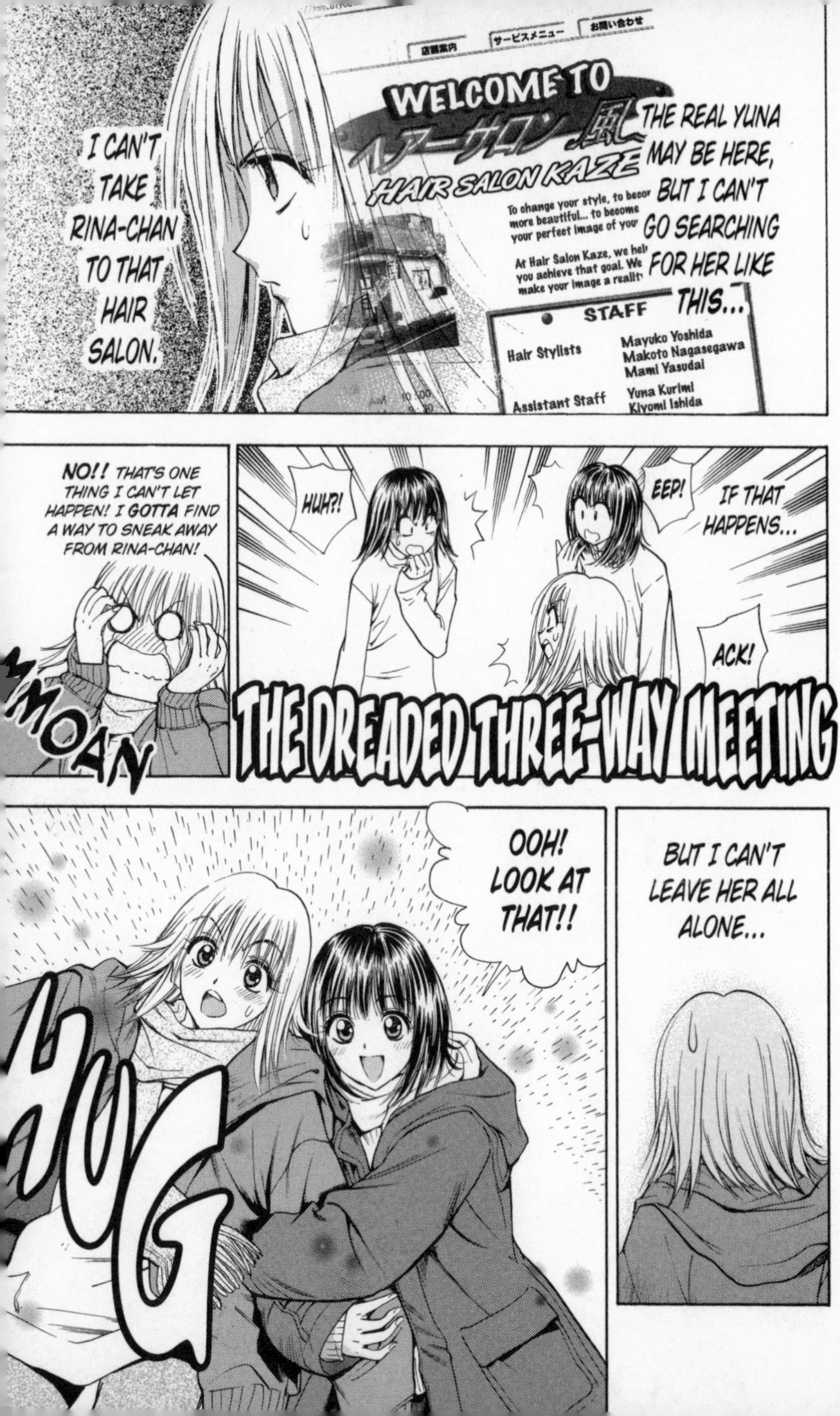

店舗案内
サービスメニュー
お問い合わせ
WELCOME TO
ヘアーサロン風
HAIR SALON KAZE
To change your style, to becor
more beautiful... to become
your perfect image of your
At Hair Salon Kaze, we help
you achieve that goal. We
make your image a reality
STAFF
Hair Stylists
Mayuko Yoshida
Makoto Nagasegawa
Mami Yasudai
Assistant Staff
Yuna Kurimi
Kiyomi Ishida
THE REAL YUNA MAY BE HERE, BUT I CAN'T GO SEARCHING FOR HER LIKE THIS...
I CAN'T TAKE RINA-CHAN TO THAT HAIR SALON.
IF THAT HAPPENS...
EEP!
HUH?!
ACK!
THE DREADED THREE-WAY MEETING
NO!! THAT'S ONE THING I CAN'T LET HAPPEN! I GOTTA FIND A WAY TO SNEAK AWAY FROM RINA-CHAN!
MMOAN
BUT I CAN'T LEAVE HER ALL ALONE...
OOH! LOOK AT THAT!!
HUG

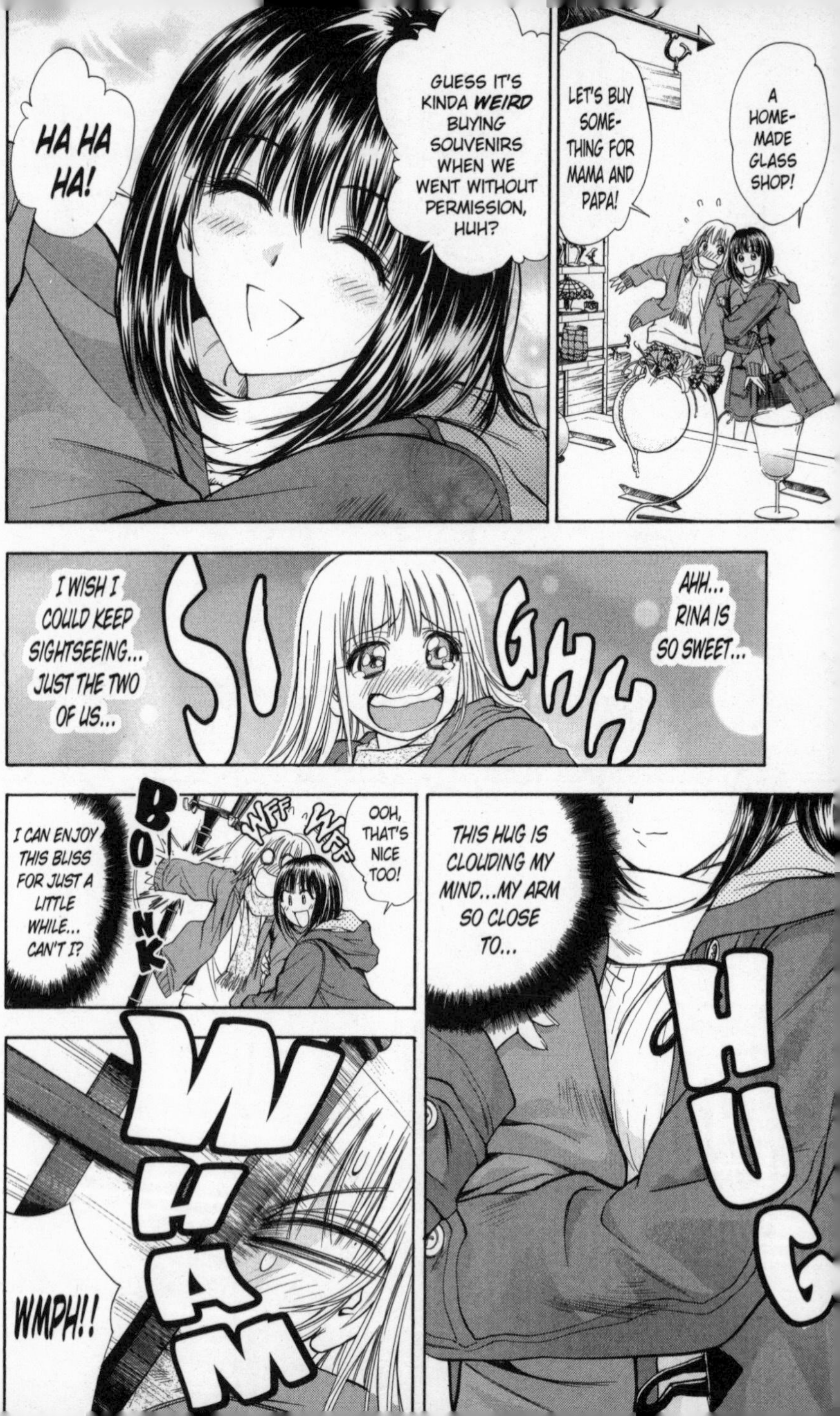
A HOME-MADE GLASS SHOP!
LET'S BUY SOME-THING FOR MAMA AND PAPA!
GUESS IT'S KINDA *WEIRD* BUYING SOUVENIRS WHEN WE WENT WITHOUT PERMISSION, HUH?
HA HA HA!
AHH... RINA IS SO SWEET...
SIGHHH
I WISH I COULD KEEP SIGHTSEEING... JUST THE TWO OF US...
THIS HUG IS CLOUDING MY MIND...MY ARM SO CLOSE TO...
HUG
OOH, THAT'S NICE TOO!
WFF WFF
BOINK
I CAN ENJOY THIS BLISS FOR JUST A LITTLE WHILE... CAN'T I?
WHAM
WMPH!!

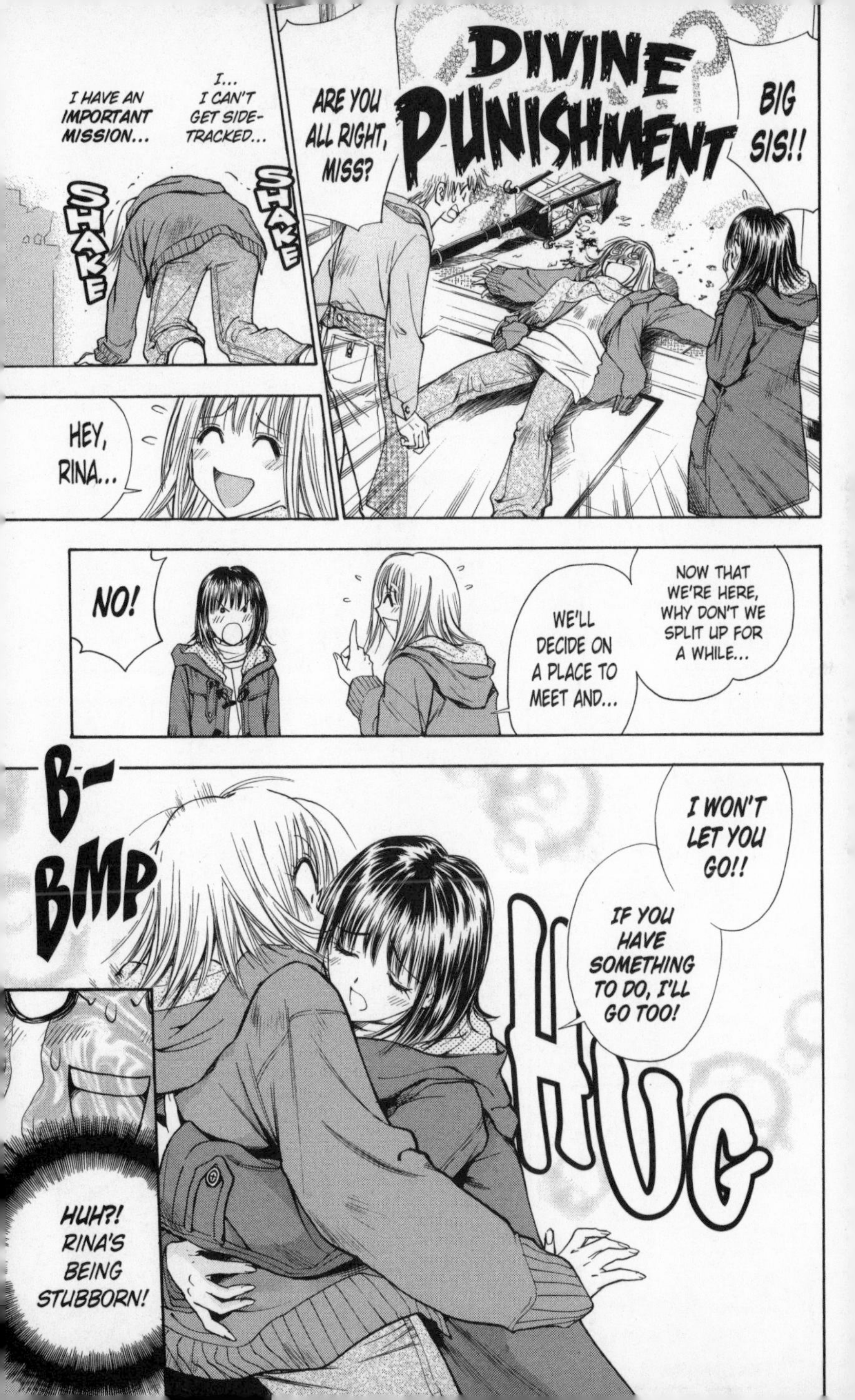
BIG SIS!!
DIVINE PUNISHMENT
ARE YOU ALL RIGHT, MISS?
I... I CAN'T GET SIDE-TRACKED...
SHAKE
I HAVE AN IMPORTANT MISSION...
SHAKE
HEY, RINA...
NOW THAT WE'RE HERE, WHY DON'T WE SPLIT UP FOR A WHILE...
WE'LL DECIDE ON A PLACE TO MEET AND...
NO!
I WON'T LET YOU GO!!
IF YOU HAVE SOMETHING TO DO, I'LL GO TOO!
HUG
B-BMP
HUH?! RINA'S BEING STUBBORN!

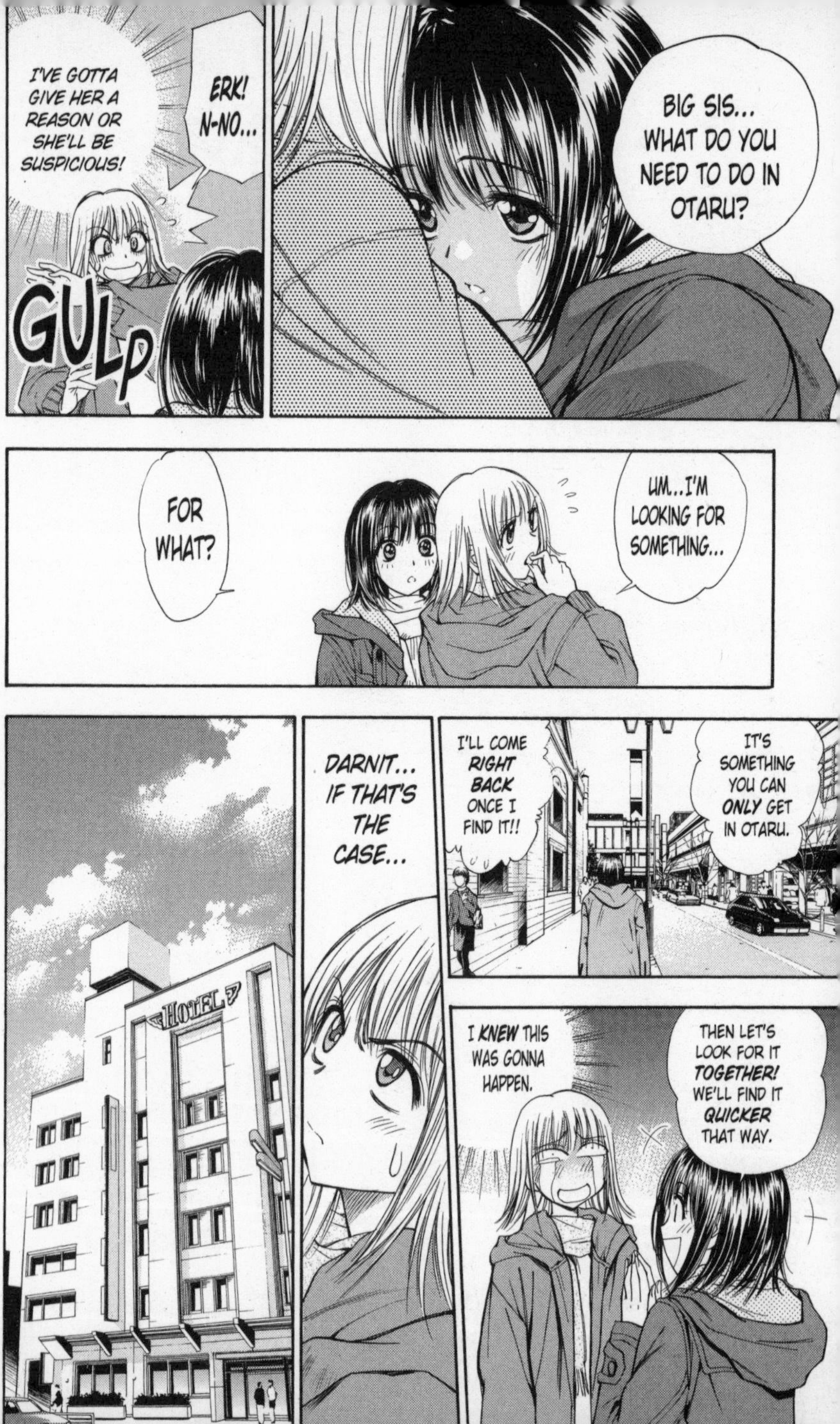
BIG SIS... WHAT DO YOU NEED TO DO IN OTARU?
ERK! N-NO...
I'VE GOTTA GIVE HER A REASON OR SHE'LL BE SUSPICIOUS!
GULP
UM...I'M LOOKING FOR SOMETHING...
FOR WHAT?
IT'S SOMETHING YOU CAN ONLY GET IN OTARU.
I'LL COME RIGHT BACK ONCE I FIND IT!!
THEN LET'S LOOK FOR IT TOGETHER! WE'LL FIND IT QUICKER THAT WAY.
I KNEW THIS WAS GONNA HAPPEN.
DARNIT... IF THAT'S THE CASE...
HOTEL

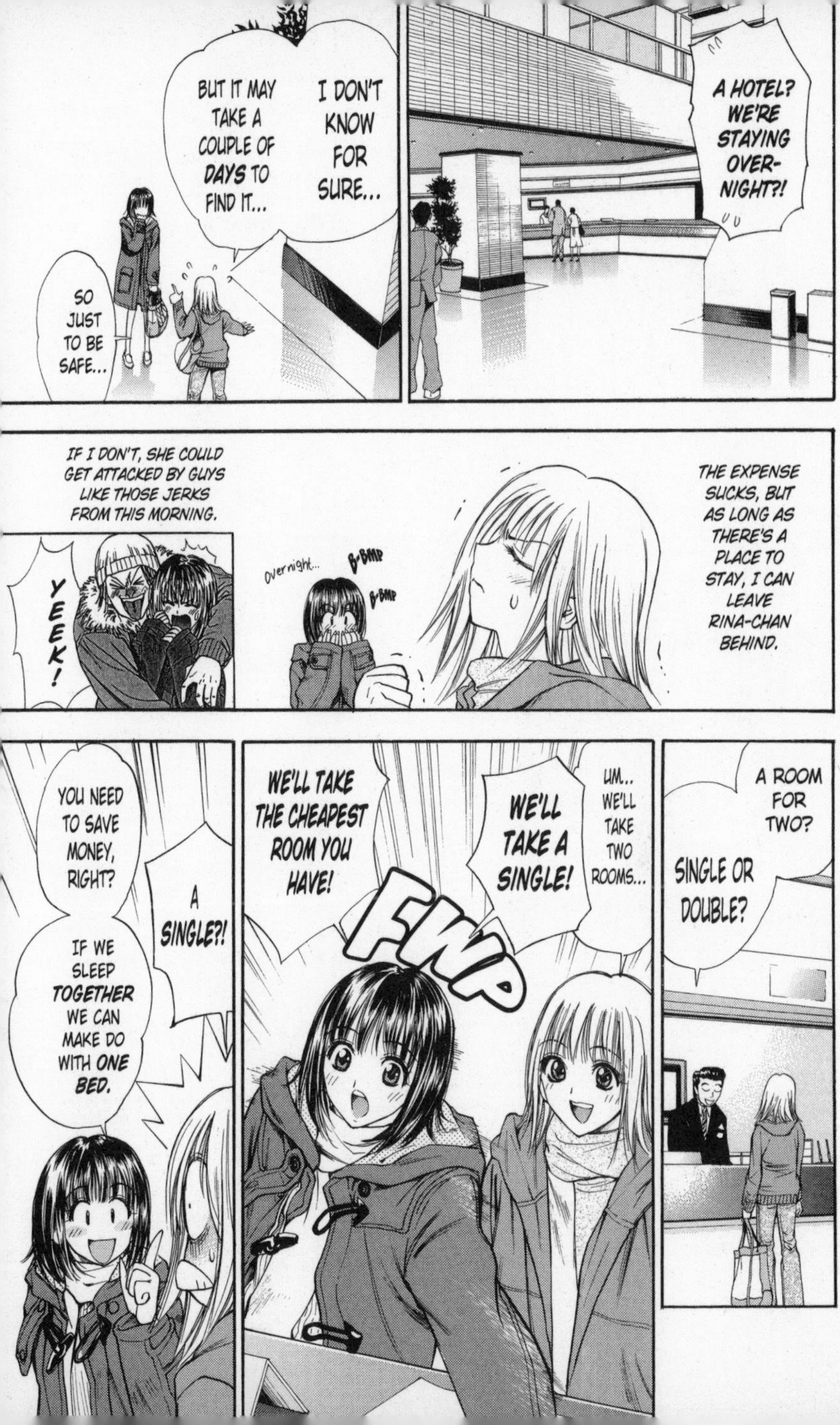
A HOTEL? WE'RE STAYING OVER-NIGHT?!
I DON'T KNOW FOR SURE...
BUT IT MAY TAKE A COUPLE OF DAYS TO FIND IT...
SO JUST TO BE SAFE...
THE EXPENSE SUCKS, BUT AS LONG AS THERE'S A PLACE TO STAY, I CAN LEAVE RINA-CHAN BEHIND.
Overnight...
B-BMP
B-BMP
IF I DON'T, SHE COULD GET ATTACKED BY GUYS LIKE THOSE JERKS FROM THIS MORNING.
YEEK!
A ROOM FOR TWO?
SINGLE OR DOUBLE?
UM.. WE'LL TAKE TWO ROOMS...
WE'LL TAKE A SINGLE!
WE'LL TAKE THE CHEAPEST ROOM YOU HAVE!
FWP
A SINGLE?!
YOU NEED TO SAVE MONEY, RIGHT?
IF WE SLEEP TOGETHER WE CAN MAKE DO WITH ONE BED.

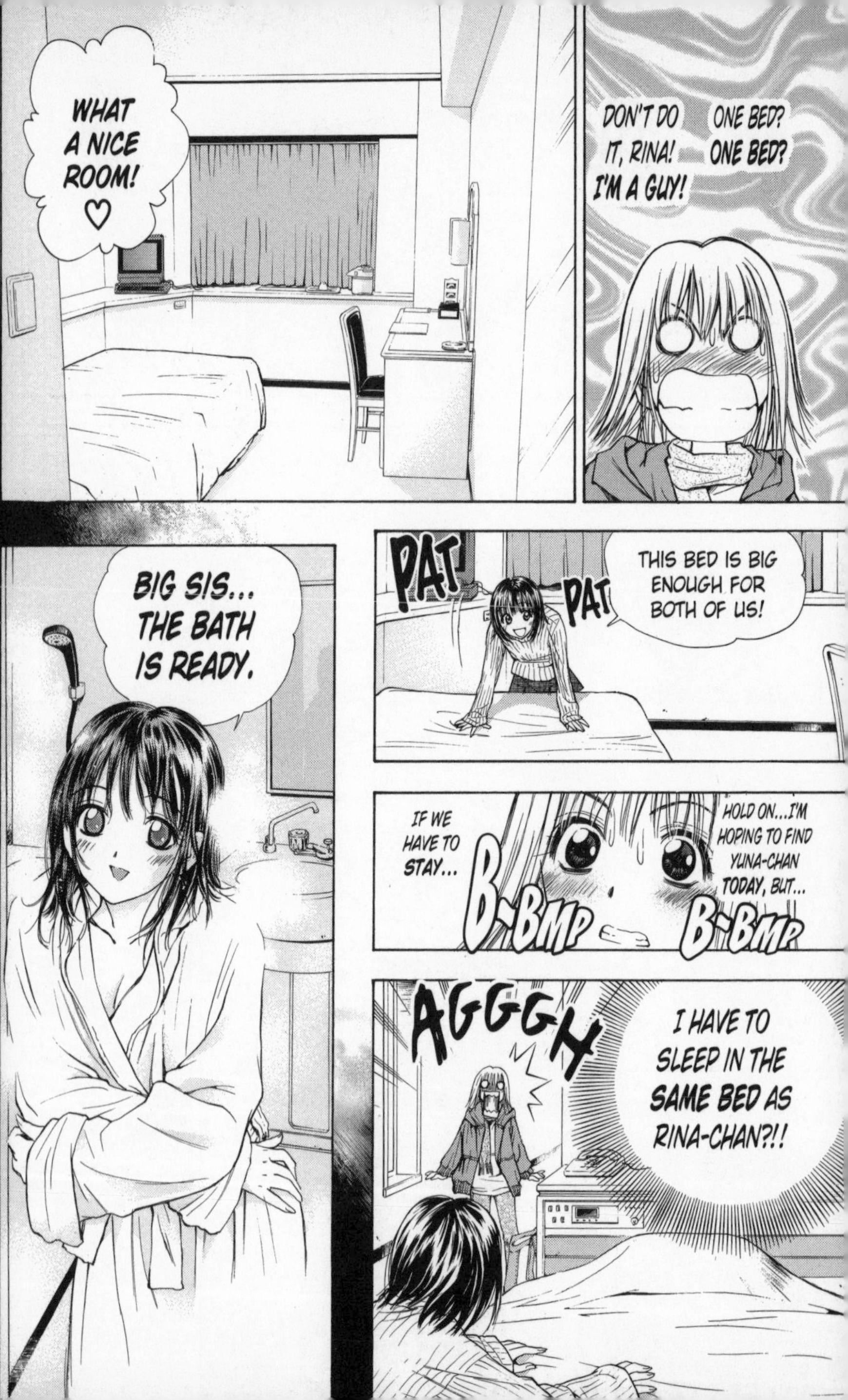
ONE BED? ONE BED?
DON'T DO IT, RINA! I'M A GUY!
WHAT A NICE ROOM! ♡
THIS BED IS BIG ENOUGH FOR BOTH OF US!
PAT
PAT
HOLD ON...I'M HOPING TO FIND YUNA-CHAN TODAY, BUT...
B-BMP
B-BMP
IF WE HAVE TO STAY...
I HAVE TO SLEEP IN THE SAME BED AS RINA-CHAN?!!
AGGGH
BIG SIS... THE BATH IS READY.

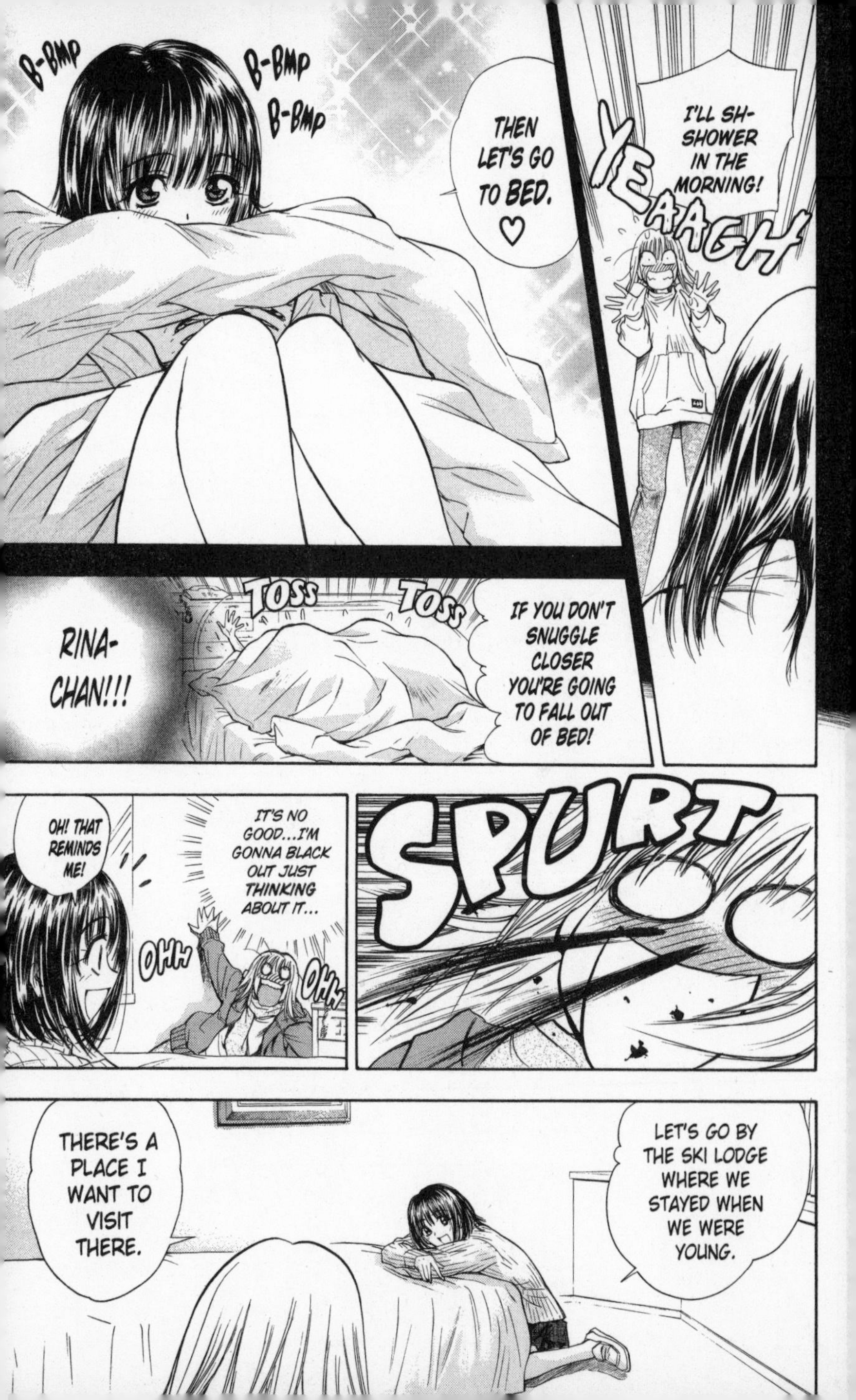
I'LL SH-SHOWER IN THE MORNING!
YEAAGH
THEN LET'S GO TO BED. ♡
B-BMP
B-BMP
B-BMP
IF YOU DON'T SNUGGLE CLOSER YOU'RE GOING TO FALL OUT OF BED!
TOSS
TOSS
RINA-CHAN!!!
SPURT
IT'S NO GOOD...I'M GONNA BLACK OUT JUST THINKING ABOUT IT...
OHH
OHH
OH! THAT REMINDS ME!
LET'S GO BY THE SKI LODGE WHERE WE STAYED WHEN WE WERE YOUNG.
THERE'S A PLACE I WANT TO VISIT THERE.

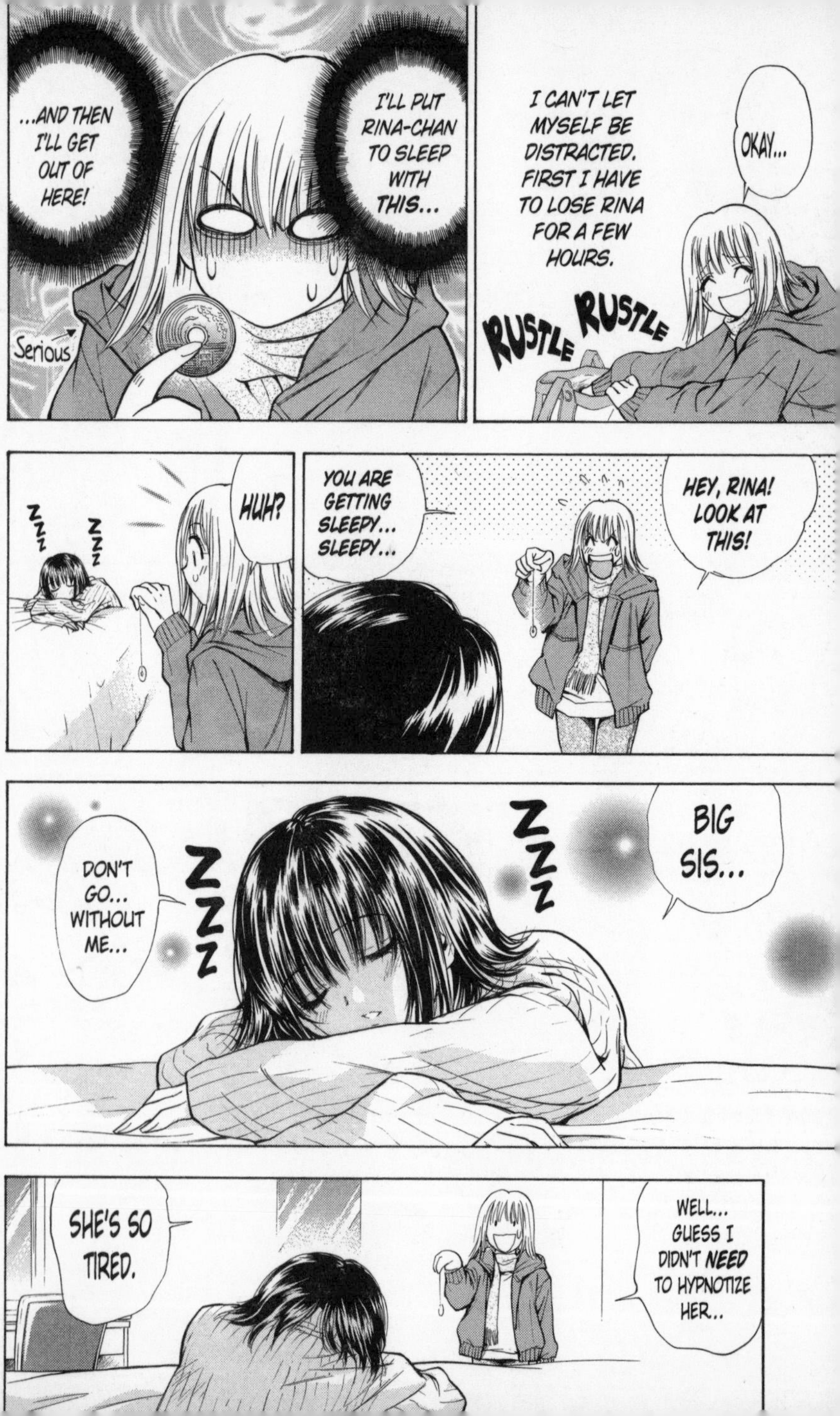
OKAY...
I CAN'T LET MYSELF BE DISTRACTED. FIRST I HAVE TO LOSE RINA FOR A FEW HOURS.
RUSTLE RUSTLE
I'LL PUT RINA-CHAN TO SLEEP WITH THIS...
...AND THEN I'LL GET OUT OF HERE!
Serious
HEY, RINA! LOOK AT THIS!
YOU ARE GETTING SLEEPY... SLEEPY...
HUH?
ZZZ
ZZZ
BIG SIS...
ZZZ
DON'T GO... WITHOUT ME...
ZZZ
WELL... GUESS I DIDN'T NEED TO HYPNOTIZE HER..
SHE'S SO TIRED.

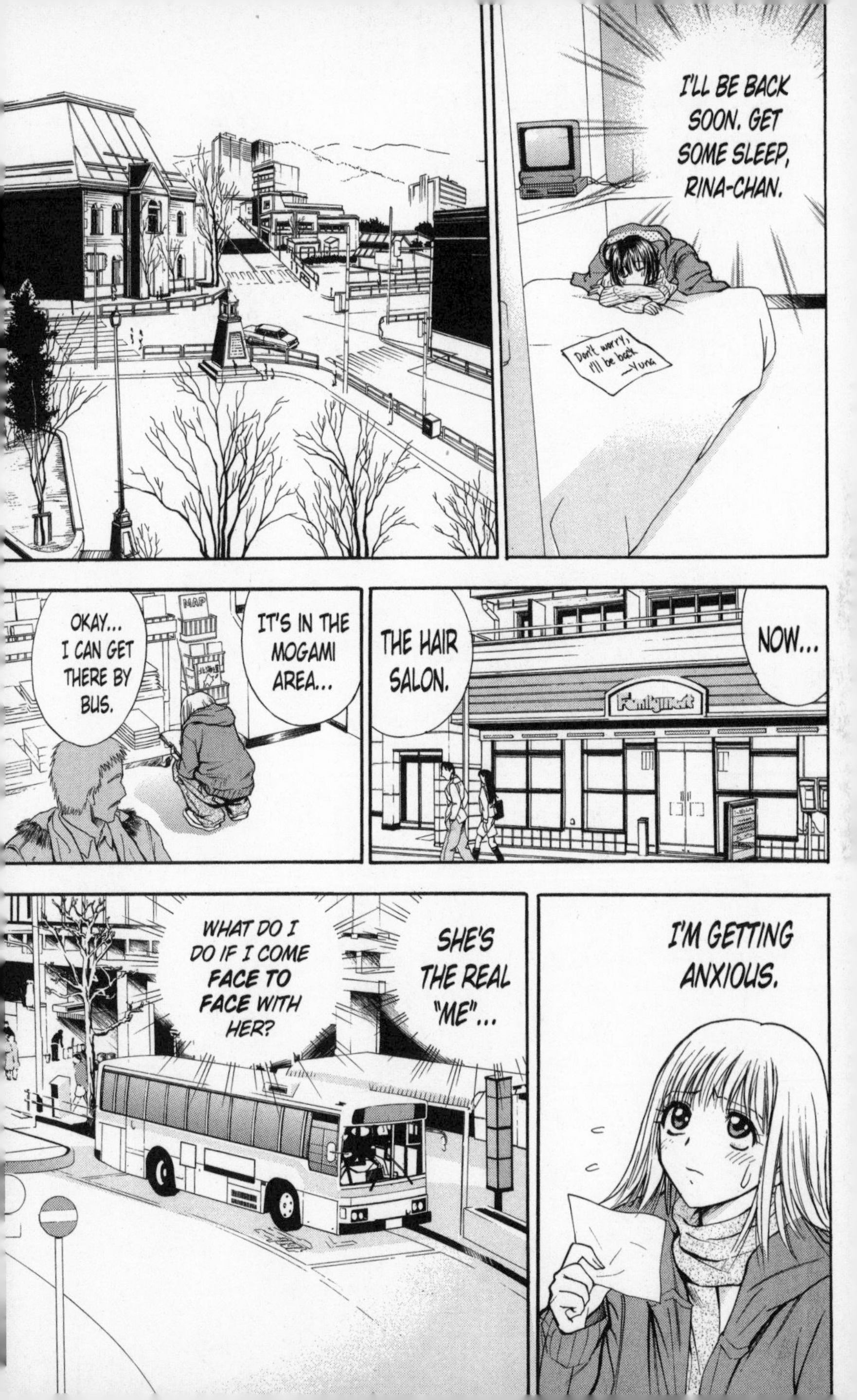
I'LL BE BACK SOON. GET SOME SLEEP, RINA-CHAN.
Don't worry, I'll be back —Yuna
NOW...
THE HAIR SALON.
IT'S IN THE MOGAMI AREA...
MAP
OKAY... I CAN GET THERE BY BUS.
I'M GETTING ANXIOUS.
SHE'S THE REAL "ME"...
WHAT DO I DO IF I COME FACE TO FACE WITH HER?

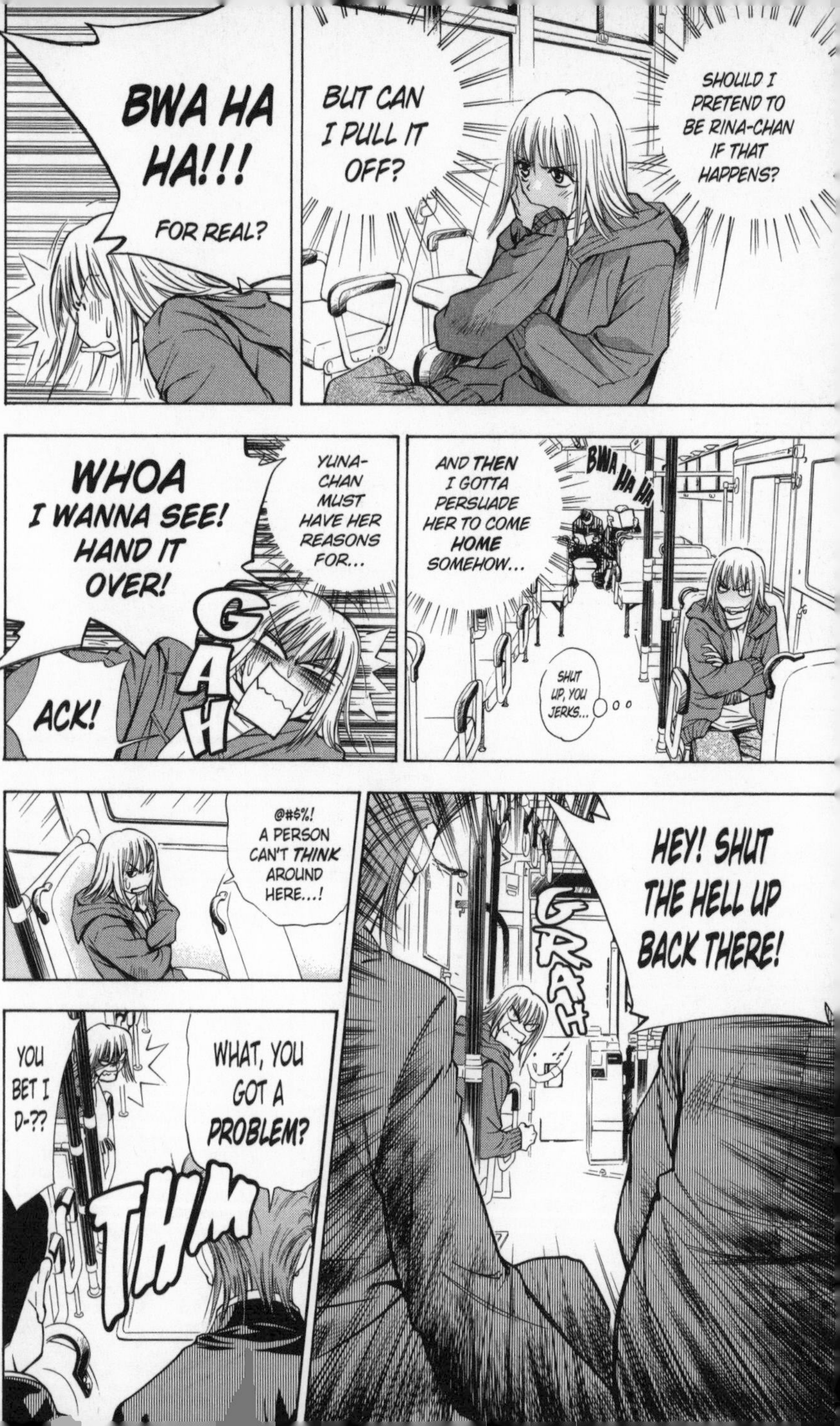
SHOULD I PRETEND TO BE RINA-CHAN IF THAT HAPPENS?
BUT CAN I PULL IT OFF?
BWA HA HA!!!
FOR REAL?
AND THEN I GOTTA PERSUADE HER TO COME HOME SOMEHOW...
BWA HA HA
SHUT UP, YOU JERKS...
YUNA-CHAN MUST HAVE HER REASONS FOR...
WHOA I WANNA SEE! HAND IT OVER!
GAH
ACK!
HEY! SHUT THE HELL UP BACK THERE!
GRAH
@#$%! A PERSON CAN'T THINK AROUND HERE...!
WHAT, YOU GOT A PROBLEM?
YOU BET I D-??
THM

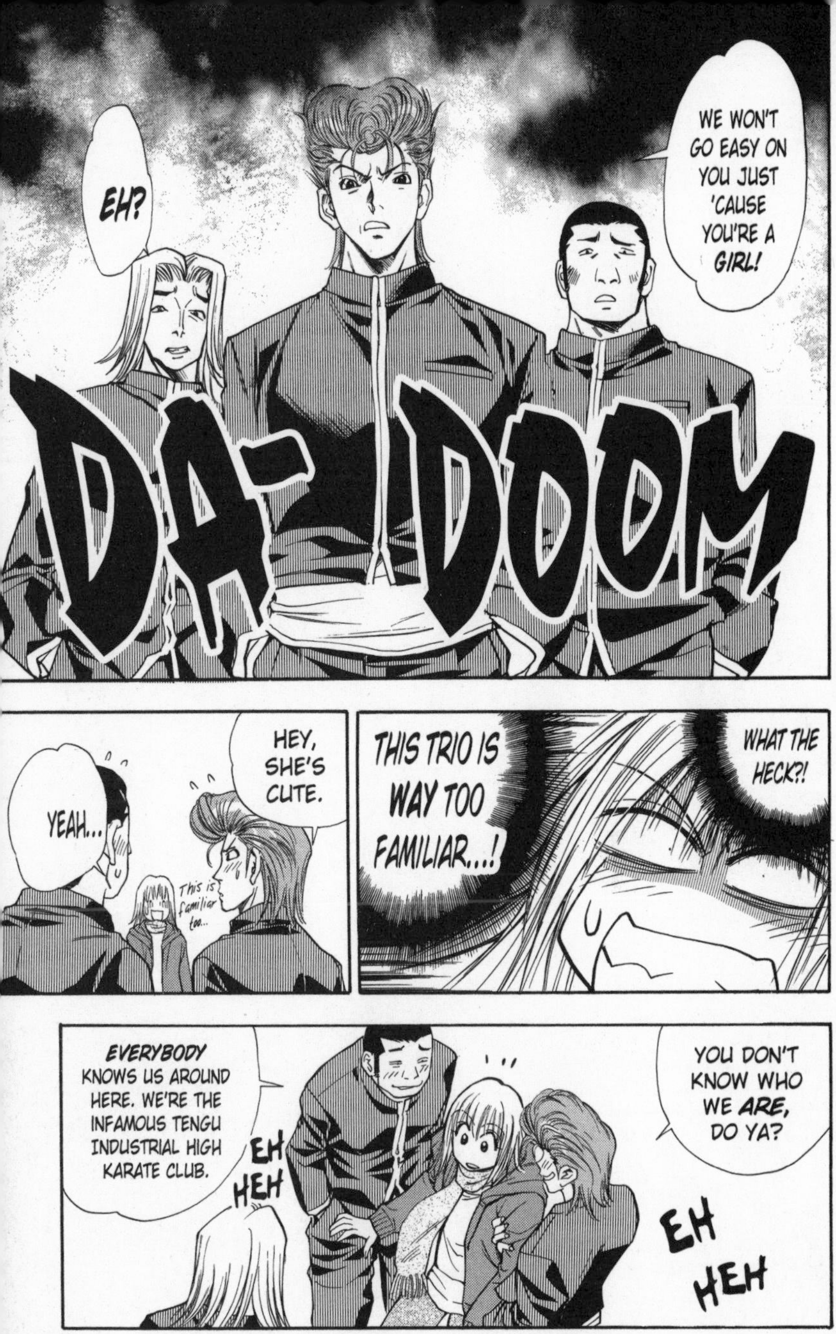
WE WON'T GO EASY ON YOU JUST 'CAUSE YOU'RE A GIRL!
EH?
DA-DOOM
WHAT THE HECK?!
THIS TRIO IS WAY TOO FAMILIAR...!
HEY, SHE'S CUTE.
YEAH...
This is familiar too...
YOU DON'T KNOW WHO WE ARE, DO YA?
EH HEH
EVERYBODY KNOWS US AROUND HERE. WE'RE THE INFAMOUS TENGU INDUSTRIAL HIGH KARATE CLUB.
EH HEH

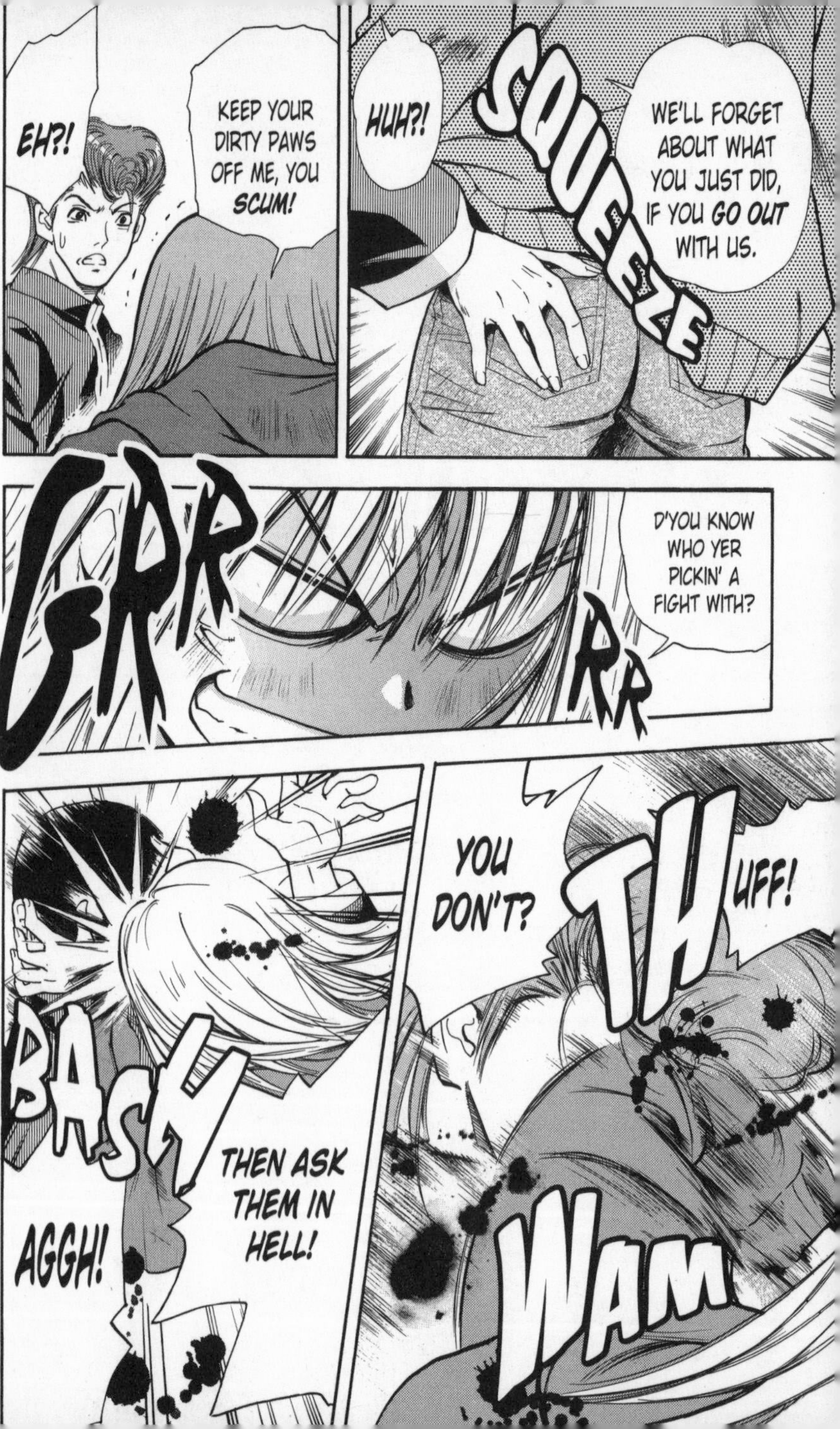

WE'LL FORGET ABOUT WHAT YOU JUST DID, IF YOU GO OUT WITH US.
SQUEEZE
HUH?!
KEEP YOUR DIRTY PAWS OFF ME, YOU SCUM!
EH?!
D'YOU KNOW WHO YER PICKIN' A FIGHT WITH?
GRRRR
THUFF!
YOU DON'T?
WAM
BASH
THEN ASK THEM IN HELL!
AGGH!

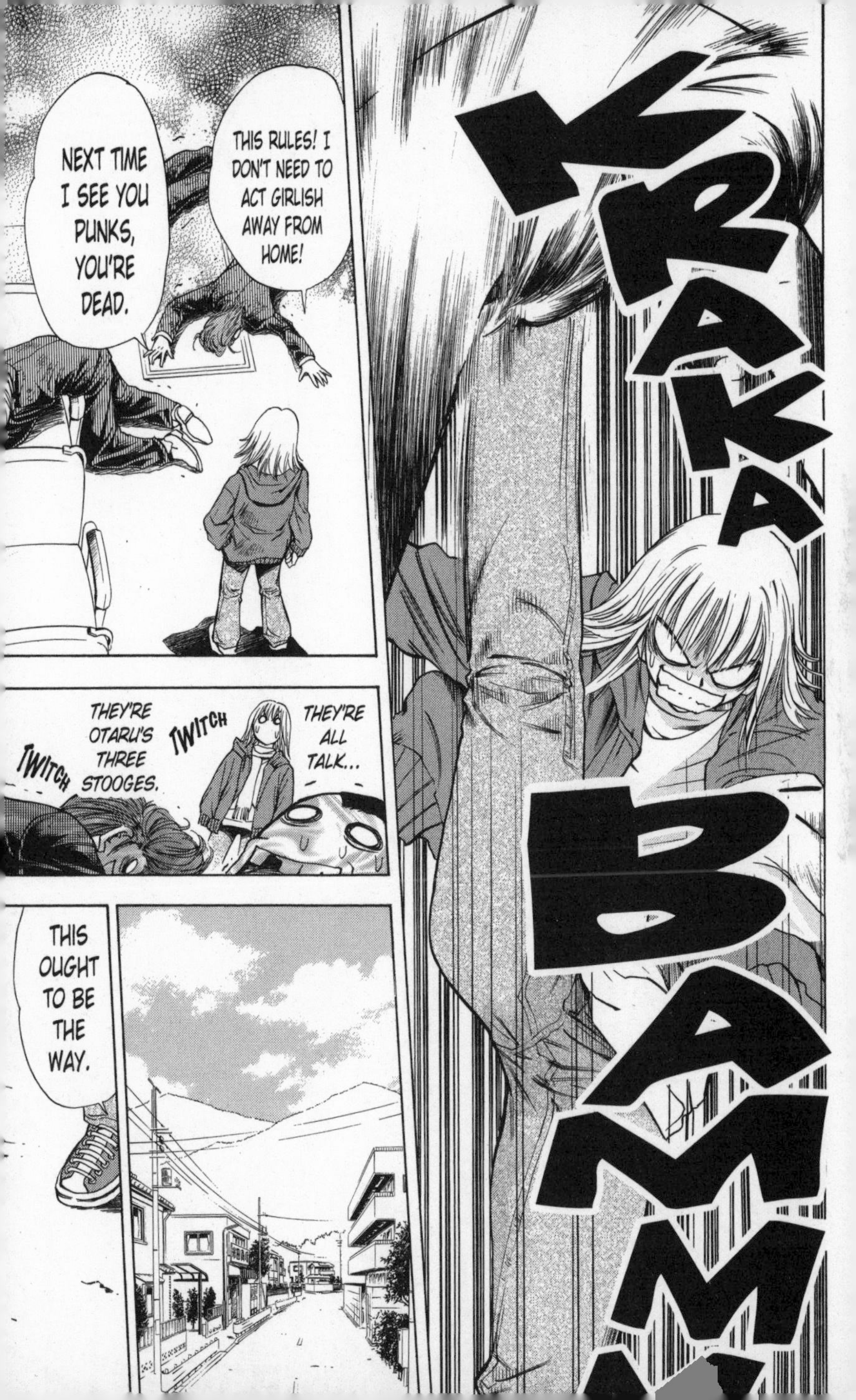
KRAKA
BAMM
THIS RULES! I DON'T NEED TO ACT GIRLISH AWAY FROM HOME!
NEXT TIME I SEE YOU PUNKS, YOU'RE DEAD.
THEY'RE ALL TALK...
TWITCH
THEY'RE OTARU'S THREE STOOGES.
TWITCH
THIS OUGHT TO BE THE WAY.

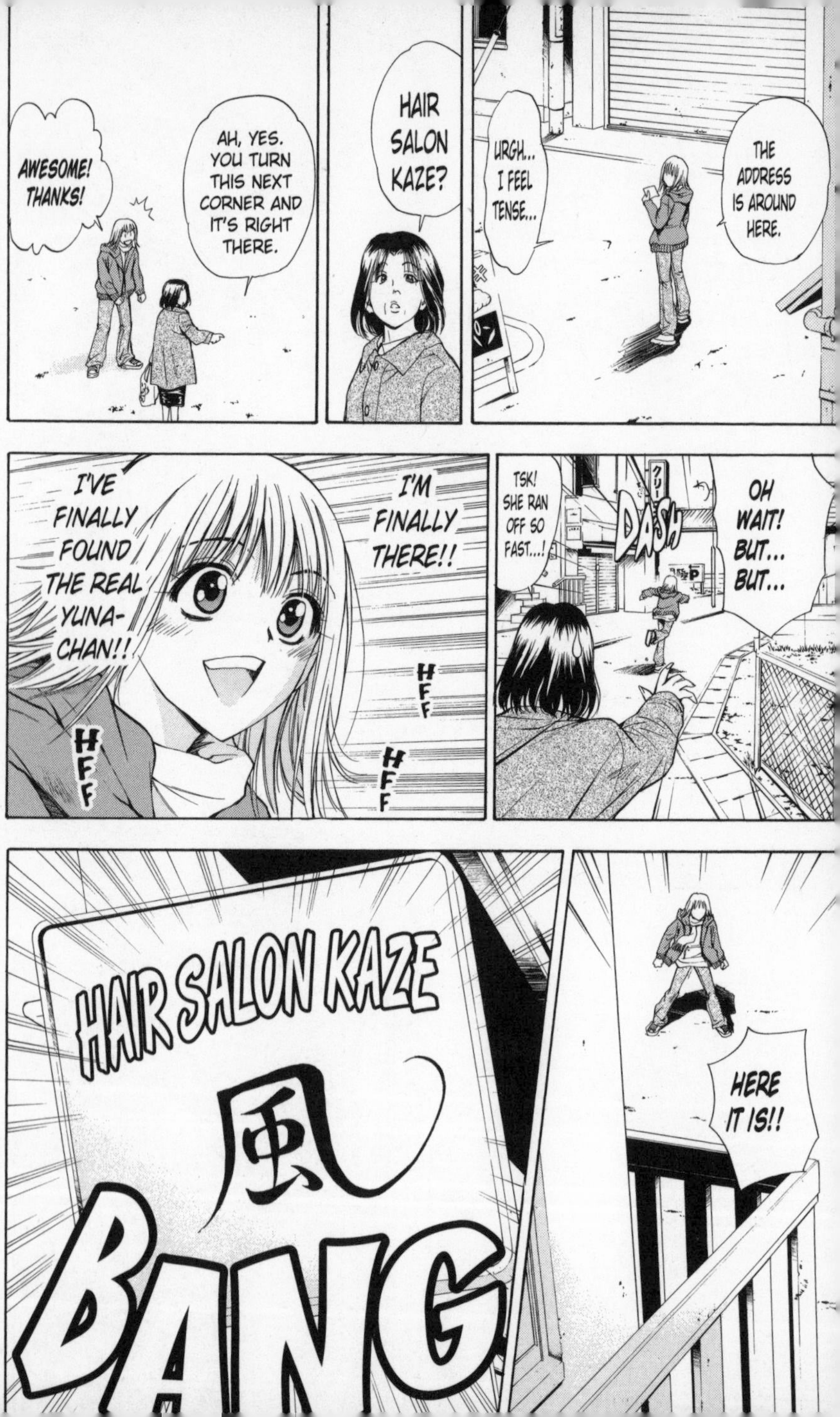
THE ADDRESS IS AROUND HERE.
URGH... I FEEL TENSE...
HAIR SALON KAZE?
AH, YES. YOU TURN THIS NEXT CORNER AND IT'S RIGHT THERE.
AWESOME! THANKS!
OH WAIT! BUT... BUT...
DASH
TSK! SHE RAN OFF SO FAST...!
I'M FINALLY THERE!!
I'VE FINALLY FOUND THE REAL YUNA-CHAN!!
HFF
HFF
HFF
HERE IT IS!!
HAIR SALON KAZE
風
BANG

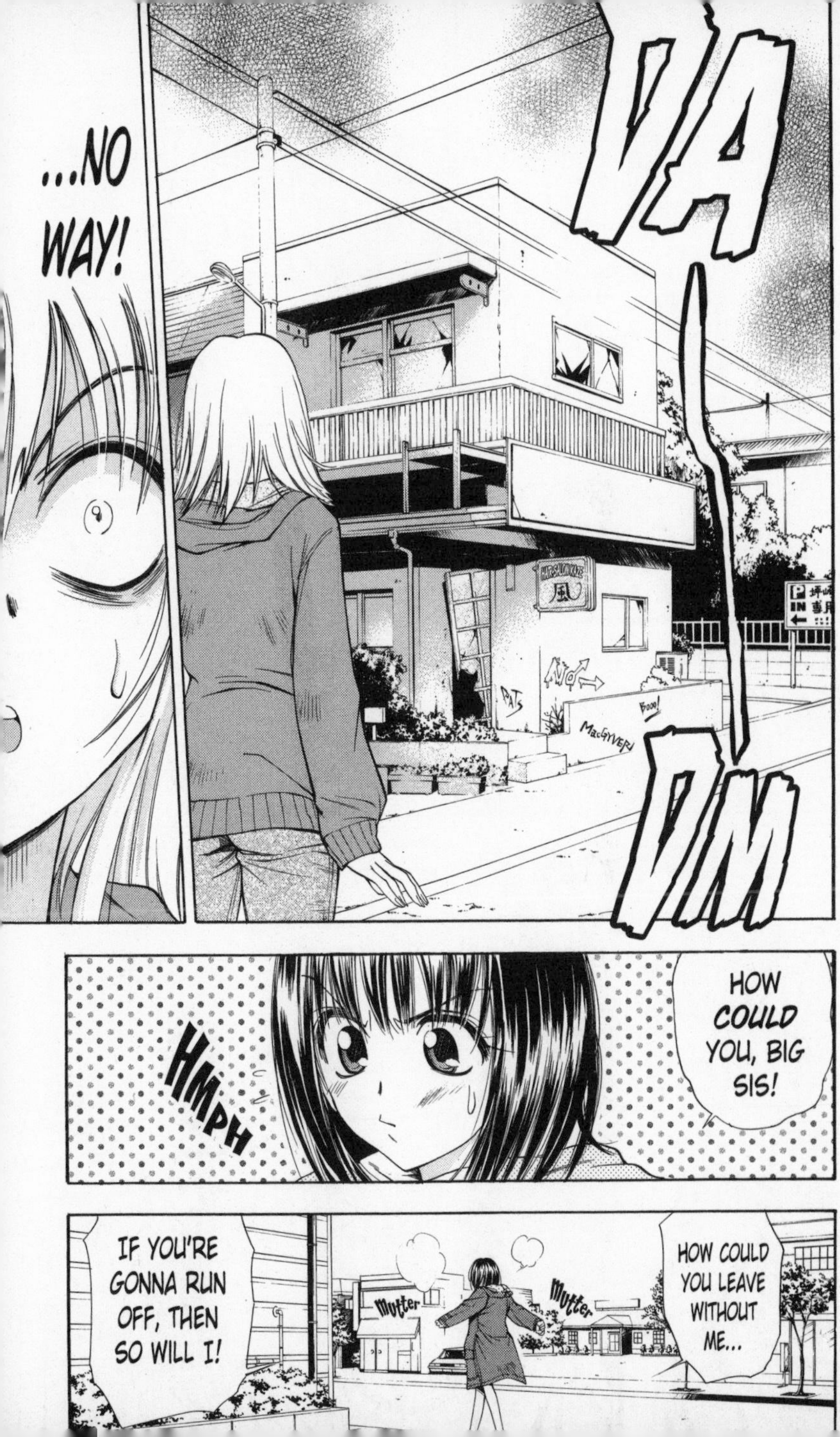
VA-DM
MacGYVER!
Boo!
...NO WAY!
HOW COULD YOU, BIG SIS!
HMPH
HOW COULD YOU LEAVE WITHOUT ME...
Mutter
Mutter
IF YOU'RE GONNA RUN OFF, THEN SO WILL I!

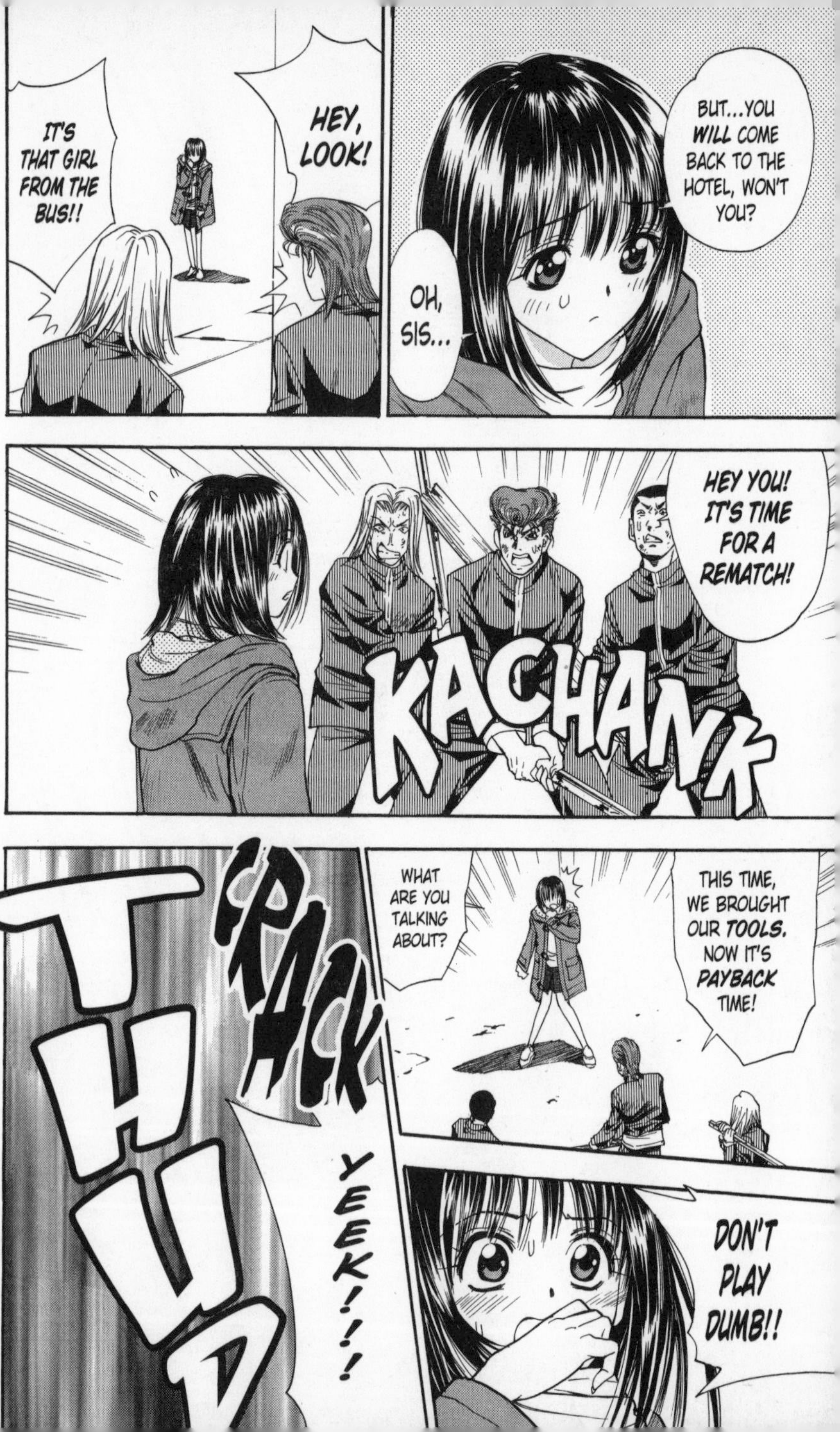
BUT...YOU WILL COME BACK TO THE HOTEL, WON'T YOU?
OH, SIS...
HEY, LOOK!
IT'S THAT GIRL FROM THE BUS!!
HEY YOU! IT'S TIME FOR A REMATCH!
KACHANK
THIS TIME, WE BROUGHT OUR TOOLS. NOW IT'S PAYBACK TIME!
WHAT ARE YOU TALKING ABOUT?
DON'T PLAY DUMB!!
CRACK
THUD
YEEK!!!

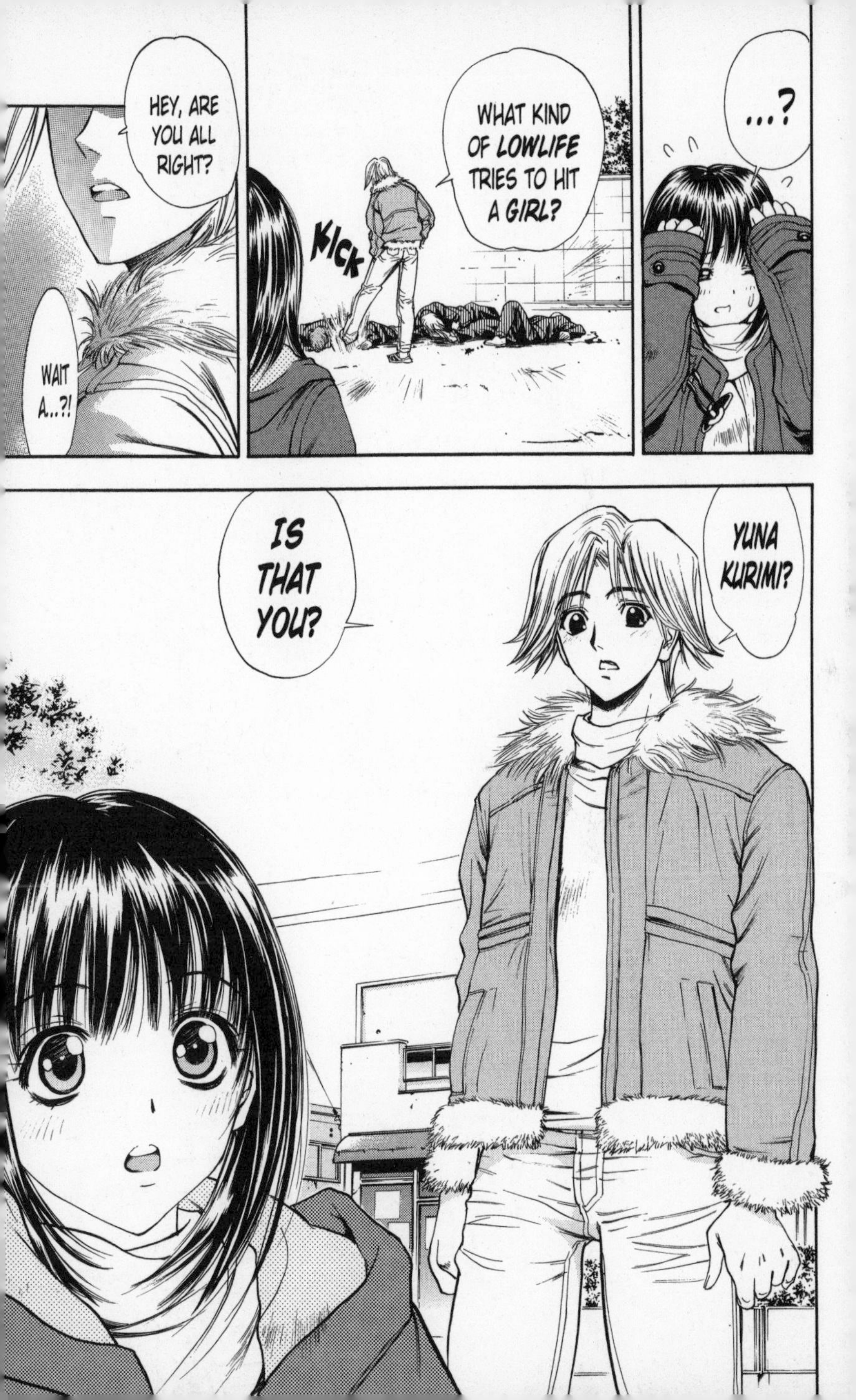
...?
WHAT KIND OF LOWLIFE TRIES TO HIT A GIRL?
KICK
HEY, ARE YOU ALL RIGHT?
WAIT A...?!
YUNA KURIMI?
IS THAT YOU?

Pretty Face

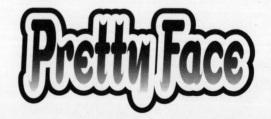

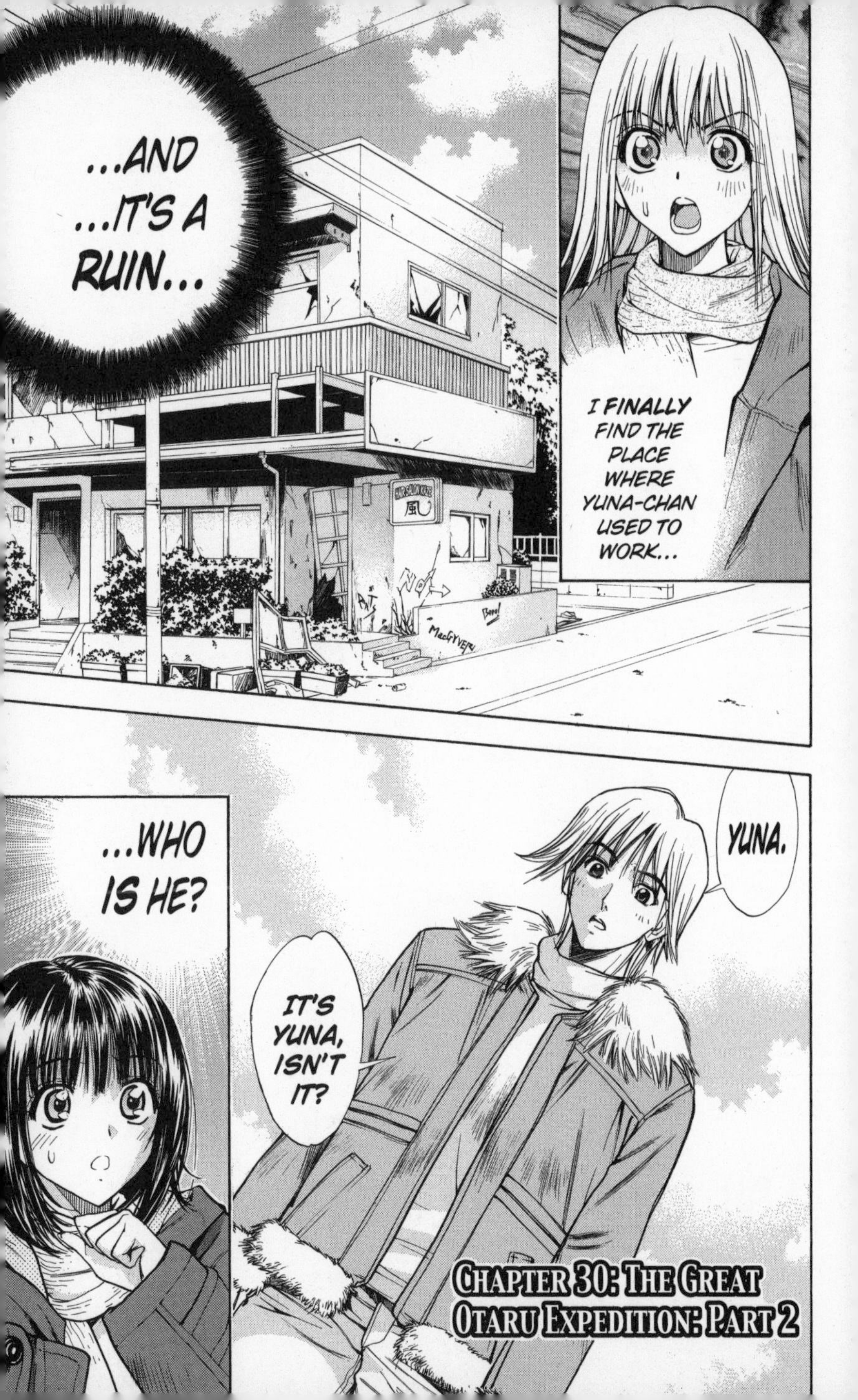
I FINALLY FIND THE PLACE WHERE YUNA-CHAN USED TO WORK...
...AND ...IT'S A RUIN...
YUNA.
IT'S YUNA, ISN'T IT?
...WHO IS HE?
CHAPTER 30: THE GREAT OTARU EXPEDITION: PART 2

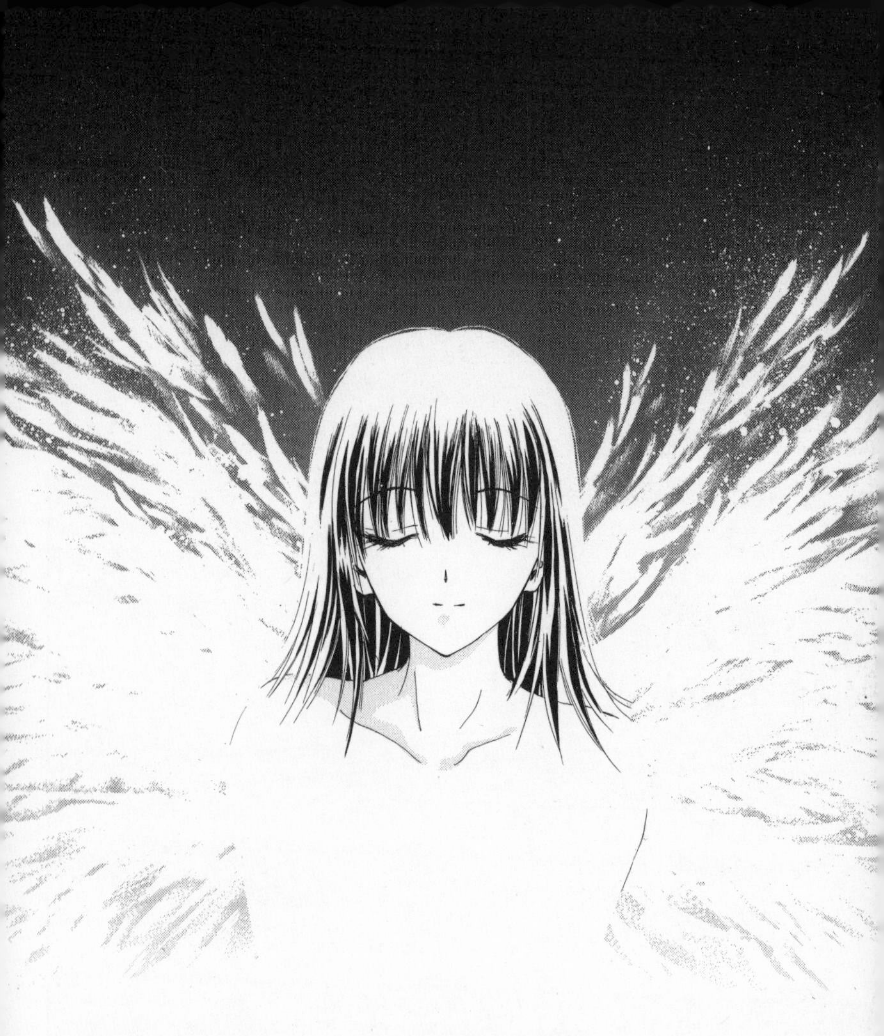

Chapter 30: The Great Otaru Expedition: Part 2

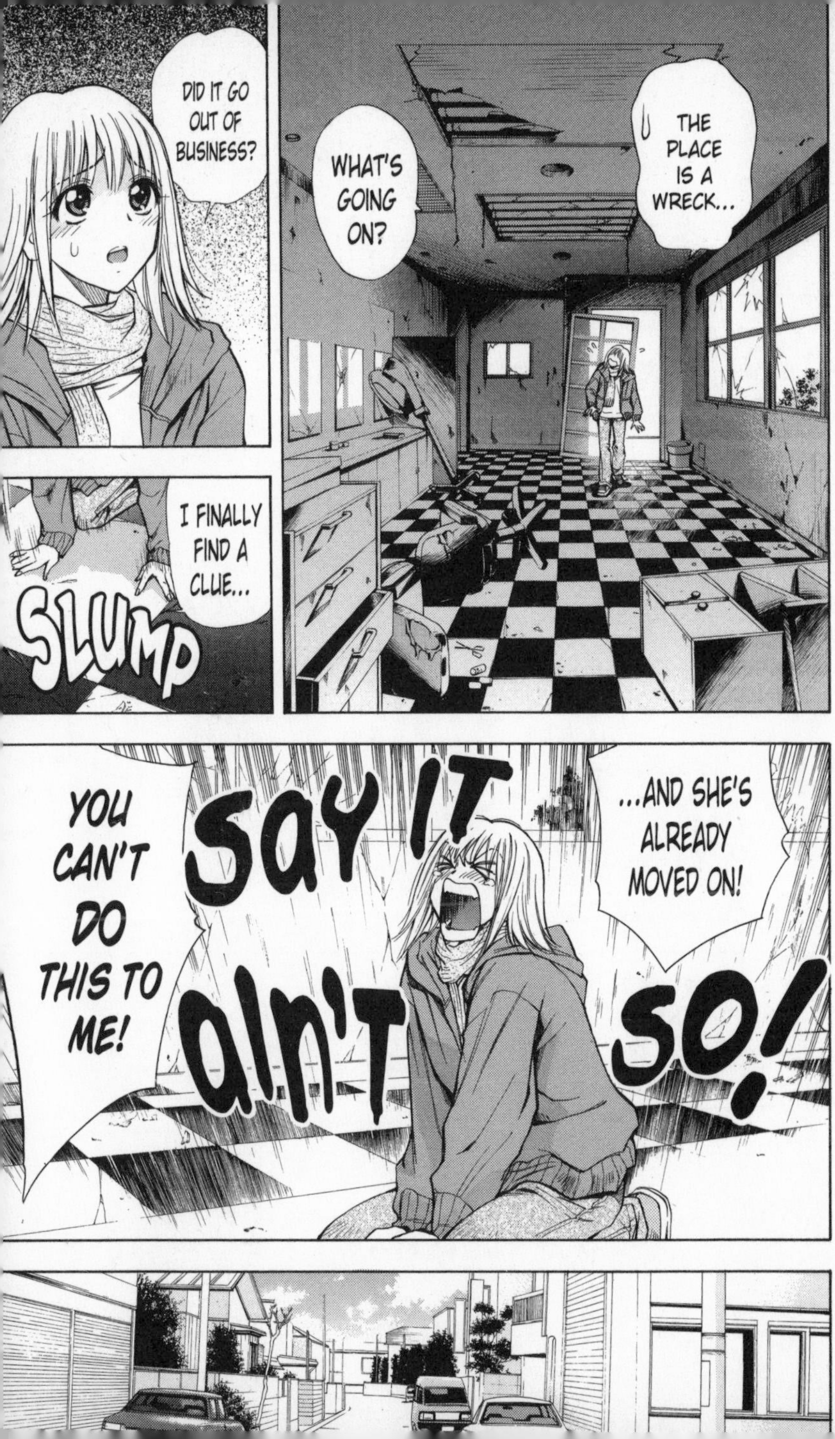
THE PLACE IS A WRECK...
WHAT'S GOING ON?
DID IT GO OUT OF BUSINESS?
I FINALLY FIND A CLUE...
SLUMP
...AND SHE'S ALREADY MOVED ON!
SAY IT AIN'T SO!
YOU CAN'T DO THIS TO ME!

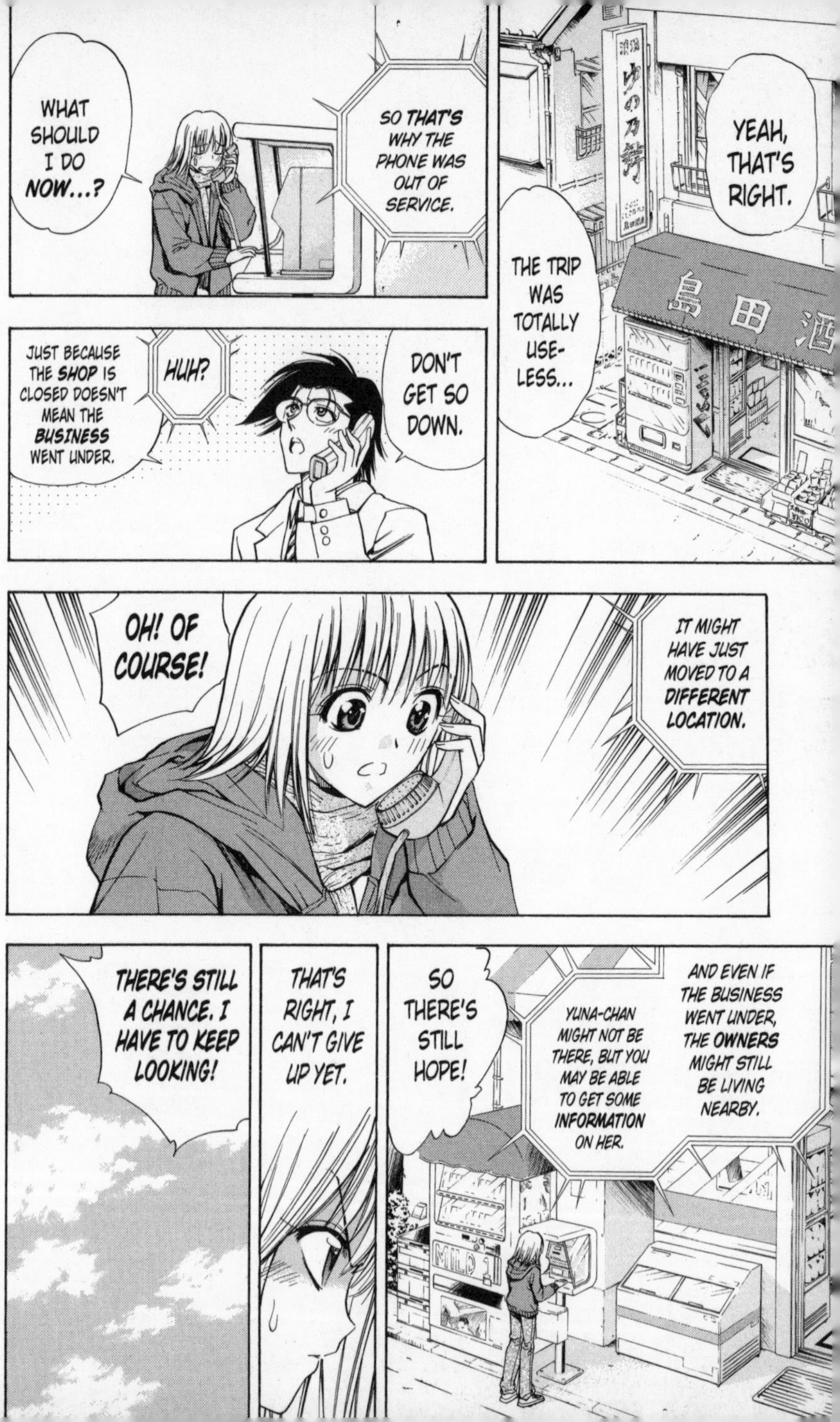
YEAH, THAT'S RIGHT.
THE TRIP WAS TOTALLY USE-LESS...
島田酒
SO THAT'S WHY THE PHONE WAS OUT OF SERVICE.
WHAT SHOULD I DO NOW...?
DON'T GET SO DOWN.
HUH?
JUST BECAUSE THE SHOP IS CLOSED DOESN'T MEAN THE BUSINESS WENT UNDER.
IT MIGHT HAVE JUST MOVED TO A DIFFERENT LOCATION.
OH! OF COURSE!
AND EVEN IF THE BUSINESS WENT UNDER, THE OWNERS MIGHT STILL BE LIVING NEARBY.
YUNA-CHAN MIGHT NOT BE THERE, BUT YOU MAY BE ABLE TO GET SOME INFORMATION ON HER.
SO THERE'S STILL HOPE!
MILD 1
THAT'S RIGHT, I CAN'T GIVE UP YET.
THERE'S STILL A CHANCE. I HAVE TO KEEP LOOKING!

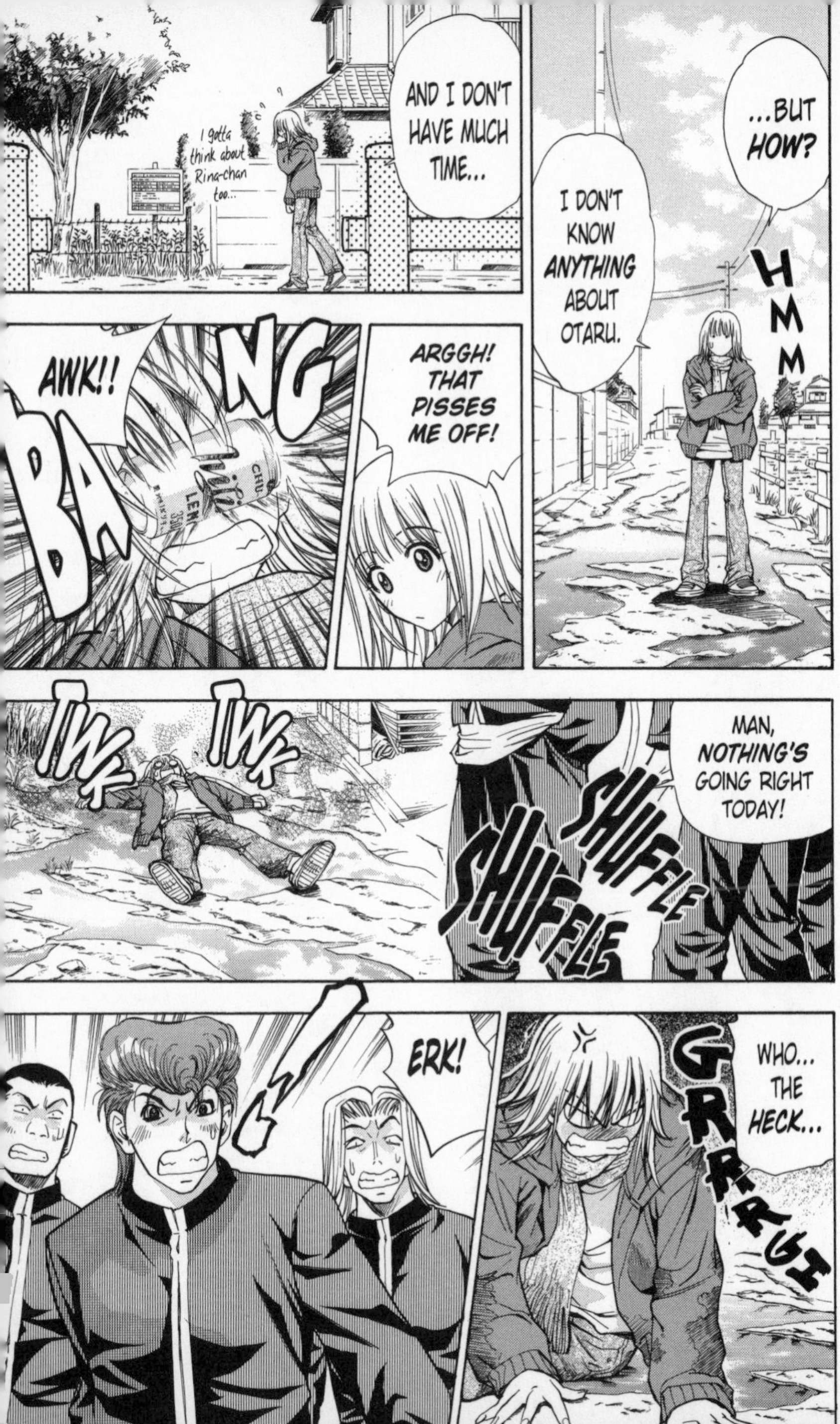
...BUT HOW?
HMMM
I DON'T KNOW ANYTHING ABOUT OTARU.
AND I DON'T HAVE MUCH TIME...
I gotta think about Rina-chan too...
ARGGH! THAT PISSES ME OFF!
BANG
AWK!!
MAN, NOTHING'S GOING RIGHT TODAY!
SHUFFLE
SHUFFLE
TWK
TWK
WHO... THE HECK...
GRRRRG!
ERK!
!

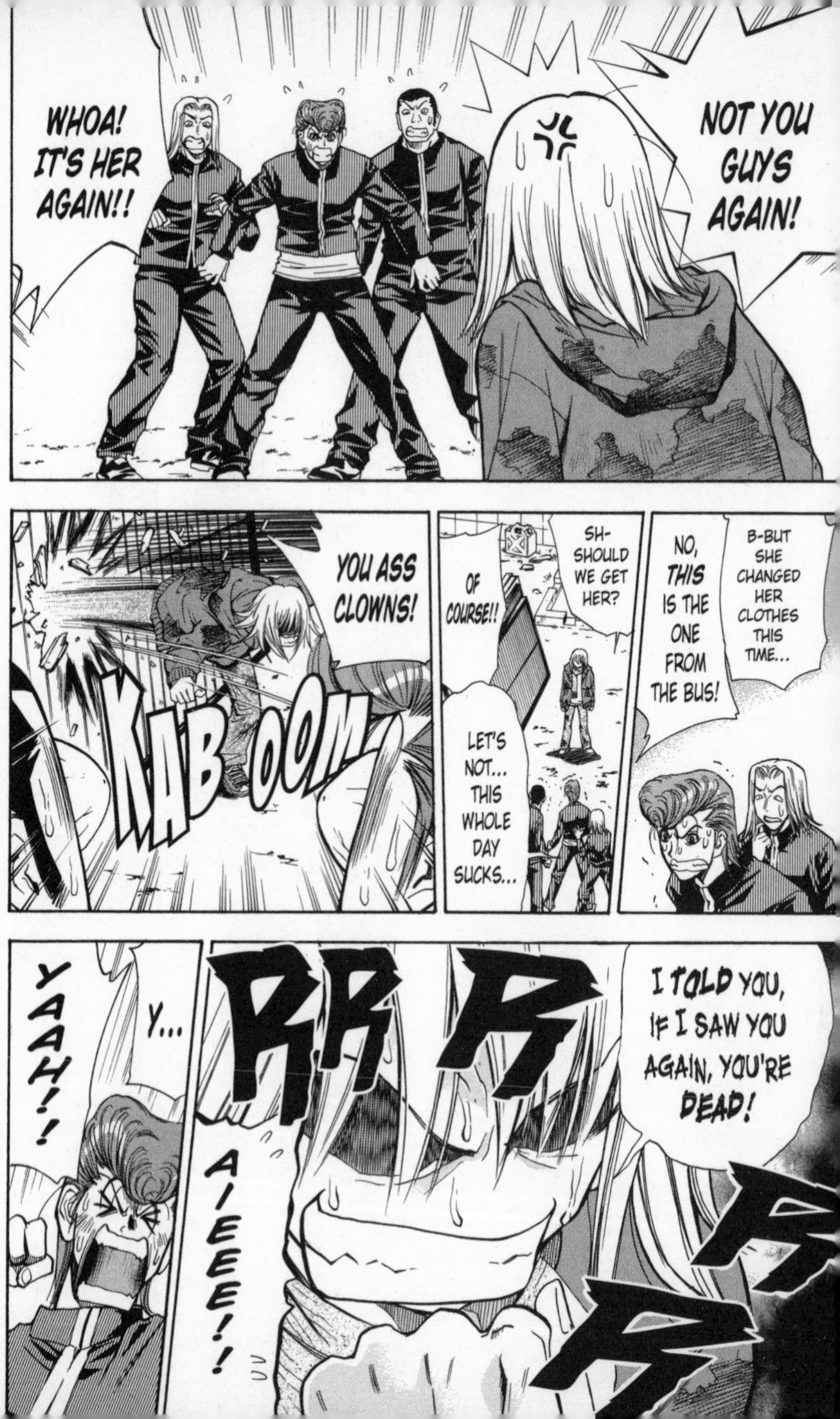
NOT YOU GUYS AGAIN!
WHOA! IT'S HER AGAIN!!
B-BUT SHE CHANGED HER CLOTHES THIS TIME...
NO, THIS IS THE ONE FROM THE BUS!
SH-SHOULD WE GET HER?
OF COURSE!!
LET'S NOT... THIS WHOLE DAY SUCKS...
YOU ASS CLOWNS!
KABOOM
I TOLD YOU, IF I SAW YOU AGAIN, YOU'RE DEAD!
RR
R
RR
Y...
AIEEEE!!
YAAAH!!!

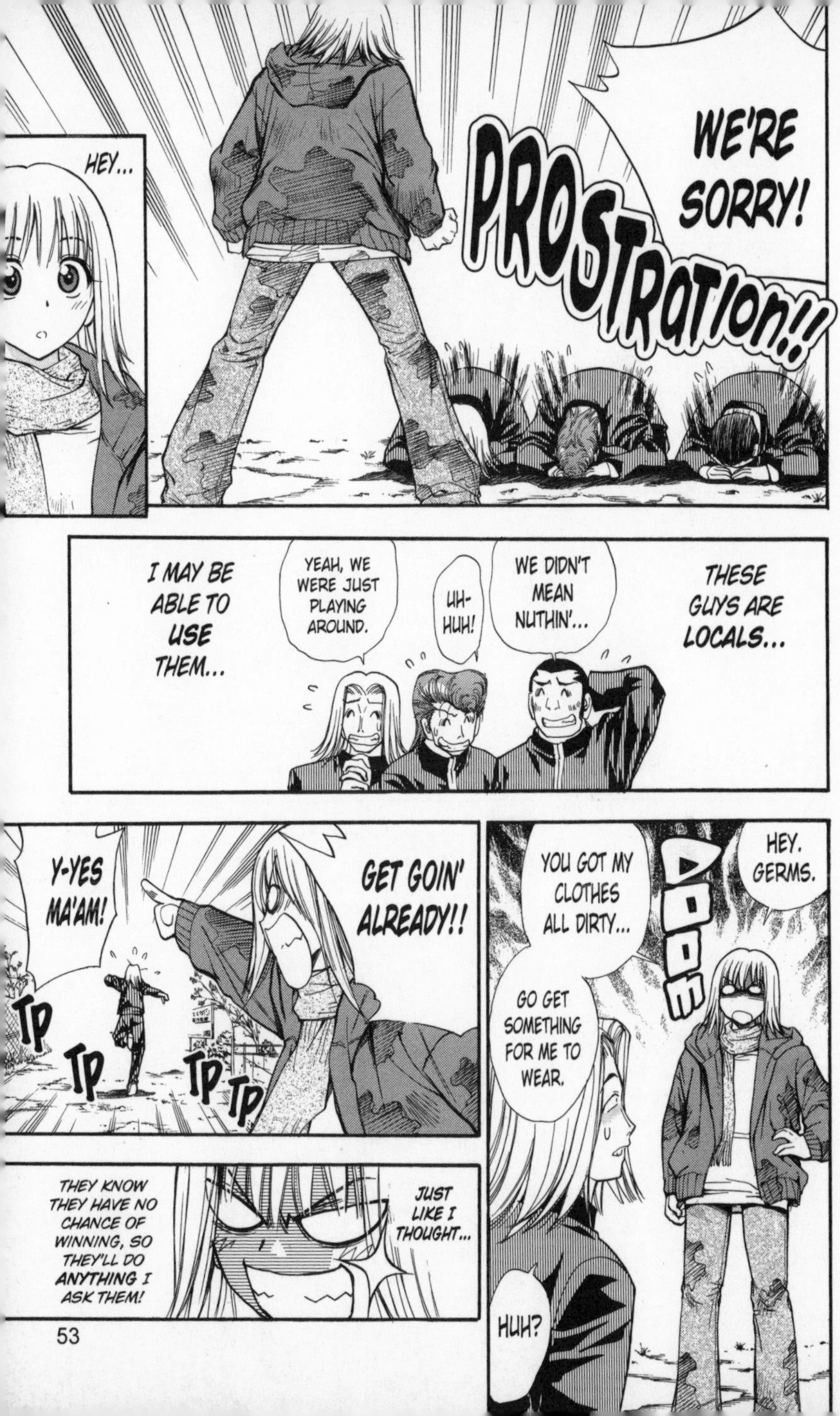
WE'RE SORRY!
PROSTRATION!!
HEY...
THESE GUYS ARE LOCALS...
WE DIDN'T MEAN NUTHIN'...
UH-HUH!
YEAH, WE WERE JUST PLAYING AROUND.
I MAY BE ABLE TO USE THEM...
HEY. GERMS.
DOOM
YOU GOT MY CLOTHES ALL DIRTY...
GO GET SOMETHING FOR ME TO WEAR.
HUH?
GET GOIN' ALREADY!!
Y-YES MA'AM!
TP TP TP TP
JUST LIKE I THOUGHT...
THEY KNOW THEY HAVE NO CHANCE OF WINNING, SO THEY'LL DO ANYTHING I ASK THEM!

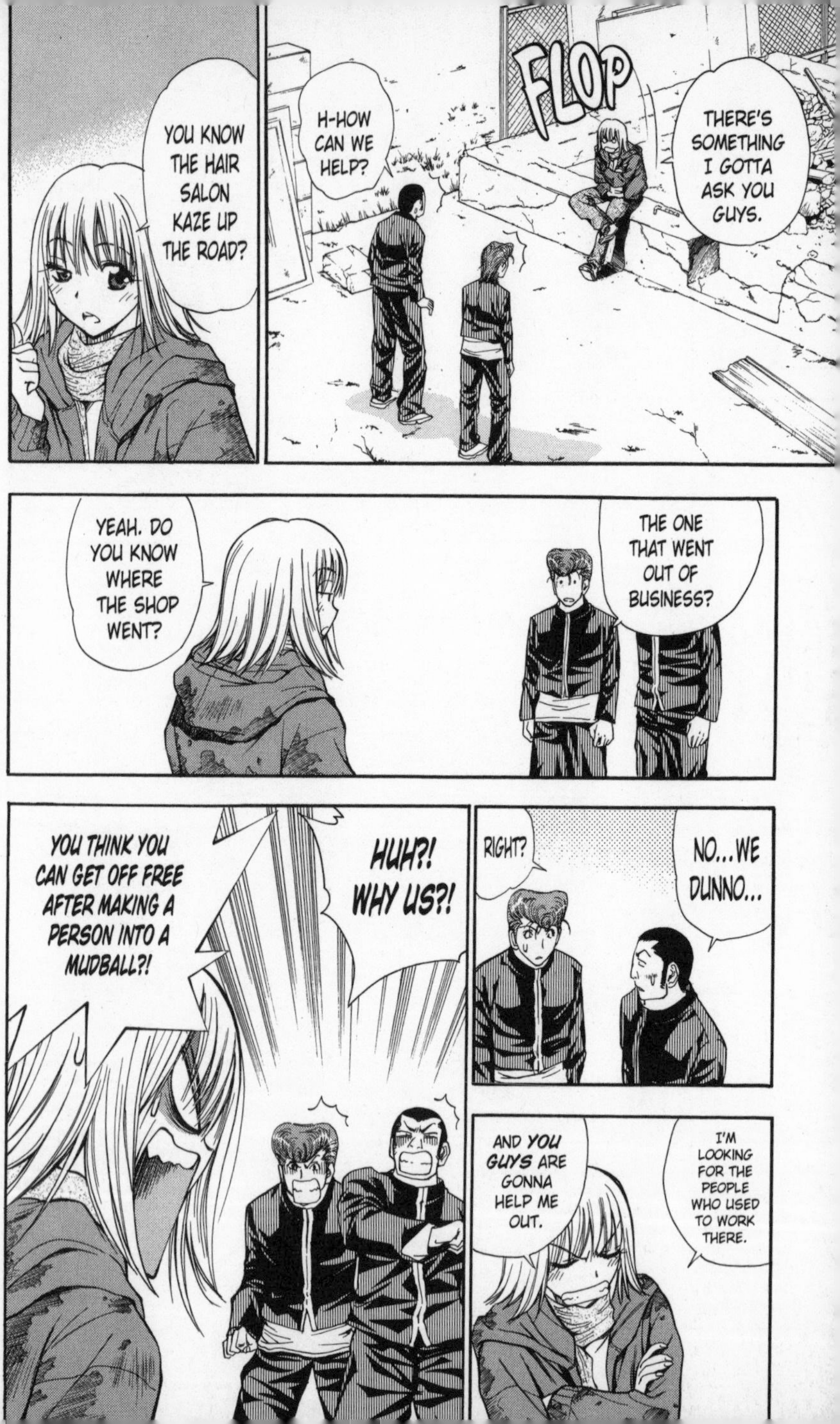
FLOP
THERE'S SOMETHING I GOTTA ASK YOU GUYS.
H-HOW CAN WE HELP?
YOU KNOW THE HAIR SALON KAZE UP THE ROAD?
THE ONE THAT WENT OUT OF BUSINESS?
YEAH. DO YOU KNOW WHERE THE SHOP WENT?
NO...WE DUNNO...
RIGHT?
I'M LOOKING FOR THE PEOPLE WHO USED TO WORK THERE.
AND *YOU GUYS* ARE GONNA HELP ME OUT.
HUH?! WHY US?!
YOU THINK YOU CAN GET OFF FREE AFTER MAKING A PERSON INTO A MUDBALL?!

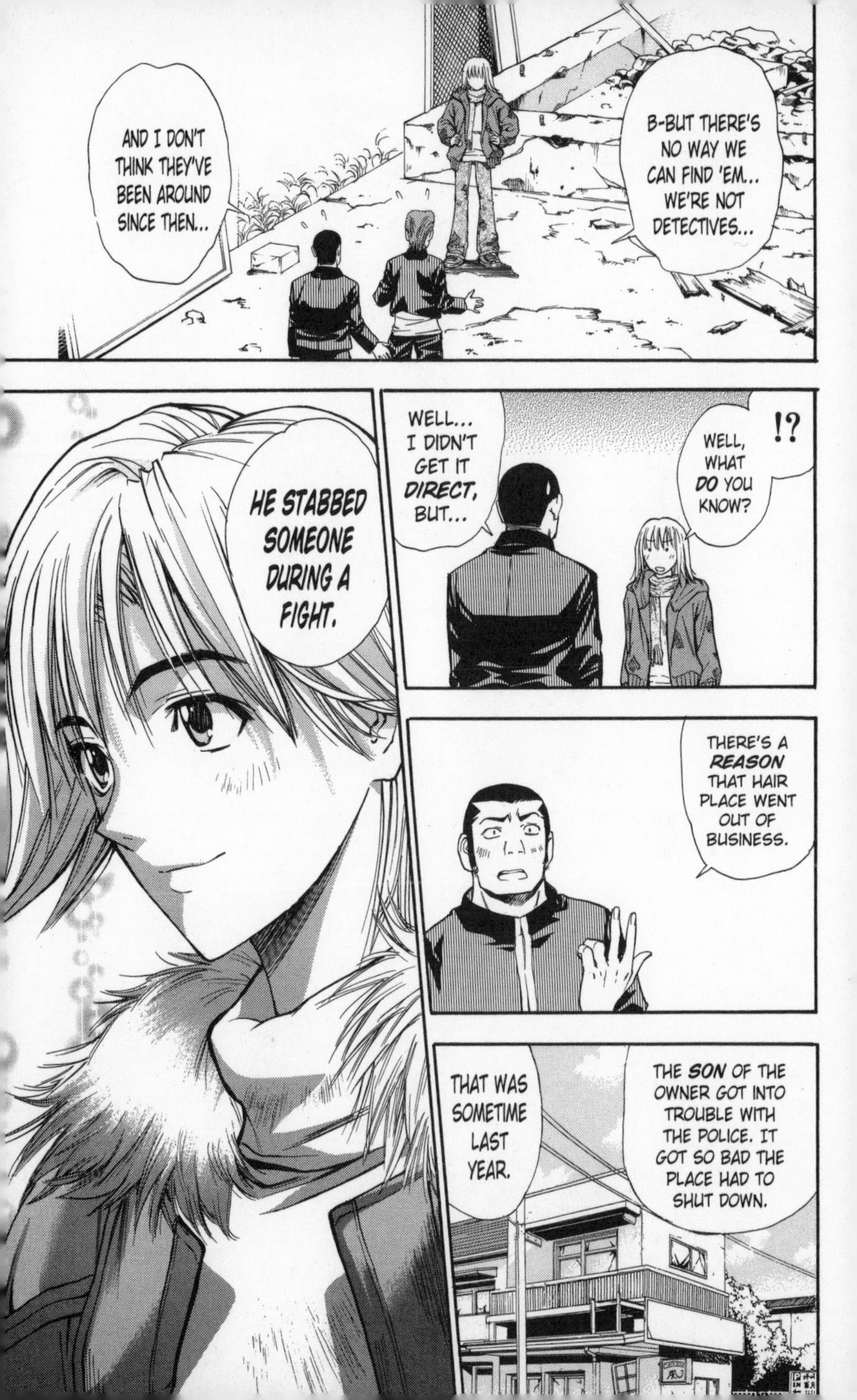
B-BUT THERE'S NO WAY WE CAN FIND 'EM... WE'RE NOT DETECTIVES...
AND I DON'T THINK THEY'VE BEEN AROUND SINCE THEN...
!?
WELL, WHAT DO YOU KNOW?
WELL... I DIDN'T GET IT DIRECT, BUT...
THERE'S A REASON THAT HAIR PLACE WENT OUT OF BUSINESS.
THE SON OF THE OWNER GOT INTO TROUBLE WITH THE POLICE. IT GOT SO BAD THE PLACE HAD TO SHUT DOWN.
THAT WAS SOMETIME LAST YEAR.
HE STABBED SOMEONE DURING A FIGHT.

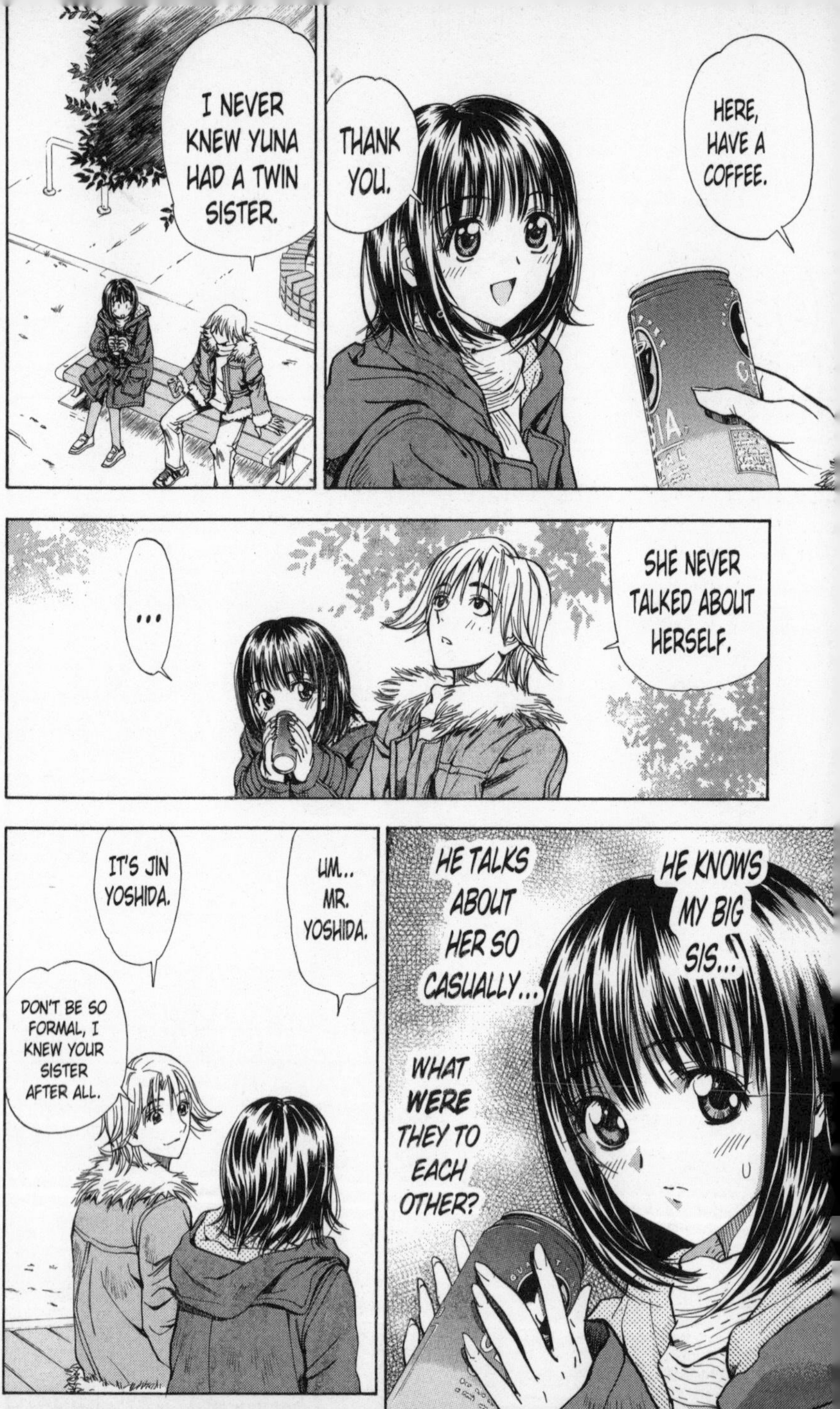
HERE, HAVE A COFFEE.
THANK YOU.
I NEVER KNEW YUNA HAD A TWIN SISTER.
SHE NEVER TALKED ABOUT HERSELF.
...
HE KNOWS MY BIG SIS...
HE TALKS ABOUT HER SO CASUALLY...
WHAT WERE THEY TO EACH OTHER?
UM... MR. YOSHIDA.
IT'S JIN YOSHIDA.
DON'T BE SO FORMAL, I KNEW YOUR SISTER AFTER ALL.

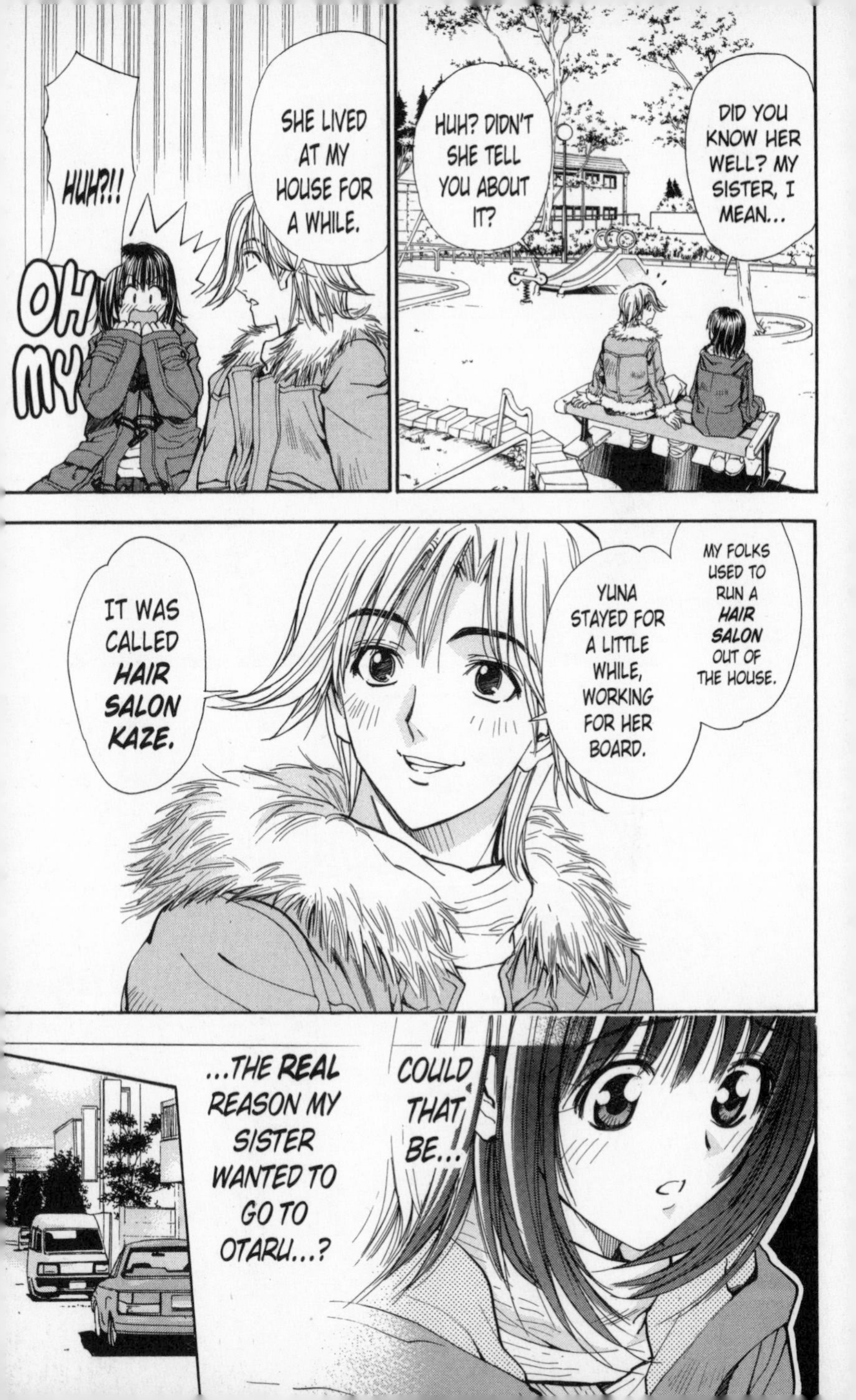
DID YOU KNOW HER WELL? MY SISTER, I MEAN...
HUH? DIDN'T SHE TELL YOU ABOUT IT?
SHE LIVED AT MY HOUSE FOR A WHILE.
HUH?!!
OH MY
MY FOLKS USED TO RUN A HAIR SALON OUT OF THE HOUSE.
YUNA STAYED FOR A LITTLE WHILE, WORKING FOR HER BOARD.
IT WAS CALLED HAIR SALON KAZE.
COULD THAT BE...
...THE REAL REASON MY SISTER WANTED TO GO TO OTARU...?

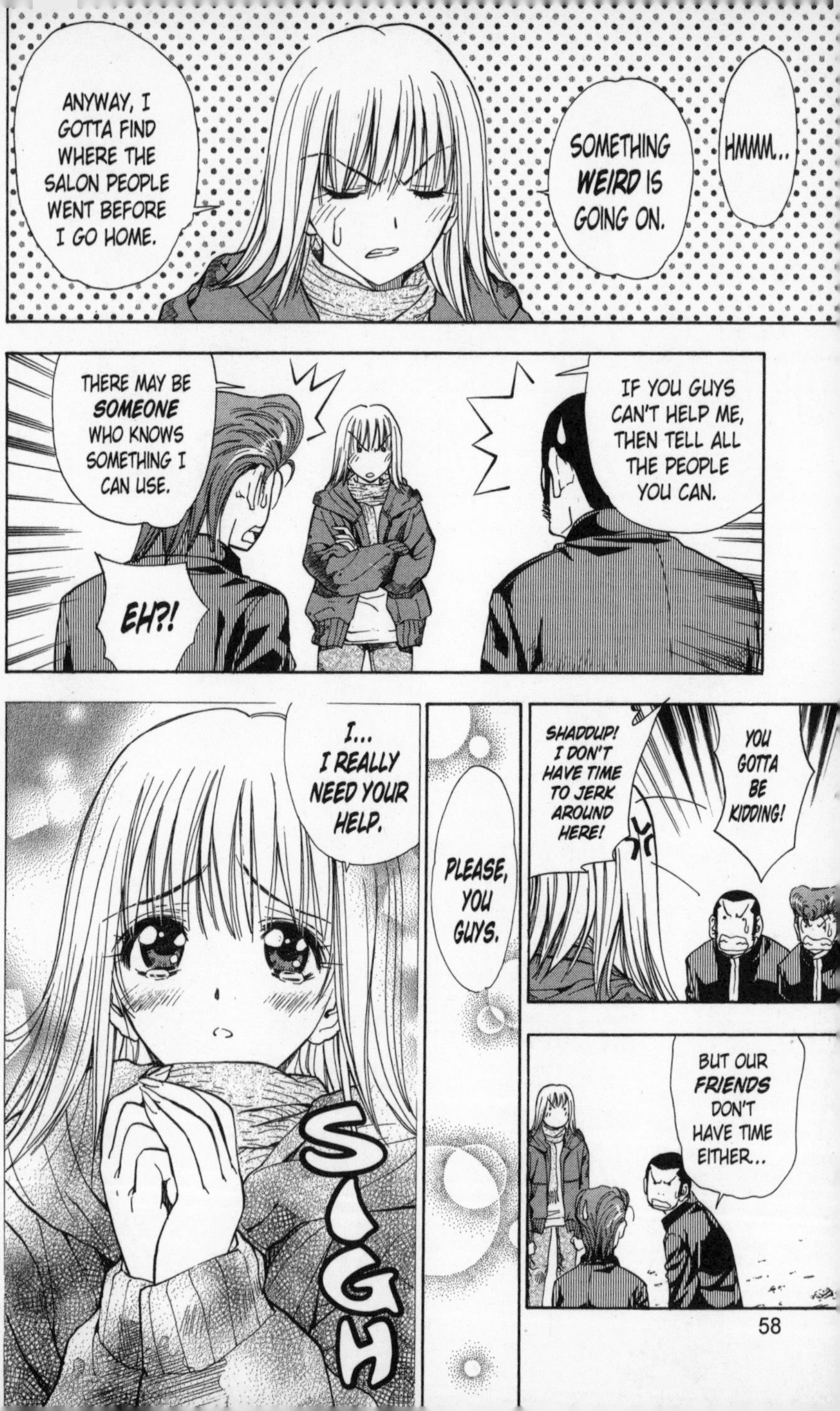
HMMM...
SOMETHING WEIRD IS GOING ON.
ANYWAY, I GOTTA FIND WHERE THE SALON PEOPLE WENT BEFORE I GO HOME.
IF YOU GUYS CAN'T HELP ME, THEN TELL ALL THE PEOPLE YOU CAN.
THERE MAY BE SOMEONE WHO KNOWS SOMETHING I CAN USE.
EH?!
YOU GOTTA BE KIDDING!
SHADDUP! I DON'T HAVE TIME TO JERK AROUND HERE!
BUT OUR FRIENDS DON'T HAVE TIME EITHER...
I... I REALLY NEED YOUR HELP.
PLEASE, YOU GUYS.
SIGH

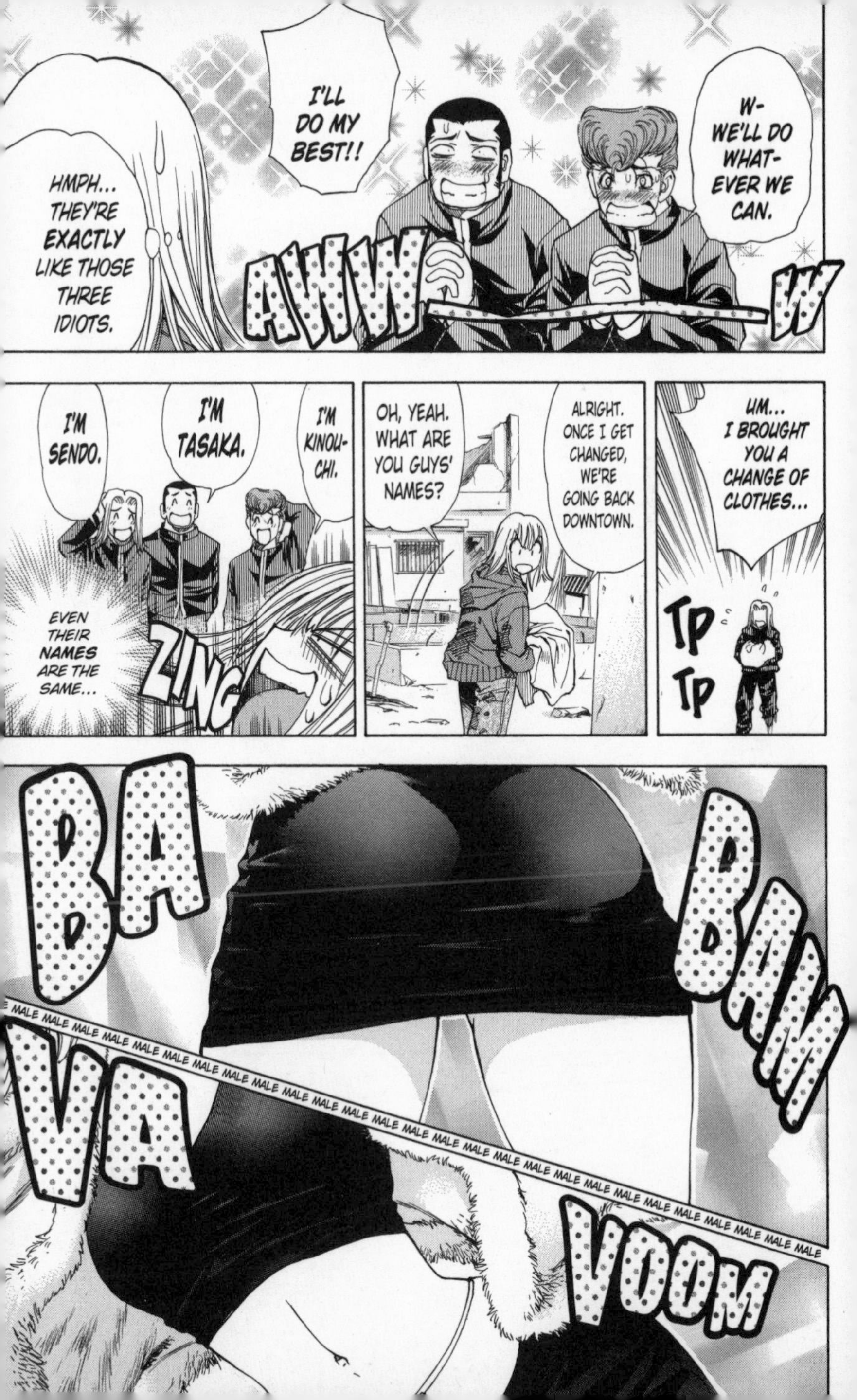
W- WE'LL DO WHAT-EVER WE CAN.
I'LL DO MY BEST!!
AWWW
HMPH... THEY'RE EXACTLY LIKE THOSE THREE IDIOTS.
UM... I BROUGHT YOU A CHANGE OF CLOTHES...
TP TP
ALRIGHT. ONCE I GET CHANGED, WE'RE GOING BACK DOWNTOWN.
OH, YEAH. WHAT ARE YOU GUYS' NAMES?
I'M KINOU-CHI.
I'M TASAKA.
I'M SENDO.
ZING
EVEN THEIR NAMES ARE THE SAME...
BAM
BA
VA
VOOM
MALE MALE MALE MALE MALE MALE MALE MALE MALE MALE MALE MALE MALE MALE MALE MALE MALE MALE MALE MALE MALE MALE MALE MALE

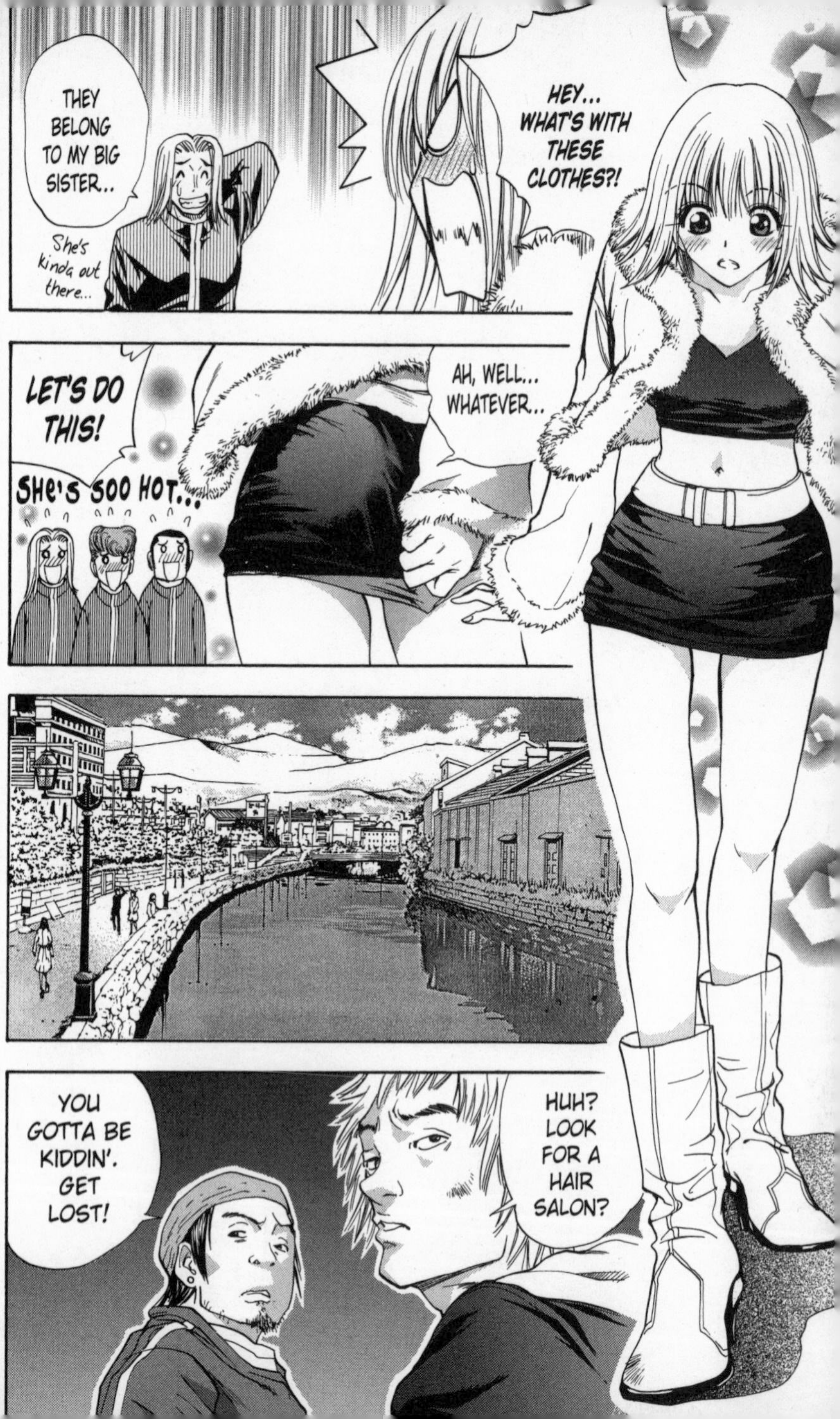
HEY... WHAT'S WITH THESE CLOTHES?!
THEY BELONG TO MY BIG SISTER..
She's kinda out there...
AH, WELL... WHATEVER...
LET'S DO THIS!
SHE'S SOO HOT...
HUH? LOOK FOR A HAIR SALON?
YOU GOTTA BE KIDDIN'. GET LOST!

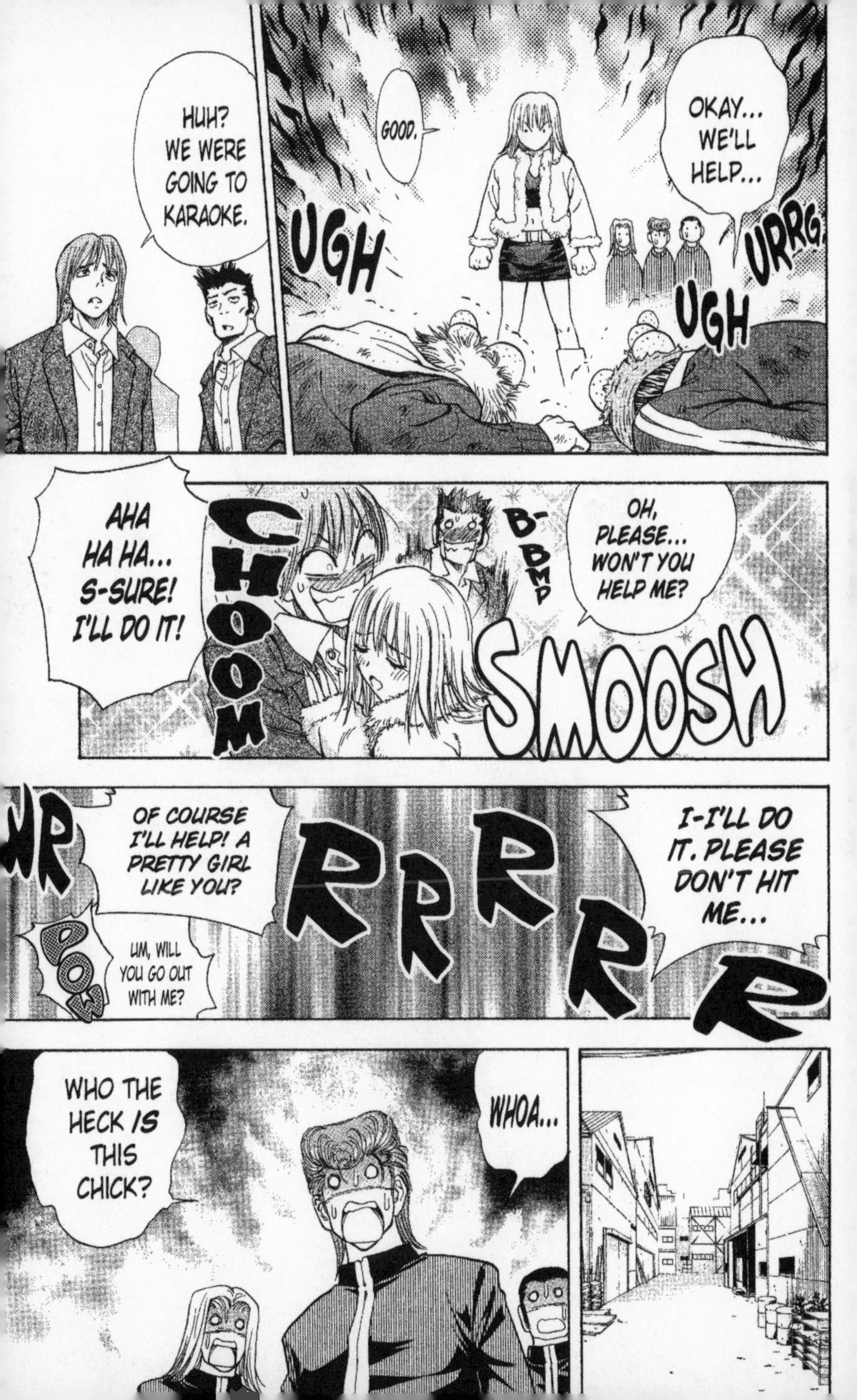
OKAY... WE'LL HELP...
URRG
GOOD.
UGH
UGH
HUH? WE WERE GOING TO KARAOKE.
OH, PLEASE... WON'T YOU HELP ME?
B-BMP
SMOOSH
CHOOM
AHA HA HA... S-SURE! I'LL DO IT!
I-I'LL DO IT. PLEASE DON'T HIT ME...
RRRRR
OF COURSE I'LL HELP! A PRETTY GIRL LIKE YOU?
UM, WILL YOU GO OUT WITH ME?
POW
WHOA...
WHO THE HECK *IS* THIS CHICK?

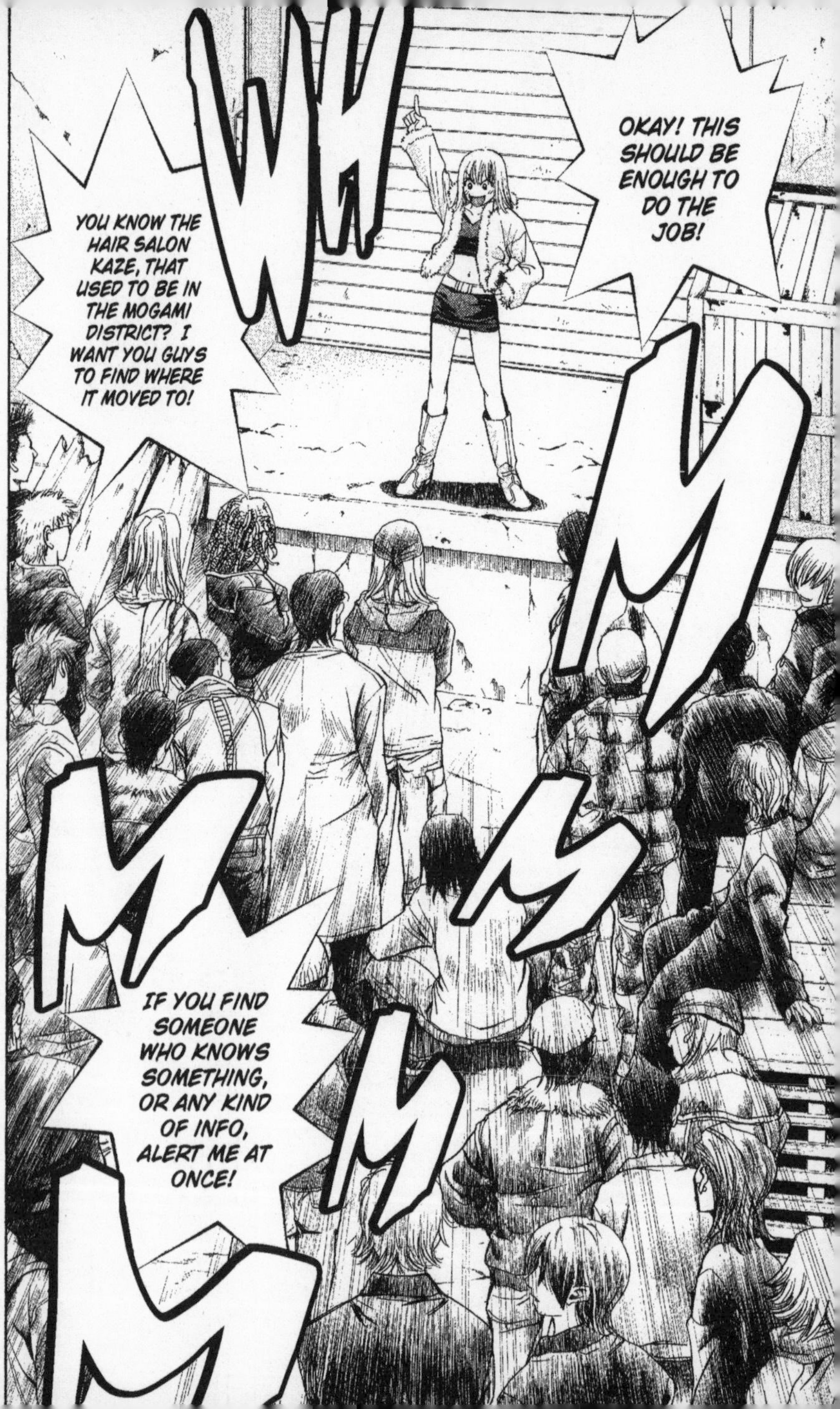
OKAY! THIS SHOULD BE ENOUGH TO DO THE JOB!
YOU KNOW THE HAIR SALON KAZE, THAT USED TO BE IN THE MOGAMI DISTRICT? I WANT YOU GUYS TO FIND WHERE IT MOVED TO!
WHMMMMM
IF YOU FIND SOMEONE WHO KNOWS SOMETHING, OR ANY KIND OF INFO, ALERT ME AT ONCE!

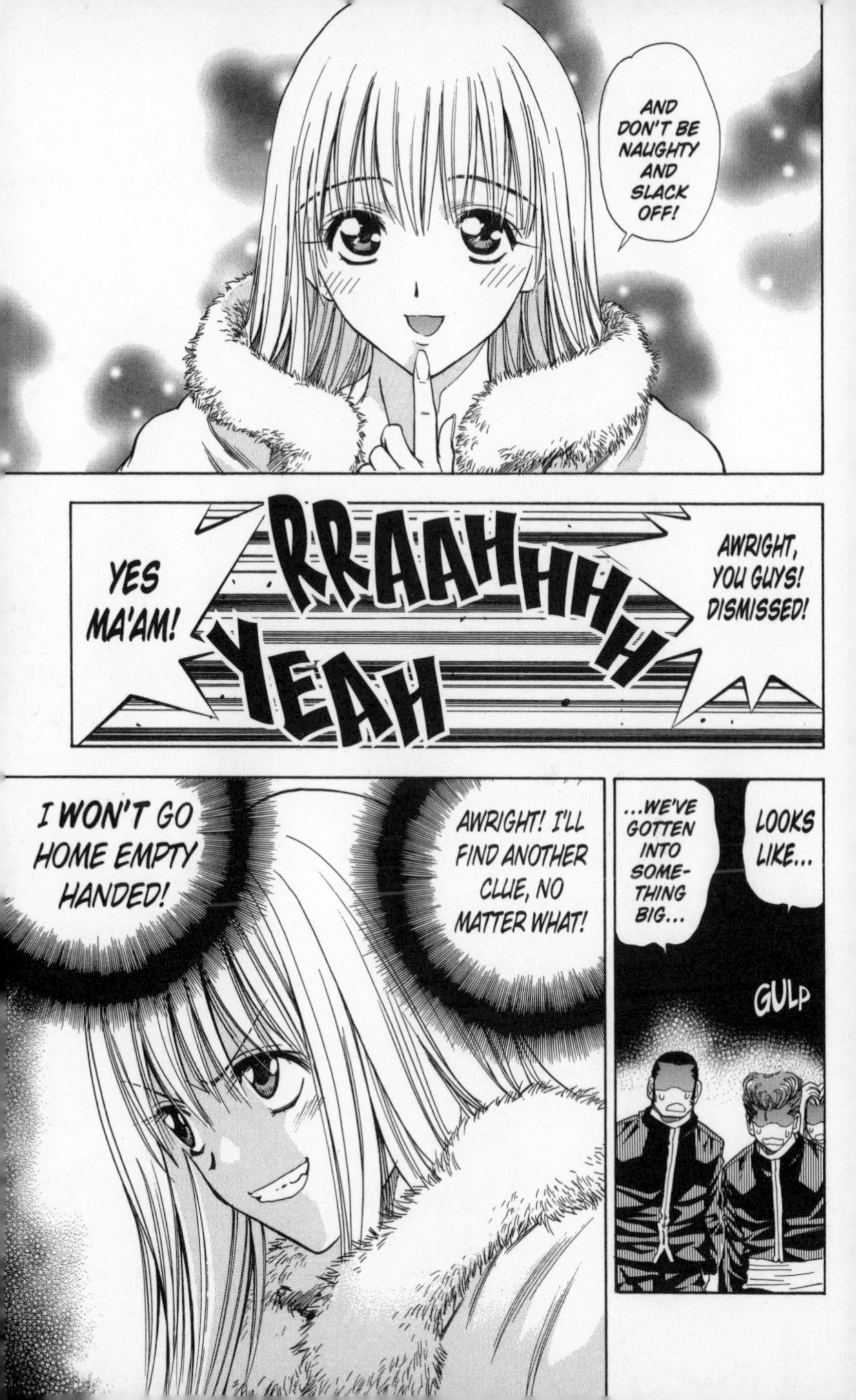
AND DON'T BE NAUGHTY AND SLACK OFF!
AWRIGHT, YOU GUYS! DISMISSED!
RRAAHHHH YEAH
YES MA'AM!
LOOKS LIKE...
...WE'VE GOTTEN INTO SOME-THING BIG...
GULP
AWRIGHT! I'LL FIND ANOTHER CLUE, NO MATTER WHAT!
I WON'T GO HOME EMPTY HANDED!

Pretty Face

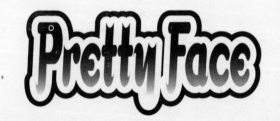

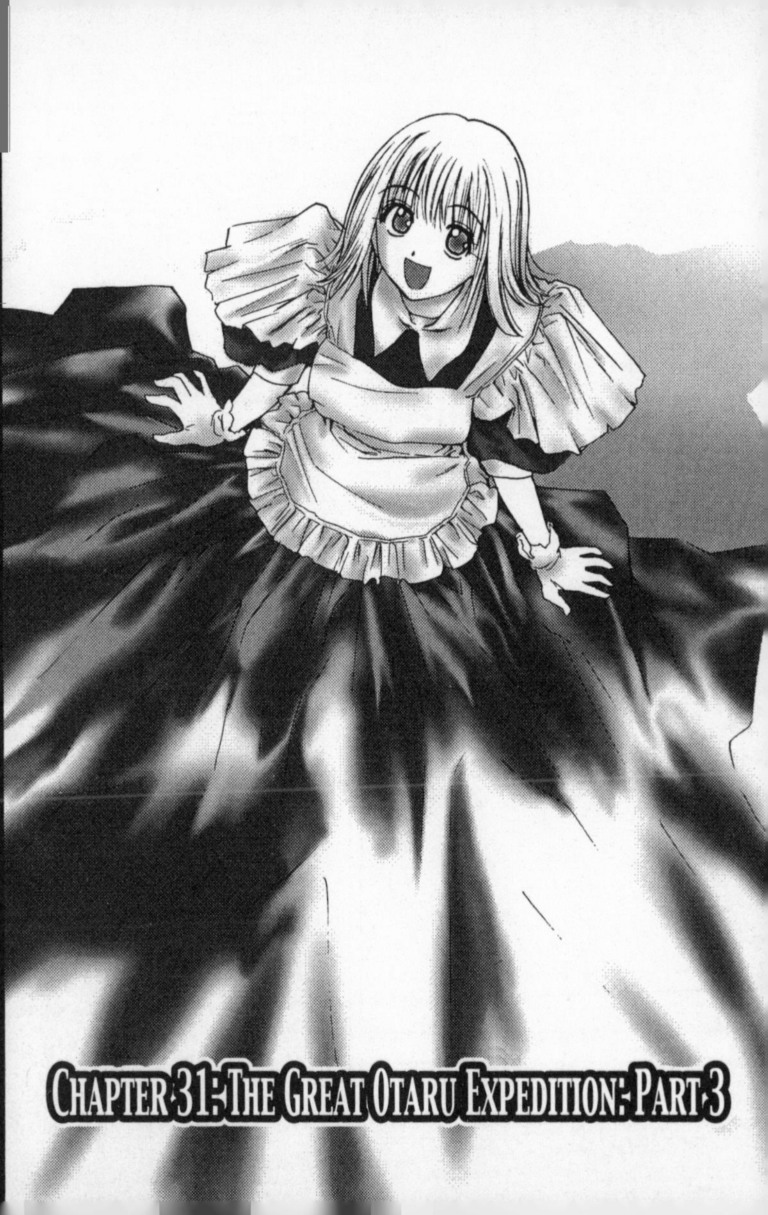
CHAPTER 31: THE GREAT OTARU EXPEDITION: PART 3

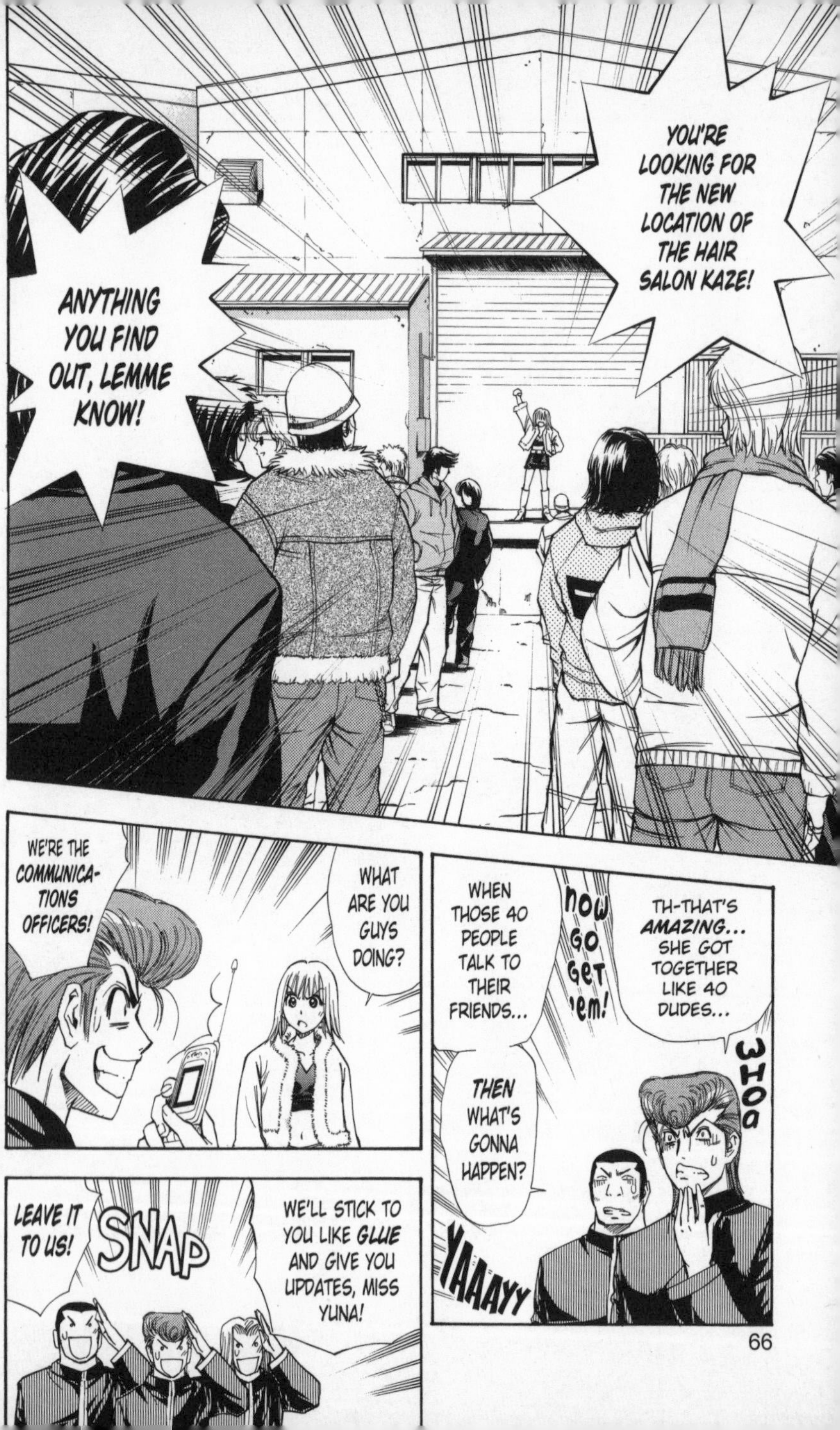
YOU'RE LOOKING FOR THE NEW LOCATION OF THE HAIR SALON KAZE!
ANYTHING YOU FIND OUT, LEMME KNOW!
TH-THAT'S *AMAZING*... SHE GOT TOGETHER LIKE 40 DUDES...
now go get 'em!
WHEN THOSE 40 PEOPLE TALK TO THEIR FRIENDS...
WHOA
THEN WHAT'S GONNA HAPPEN?
YAAAAYY
WHAT ARE YOU GUYS DOING?
WE'RE THE COMMUNICATIONS OFFICERS!
WE'LL STICK TO YOU LIKE *GLUE* AND GIVE YOU UPDATES, MISS YUNA!
SNAP
LEAVE IT TO US!

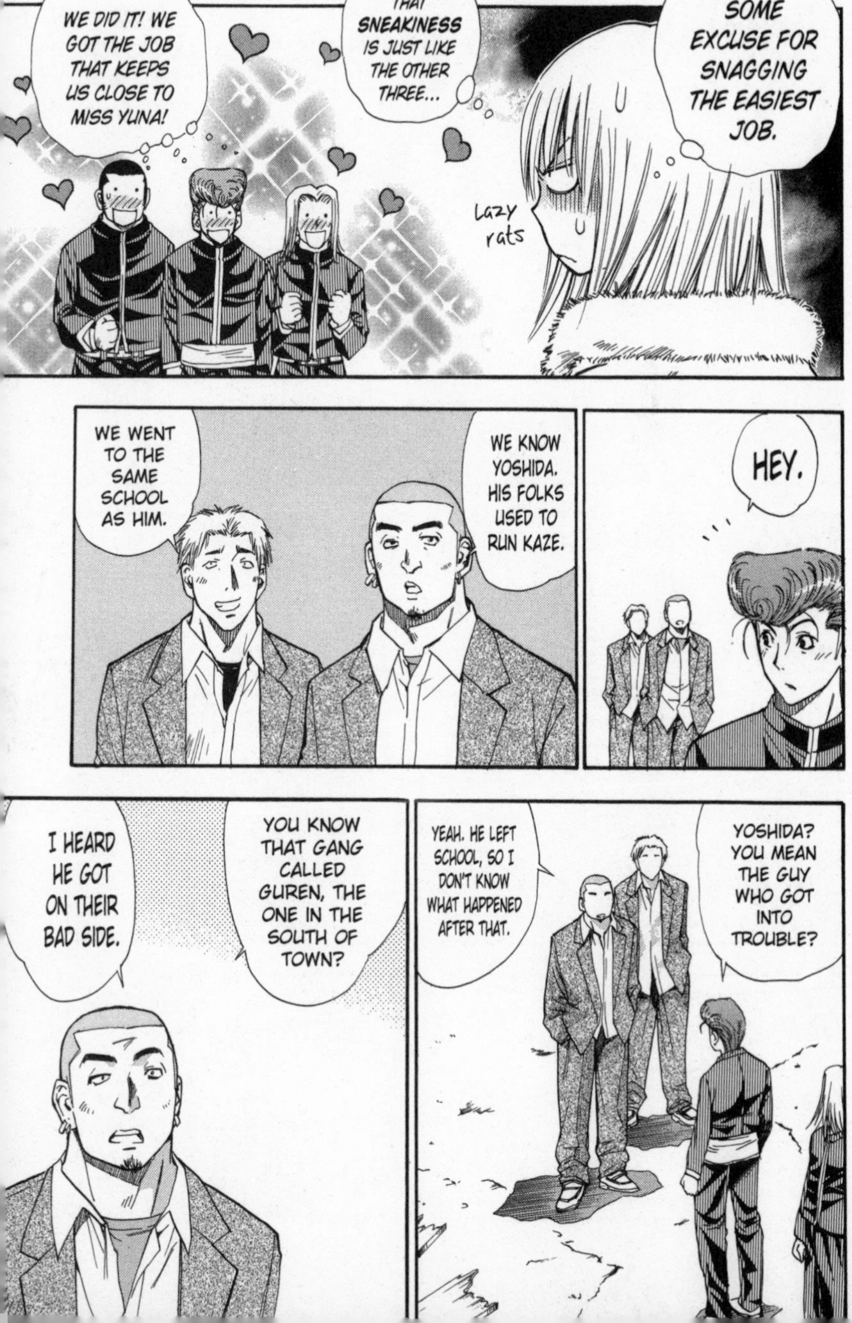
SOME EXCUSE FOR SNAGGING THE EASIEST JOB.
Lazy rats
THAT SNEAKINESS IS JUST LIKE THE OTHER THREE...
WE DID IT! WE GOT THE JOB THAT KEEPS US CLOSE TO MISS YUNA!
HEY.
WE KNOW YOSHIDA. HIS FOLKS USED TO RUN KAZE.
WE WENT TO THE SAME SCHOOL AS HIM.
YOSHIDA? YOU MEAN THE GUY WHO GOT INTO TROUBLE?
YEAH. HE LEFT SCHOOL, SO I DON'T KNOW WHAT HAPPENED AFTER THAT.
YOU KNOW THAT GANG CALLED GUREN, THE ONE IN THE SOUTH OF TOWN?
I HEARD HE GOT ON THEIR BAD SIDE.

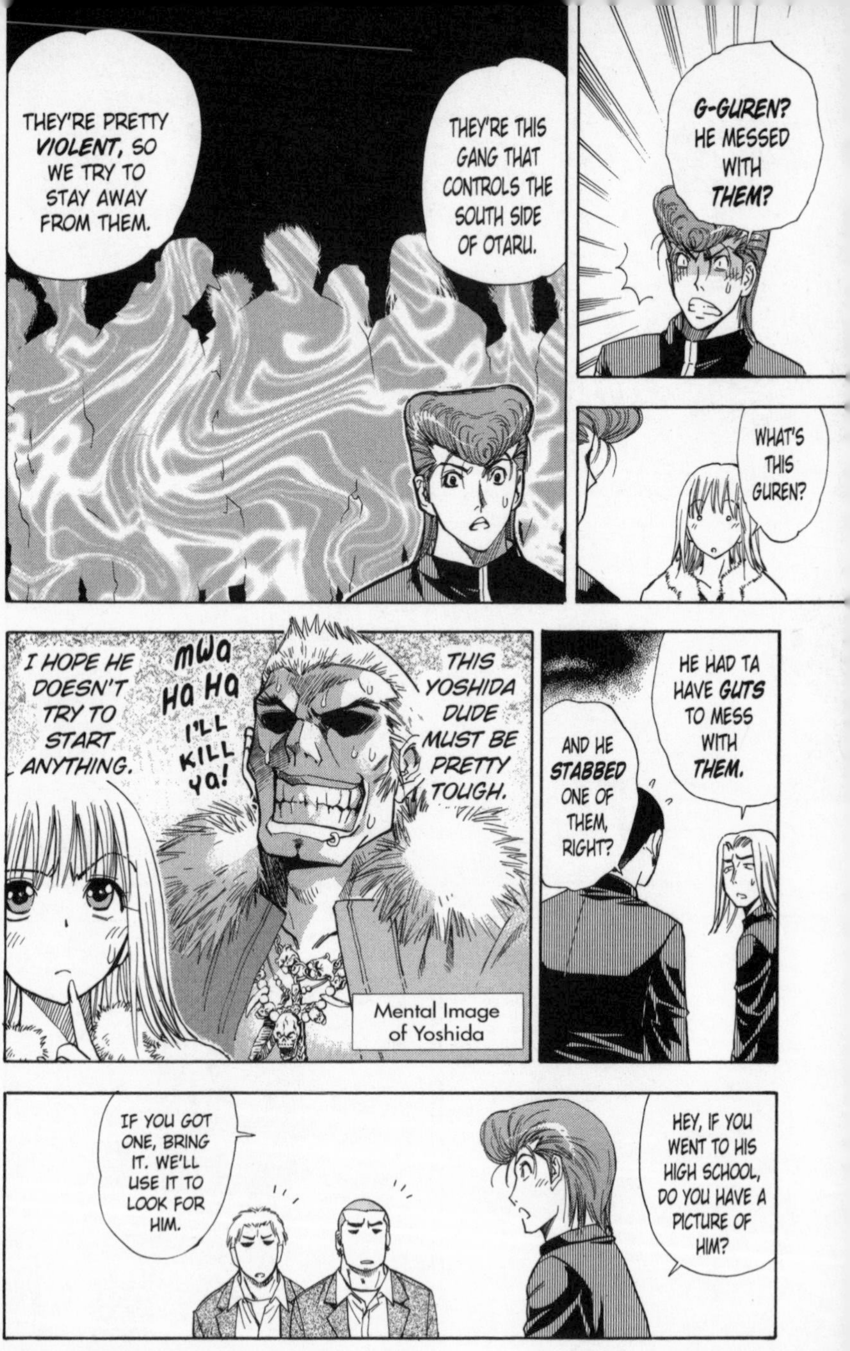
G-GUREN? HE MESSED WITH THEM?
WHAT'S THIS GUREN?
THEY'RE THIS GANG THAT CONTROLS THE SOUTH SIDE OF OTARU.
THEY'RE PRETTY VIOLENT, SO WE TRY TO STAY AWAY FROM THEM.
HE HAD TA HAVE GUTS TO MESS WITH THEM.
AND HE STABBED ONE OF THEM, RIGHT?
THIS YOSHIDA DUDE MUST BE PRETTY TOUGH.
mwa Ha Ha
I'LL KILL ya!
I HOPE HE DOESN'T TRY TO START ANYTHING.
Mental Image of Yoshida
HEY, IF YOU WENT TO HIS HIGH SCHOOL, DO YOU HAVE A PICTURE OF HIM?
IF YOU GOT ONE, BRING IT. WE'LL USE IT TO LOOK FOR HIM.

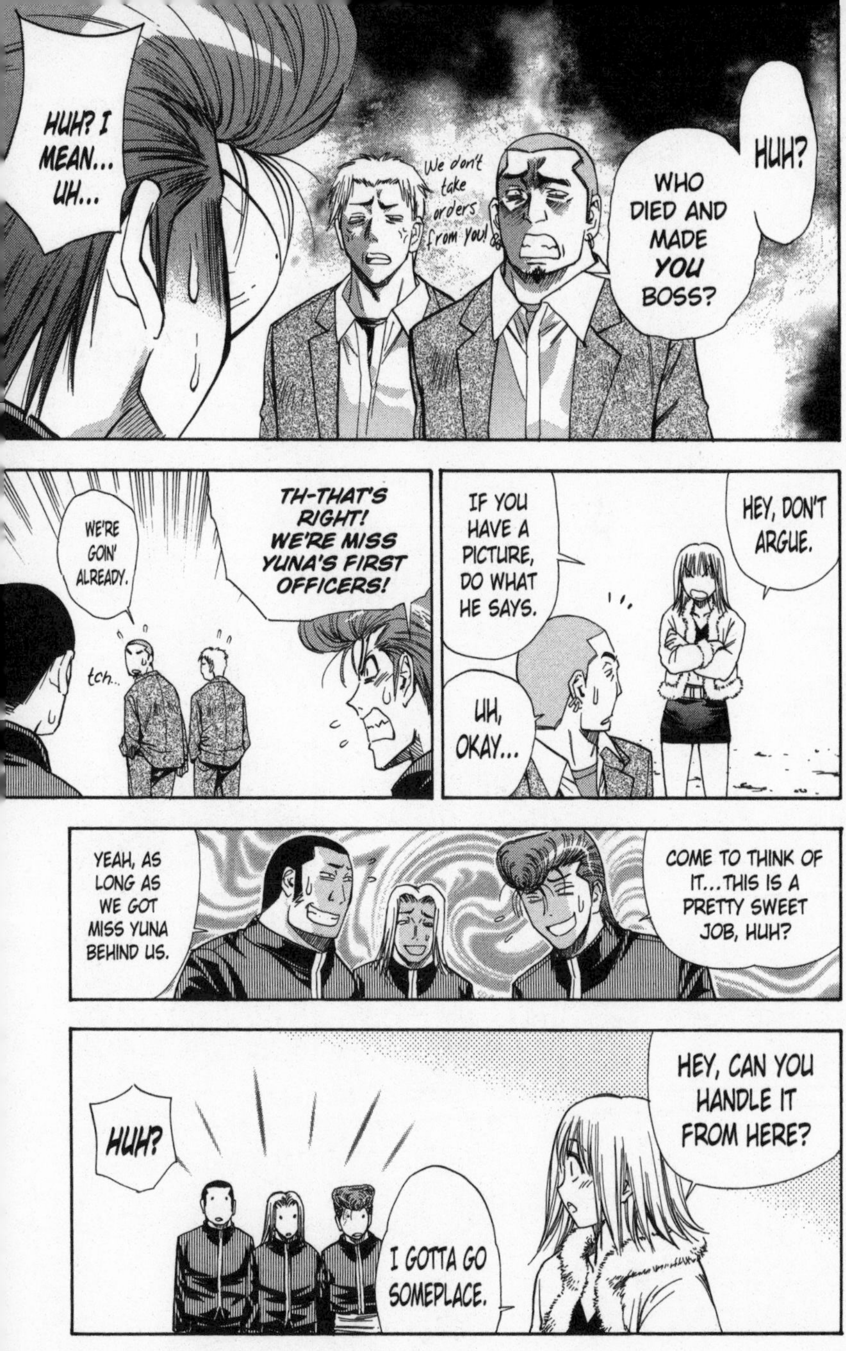
HUH?
WHO DIED AND MADE YOU BOSS?
We don't take orders from you!
HUH? I MEAN... UH...
HEY, DON'T ARGUE.
IF YOU HAVE A PICTURE, DO WHAT HE SAYS.
UH, OKAY...
TH-THAT'S RIGHT! WE'RE MISS YUNA'S FIRST OFFICERS!
WE'RE GOIN' ALREADY.
tch...
COME TO THINK OF IT...THIS IS A PRETTY SWEET JOB, HUH?
YEAH, AS LONG AS WE GOT MISS YUNA BEHIND US.
HEY, CAN YOU HANDLE IT FROM HERE?
I GOTTA GO SOMEPLACE.
HUH?

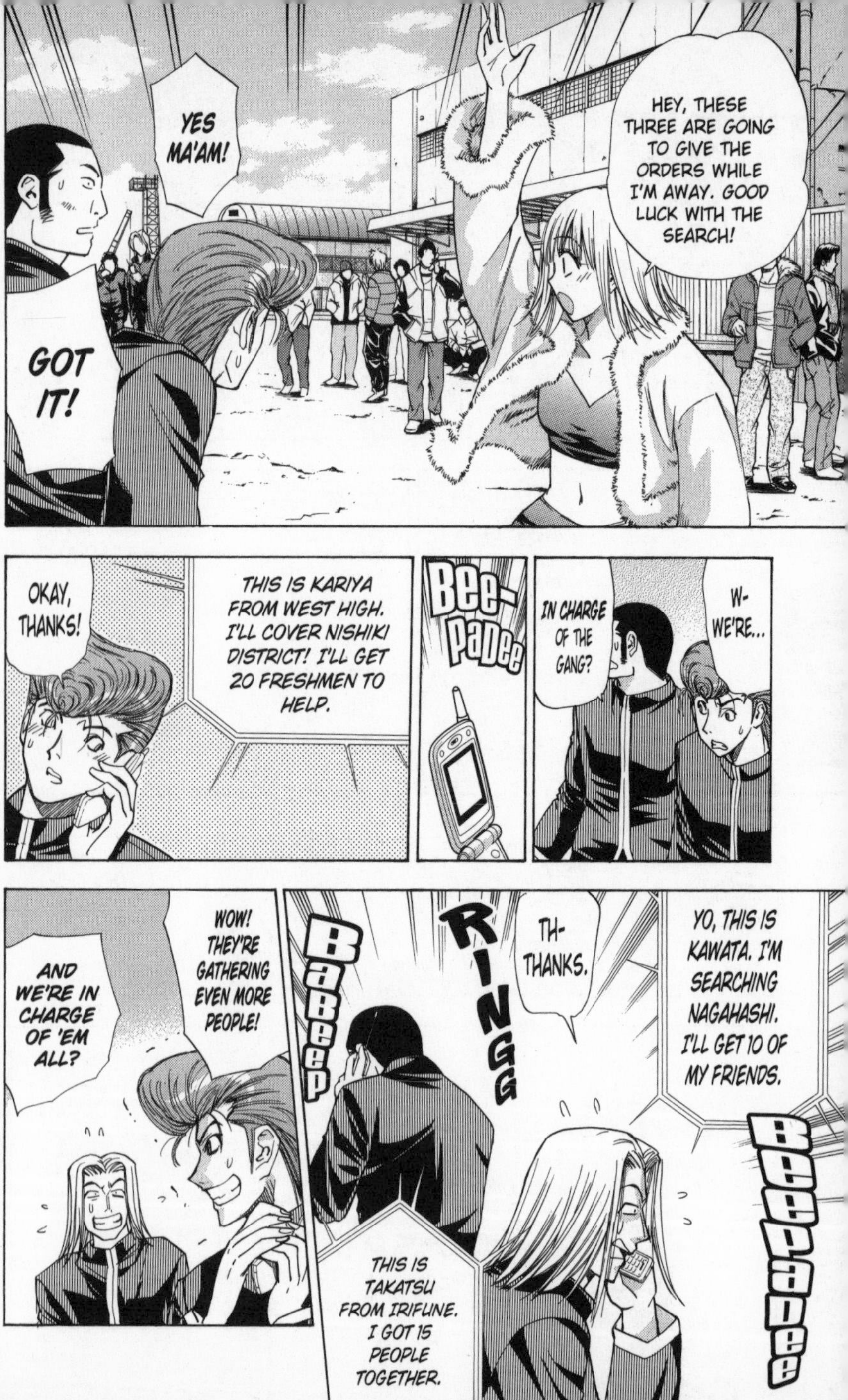
HEY, THESE THREE ARE GOING TO GIVE THE ORDERS WHILE I'M AWAY. GOOD LUCK WITH THE SEARCH!
YES MA'AM!
GOT IT!
W- WE'RE...
IN CHARGE OF THE GANG?
Bee-padee
THIS IS KARIYA FROM WEST HIGH. I'LL COVER NISHIKI DISTRICT! I'LL GET 20 FRESHMEN TO HELP.
OKAY, THANKS!
YO, THIS IS KAWATA. I'M SEARCHING NAGAHASHI. I'LL GET 10 OF MY FRIENDS.
TH- THANKS.
Beepadee
RINGG
Babeep
THIS IS TAKATSU FROM IRIFUNE. I GOT 15 PEOPLE TOGETHER.
WOW! THEY'RE GATHERING EVEN MORE PEOPLE!
AND WE'RE IN CHARGE OF 'EM ALL?

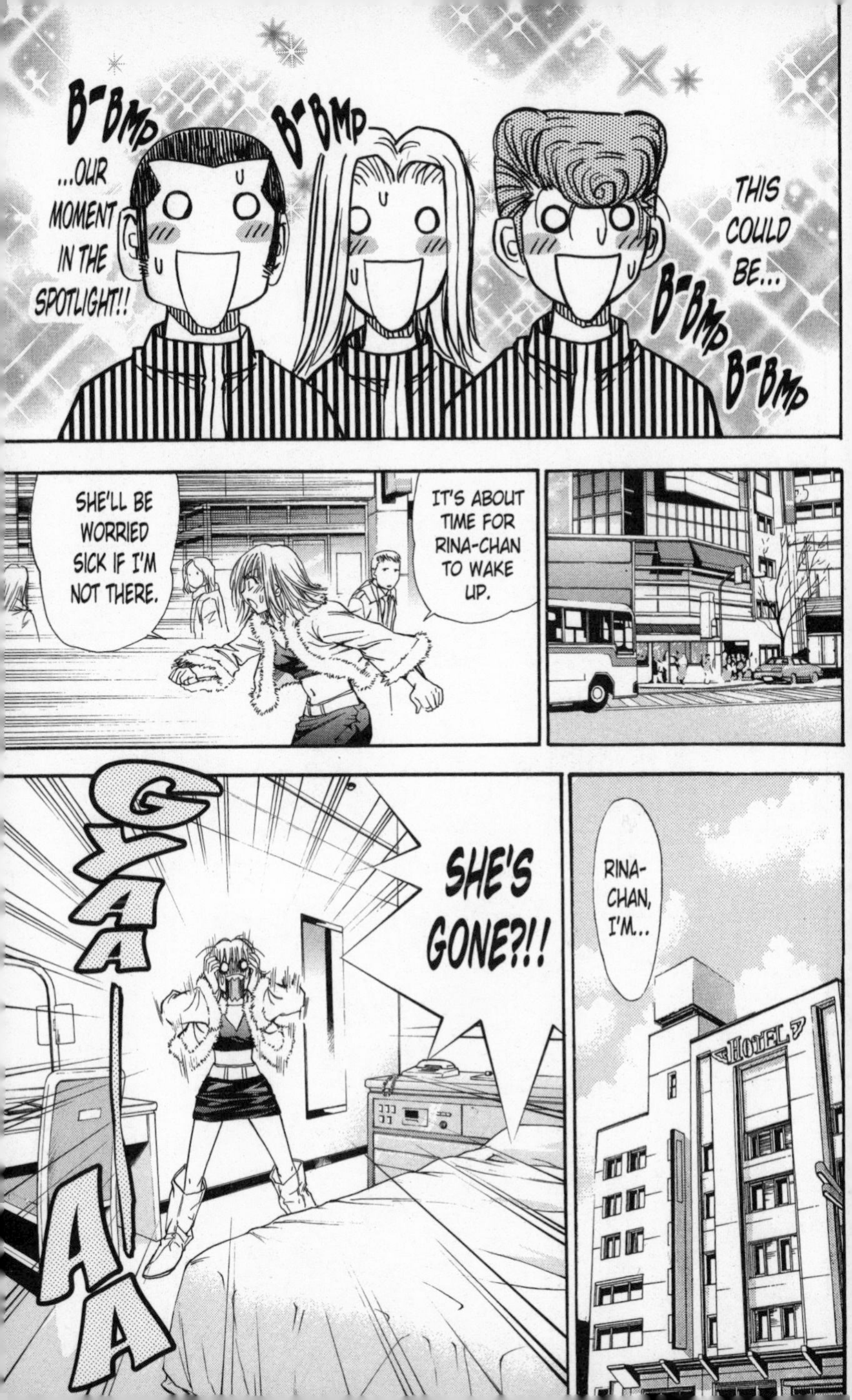
THIS COULD BE...
B-BMP
B-BMP
B-BMP
B-BMP
...OUR MOMENT IN THE SPOTLIGHT!!
IT'S ABOUT TIME FOR RINA-CHAN TO WAKE UP.
SHE'LL BE WORRIED SICK IF I'M NOT THERE.
RINA-CHAN, I'M...
HOTEL
SHE'S GONE?!!
GYAAAA

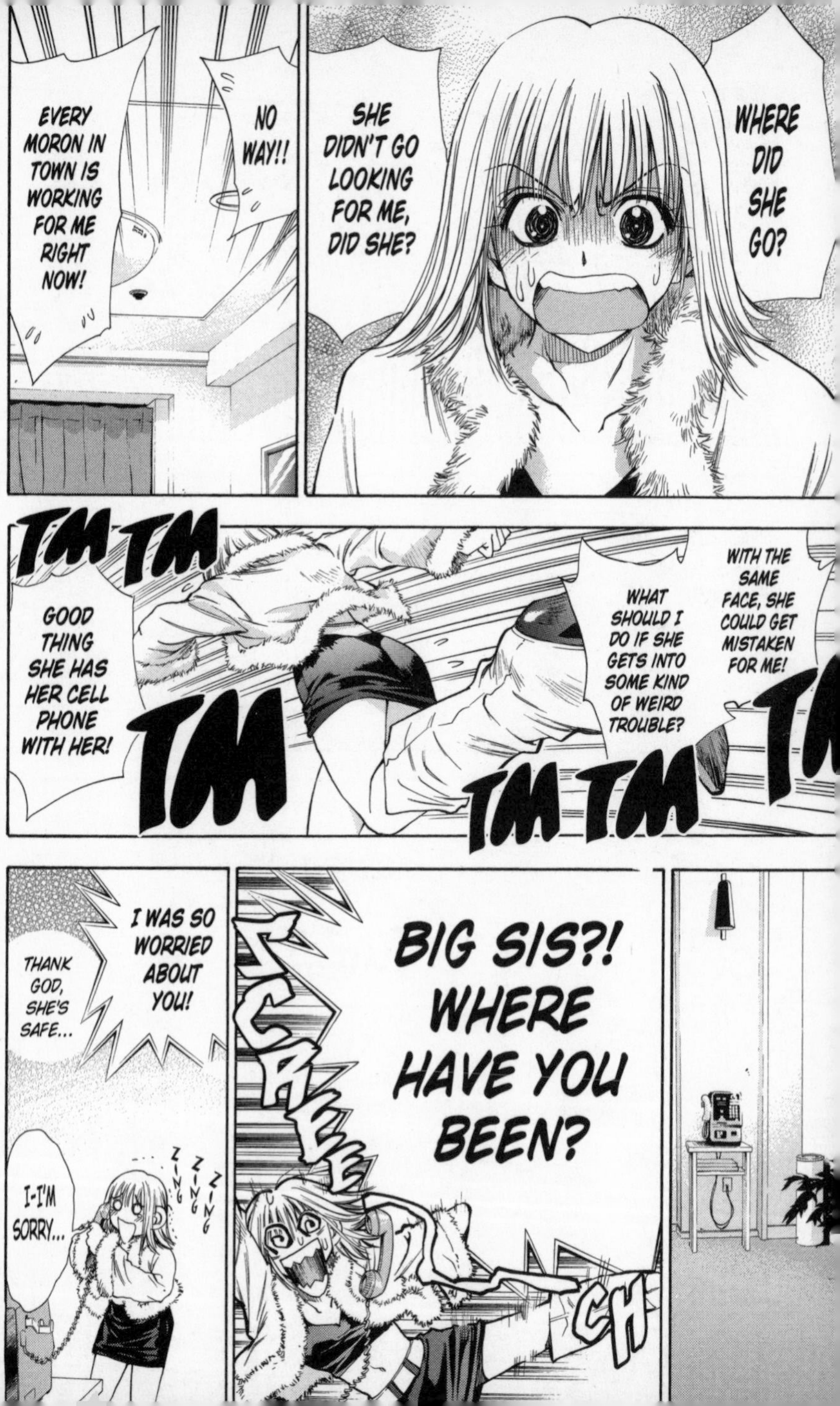
WHERE DID SHE GO?
SHE DIDN'T GO LOOKING FOR ME, DID SHE?
NO WAY!!
EVERY MORON IN TOWN IS WORKING FOR ME RIGHT NOW!
WITH THE SAME FACE, SHE COULD GET MISTAKEN FOR ME!
WHAT SHOULD I DO IF SHE GETS INTO SOME KIND OF WEIRD TROUBLE?
TM TM TM
TM TM
GOOD THING SHE HAS HER CELL PHONE WITH HER!
BIG SIS?! WHERE HAVE YOU BEEN?
CH
I WAS SO WORRIED ABOUT YOU!
THANK GOD, SHE'S SAFE...
ZING ZING ZING
I-I'M SORRY...

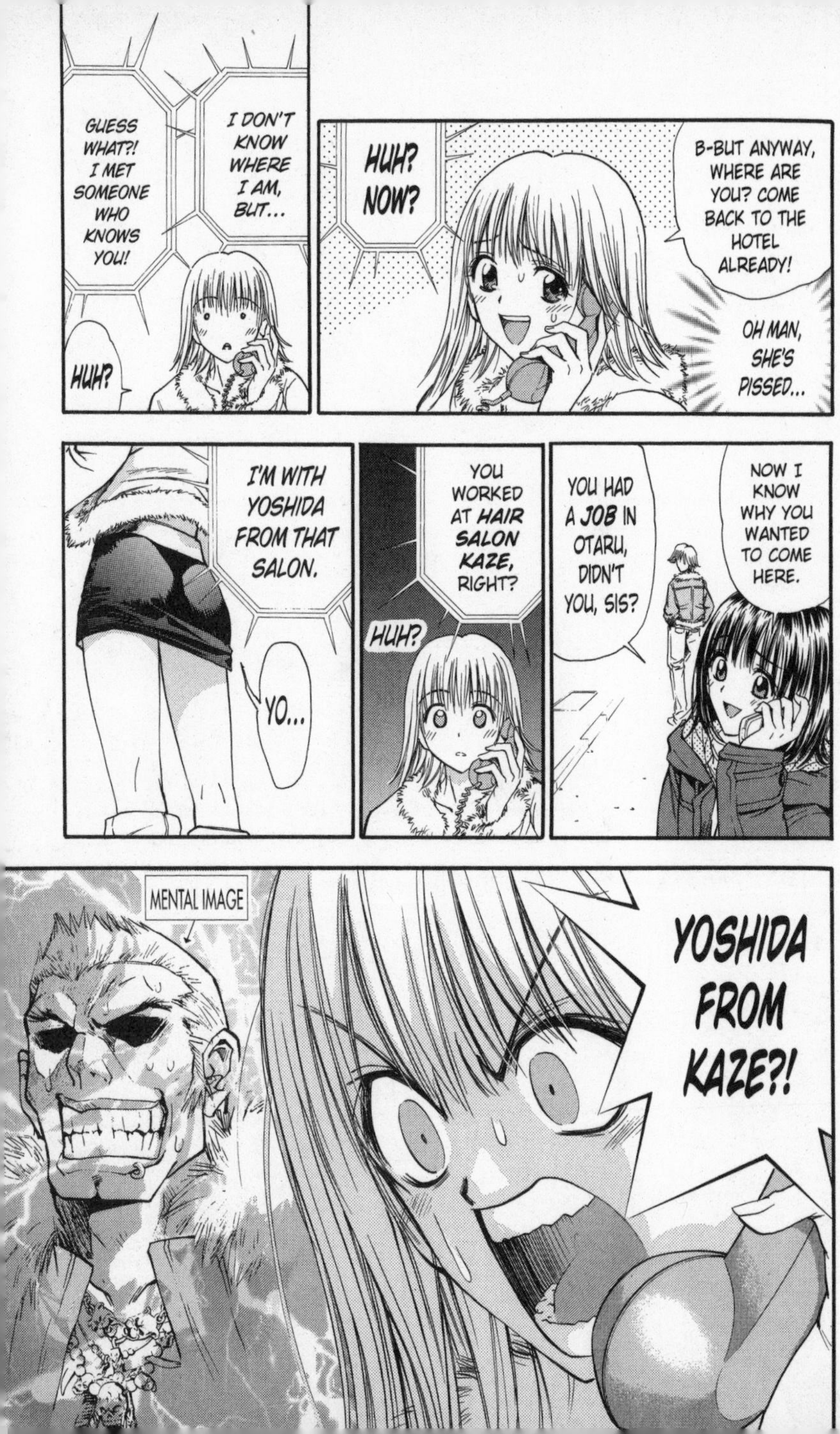
B-BUT ANYWAY, WHERE ARE YOU? COME BACK TO THE HOTEL ALREADY!
HUH? NOW?
OH MAN, SHE'S PISSED...
I DON'T KNOW WHERE I AM, BUT...
GUESS WHAT?! I MET SOMEONE WHO KNOWS YOU!
HUH?
NOW I KNOW WHY YOU WANTED TO COME HERE.
YOU HAD A JOB IN OTARU, DIDN'T YOU, SIS?
YOU WORKED AT HAIR SALON KAZE, RIGHT?
HUH?
I'M WITH YOSHIDA FROM THAT SALON.
YO...
YOSHIDA FROM KAZE?!
MENTAL IMAGE

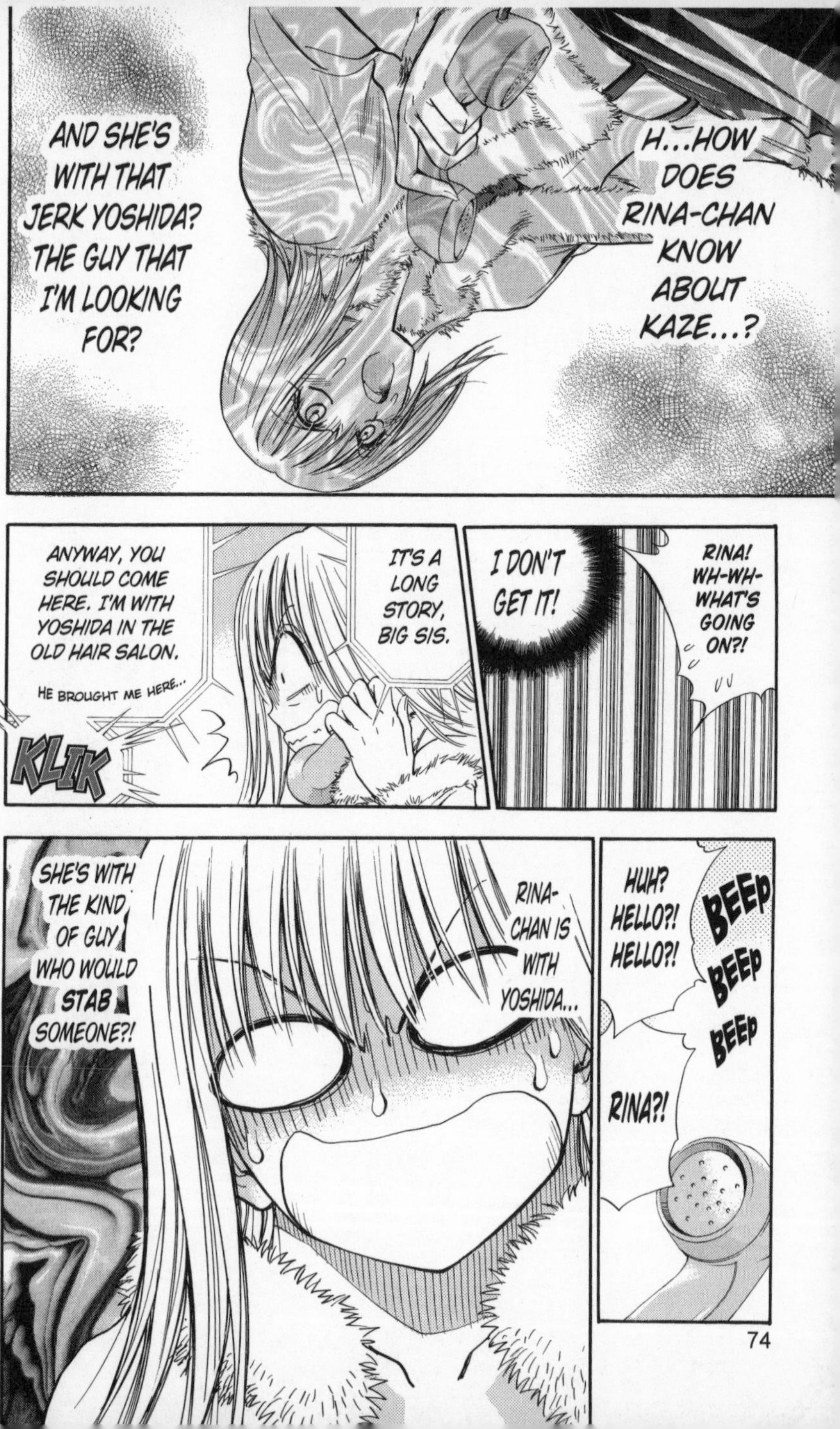
H...HOW DOES RINA-CHAN KNOW ABOUT KAZE...?
AND SHE'S WITH THAT JERK YOSHIDA? THE GUY THAT I'M LOOKING FOR?
RINA! WH-WH-WHAT'S GOING ON?!
I DON'T GET IT!
IT'S A LONG STORY, BIG SIS.
ANYWAY, YOU SHOULD COME HERE. I'M WITH YOSHIDA IN THE OLD HAIR SALON.
HE BROUGHT ME HERE...
KLIK
HUH? HELLO?! HELLO?!
BEEP
BEEP
BEEP
RINA?!
RINA-CHAN IS WITH YOSHIDA...
SHE'S WITH THE KIND OF GUY WHO WOULD STAB SOMEONE?!

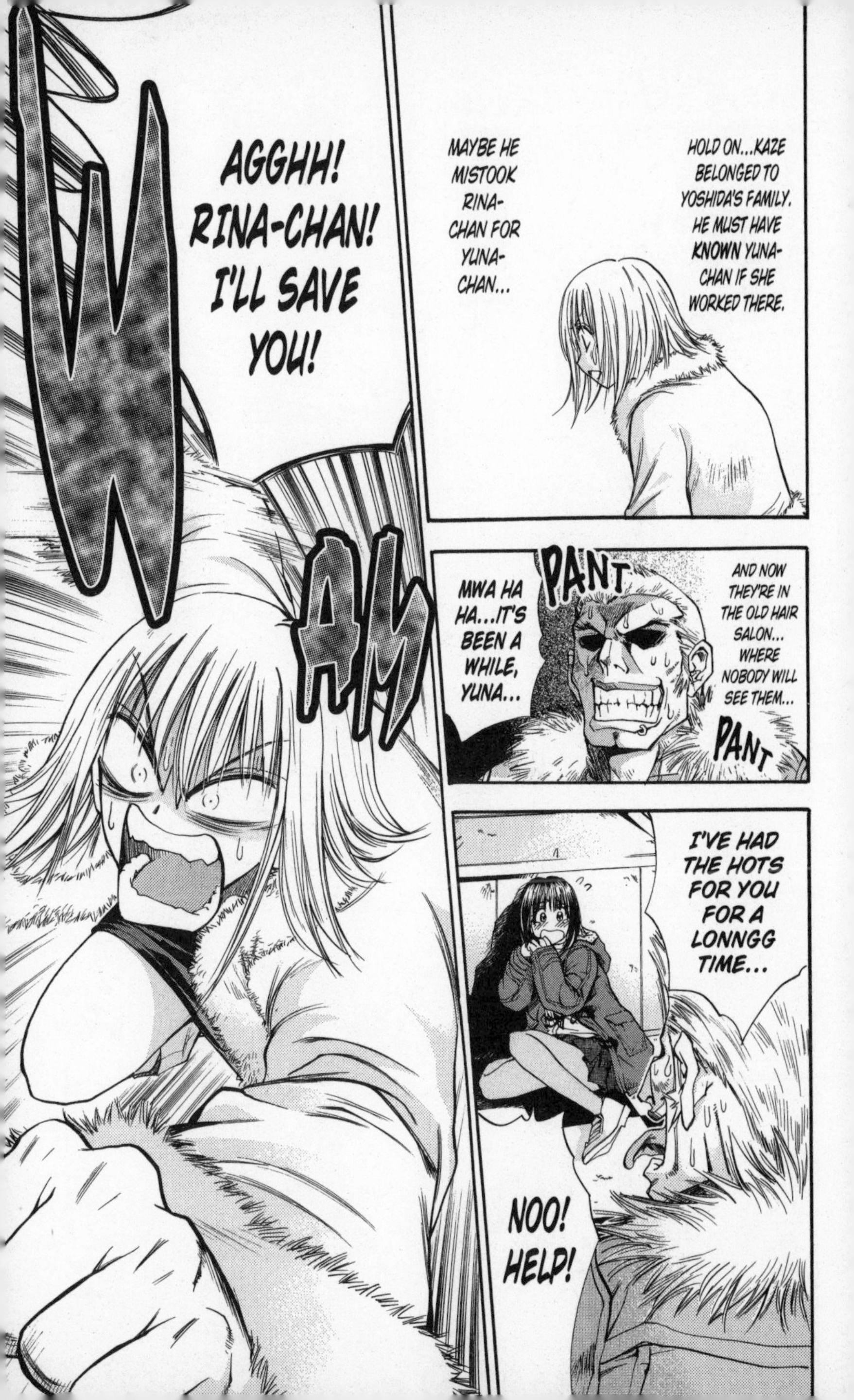
HOLD ON...KAZE BELONGED TO YOSHIDA'S FAMILY. HE MUST HAVE KNOWN YUNA-CHAN IF SHE WORKED THERE.
MAYBE HE MISTOOK RINA-CHAN FOR YUNA-CHAN...
AND NOW THEY'RE IN THE OLD HAIR SALON... WHERE NOBODY WILL SEE THEM...
PANT
MWA HA HA...IT'S BEEN A WHILE, YUNA...
PANT
I'VE HAD THE HOTS FOR YOU FOR A LONNGG TIME...
NOO! HELP!
AGGHH! RINA-CHAN! I'LL SAVE YOU!
WHAM

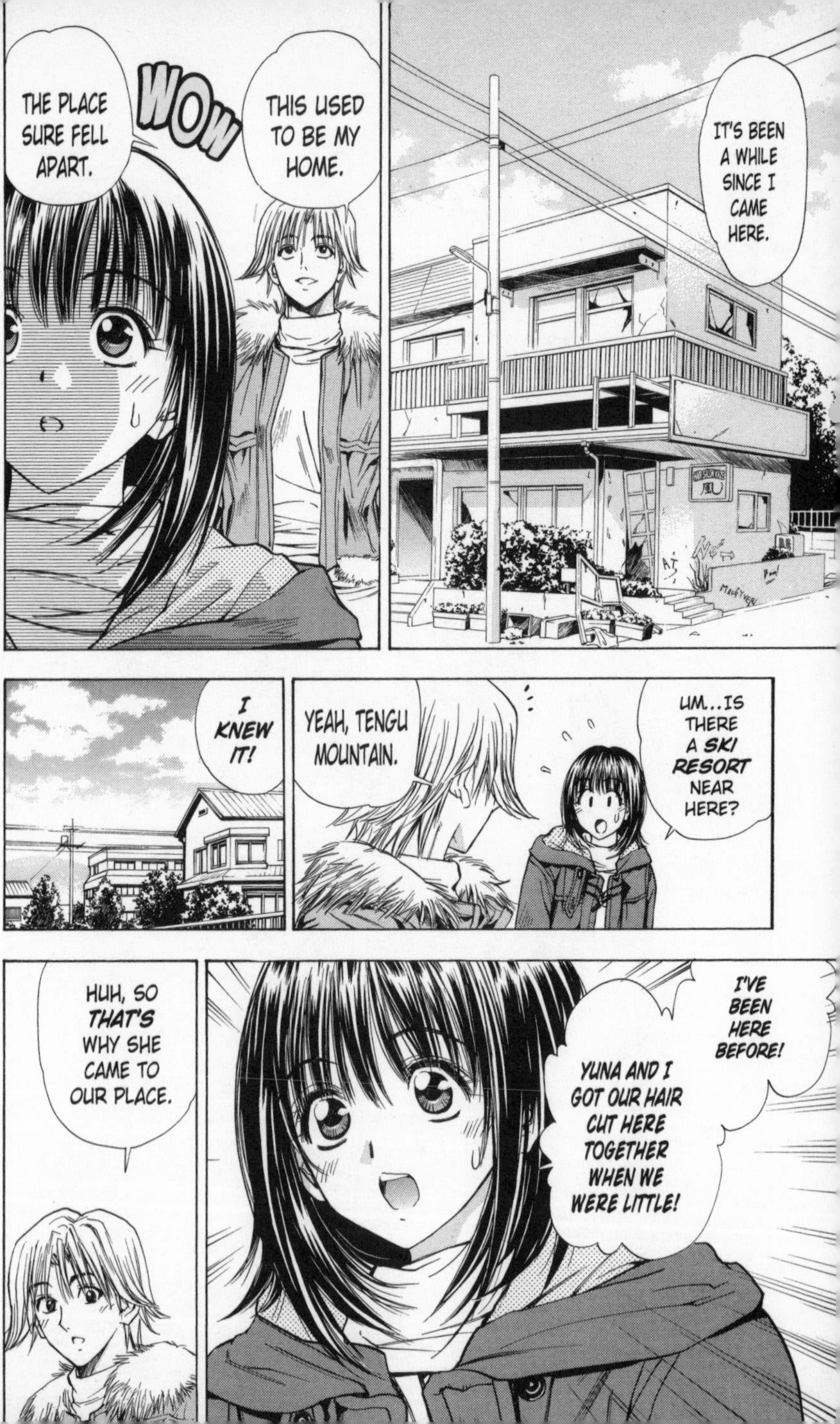
IT'S BEEN A WHILE SINCE I CAME HERE.
THIS USED TO BE MY HOME.
WOW
THE PLACE SURE FELL APART.
UM...IS THERE A SKI RESORT NEAR HERE?
YEAH, TENGU MOUNTAIN.
I KNEW IT!
I'VE BEEN HERE BEFORE!
YUNA AND I GOT OUR HAIR CUT HERE TOGETHER WHEN WE WERE LITTLE!
HUH, SO THAT'S WHY SHE CAME TO OUR PLACE.

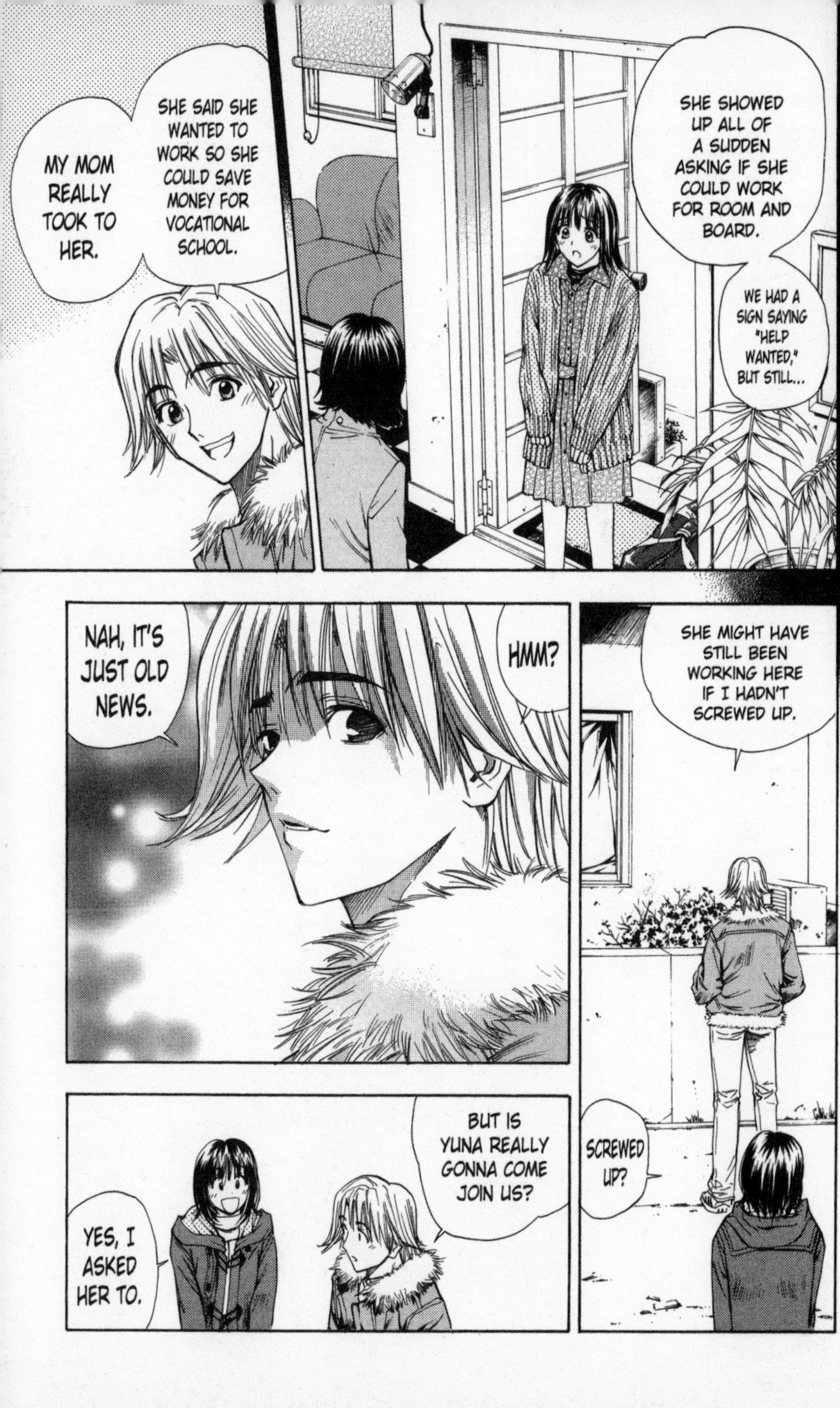
SHE SHOWED UP ALL OF A SUDDEN ASKING IF SHE COULD WORK FOR ROOM AND BOARD.
WE HAD A SIGN SAYING "HELP WANTED," BUT STILL...
SHE SAID SHE WANTED TO WORK SO SHE COULD SAVE MONEY FOR VOCATIONAL SCHOOL.
MY MOM REALLY TOOK TO HER.
SHE MIGHT HAVE STILL BEEN WORKING HERE IF I HADN'T SCREWED UP.
SCREWED UP?
HMM?
NAH, IT'S JUST OLD NEWS.
BUT IS YUNA REALLY GONNA COME JOIN US?
YES, I ASKED HER TO.

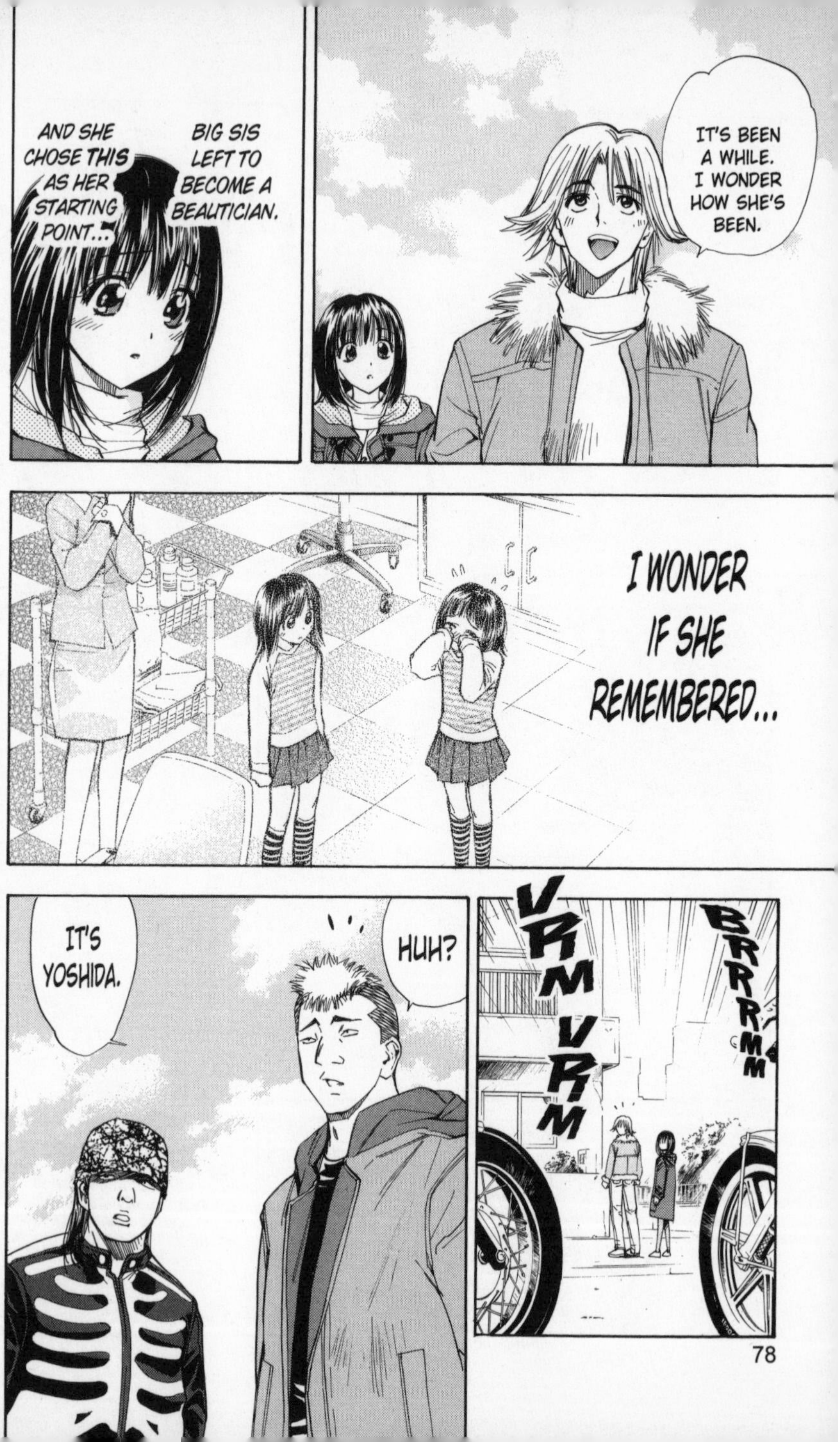
IT'S BEEN A WHILE. I WONDER HOW SHE'S BEEN.
BIG SIS LEFT TO BECOME A BEAUTICIAN.
AND SHE CHOSE THIS AS HER STARTING POINT...
I WONDER IF SHE REMEMBERED...
BRRRRMM
VRM VRM
HUH?
IT'S YOSHIDA.

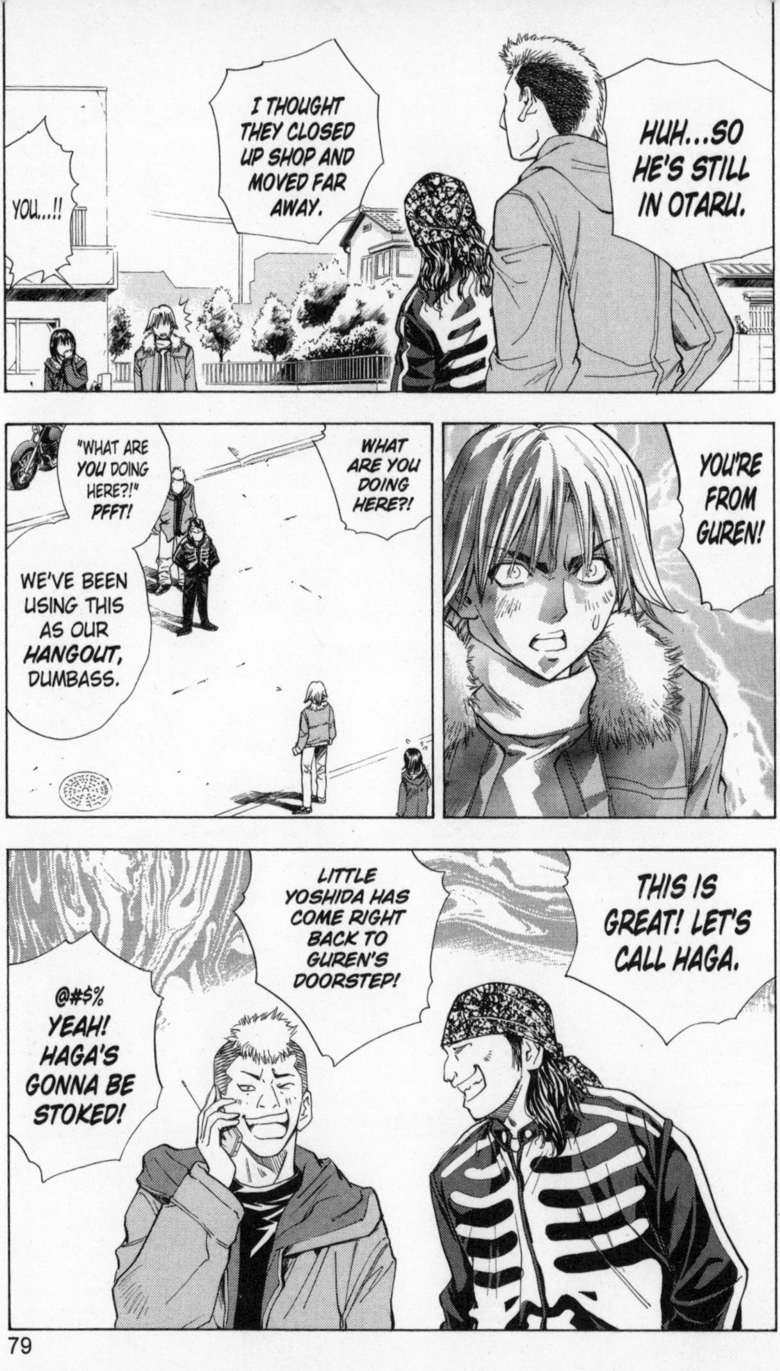
HUH...SO HE'S STILL IN OTARU.
I THOUGHT THEY CLOSED UP SHOP AND MOVED FAR AWAY.
YOU...!!
YOU'RE FROM GUREN!
WHAT ARE YOU DOING HERE?!
"WHAT ARE YOU DOING HERE?!" PFFT!
WE'VE BEEN USING THIS AS OUR HANGOUT, DUMBASS.
THIS IS GREAT! LET'S CALL HAGA.
LITTLE YOSHIDA HAS COME RIGHT BACK TO GUREN'S DOORSTEP!
@#$% YEAH! HAGA'S GONNA BE STOKED!

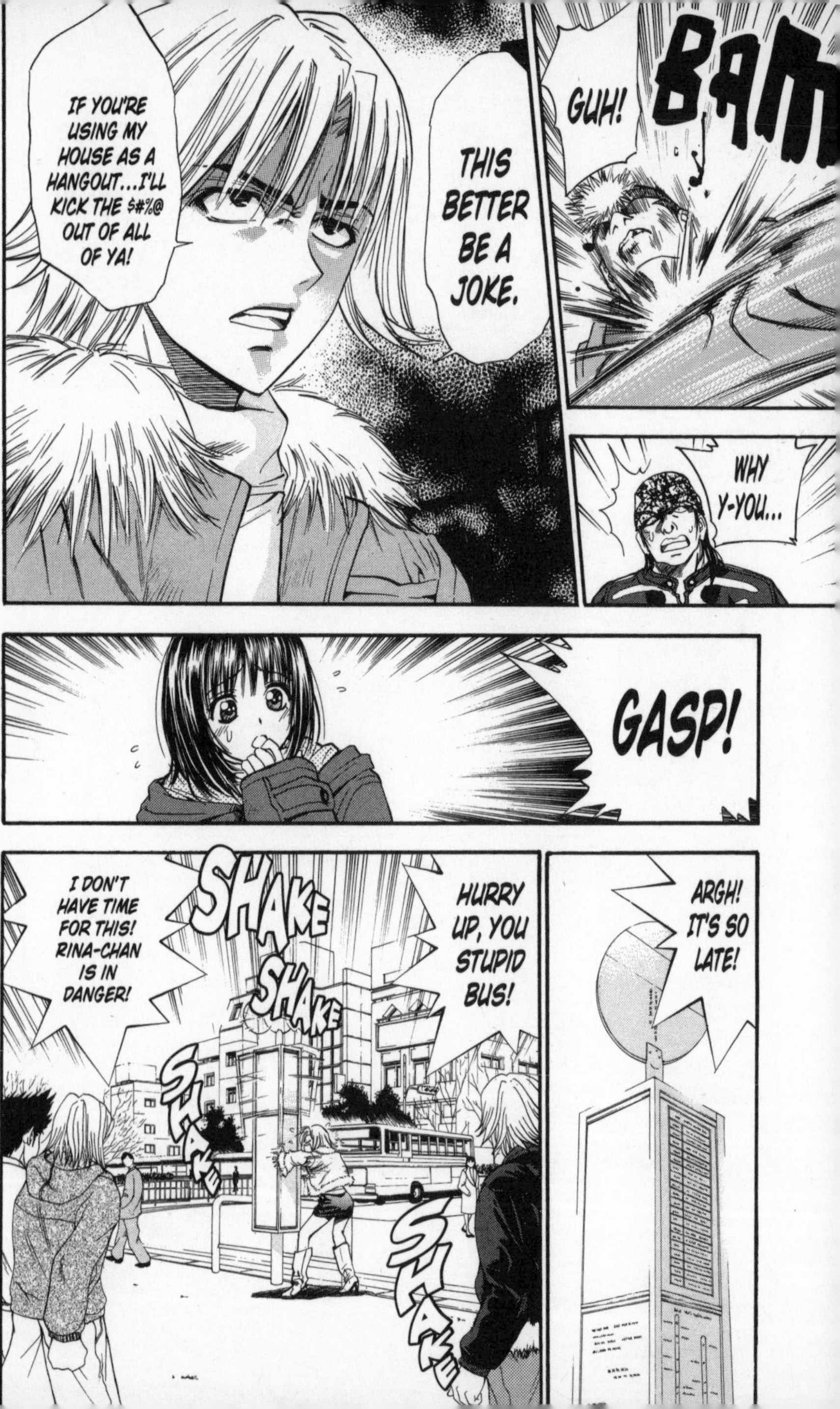
BAM
GUH!
WHY Y-YOU...
THIS BETTER BE A JOKE.
IF YOU'RE USING MY HOUSE AS A HANGOUT...I'LL KICK THE $#%@ OUT OF ALL OF YA!
GASP!
ARGH! IT'S SO LATE!
HURRY UP, YOU STUPID BUS!
SHAKE
SHAKE
SHAKE
SHAKE
I DON'T HAVE TIME FOR THIS! RINA-CHAN IS IN DANGER!

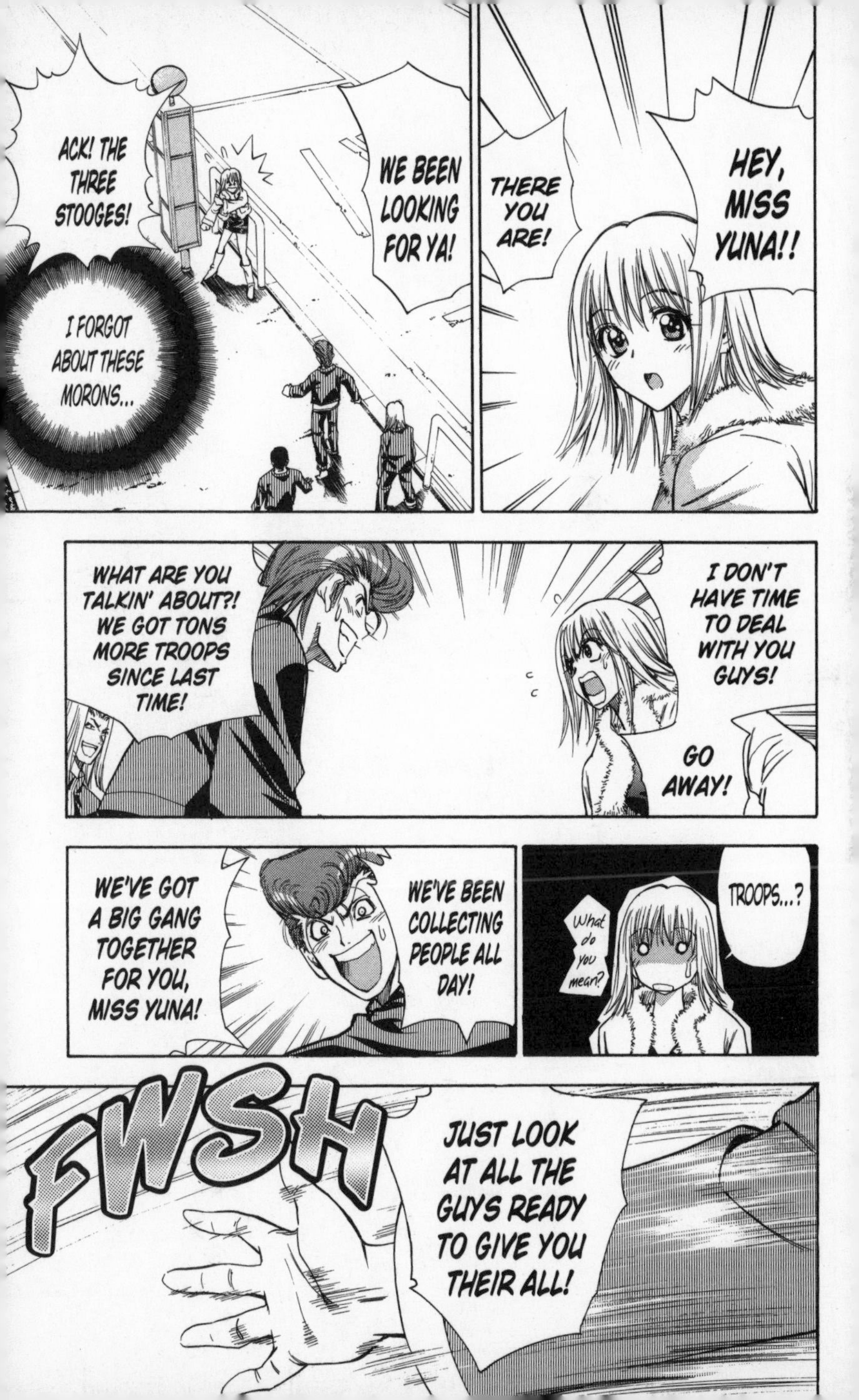
HEY, MISS YUNA!!
THERE YOU ARE!
WE BEEN LOOKING FOR YA!
ACK! THE THREE STOOGES!
I FORGOT ABOUT THESE MORONS...
I DON'T HAVE TIME TO DEAL WITH YOU GUYS!
GO AWAY!
WHAT ARE YOU TALKIN' ABOUT?! WE GOT TONS MORE TROOPS SINCE LAST TIME!
TROOPS...?
What do you mean?
WE'VE BEEN COLLECTING PEOPLE ALL DAY!
WE'VE GOT A BIG GANG TOGETHER FOR YOU, MISS YUNA!
JUST LOOK AT ALL THE GUYS READY TO GIVE YOU THEIR ALL!
FWSH

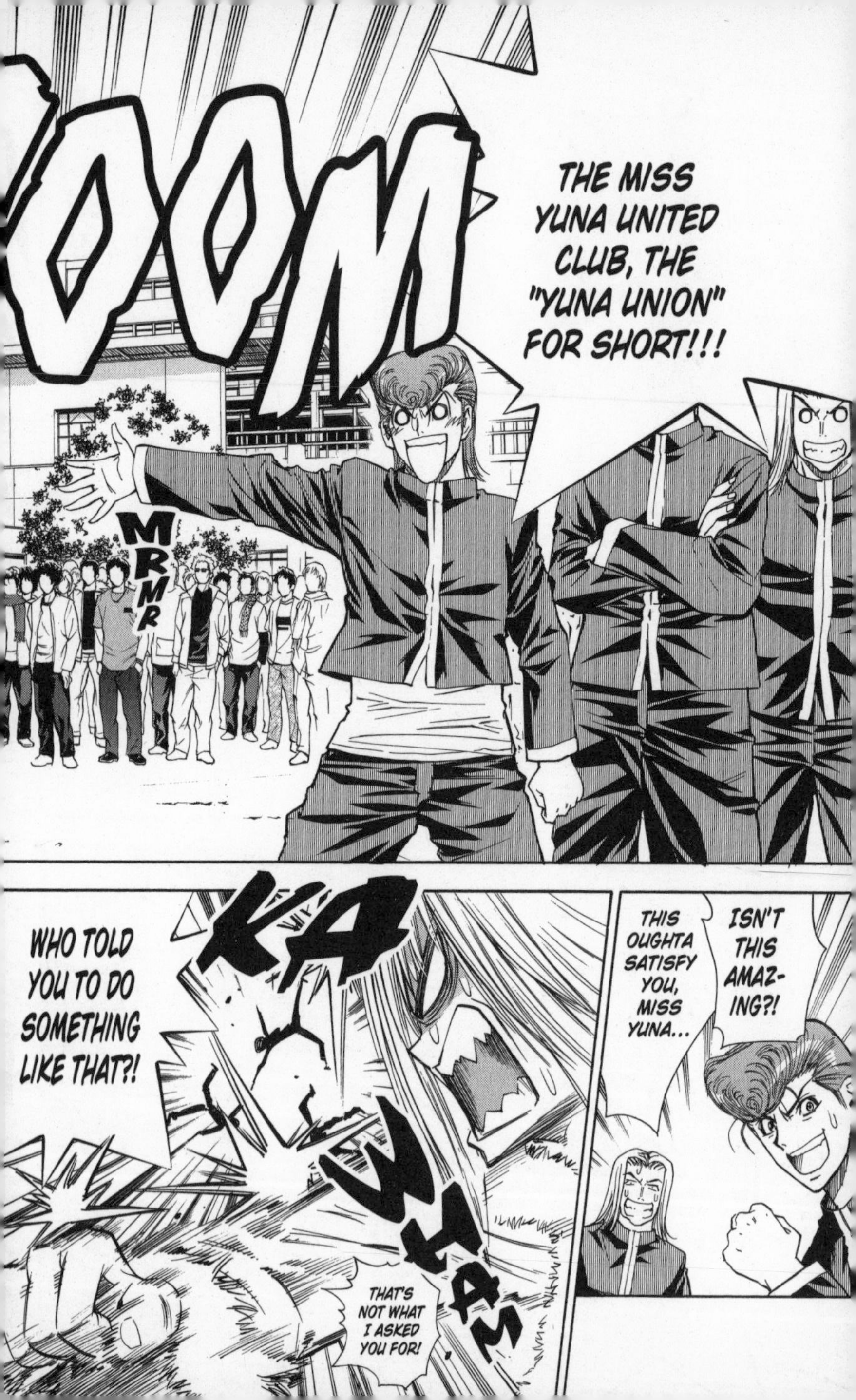
OOM
THE MISS YUNA UNITED CLUB, THE "YUNA UNION" FOR SHORT!!!
MRMR
ISN'T THIS AMAZ-ING?!
THIS OUGHTA SATISFY YOU, MISS YUNA...
KA
WHO TOLD YOU TO DO SOMETHING LIKE THAT?!
WHAM
THAT'S NOT WHAT I ASKED YOU FOR!

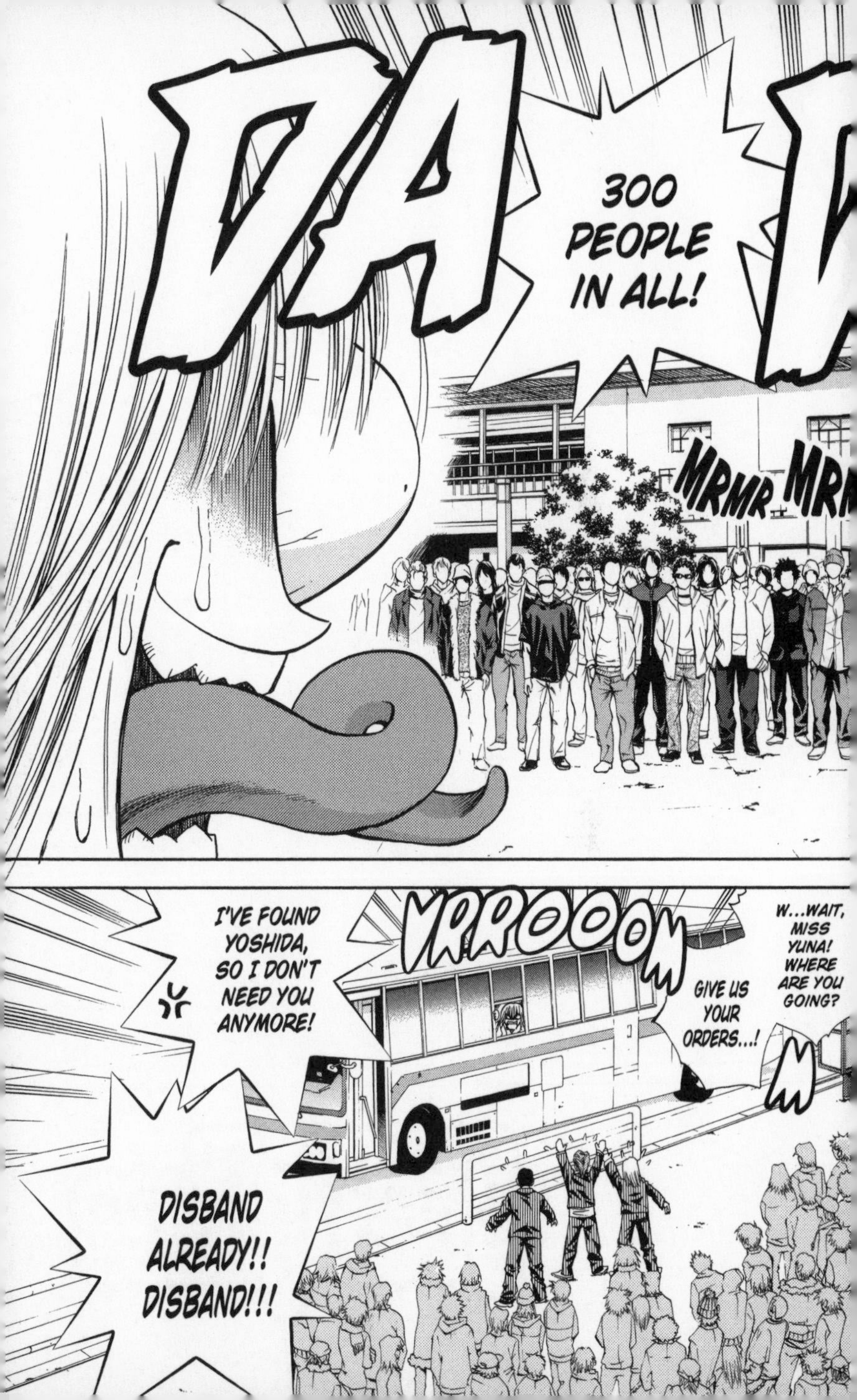
DA
300 PEOPLE IN ALL!
MRMR
W...WAIT, MISS YUNA! WHERE ARE YOU GOING?
GIVE US YOUR ORDERS...!
VRROOOOM
I'VE FOUND YOSHIDA, SO I DON'T NEED YOU ANYMORE!
DISBAND ALREADY!! DISBAND!!!

Pretty Face

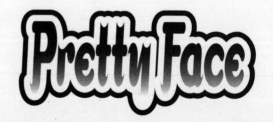

Chapter 32: The Great Otaru Expedition: Part 4

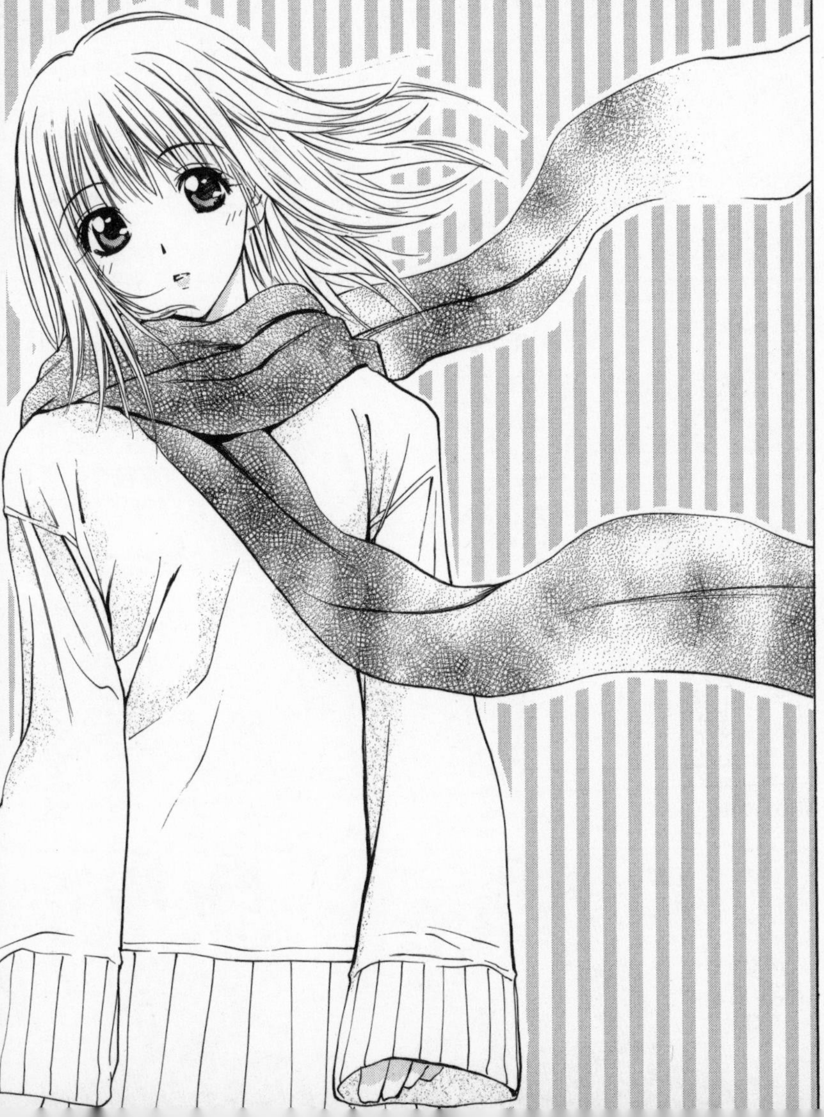

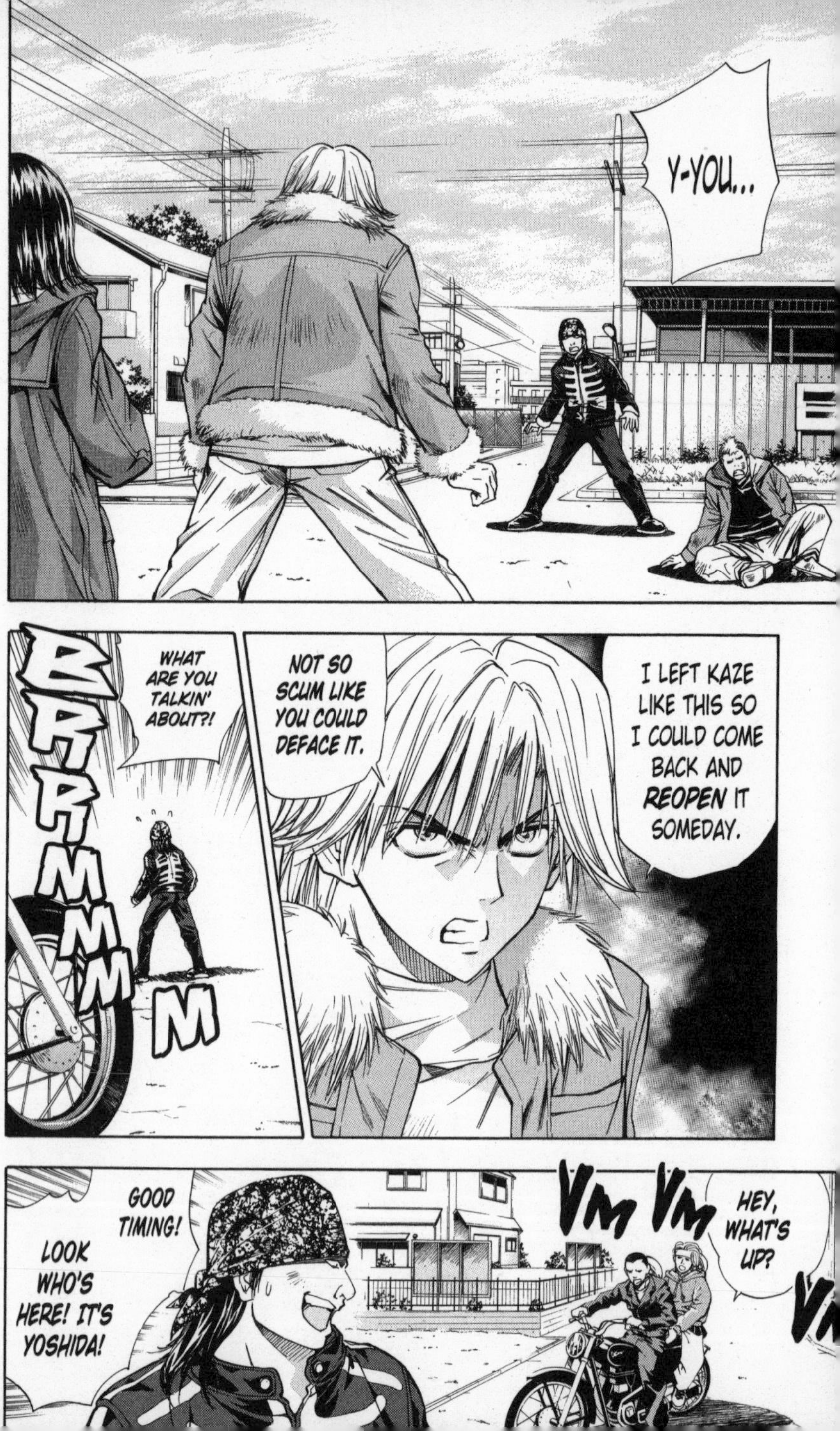
Y-YOU...
I LEFT KAZE LIKE THIS SO I COULD COME BACK AND REOPEN IT SOMEDAY.
NOT SO SCUM LIKE YOU COULD DEFACE IT.
WHAT ARE YOU TALKIN' ABOUT?!
BRRMMMMM
VM VM
HEY, WHAT'S UP?
GOOD TIMING!
LOOK WHO'S HERE! IT'S YOSHIDA!

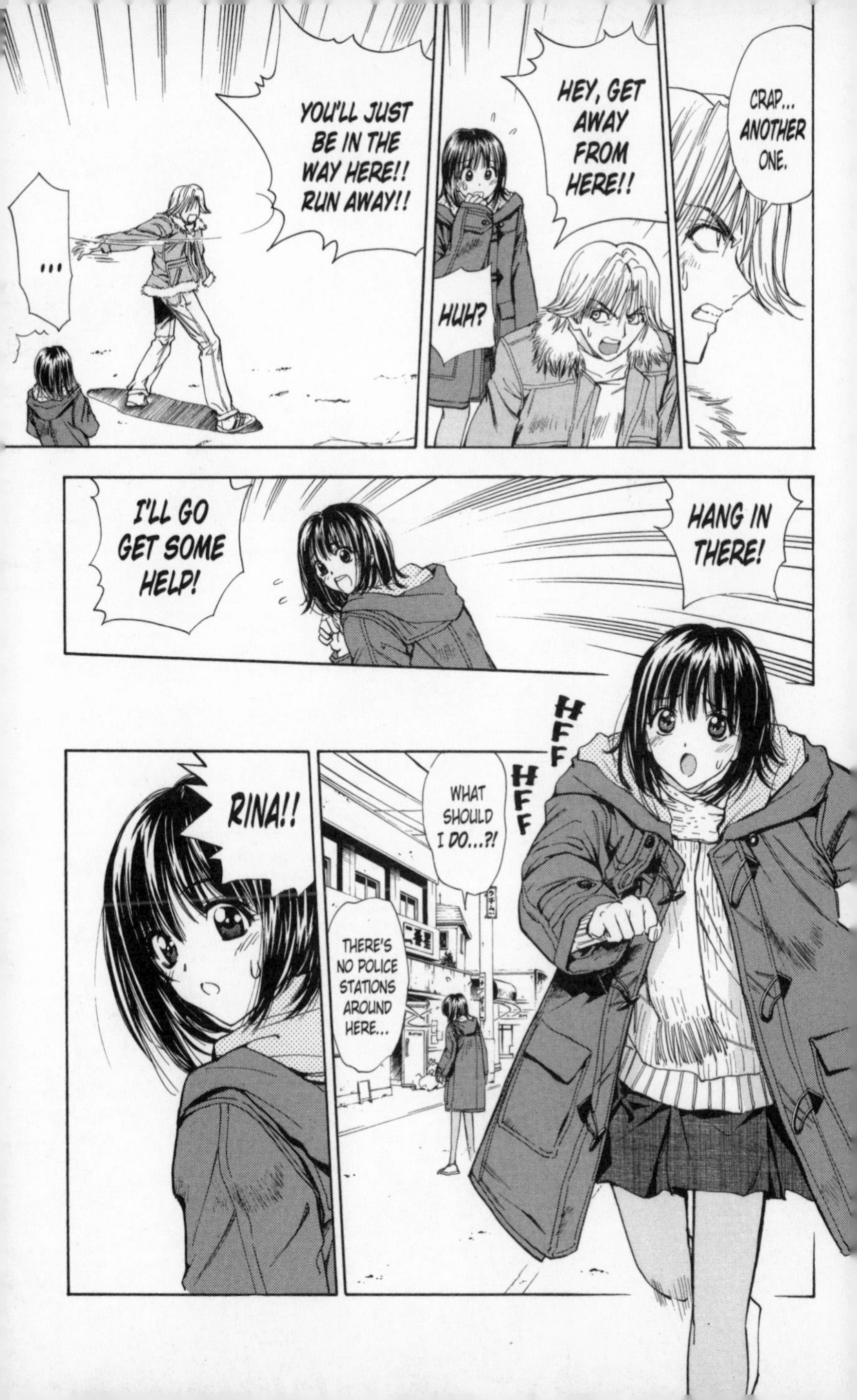
CRAP... ANOTHER ONE.
HEY, GET AWAY FROM HERE!!
HUH?
YOU'LL JUST BE IN THE WAY HERE!! RUN AWAY!!
...
HANG IN THERE!
I'LL GO GET SOME HELP!
HFF HFF
WHAT SHOULD I DO...?!
THERE'S NO POLICE STATIONS AROUND HERE...
RINA!!

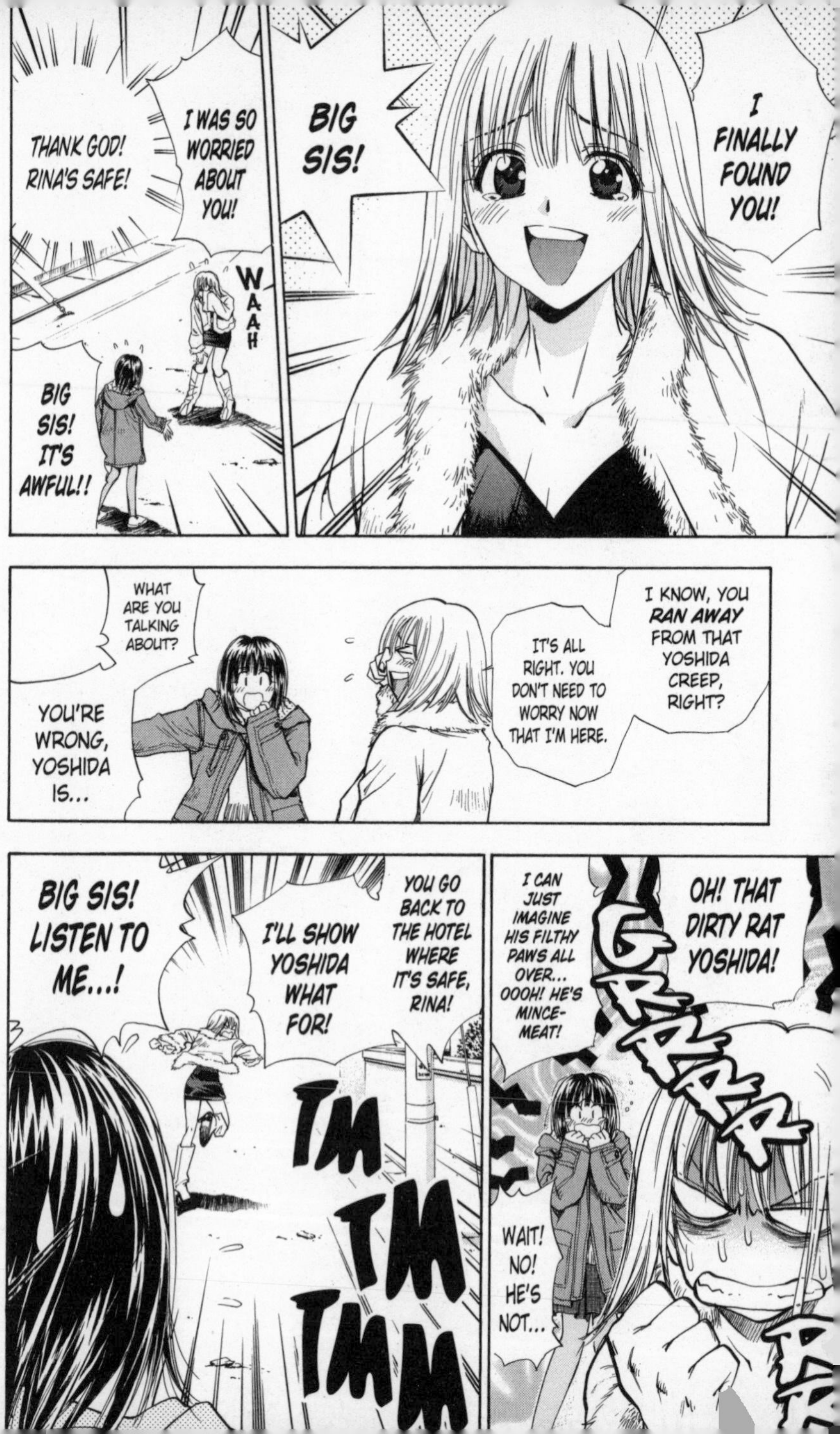
I FINALLY FOUND YOU!
BIG SIS!
I WAS SO WORRIED ABOUT YOU!
THANK GOD! RINA'S SAFE!
WAAH
BIG SIS! IT'S AWFUL!!
I KNOW, YOU RAN AWAY FROM THAT YOSHIDA CREEP, RIGHT?
IT'S ALL RIGHT. YOU DON'T NEED TO WORRY NOW THAT I'M HERE.
WHAT ARE YOU TALKING ABOUT?
YOU'RE WRONG, YOSHIDA IS...
OH! THAT DIRTY RAT YOSHIDA!
I CAN JUST IMAGINE HIS FILTHY PAWS ALL OVER... OOOH! HE'S MINCE-MEAT!
WAIT! NO! HE'S NOT...
YOU GO BACK TO THE HOTEL WHERE IT'S SAFE, RINA!
I'LL SHOW YOSHIDA WHAT FOR!
BIG SIS! LISTEN TO ME...!
TM TM TMM

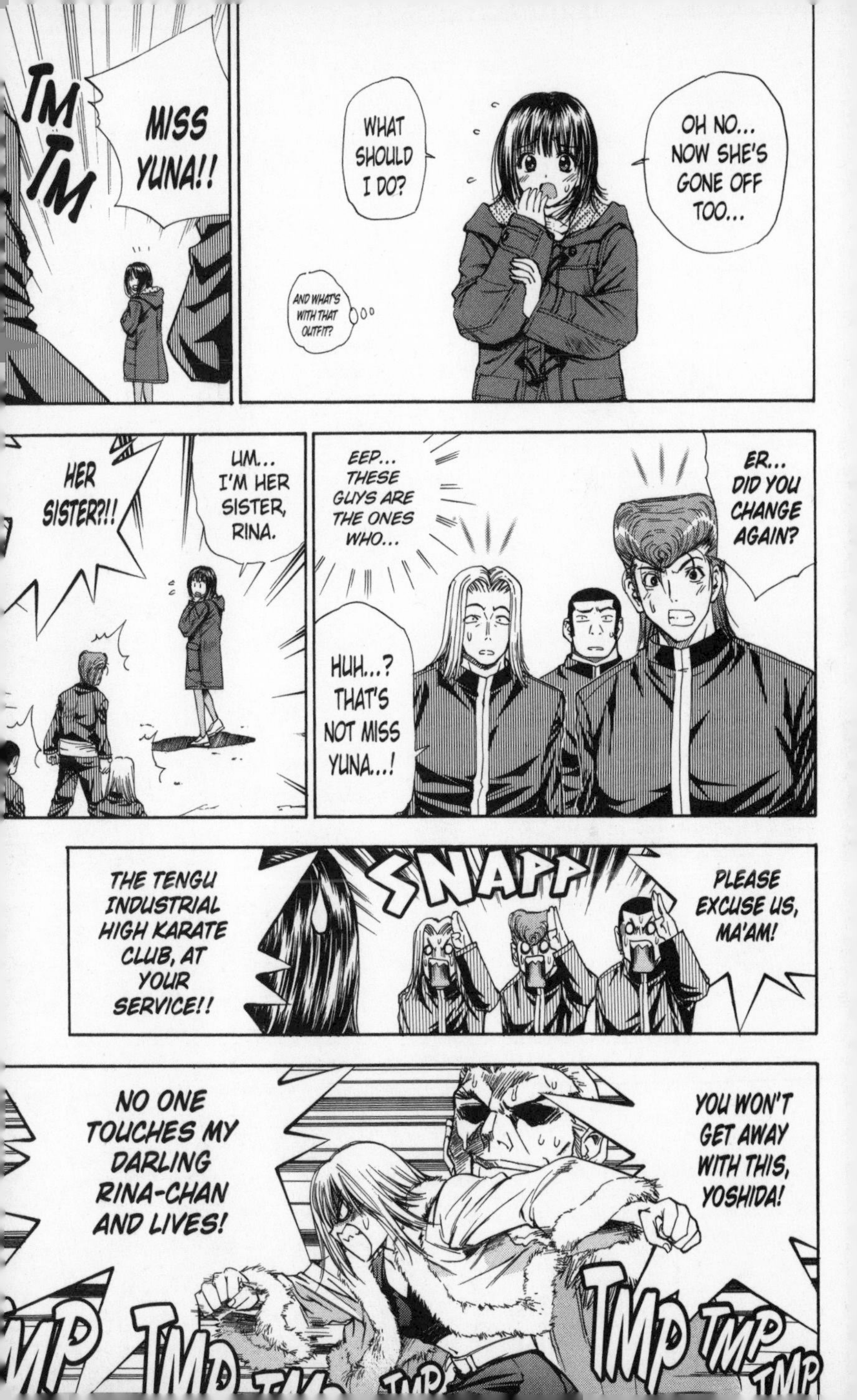
OH NO... NOW SHE'S GONE OFF TOO...
WHAT SHOULD I DO?
AND WHAT'S WITH THAT OUTFIT?
MISS YUNA!!
TM TM
ER... DID YOU CHANGE AGAIN?
EEP... THESE GUYS ARE THE ONES WHO...
HUH...? THAT'S NOT MISS YUNA...!
UM... I'M HER SISTER, RINA.
HER SISTER?!!
PLEASE EXCUSE US, MA'AM!
SNAPP
THE TENGU INDUSTRIAL HIGH KARATE CLUB, AT YOUR SERVICE!!
YOU WON'T GET AWAY WITH THIS, YOSHIDA!
TMP TMP TMP
NO ONE TOUCHES MY DARLING RINA-CHAN AND LIVES!
TMP

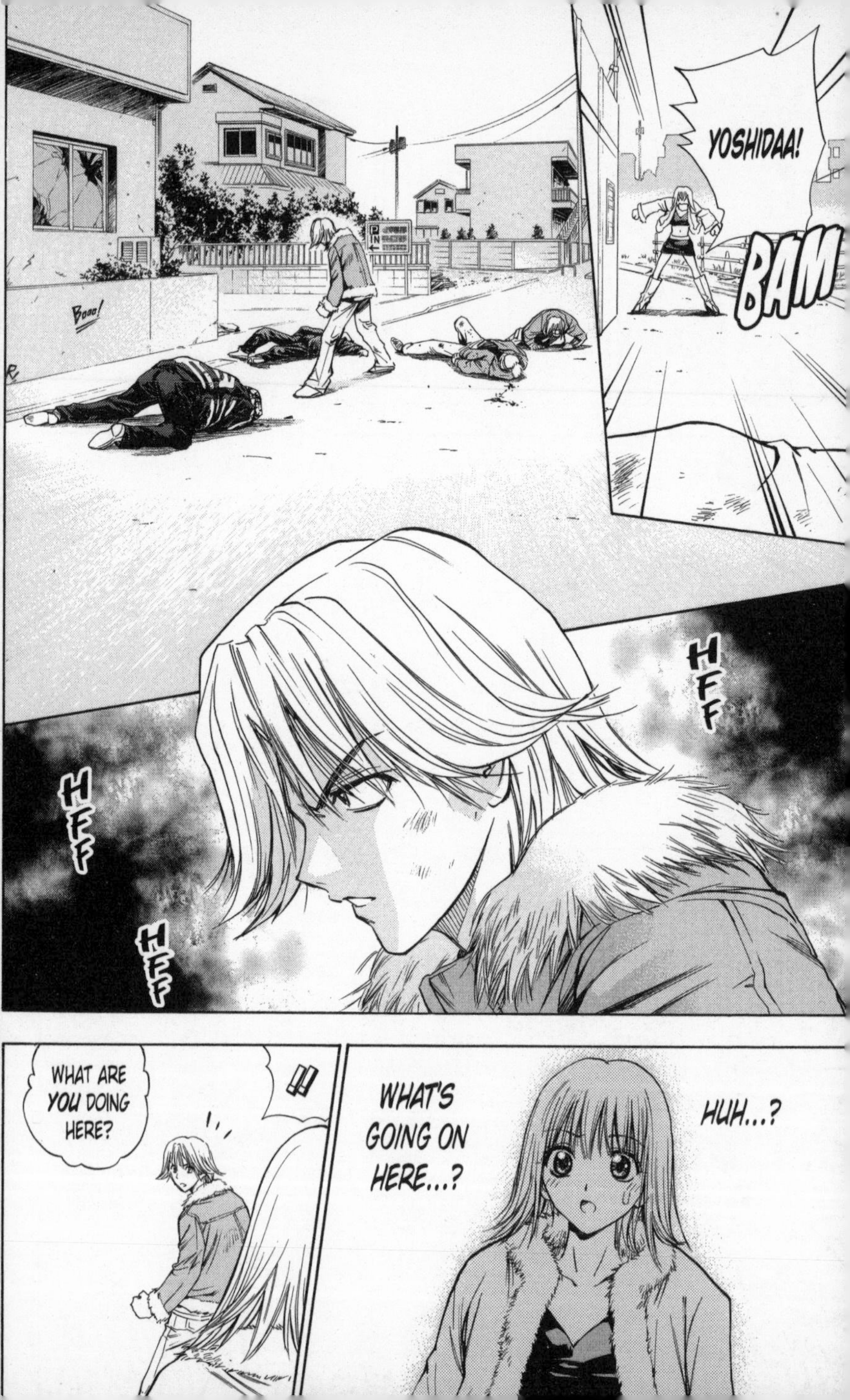
YOSHIDAA!
BAM
HFF
HFF
HFF
HUH...?
WHAT'S GOING ON HERE...?
!!
WHAT ARE YOU DOING HERE?

READ THIS WAY

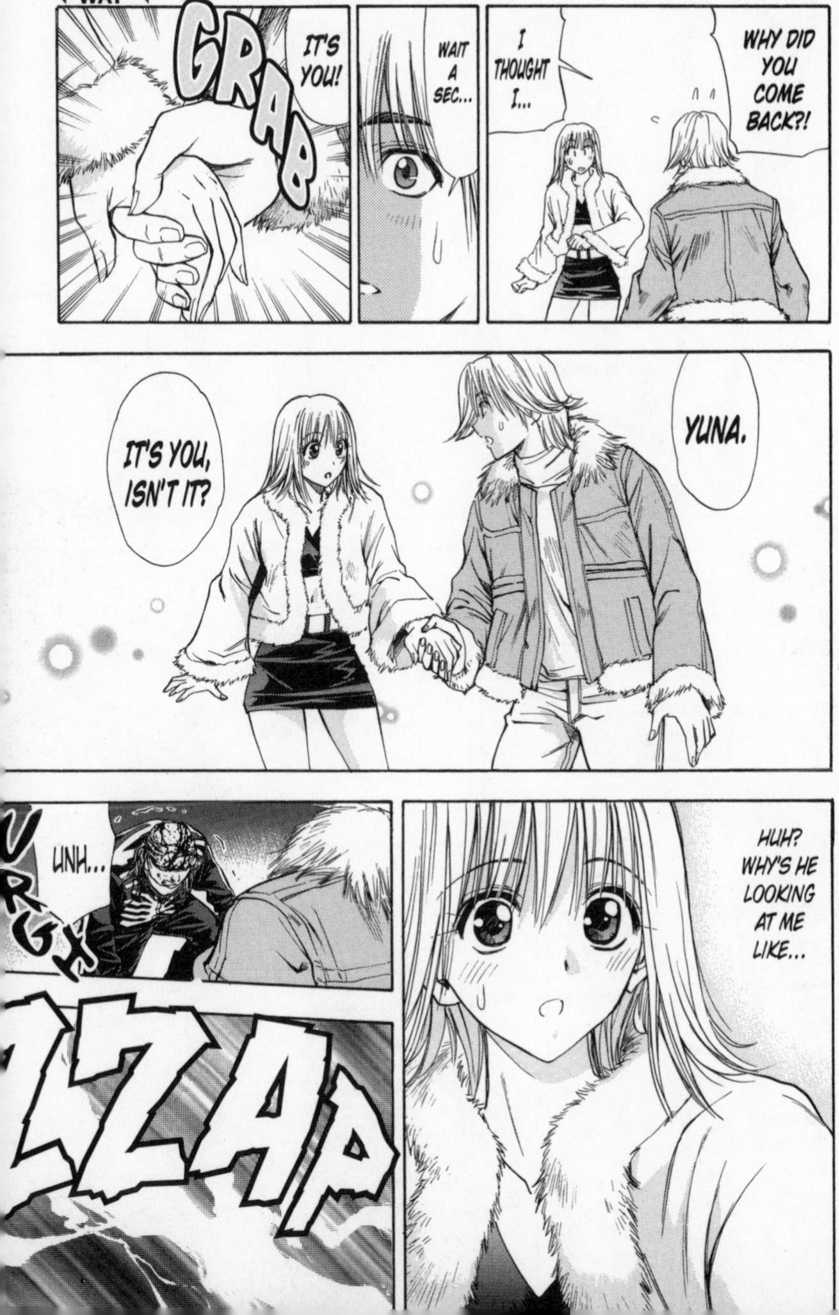
WHY DID YOU COME BACK?!
I THOUGHT I...
WAIT A SEC...
IT'S YOU!
GRAB
YUNA.
IT'S YOU, ISN'T IT?
HUH? WHY'S HE LOOKING AT ME LIKE...
UNH...
URGH
ZAP

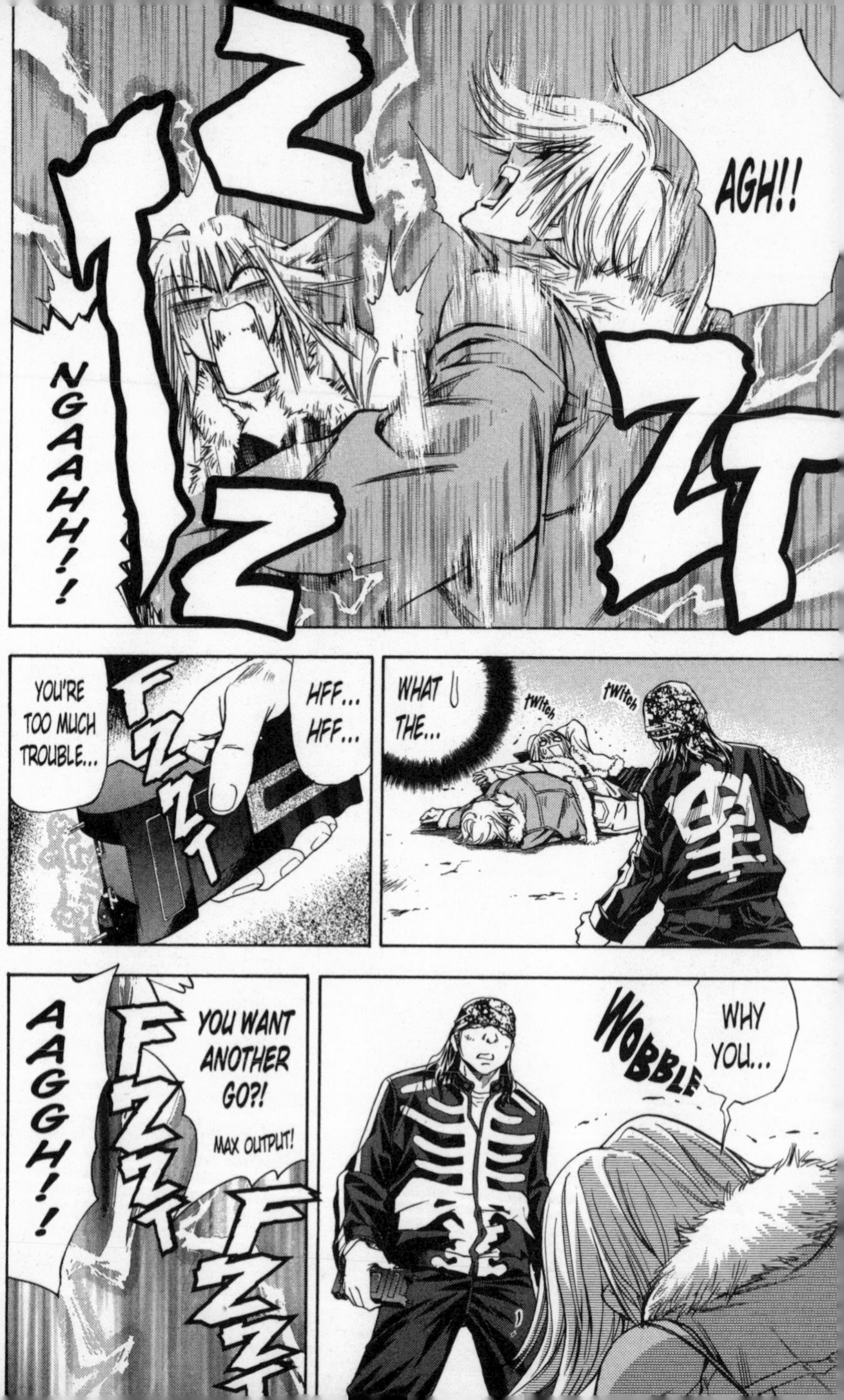
AGH!!
ZZT
ZZZ
NGAAHH!!
WHAT THE...
twitch
twitch
HFF... HFF...
FZZT
YOU'RE TOO MUCH TROUBLE...
WHY YOU...
WOBBLE
YOU WANT ANOTHER GO?!
MAX OUTPUT!
FZZT
FZZZ
AAGGH!!

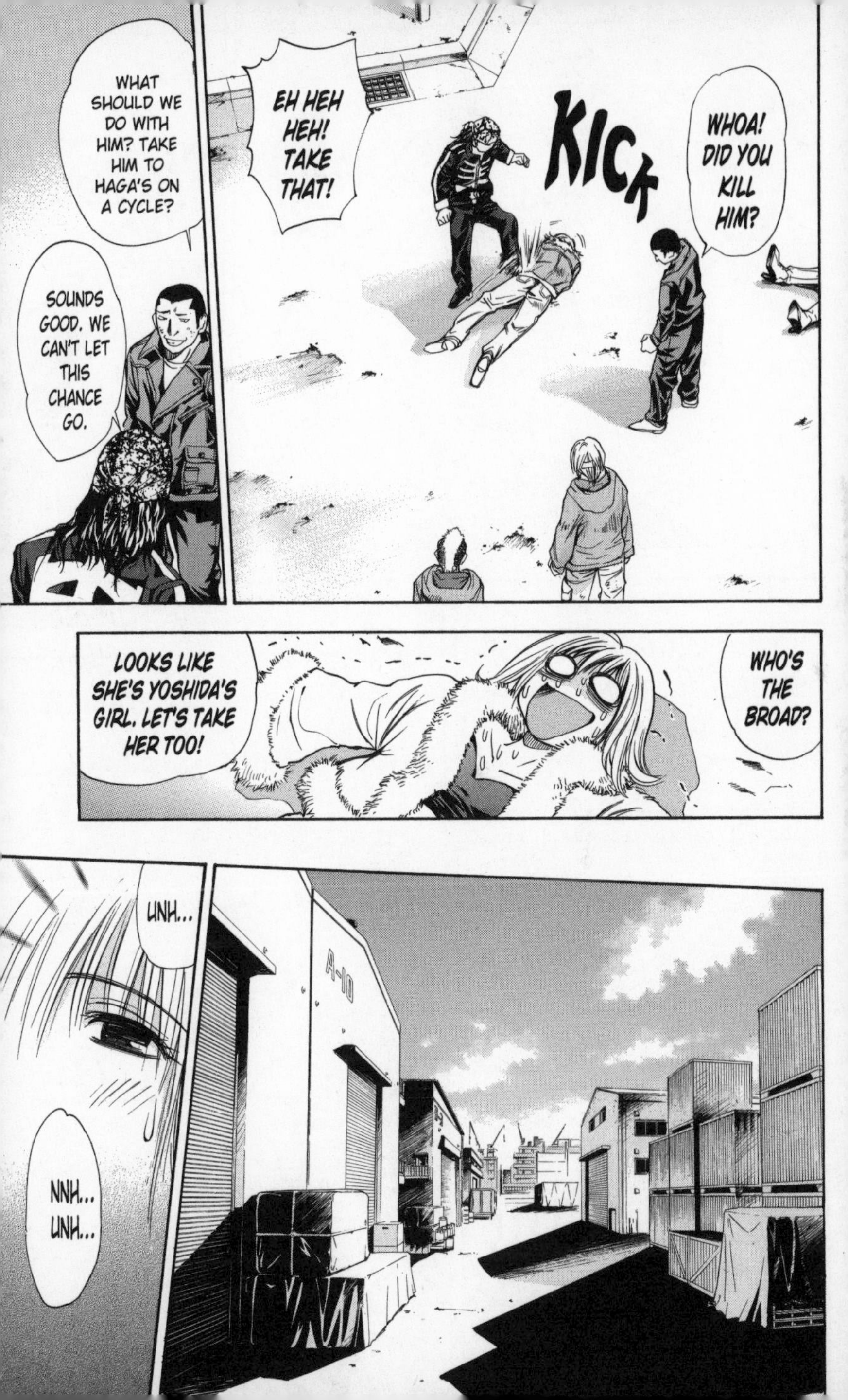
WHOA! DID YOU KILL HIM?
KICK
EH HEH HEH! TAKE THAT!
WHAT SHOULD WE DO WITH HIM? TAKE HIM TO HAGA'S ON A CYCLE?
SOUNDS GOOD. WE CAN'T LET THIS CHANCE GO.
WHO'S THE BROAD?
LOOKS LIKE SHE'S YOSHIDA'S GIRL. LET'S TAKE HER TOO!
UNH...
NNH... UNH...

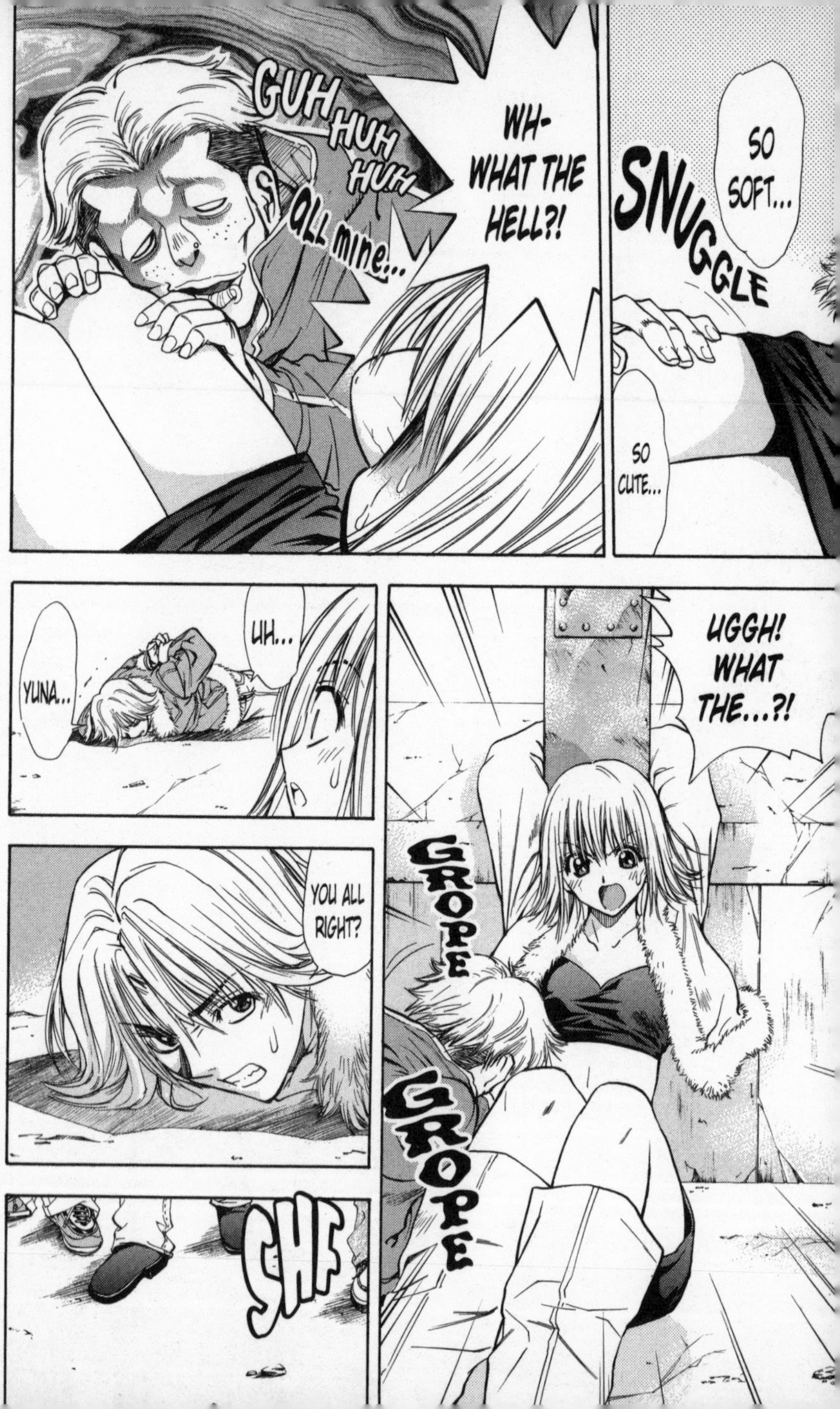
SO SOFT...
SNUGGLE
SO CUTE...
WH- WHAT THE HELL?!
GUH HUH HUH
ALL mine...
UGGH! WHAT THE...?!
GROPE
GROPE
UH...
YUNA...
YOU ALL RIGHT?
SHF

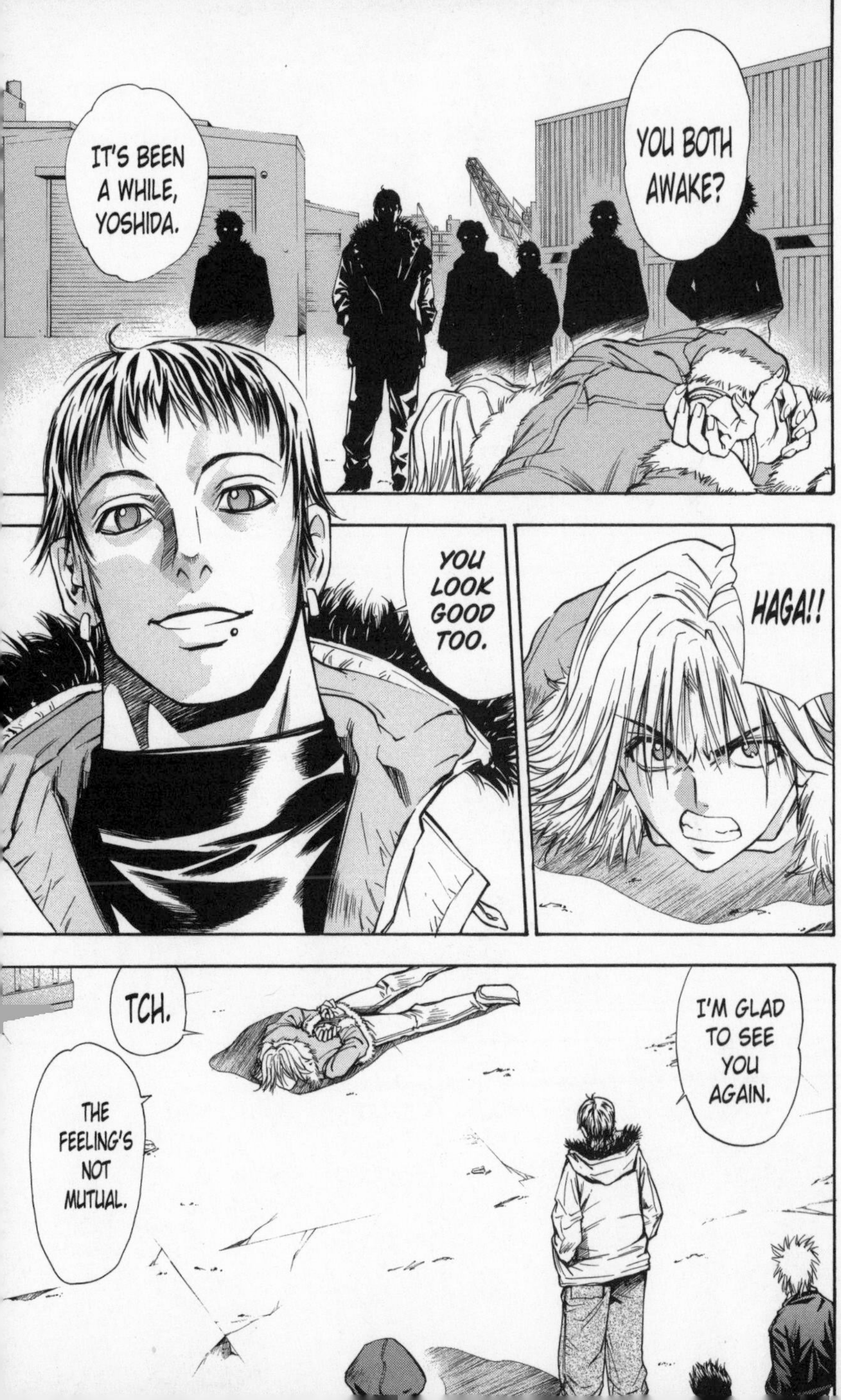
YOU BOTH AWAKE?
IT'S BEEN A WHILE, YOSHIDA.
HAGA!!
YOU LOOK GOOD TOO.
I'M GLAD TO SEE YOU AGAIN.
TCH.
THE FEELING'S NOT MUTUAL.

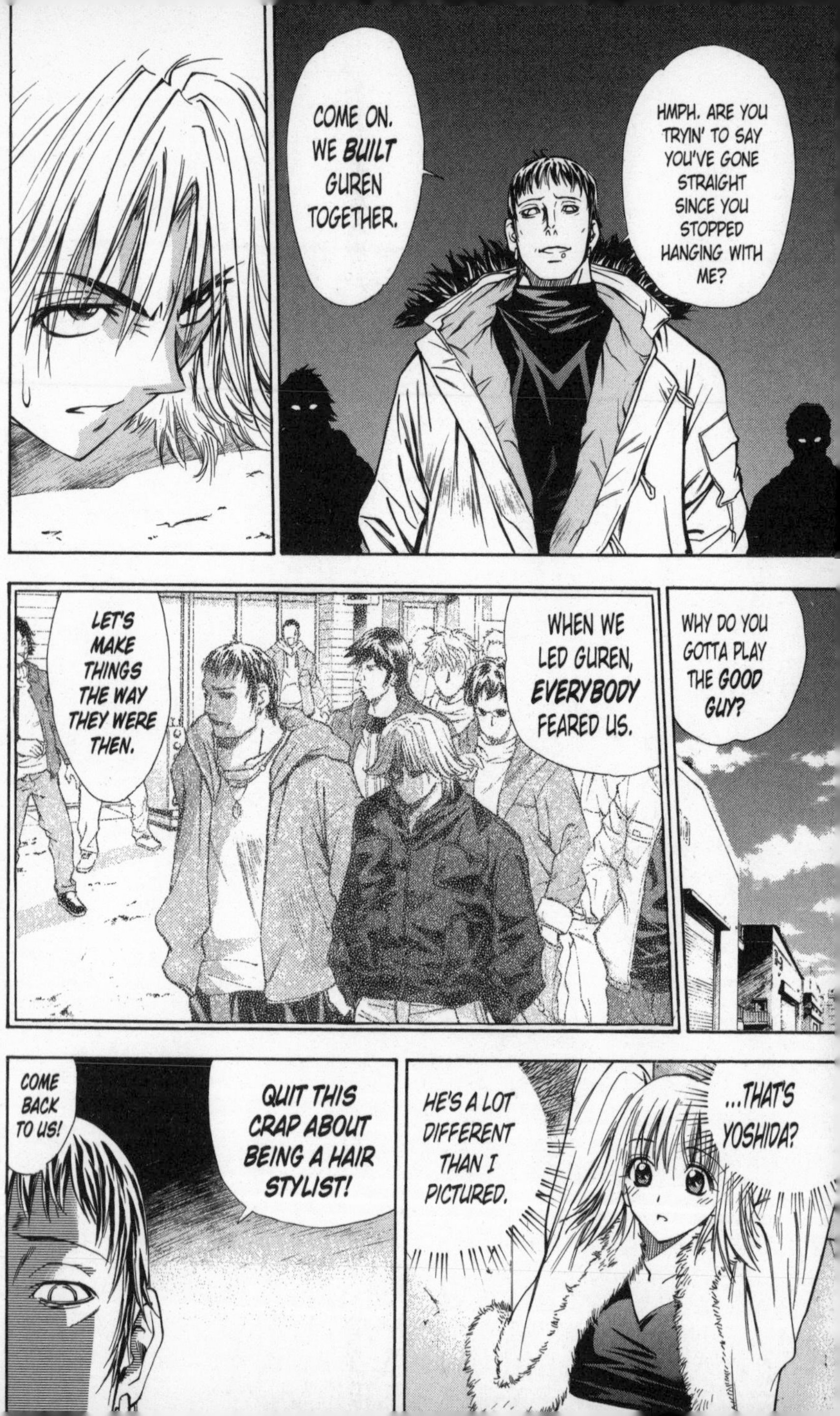
HMPH. ARE YOU TRYIN' TO SAY YOU'VE GONE STRAIGHT SINCE YOU STOPPED HANGING WITH ME?
COME ON. WE *BUILT* GUREN TOGETHER.
WHY DO YOU GOTTA PLAY THE *GOOD GUY?*
WHEN WE LED GUREN, *EVERYBODY* FEARED US.
LET'S MAKE THINGS THE WAY THEY WERE THEN.
...THAT'S YOSHIDA?
HE'S A LOT DIFFERENT THAN I PICTURED.
QUIT THIS CRAP ABOUT BEING A HAIR STYLIST!
COME BACK TO US!

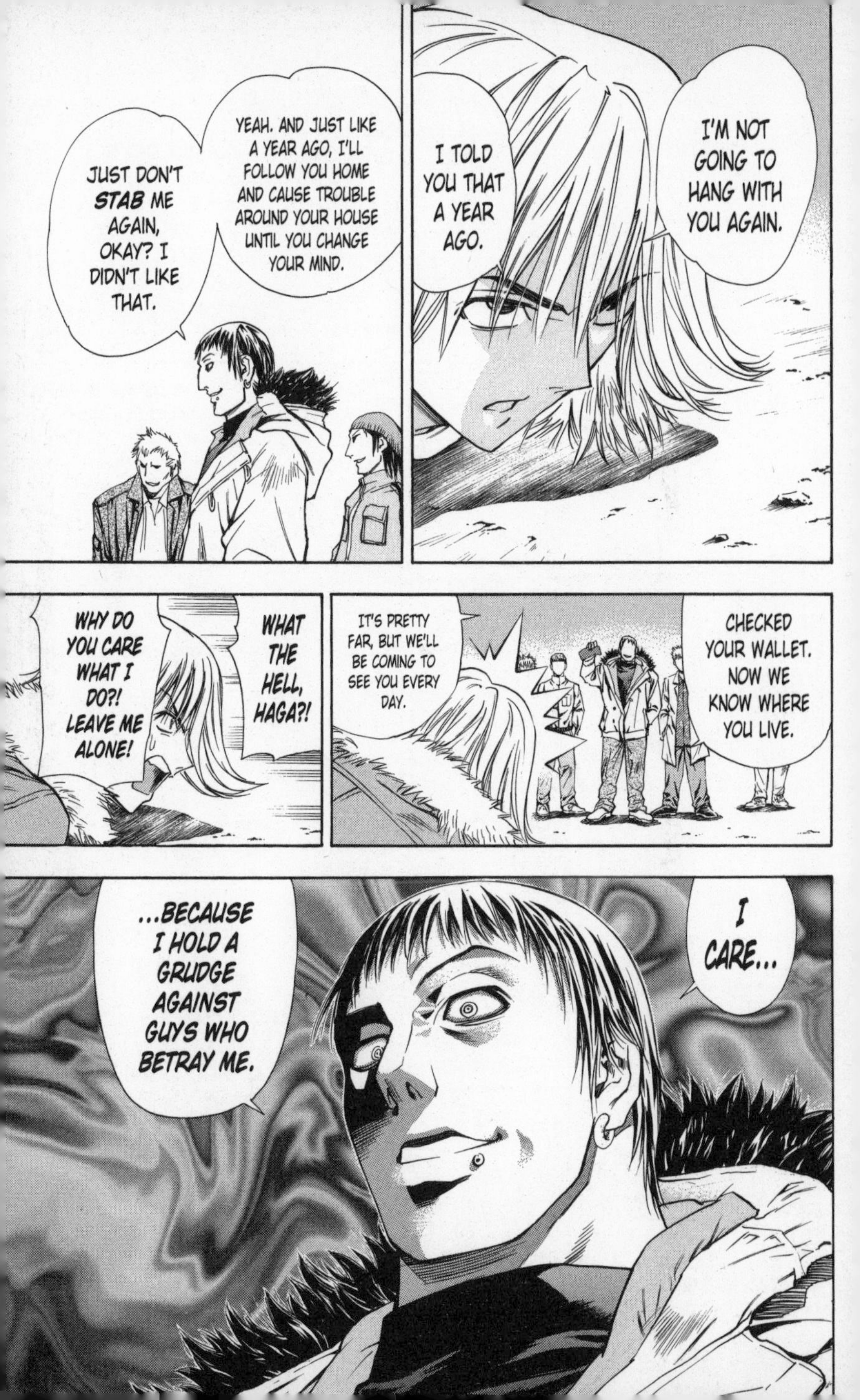
I'M NOT GOING TO HANG WITH YOU AGAIN.
I TOLD YOU THAT A YEAR AGO.
YEAH. AND JUST LIKE A YEAR AGO, I'LL FOLLOW YOU HOME AND CAUSE TROUBLE AROUND YOUR HOUSE UNTIL YOU CHANGE YOUR MIND.
JUST DON'T **STAB** ME AGAIN, OKAY? I DIDN'T LIKE THAT.
CHECKED YOUR WALLET. NOW WE KNOW WHERE YOU LIVE.
IT'S PRETTY FAR, BUT WE'LL BE COMING TO SEE YOU EVERY DAY.
WHAT THE HELL, HAGA?!
WHY DO YOU CARE WHAT I DO?! LEAVE ME ALONE!
I CARE...
...BECAUSE I HOLD A GRUDGE AGAINST GUYS WHO BETRAY ME.

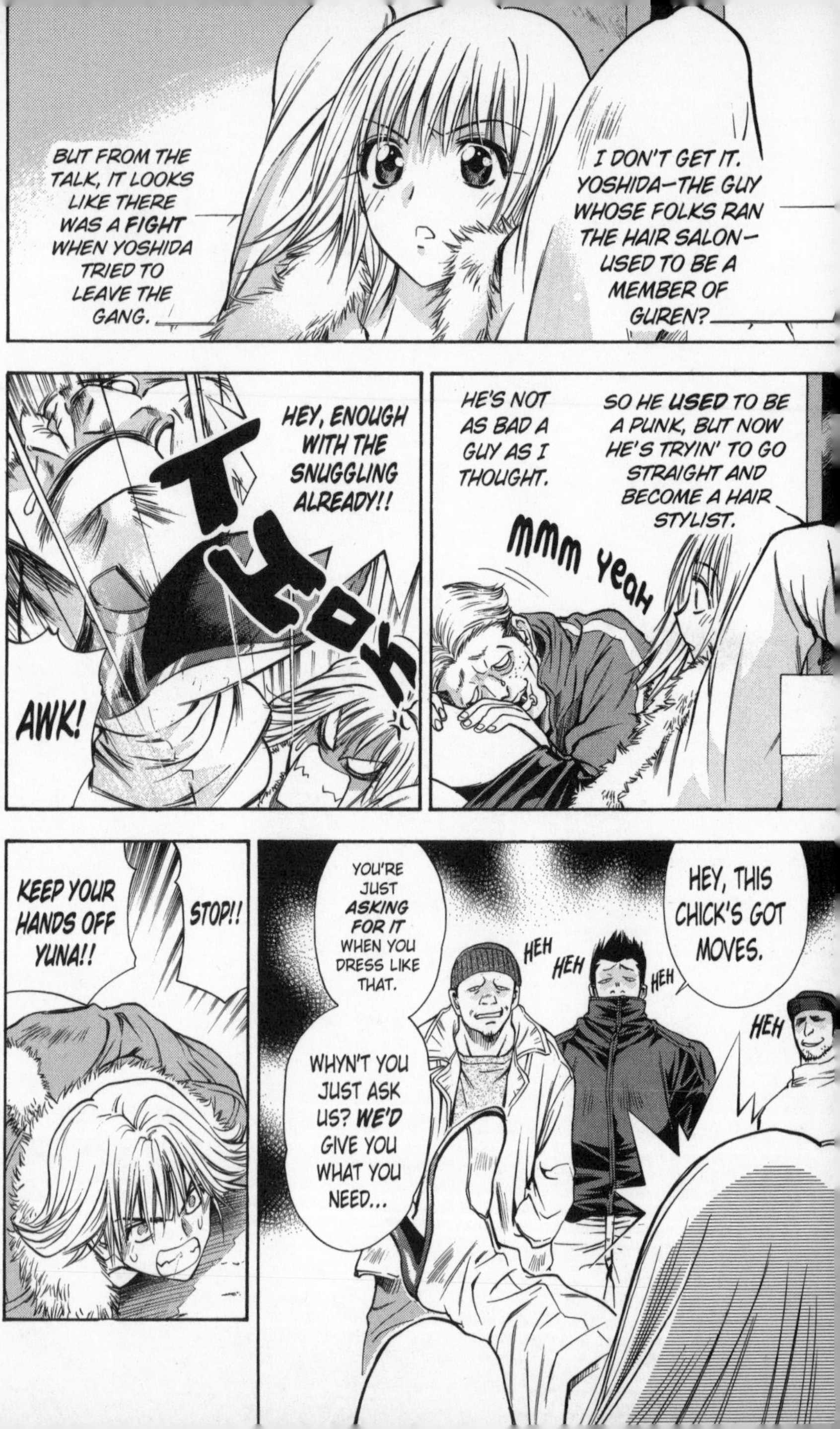
I DON'T GET IT. YOSHIDA—THE GUY WHOSE FOLKS RAN THE HAIR SALON—USED TO BE A MEMBER OF GUREN?
BUT FROM THE TALK, IT LOOKS LIKE THERE WAS A FIGHT WHEN YOSHIDA TRIED TO LEAVE THE GANG.
SO HE USED TO BE A PUNK, BUT NOW HE'S TRYIN' TO GO STRAIGHT AND BECOME A HAIR STYLIST.
HE'S NOT AS BAD A GUY AS I THOUGHT.
MMM YEAH
HEY, ENOUGH WITH THE SNUGGLING ALREADY!!
THOK
AWK!
HEY, THIS CHICK'S GOT MOVES.
HEH
HEH
HEH
HEH
YOU'RE JUST ASKING FOR IT WHEN YOU DRESS LIKE THAT.
WHYN'T YOU JUST ASK US? WE'D GIVE YOU WHAT YOU NEED...
STOP!!
KEEP YOUR HANDS OFF YUNA!!

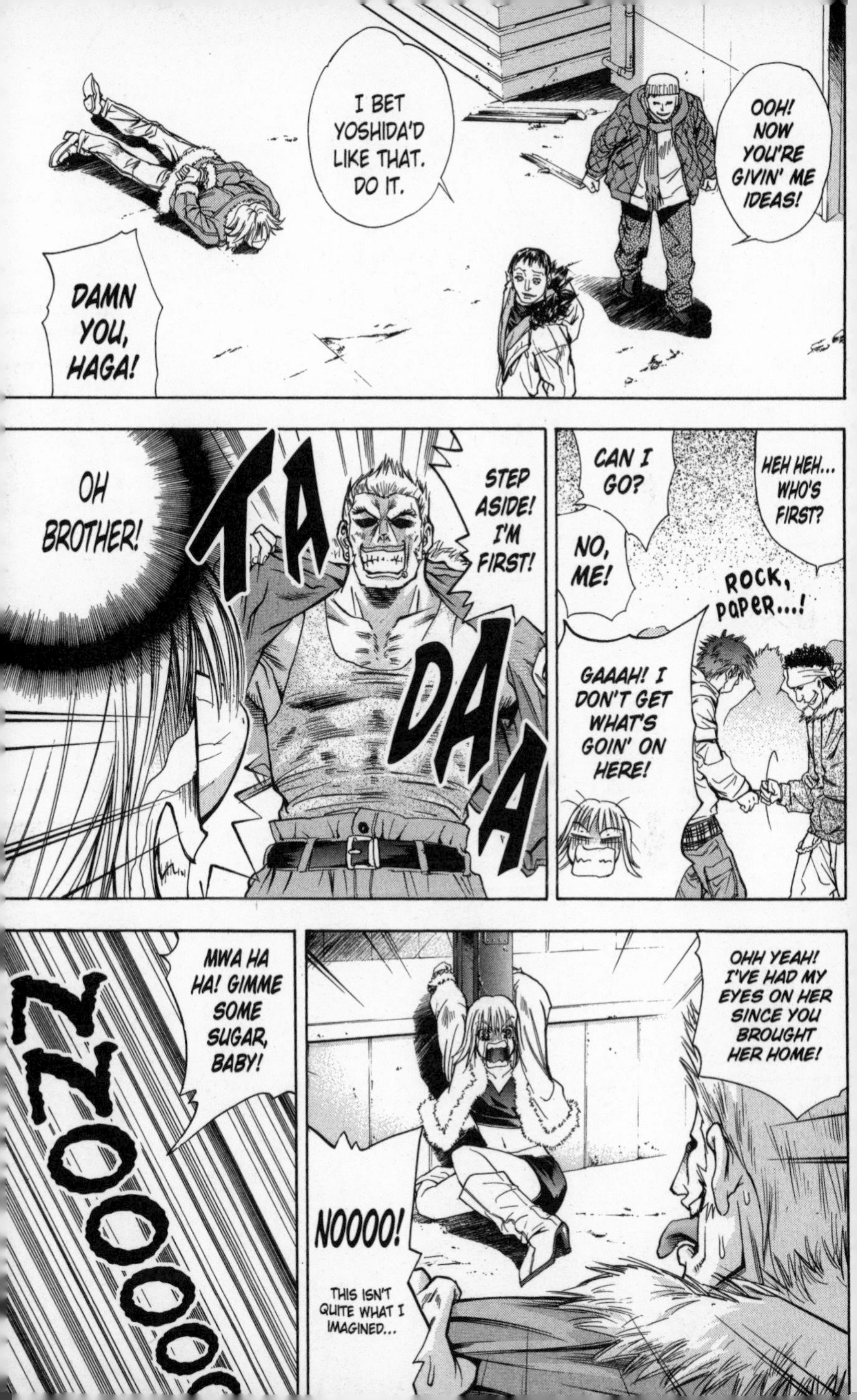
I BET YOSHIDA'D LIKE THAT. DO IT.
OOH! NOW YOU'RE GIVIN' ME IDEAS!
DAMN YOU, HAGA!
HEH HEH... WHO'S FIRST?
CAN I GO?
NO, ME!
ROCK, PAPER...!
GAAAH! I DON'T GET WHAT'S GOIN' ON HERE!
STEP ASIDE! I'M FIRST!
TA
DA
A
OH BROTHER!
OHH YEAH! I'VE HAD MY EYES ON HER SINCE YOU BROUGHT HER HOME!
NOOOO!
THIS ISN'T QUITE WHAT I IMAGINED...
MWA HA HA! GIMME SOME SUGAR, BABY!
ZOOOO

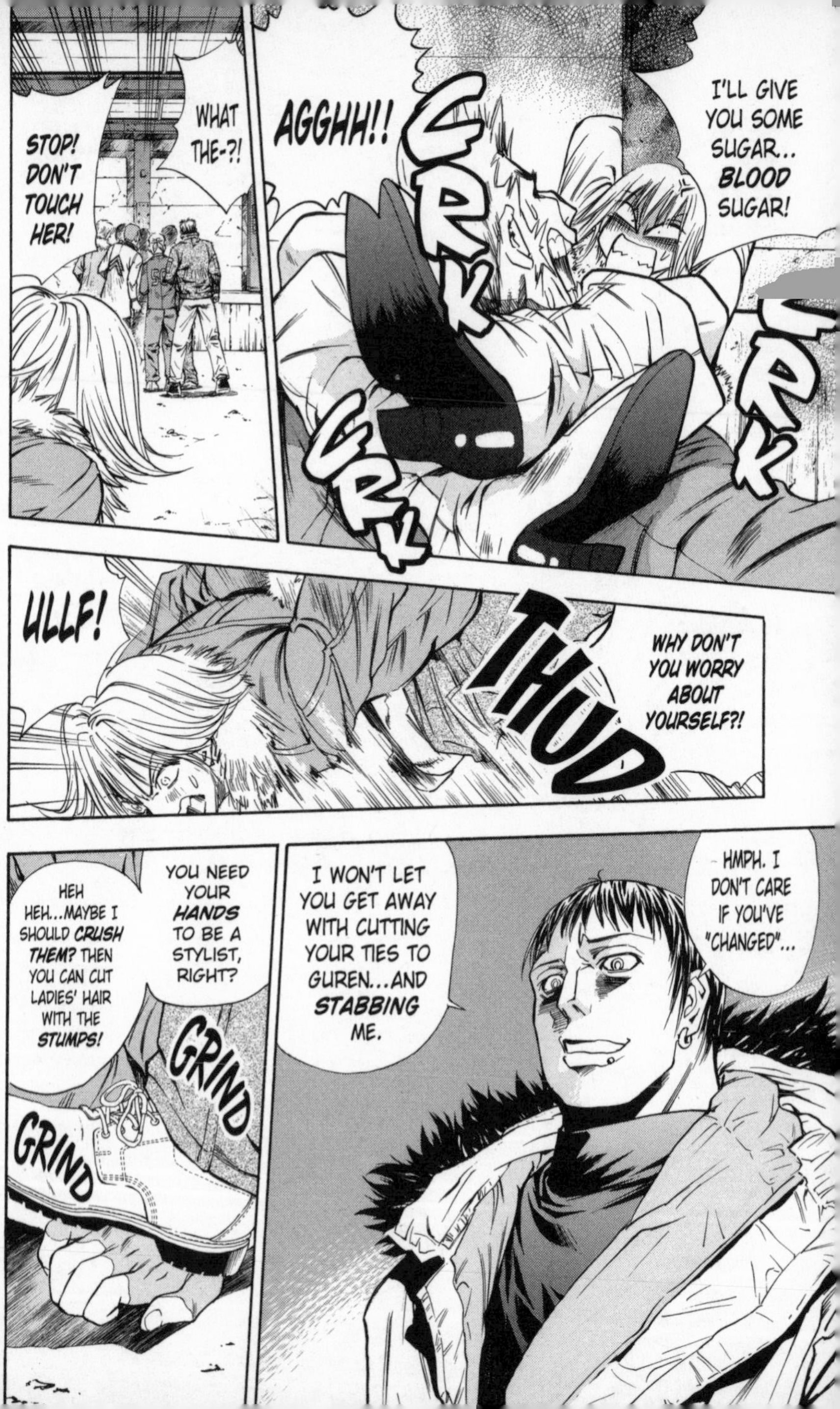
I'LL GIVE YOU SOME SUGAR... BLOOD SUGAR!
CRK
AGGHH!!
CRK
CRK
WHAT THE-?!
STOP! DON'T TOUCH HER!
WHY DON'T YOU WORRY ABOUT YOURSELF?!
THUD
ULLF!
HMPH. I DON'T CARE IF YOU'VE "CHANGED"...
I WON'T LET YOU GET AWAY WITH CUTTING YOUR TIES TO GUREN...AND STABBING ME.
YOU NEED YOUR HANDS TO BE A STYLIST, RIGHT?
HEH HEH...MAYBE I SHOULD CRUSH THEM? THEN YOU CAN CUT LADIES' HAIR WITH THE STUMPS!
GRIND
GRIND

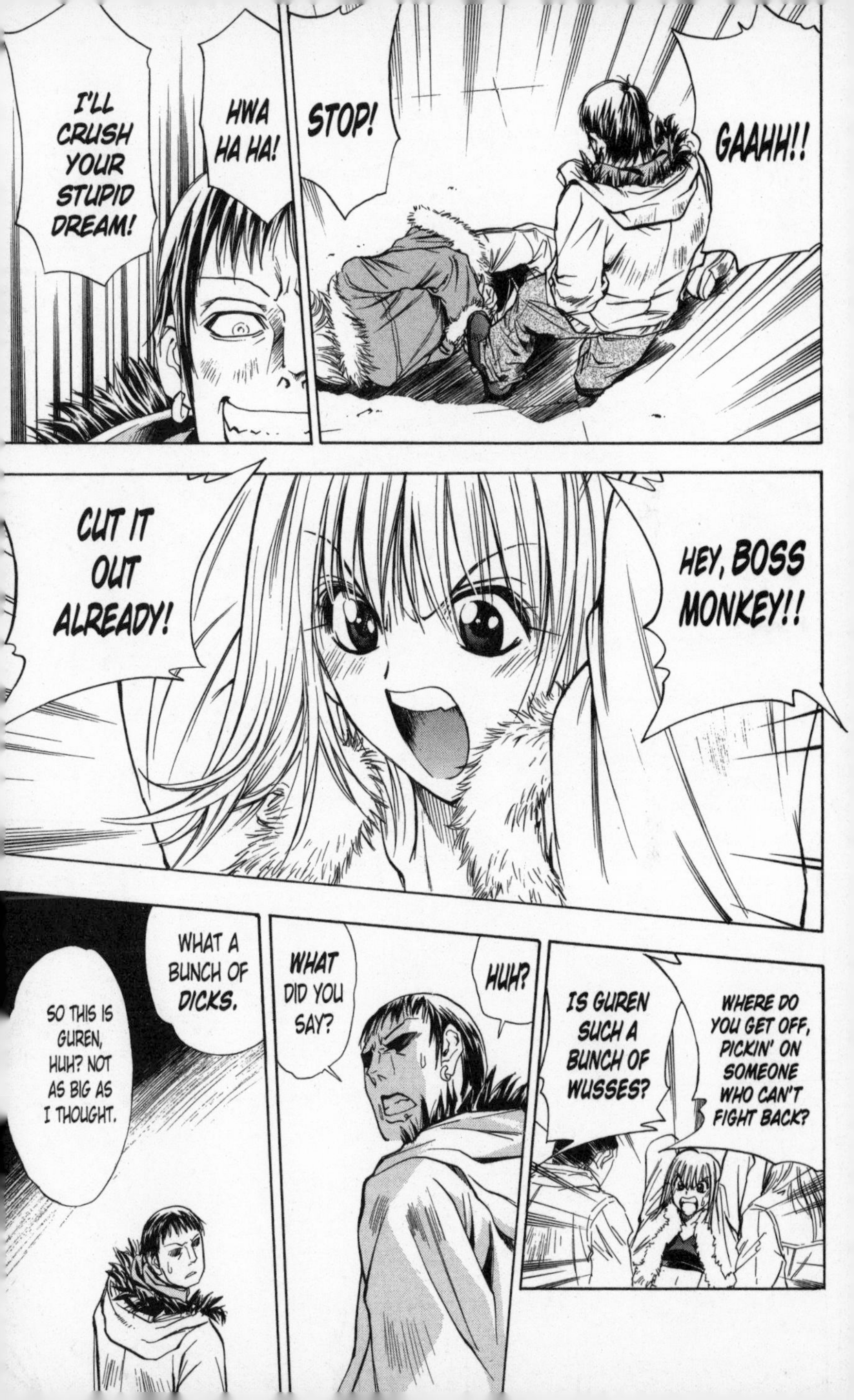
GAAHH!!
STOP!
HWA HA HA!
I'LL CRUSH YOUR STUPID DREAM!
HEY, BOSS MONKEY!!
CUT IT OUT ALREADY!
WHERE DO YOU GET OFF, PICKIN' ON SOMEONE WHO CAN'T FIGHT BACK?
IS GUREN SUCH A BUNCH OF WUSSES?
HUH?
WHAT DID YOU SAY?
WHAT A BUNCH OF DICKS.
SO THIS IS GUREN, HUH? NOT AS BIG AS I THOUGHT.

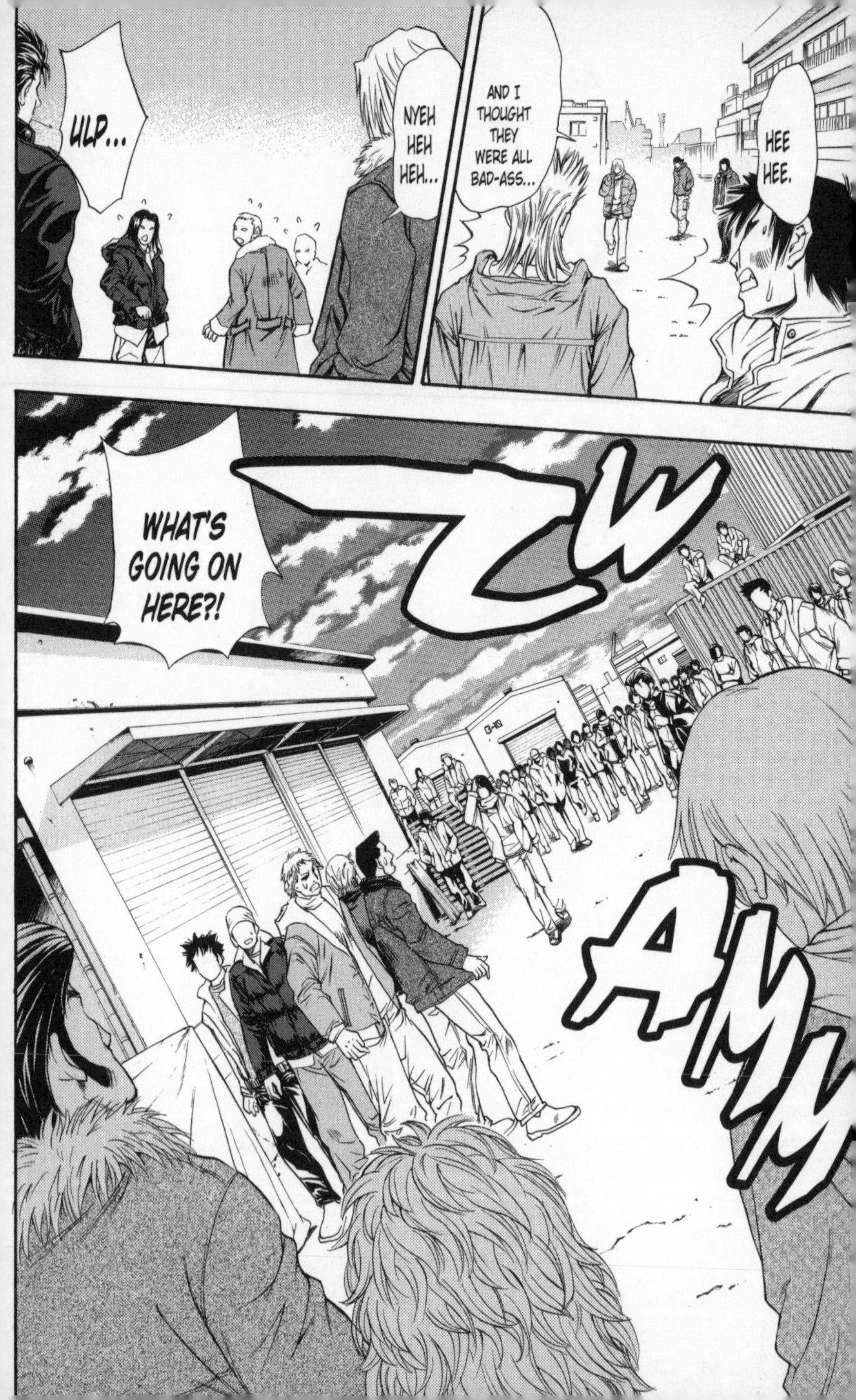
HEE HEE.
AND I THOUGHT THEY WERE ALL BAD-ASS...
NYEH HEH HEH...
ULP...
ZW
WHAT'S GOING ON HERE?!
AMM

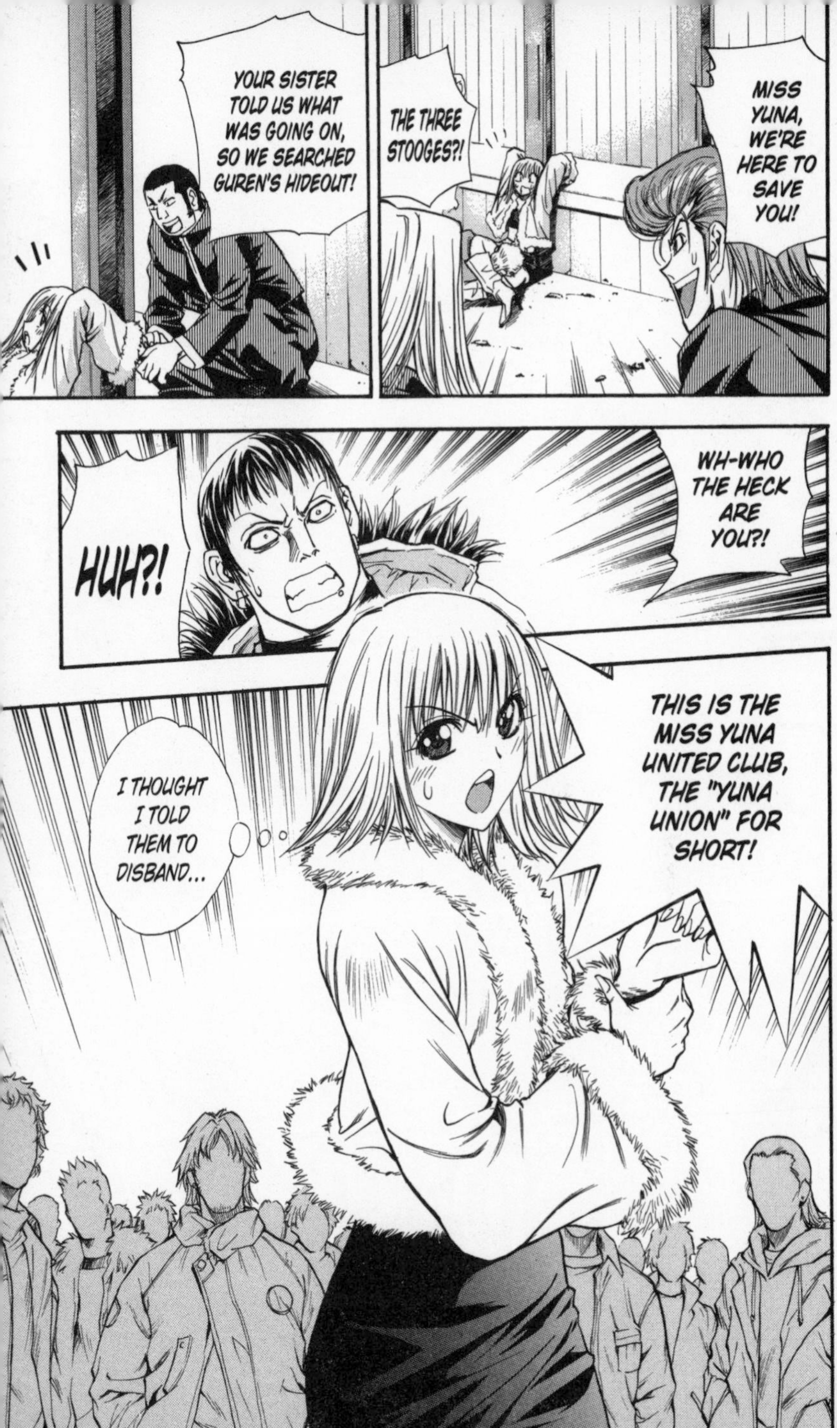
MISS YUNA, WE'RE HERE TO SAVE YOU!
THE THREE STOOGES?!
YOUR SISTER TOLD US WHAT WAS GOING ON, SO WE SEARCHED GUREN'S HIDEOUT!
WH-WHO THE HECK ARE YOU?!
HUH?!
THIS IS THE MISS YUNA UNITED CLUB, THE "YUNA UNION" FOR SHORT!
I THOUGHT I TOLD THEM TO DISBAND...

Pretty Face

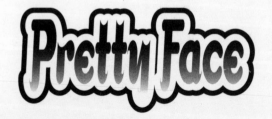

Chapter 33:
The Great Otaru Expedition: Part 5

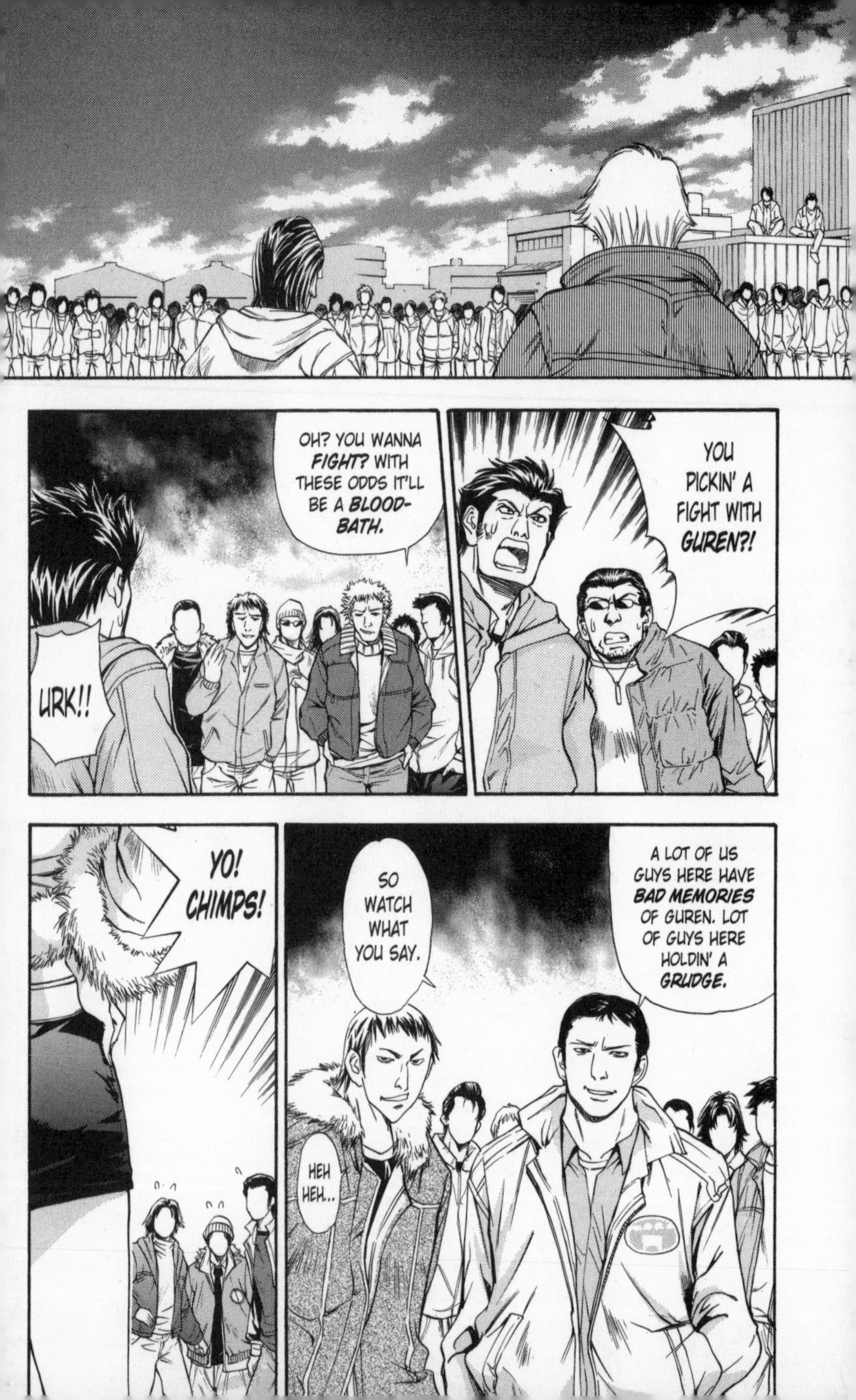
YOU PICKIN' A FIGHT WITH GUREN?!
OH? YOU WANNA FIGHT? WITH THESE ODDS IT'LL BE A BLOOD-BATH.
URK!!
A LOT OF US GUYS HERE HAVE BAD MEMORIES OF GUREN. LOT OF GUYS HERE HOLDIN' A GRUDGE.
SO WATCH WHAT YOU SAY.
HEH HEH...
YO! CHIMPS!

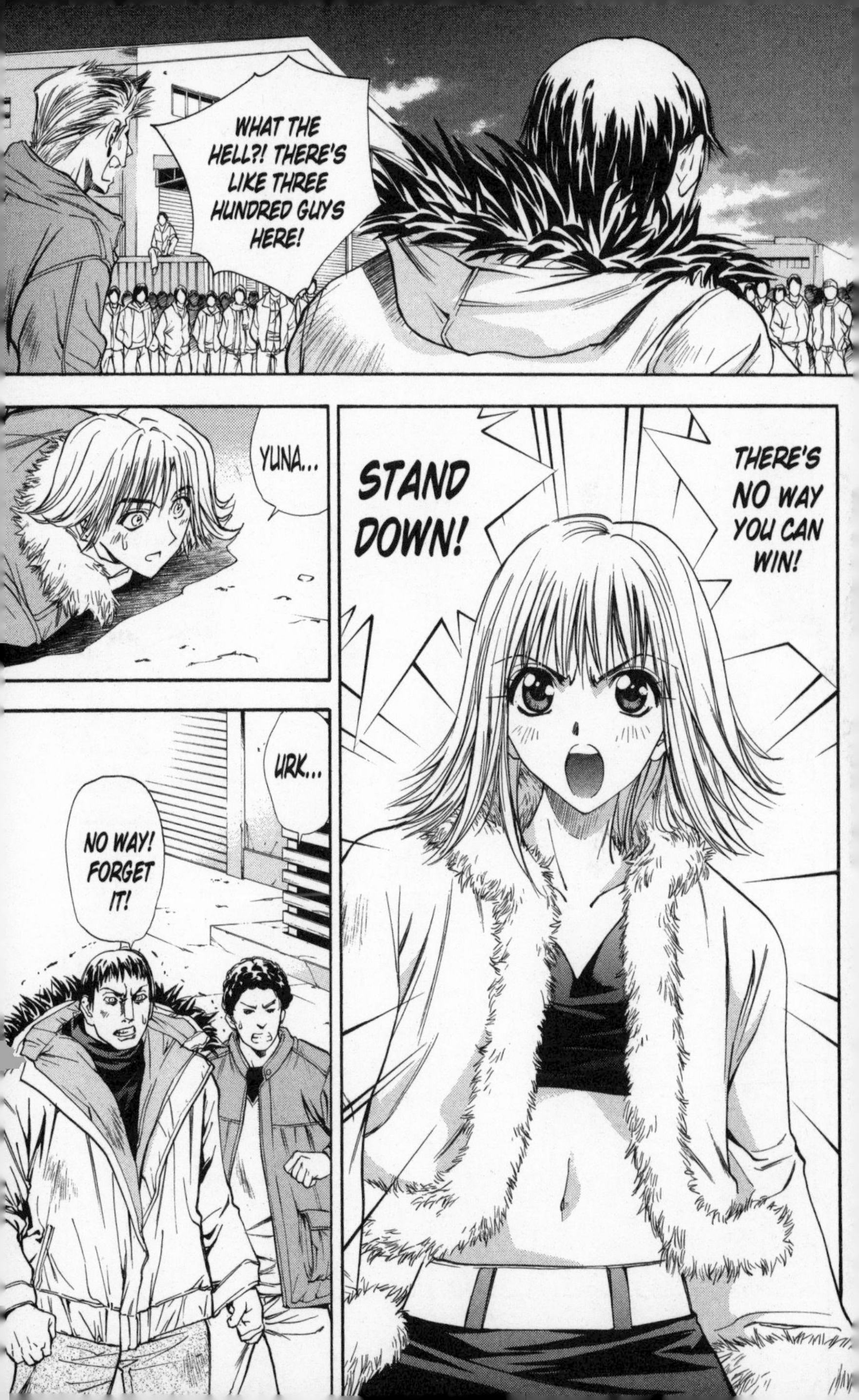
WHAT THE HELL?! THERE'S LIKE THREE HUNDRED GUYS HERE!
THERE'S NO WAY YOU CAN WIN!
STAND DOWN!
YUNA...
URK...
NO WAY! FORGET IT!

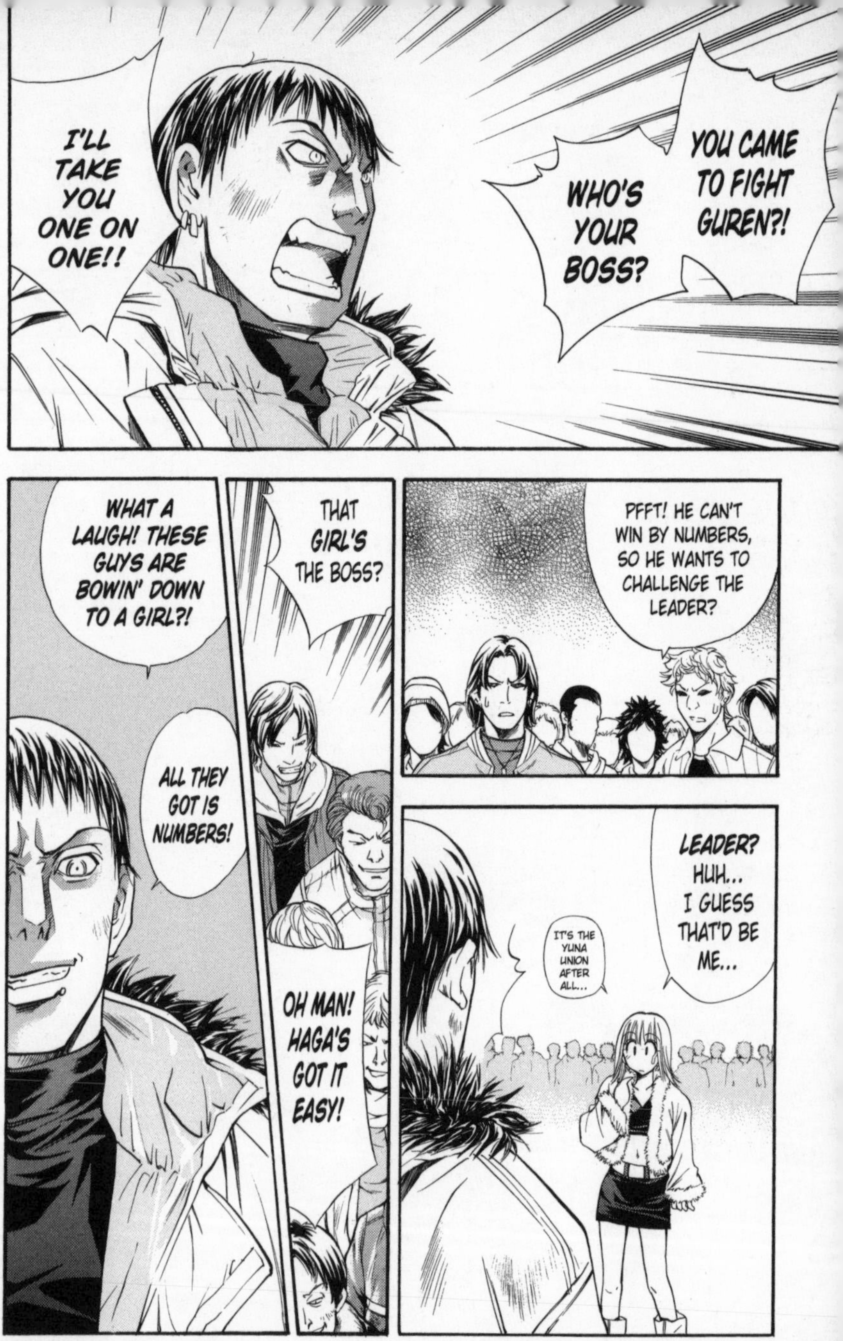
YOU CAME TO FIGHT GUREN?!
WHO'S YOUR BOSS?
I'LL TAKE YOU ONE ON ONE!!
PFFT! HE CAN'T WIN BY NUMBERS, SO HE WANTS TO CHALLENGE THE LEADER?
LEADER? HUH... I GUESS THAT'D BE ME...
IT'S THE YUNA UNION AFTER ALL...
THAT GIRL'S THE BOSS?
OH MAN! HAGA'S GOT IT EASY!
WHAT A LAUGH! THESE GUYS ARE BOWIN' DOWN TO A GIRL?!
ALL THEY GOT IS NUMBERS!

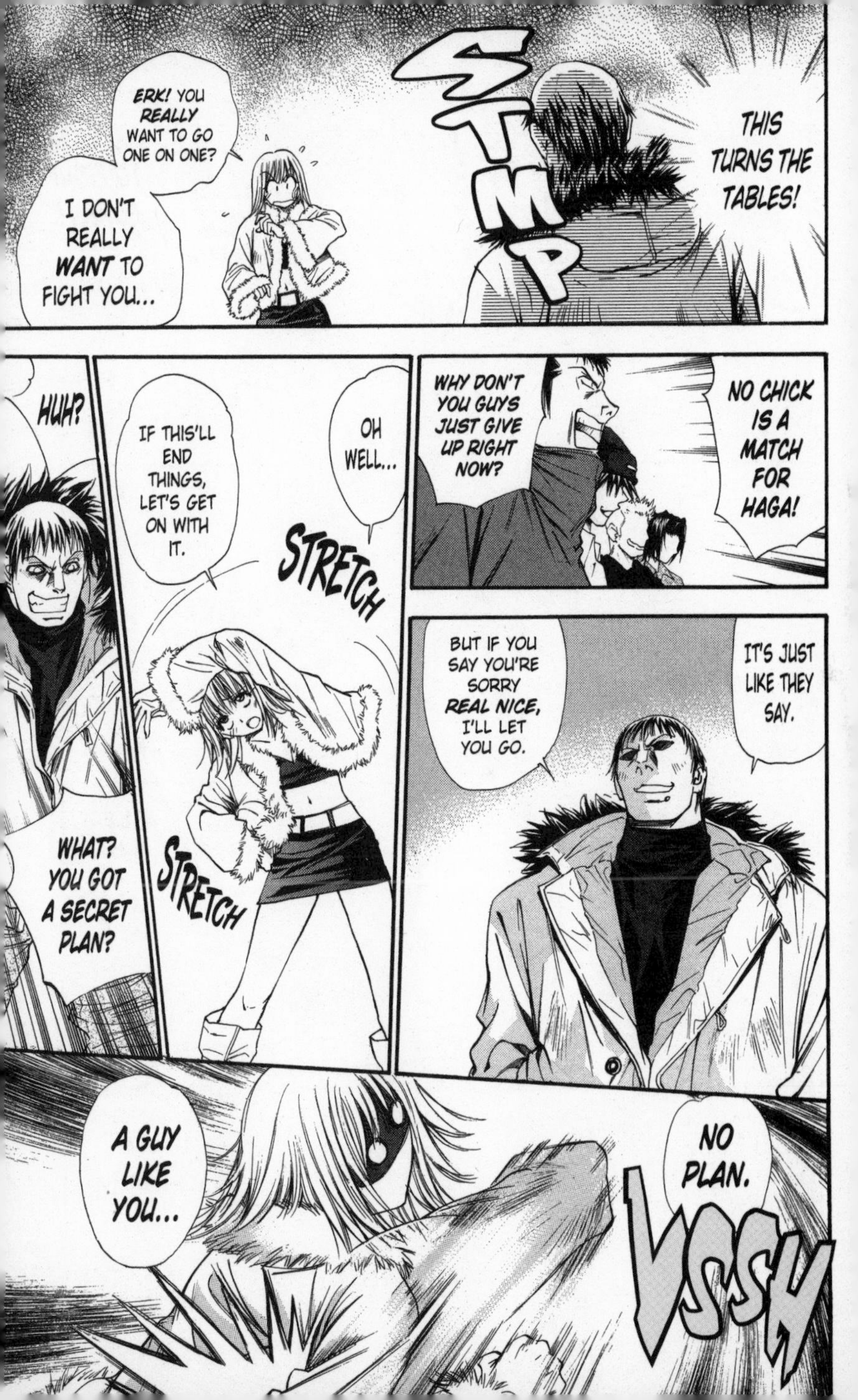
THIS TURNS THE TABLES!
STMP
ERK! YOU REALLY WANT TO GO ONE ON ONE?
I DON'T REALLY WANT TO FIGHT YOU...
NO CHICK IS A MATCH FOR HAGA!
WHY DON'T YOU GUYS JUST GIVE UP RIGHT NOW?
IT'S JUST LIKE THEY SAY.
BUT IF YOU SAY YOU'RE SORRY REAL NICE, I'LL LET YOU GO.
OH WELL...
IF THIS'LL END THINGS, LET'S GET ON WITH IT.
STRETCH
STRETCH
HUH?
WHAT? YOU GOT A SECRET PLAN?
NO PLAN.
VSSH
A GUY LIKE YOU...

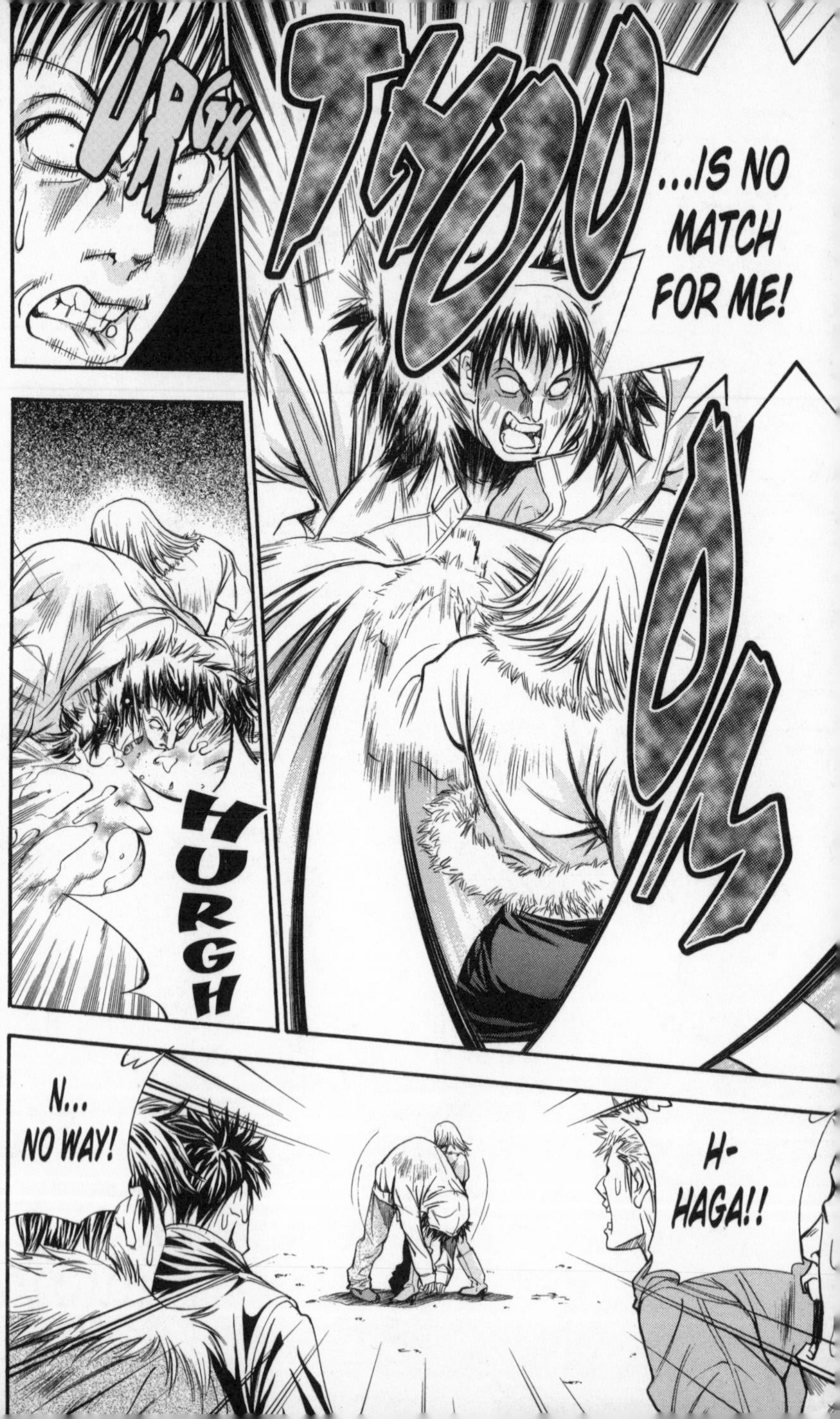
...IS NO MATCH FOR ME!
URGH
HURGH
H- HAGA!!
N... NO WAY!

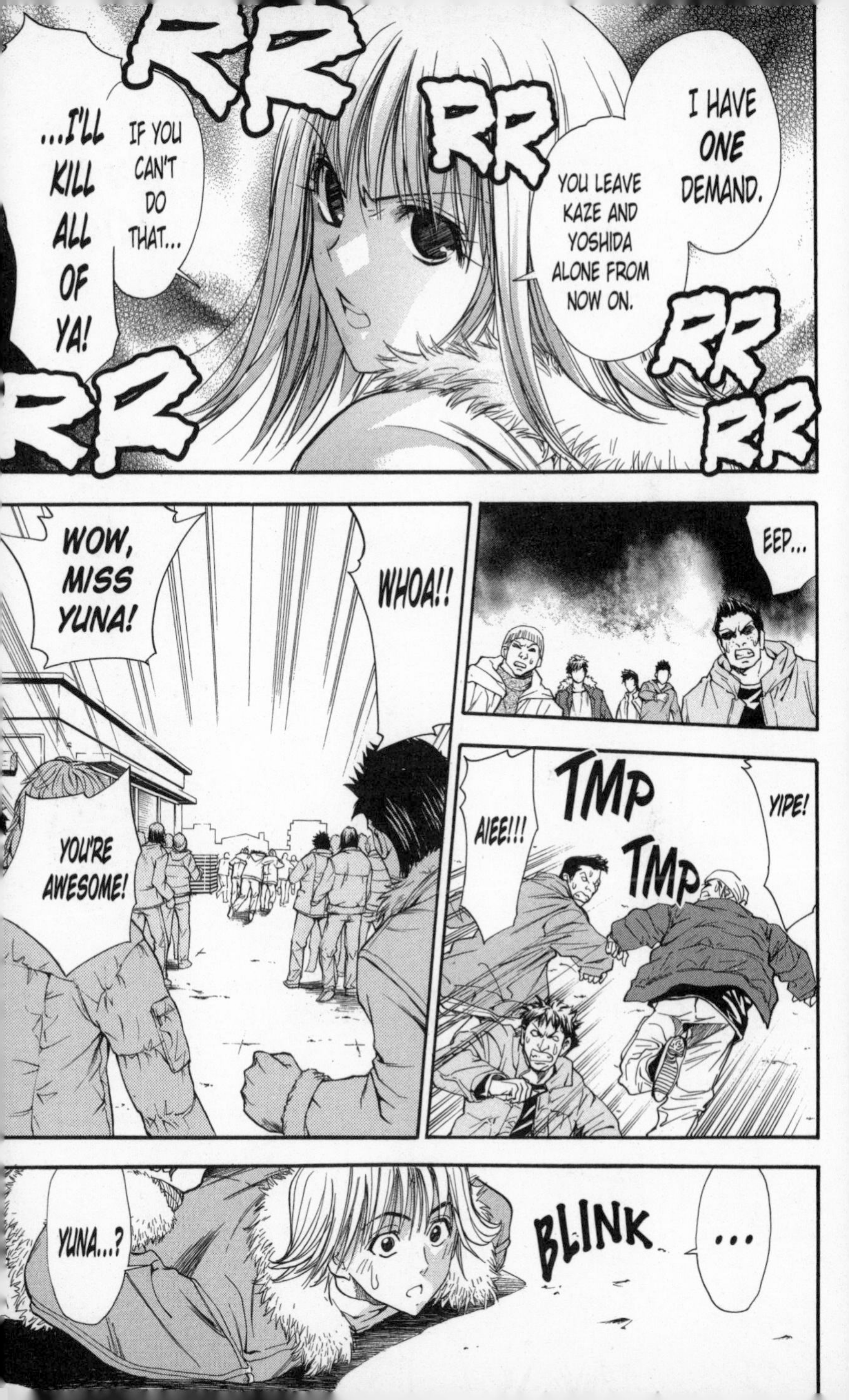
RR
RR
I HAVE ONE DEMAND.
YOU LEAVE KAZE AND YOSHIDA ALONE FROM NOW ON.
RR
RR
IF YOU CAN'T DO THAT...
...I'LL KILL ALL OF YA!
RR
EEP...
YIPE!
TMP
TMP
AIEE!!!
WHOA!!
WOW, MISS YUNA!
YOU'RE AWESOME!
...
BLINK
YUNA...?

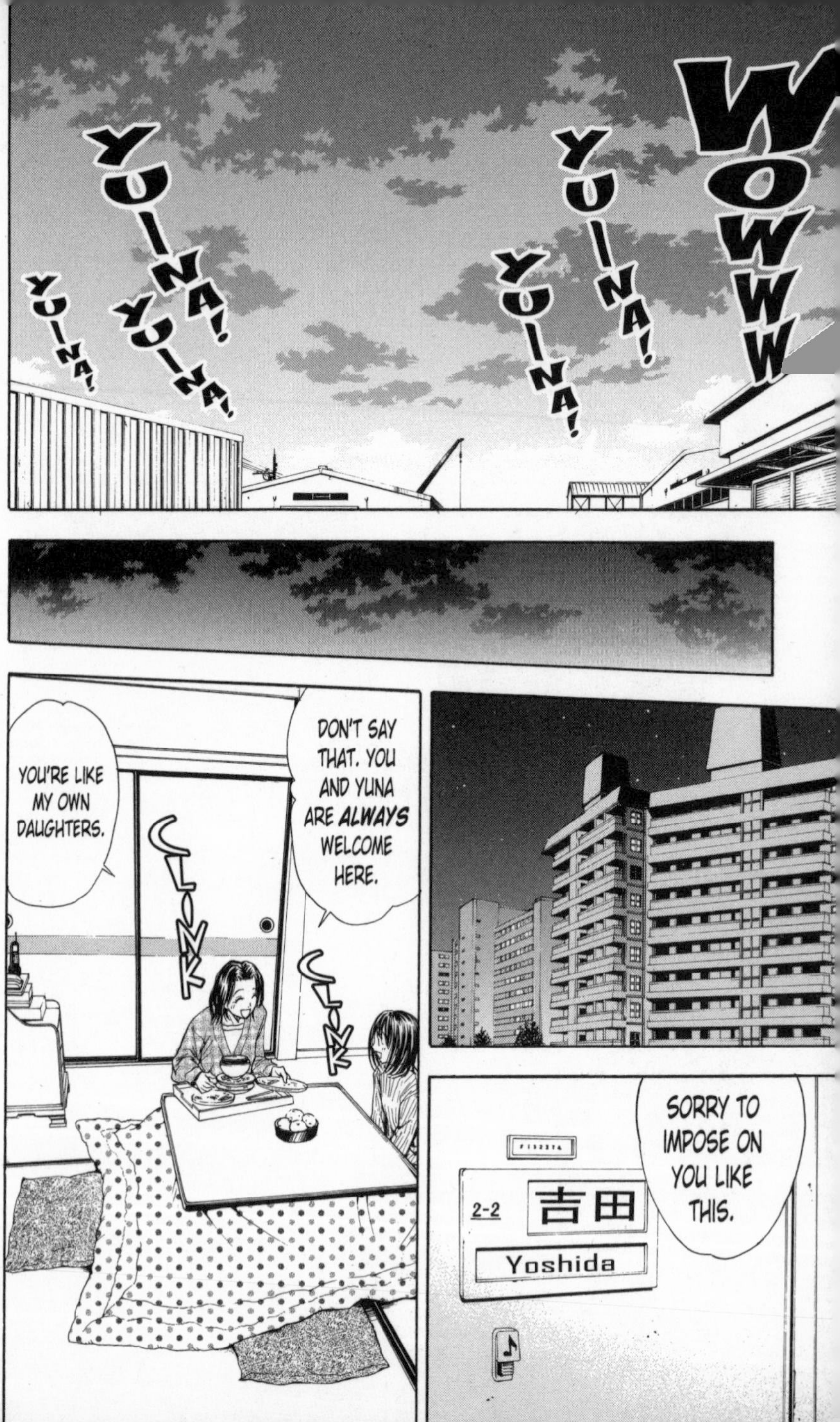
WOWWW
YUINA!
YUINA!
YUINA!
YUINA!
YUINA!
SORRY TO IMPOSE ON YOU LIKE THIS.
2-2
吉田
Yoshida
DON'T SAY THAT. YOU AND YUNA ARE *ALWAYS* WELCOME HERE.
CLONK
YOU'RE LIKE MY OWN DAUGHTERS.
CLONK

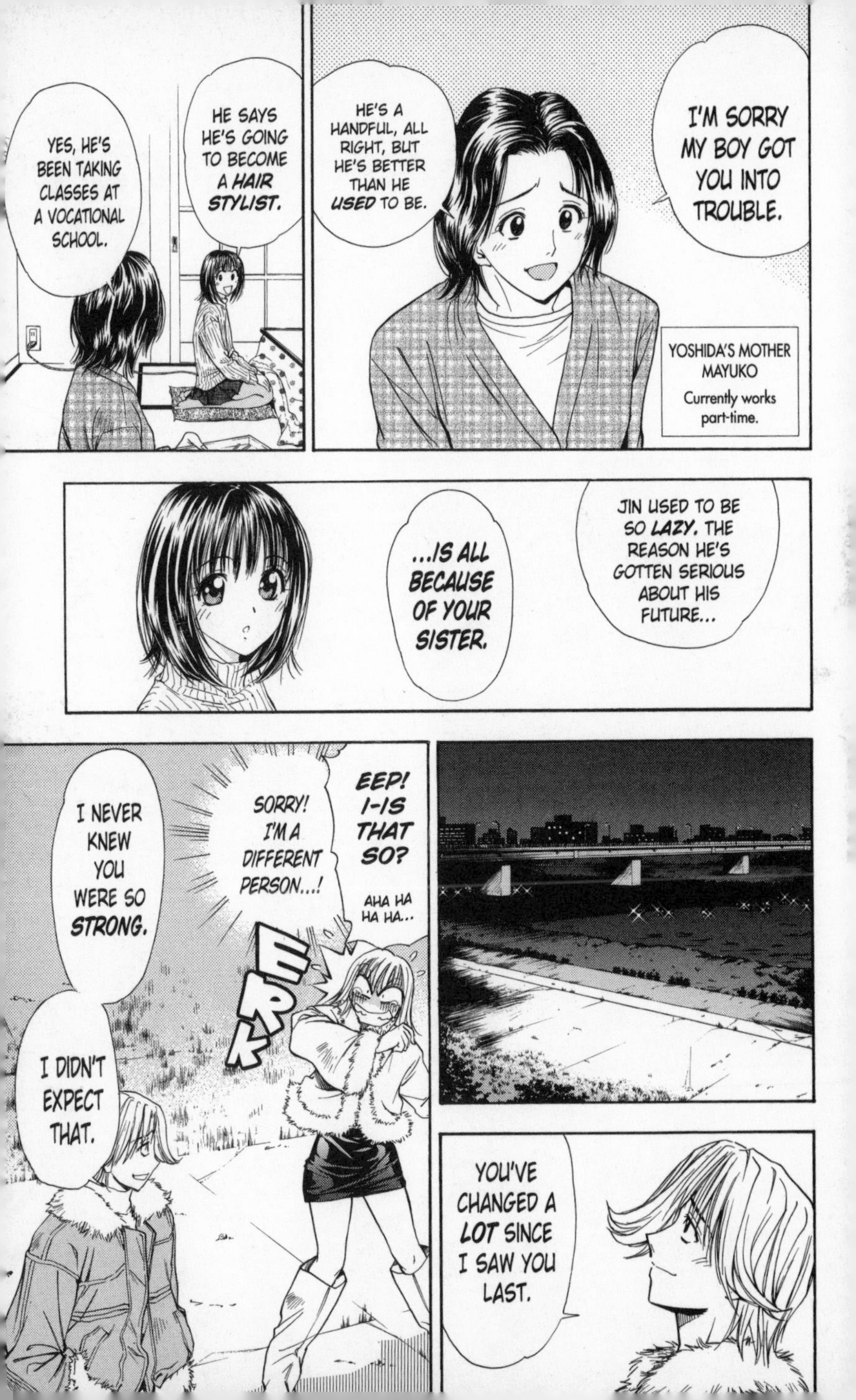
I'M SORRY MY BOY GOT YOU INTO TROUBLE.
YOSHIDA'S MOTHER MAYUKO
Currently works part-time.
HE'S A HANDFUL, ALL RIGHT, BUT HE'S BETTER THAN HE USED TO BE.
HE SAYS HE'S GOING TO BECOME A HAIR STYLIST.
YES, HE'S BEEN TAKING CLASSES AT A VOCATIONAL SCHOOL.
JIN USED TO BE SO LAZY. THE REASON HE'S GOTTEN SERIOUS ABOUT HIS FUTURE...
...IS ALL BECAUSE OF YOUR SISTER.
YOU'VE CHANGED A LOT SINCE I SAW YOU LAST.
I NEVER KNEW YOU WERE SO STRONG.
I DIDN'T EXPECT THAT.
EERK
EEP! I-IS THAT SO?
AHA HA HA HA...
SORRY! I'M A DIFFERENT PERSON...!

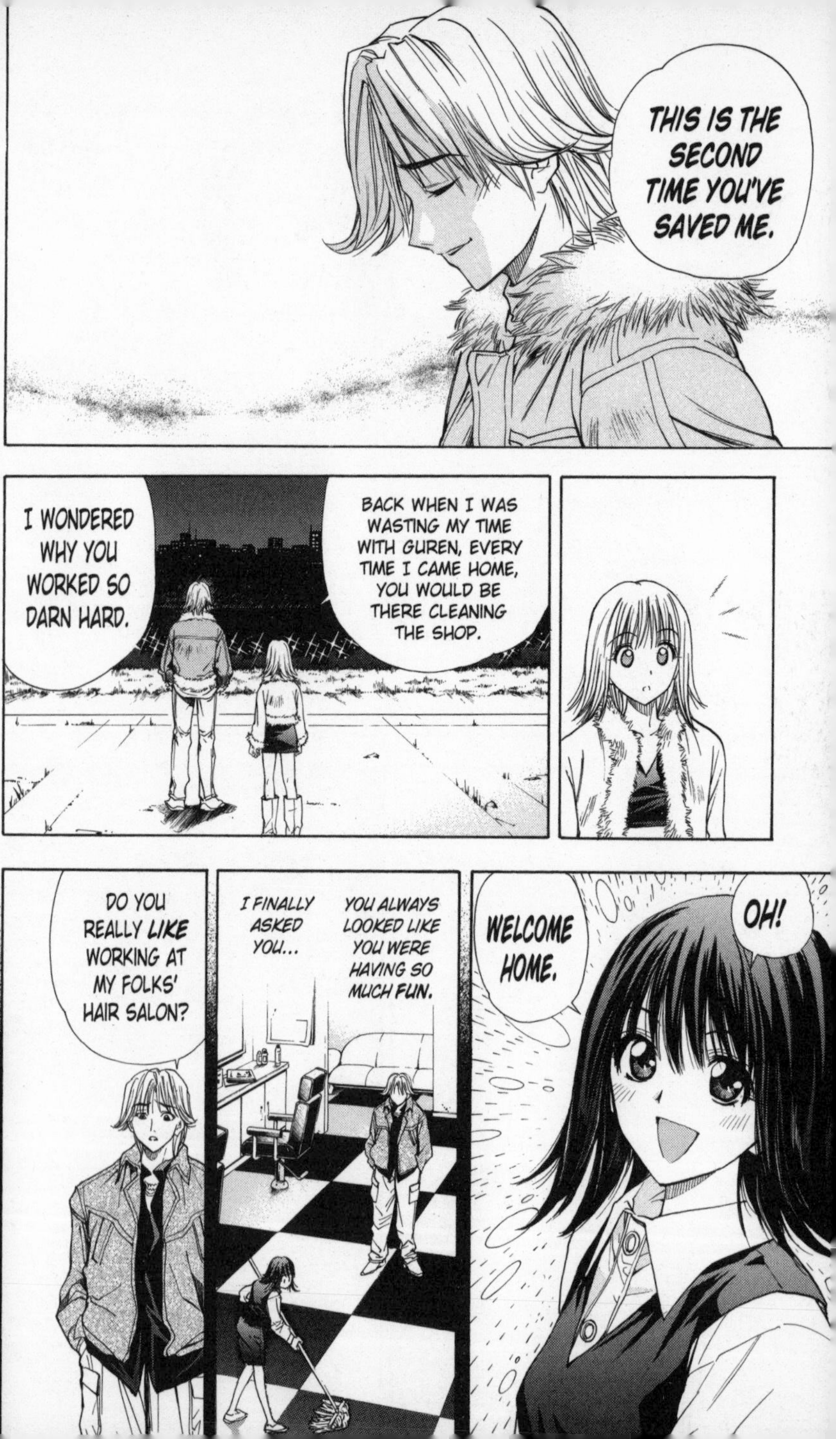
THIS IS THE SECOND TIME YOU'VE SAVED ME.
BACK WHEN I WAS WASTING MY TIME WITH GUREN, EVERY TIME I CAME HOME, YOU WOULD BE THERE CLEANING THE SHOP.
I WONDERED WHY YOU WORKED SO DARN HARD.
OH!
WELCOME HOME.
YOU ALWAYS LOOKED LIKE YOU WERE HAVING SO MUCH **FUN**.
I FINALLY ASKED YOU...
DO YOU REALLY **LIKE** WORKING AT MY FOLKS' HAIR SALON?

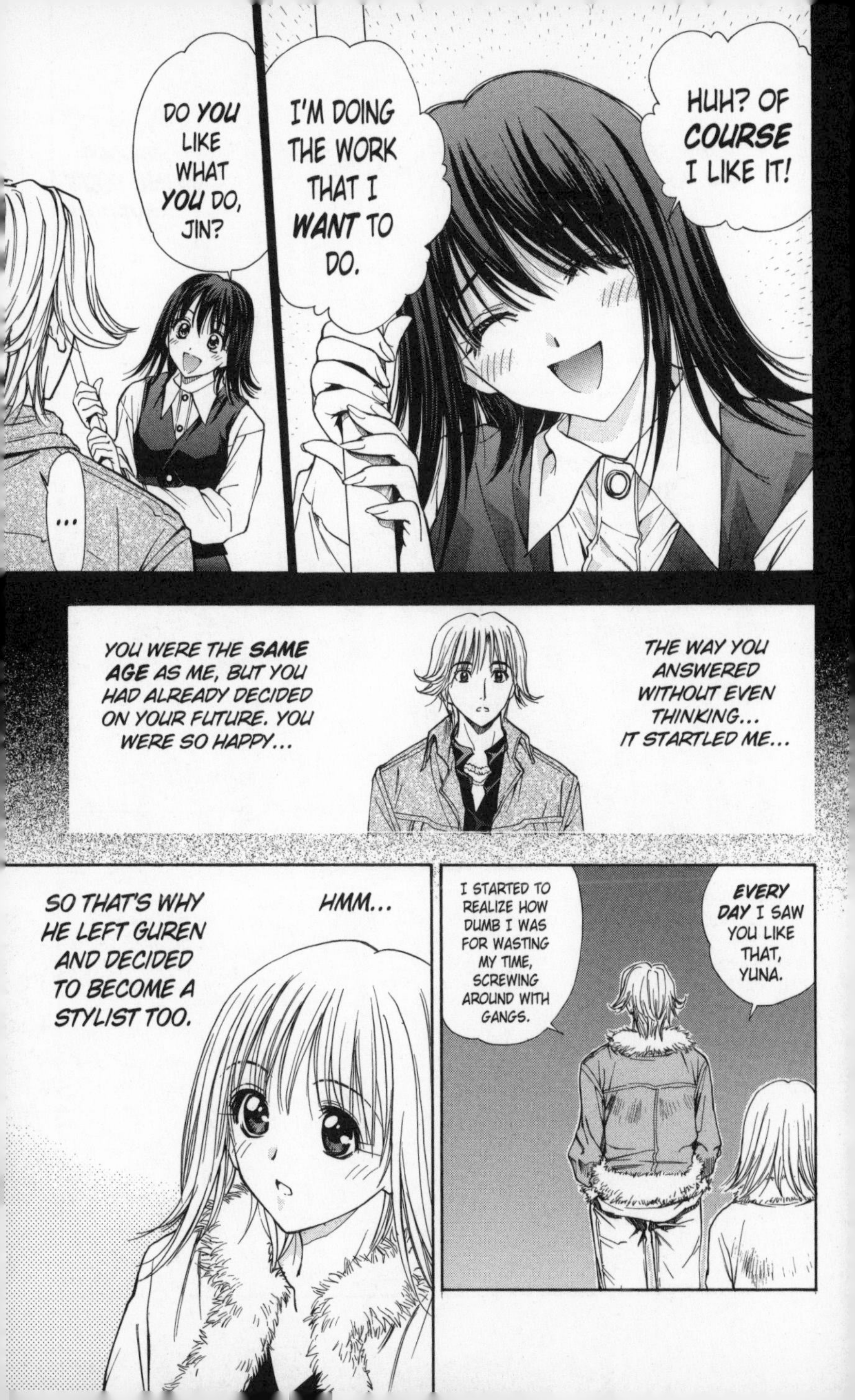

HUH? OF COURSE I LIKE IT!
I'M DOING THE WORK THAT I WANT TO DO.
DO YOU LIKE WHAT YOU DO, JIN?
...
THE WAY YOU ANSWERED WITHOUT EVEN THINKING... IT STARTLED ME...
YOU WERE THE SAME AGE AS ME, BUT YOU HAD ALREADY DECIDED ON YOUR FUTURE. YOU WERE SO HAPPY...
EVERY DAY I SAW YOU LIKE THAT, YUNA.
I STARTED TO REALIZE HOW DUMB I WAS FOR WASTING MY TIME, SCREWING AROUND WITH GANGS.
HMM...
SO THAT'S WHY HE LEFT GUREN AND DECIDED TO BECOME A STYLIST TOO.

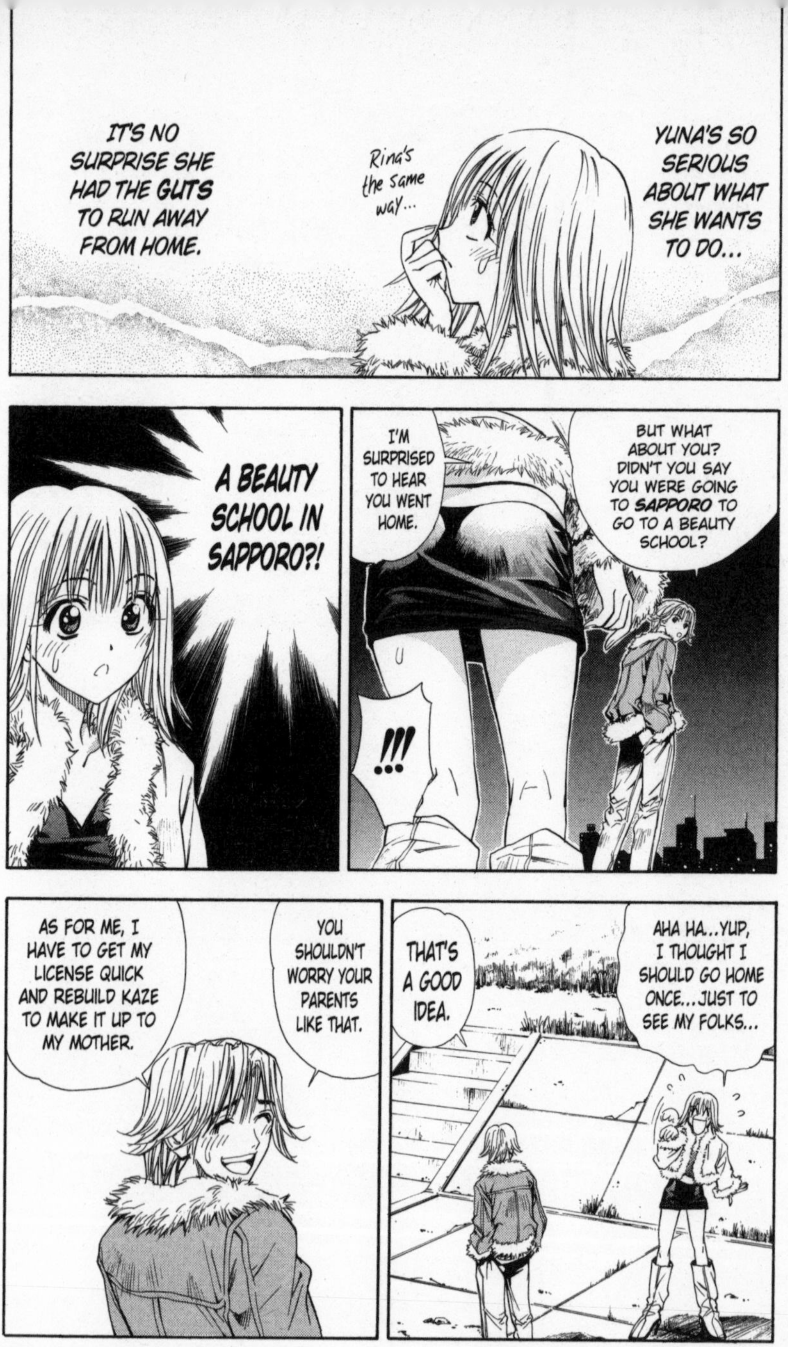
YUNA'S SO SERIOUS ABOUT WHAT SHE WANTS TO DO...
Rina's the same way...
IT'S NO SURPRISE SHE HAD THE GUTS TO RUN AWAY FROM HOME.
BUT WHAT ABOUT YOU? DIDN'T YOU SAY YOU WERE GOING TO SAPPORO TO GO TO A BEAUTY SCHOOL?
I'M SURPRISED TO HEAR YOU WENT HOME.
!!!
A BEAUTY SCHOOL IN SAPPORO?!
AHA HA...YUP, I THOUGHT I SHOULD GO HOME ONCE...JUST TO SEE MY FOLKS...
THAT'S A GOOD IDEA.
YOU SHOULDN'T WORRY YOUR PARENTS LIKE THAT.
AS FOR ME, I HAVE TO GET MY LICENSE QUICK AND REBUILD KAZE TO MAKE IT UP TO MY MOTHER.

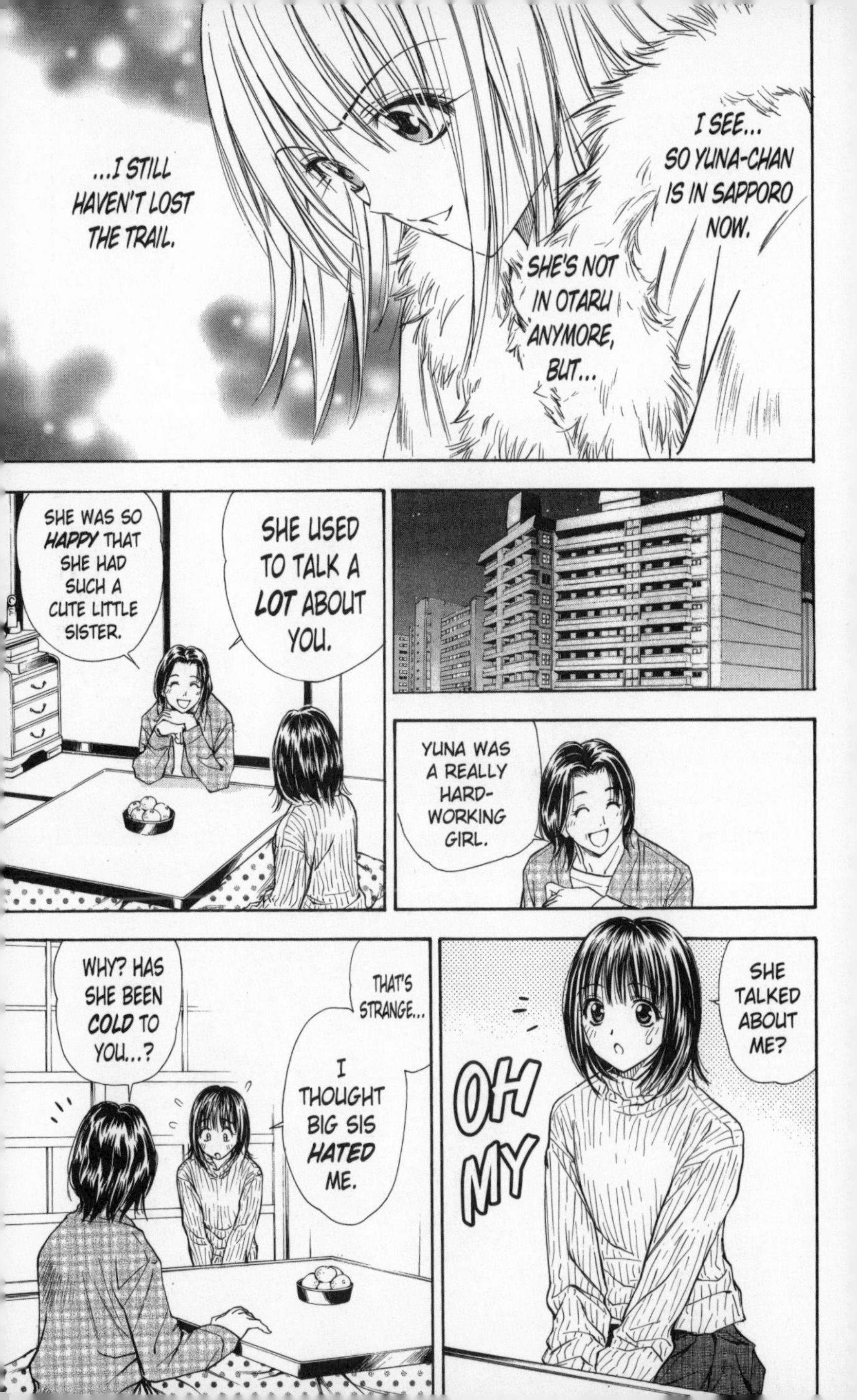
I SEE... SO YUNA-CHAN IS IN SAPPORO NOW.
SHE'S NOT IN OTARU ANYMORE, BUT...
...I STILL HAVEN'T LOST THE TRAIL.
YUNA WAS A REALLY HARD-WORKING GIRL.
SHE USED TO TALK A LOT ABOUT YOU.
SHE WAS SO HAPPY THAT SHE HAD SUCH A CUTE LITTLE SISTER.
SHE TALKED ABOUT ME?
OH MY
THAT'S STRANGE...
I THOUGHT BIG SIS HATED ME.
WHY? HAS SHE BEEN COLD TO YOU...?

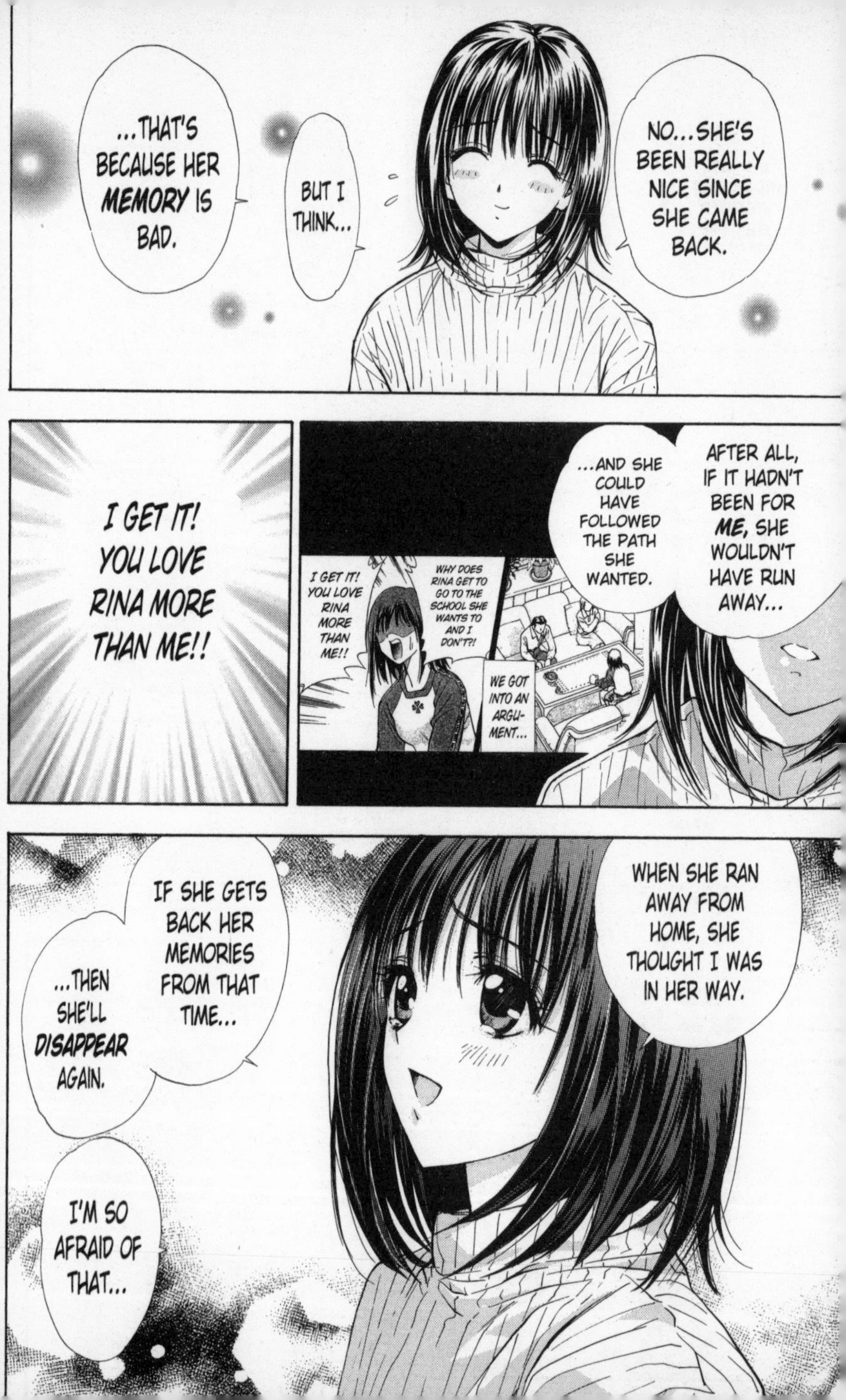
NO... SHE'S BEEN REALLY NICE SINCE SHE CAME BACK.
BUT I THINK...
...THAT'S BECAUSE HER MEMORY IS BAD.
AFTER ALL, IF IT HADN'T BEEN FOR ME, SHE WOULDN'T HAVE RUN AWAY...
...AND SHE COULD HAVE FOLLOWED THE PATH SHE WANTED.
WE GOT INTO AN ARGUMENT...
WHY DOES RINA GET TO GO TO THE SCHOOL SHE WANTS TO AND I DON'T?!
I GET IT! YOU LOVE RINA MORE THAN ME!!
I GET IT! YOU LOVE RINA MORE THAN ME!!
WHEN SHE RAN AWAY FROM HOME, SHE THOUGHT I WAS IN HER WAY.
IF SHE GETS BACK HER MEMORIES FROM THAT TIME...
...THEN SHE'LL DISAPPEAR AGAIN.
I'M SO AFRAID OF THAT...

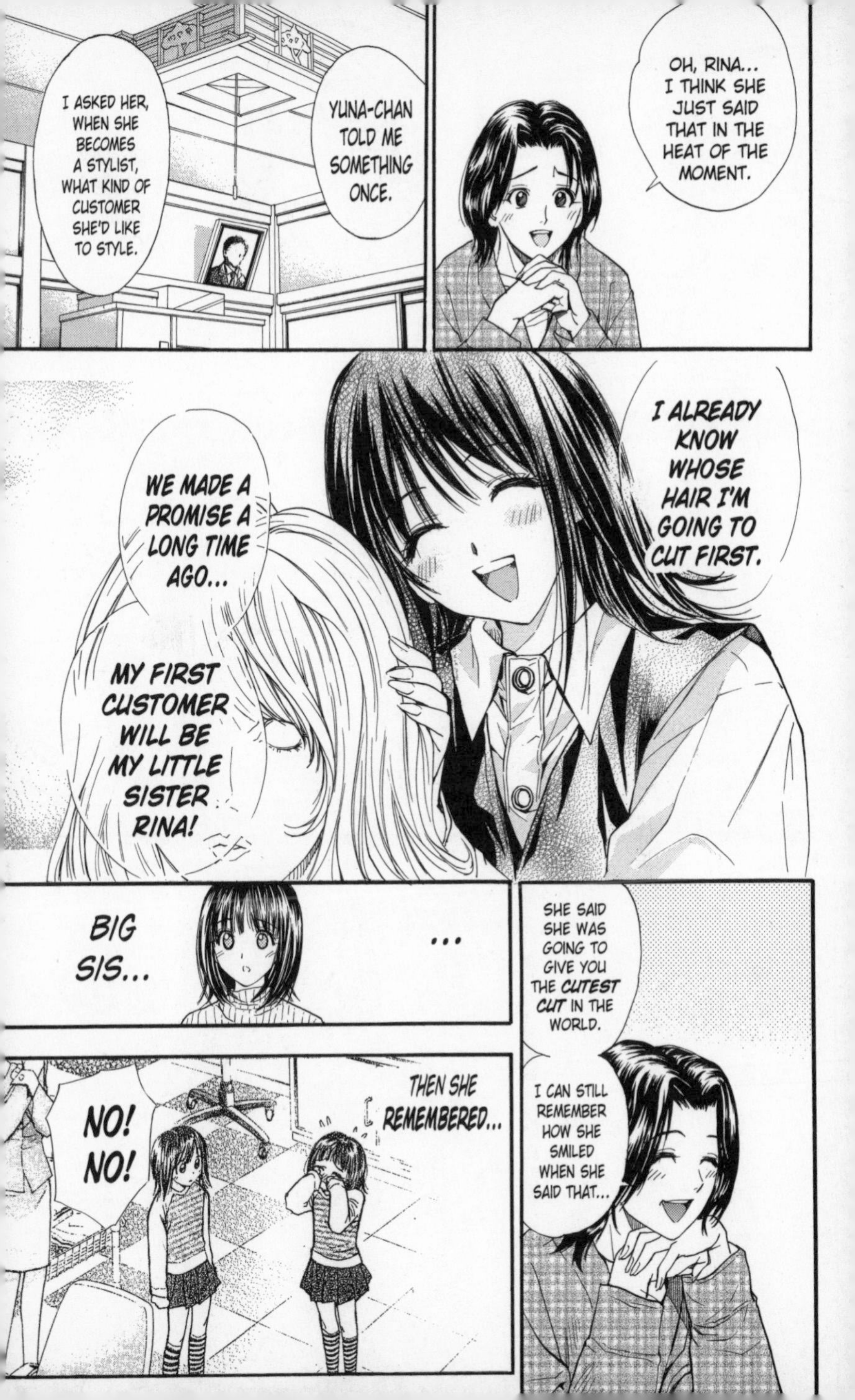
OH, RINA... I THINK SHE JUST SAID THAT IN THE HEAT OF THE MOMENT.
YUNA-CHAN TOLD ME SOMETHING ONCE.
I ASKED HER, WHEN SHE BECOMES A STYLIST, WHAT KIND OF CUSTOMER SHE'D LIKE TO STYLE.
I ALREADY KNOW WHOSE HAIR I'M GOING TO CUT FIRST.
WE MADE A PROMISE A LONG TIME AGO...
MY FIRST CUSTOMER WILL BE MY LITTLE SISTER RINA!
SHE SAID SHE WAS GOING TO GIVE YOU THE CUTEST CUT IN THE WORLD.
I CAN STILL REMEMBER HOW SHE SMILED WHEN SHE SAID THAT...
...
BIG SIS...
THEN SHE REMEMBERED...
NO! NO!

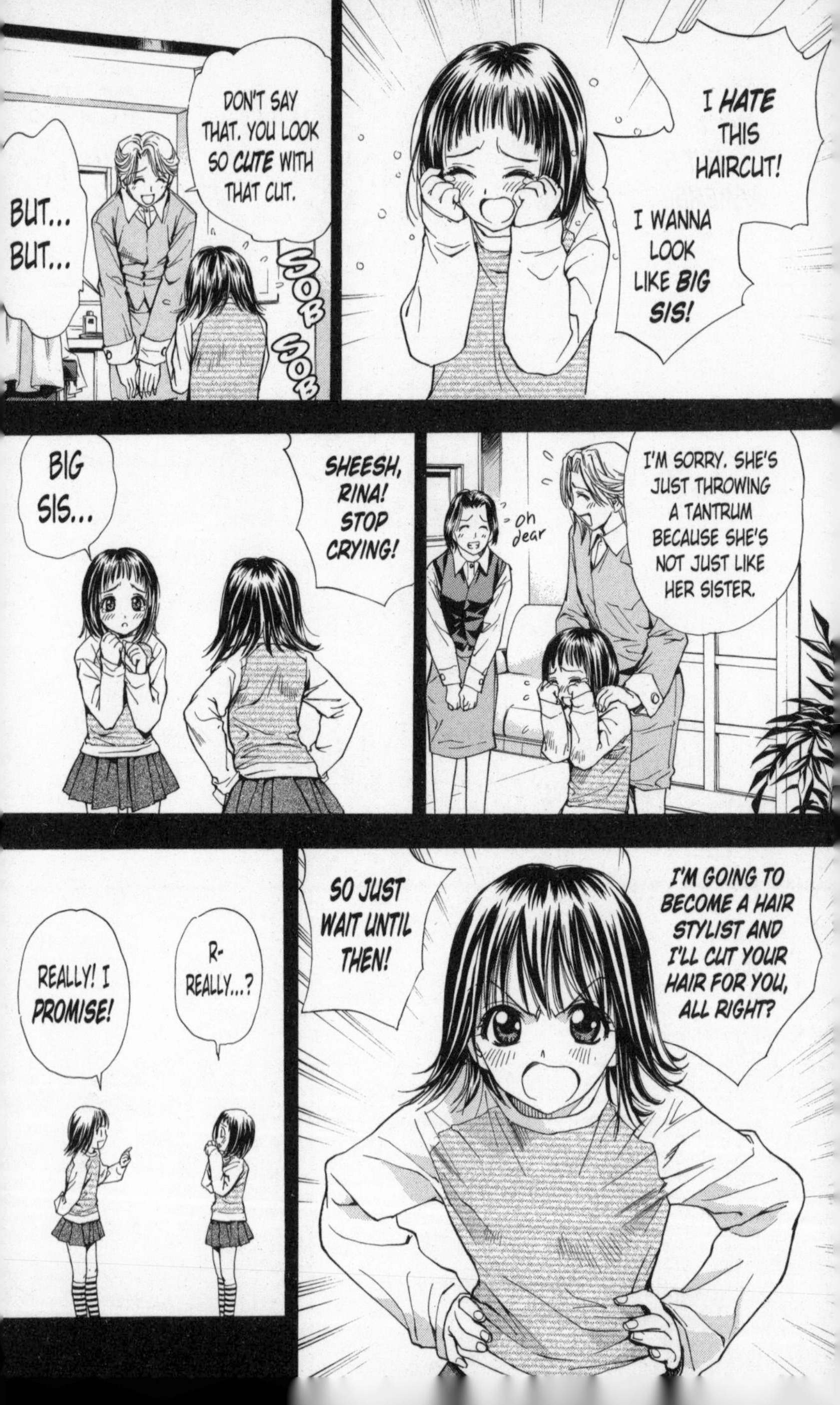
I HATE THIS HAIRCUT!
I WANNA LOOK LIKE BIG SIS!
DON'T SAY THAT. YOU LOOK SO CUTE WITH THAT CUT.
SOB SOB
BUT... BUT...
I'M SORRY. SHE'S JUST THROWING A TANTRUM BECAUSE SHE'S NOT JUST LIKE HER SISTER.
oh dear
SHEESH, RINA! STOP CRYING!
BIG SIS...
I'M GOING TO BECOME A HAIR STYLIST AND I'LL CUT YOUR HAIR FOR YOU, ALL RIGHT?
SO JUST WAIT UNTIL THEN!
R- REALLY...?
REALLY! I PROMISE!

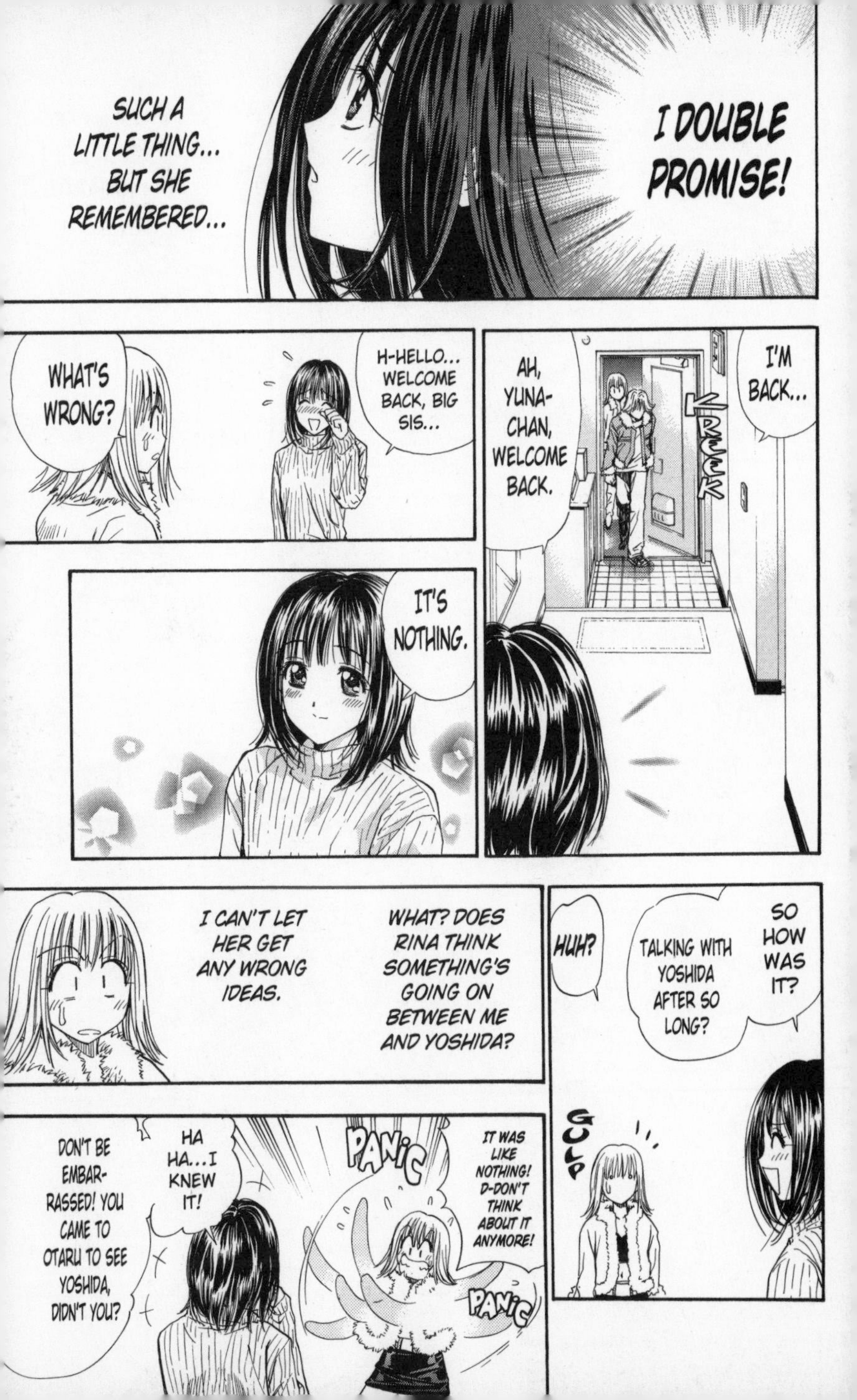
I DOUBLE PROMISE!
SUCH A LITTLE THING... BUT SHE REMEMBERED...
I'M BACK...
KRECK
AH, YUNA-CHAN, WELCOME BACK.
H-HELLO... WELCOME BACK, BIG SIS...
WHAT'S WRONG?
IT'S NOTHING.
SO HOW WAS IT?
TALKING WITH YOSHIDA AFTER SO LONG?
HUH?
GULP
WHAT? DOES RINA THINK SOMETHING'S GOING ON BETWEEN ME AND YOSHIDA?
I CAN'T LET HER GET ANY WRONG IDEAS.
IT WAS LIKE NOTHING! D-DON'T THINK ABOUT IT ANYMORE!
PANIC
PANIC
HA HA...I KNEW IT!
DON'T BE EMBAR-RASSED! YOU CAME TO OTARU TO SEE YOSHIDA, DIDN'T YOU?

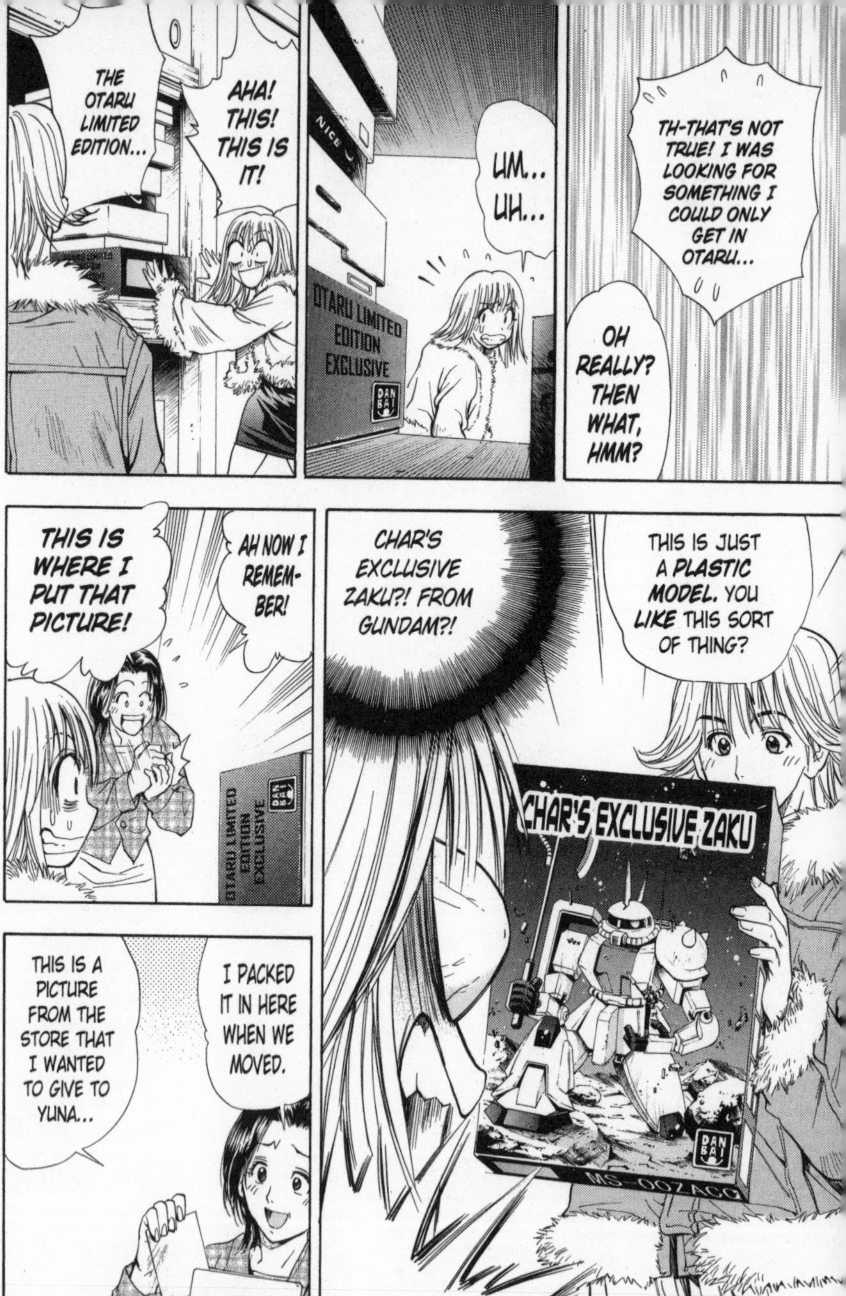
TH-THAT'S NOT TRUE! I WAS LOOKING FOR SOMETHING I COULD ONLY GET IN OTARU...
OH REALLY? THEN WHAT, HMM?
UM... UH...
NICE
OTARU LIMITED EDITION EXCLUSIVE
DAN BAI
AHA! THIS! THIS IS IT!
THE OTARU LIMITED EDITION...
THIS IS JUST A PLASTIC MODEL. YOU LIKE THIS SORT OF THING?
CHAR'S EXCLUSIVE ZAKU?! FROM GUNDAM?!
CHAR'S EXCLUSIVE ZAKU
DAN BAI
AH NOW I REMEMBER!
THIS IS WHERE I PUT THAT PICTURE!
DAN BAI
OTARU LIMITED EDITION EXCLUSIVE
I PACKED IT IN HERE WHEN WE MOVED.
THIS IS A PICTURE FROM THE STORE THAT I WANTED TO GIVE TO YUNA...
pocket album

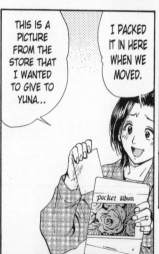

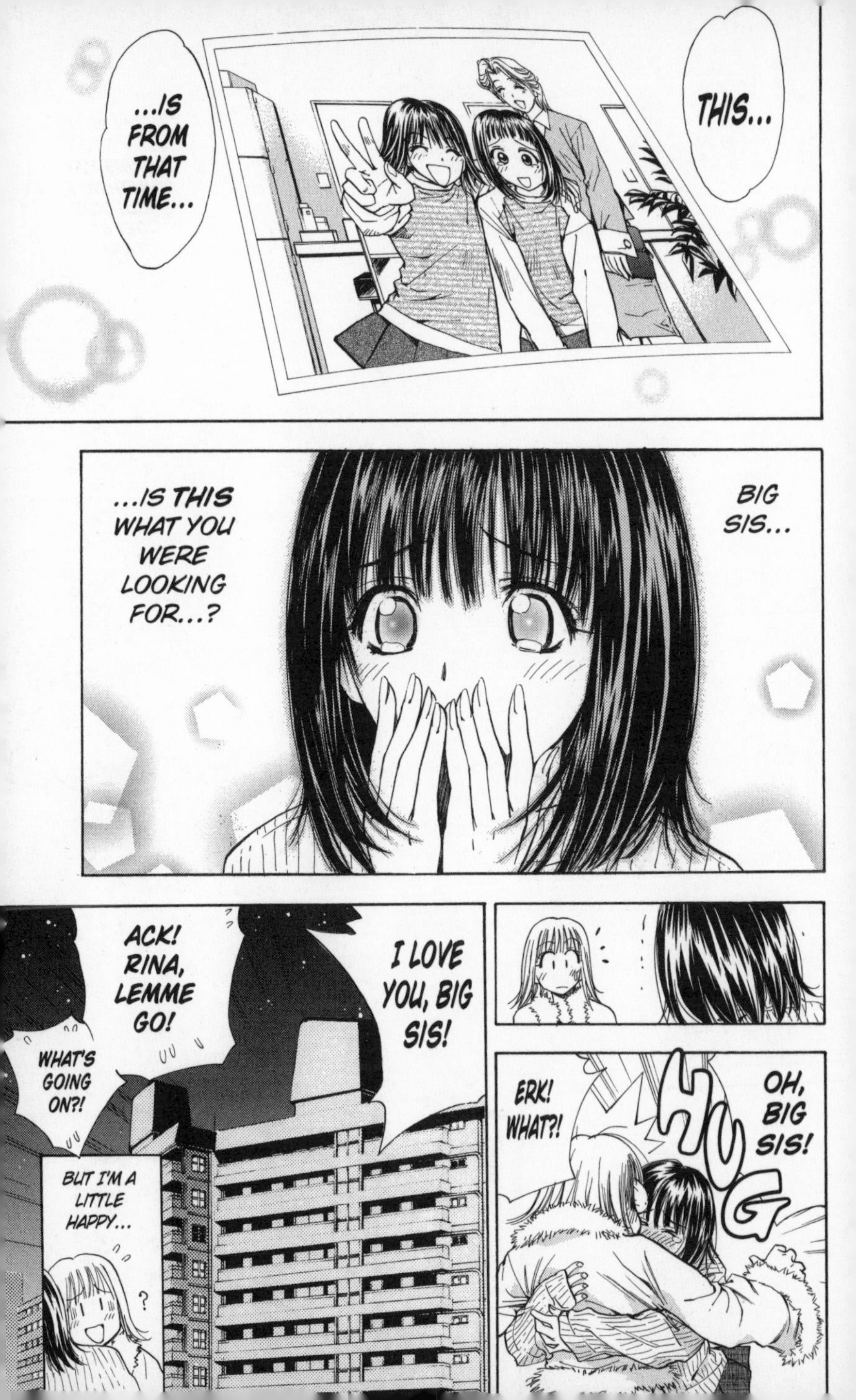
THIS...
...IS FROM THAT TIME...
BIG SIS...
...IS THIS WHAT YOU WERE LOOKING FOR...?
OH, BIG SIS!
HUG
ERK! WHAT?!
I LOVE YOU, BIG SIS!
ACK! RINA, LEMME GO!
WHAT'S GOING ON?!
BUT I'M A LITTLE HAPPY...
?

Pretty Face

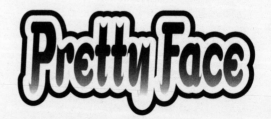

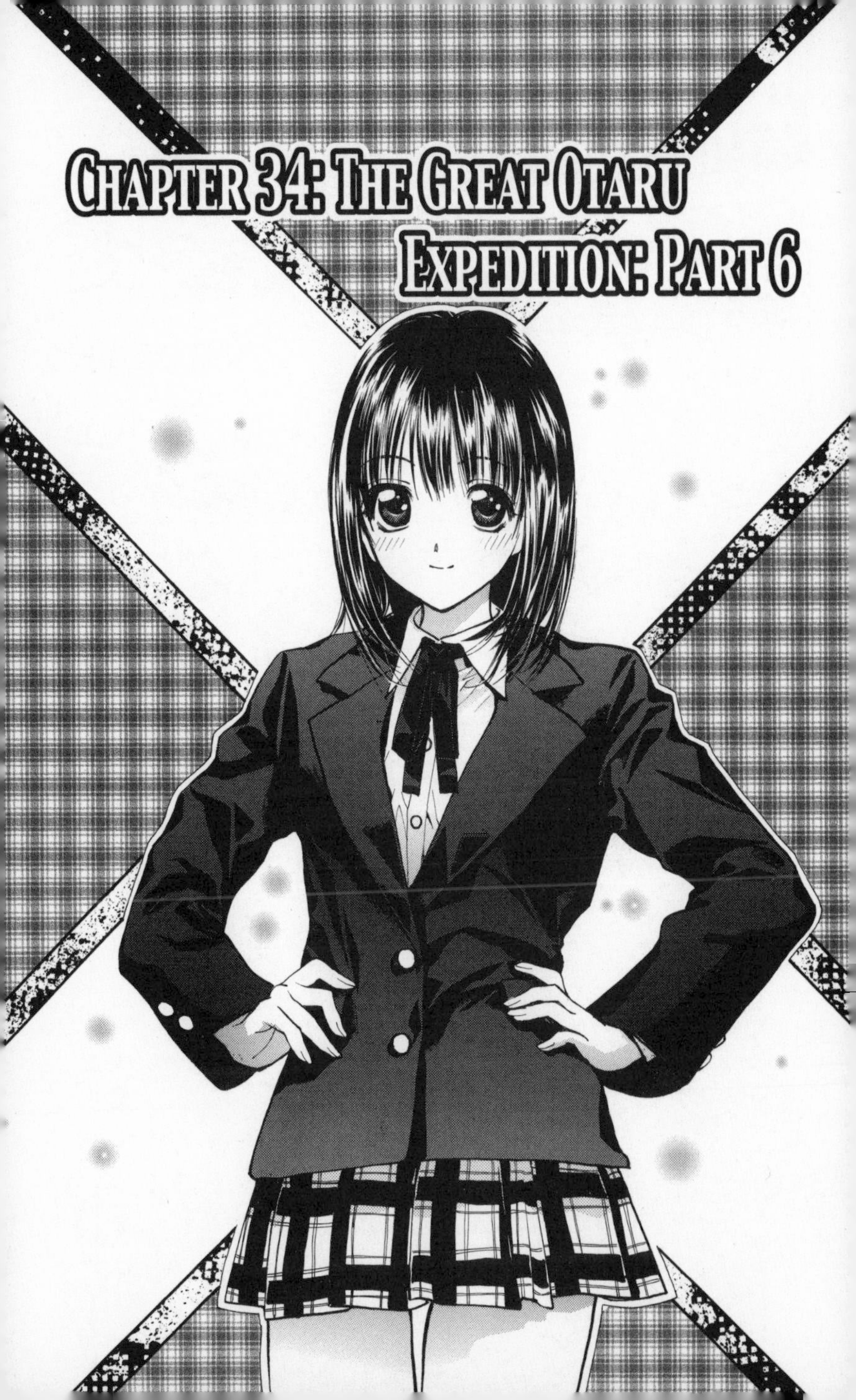
CHAPTER 34: THE GREAT OTARU
EXPEDITION: PART 6

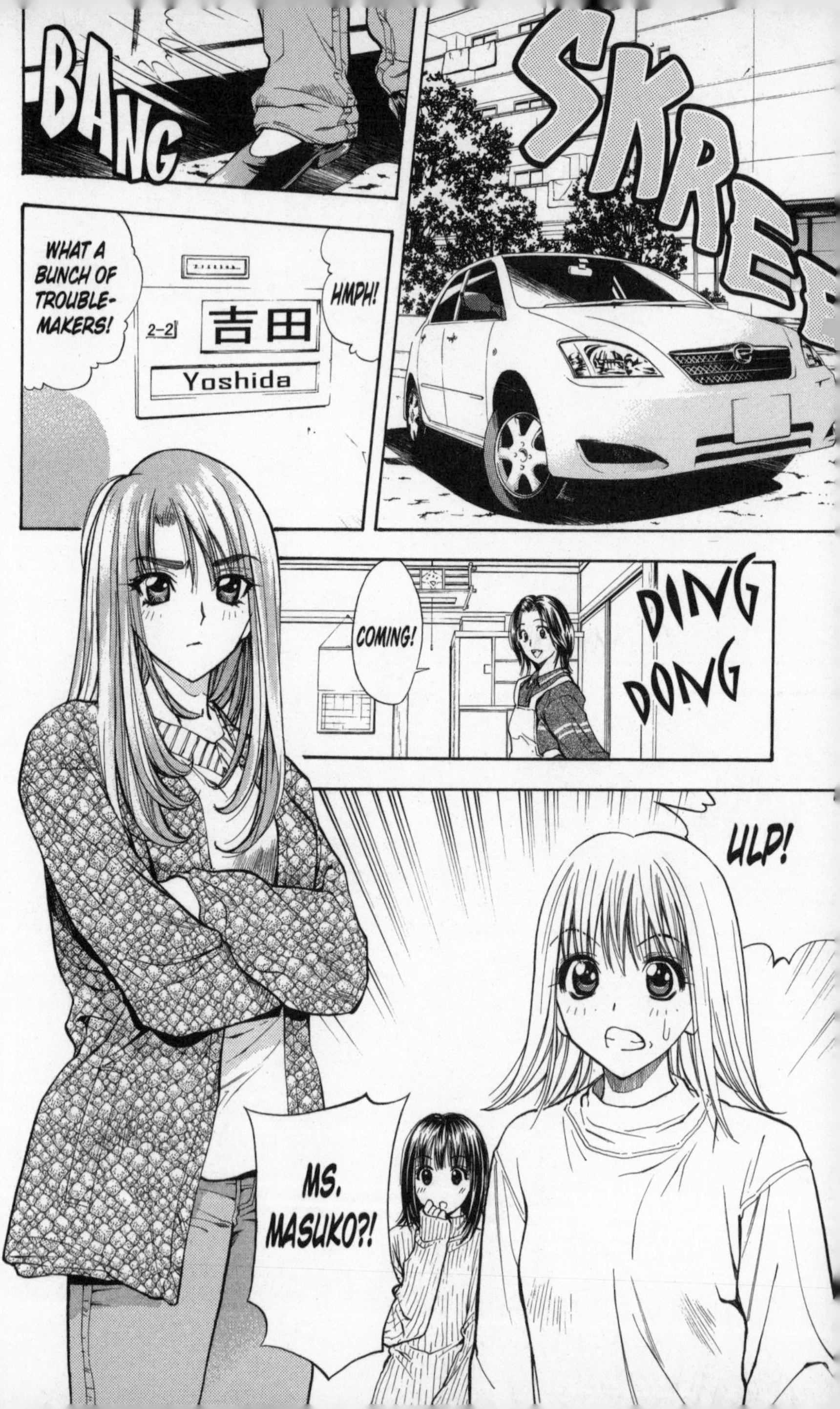

SKREE
BANG
HMPH!
WHAT A BUNCH OF TROUBLE-MAKERS!
吉田
2-2
Yoshida
DING DONG
COMING!
ULP!
MS. MASUKO?!

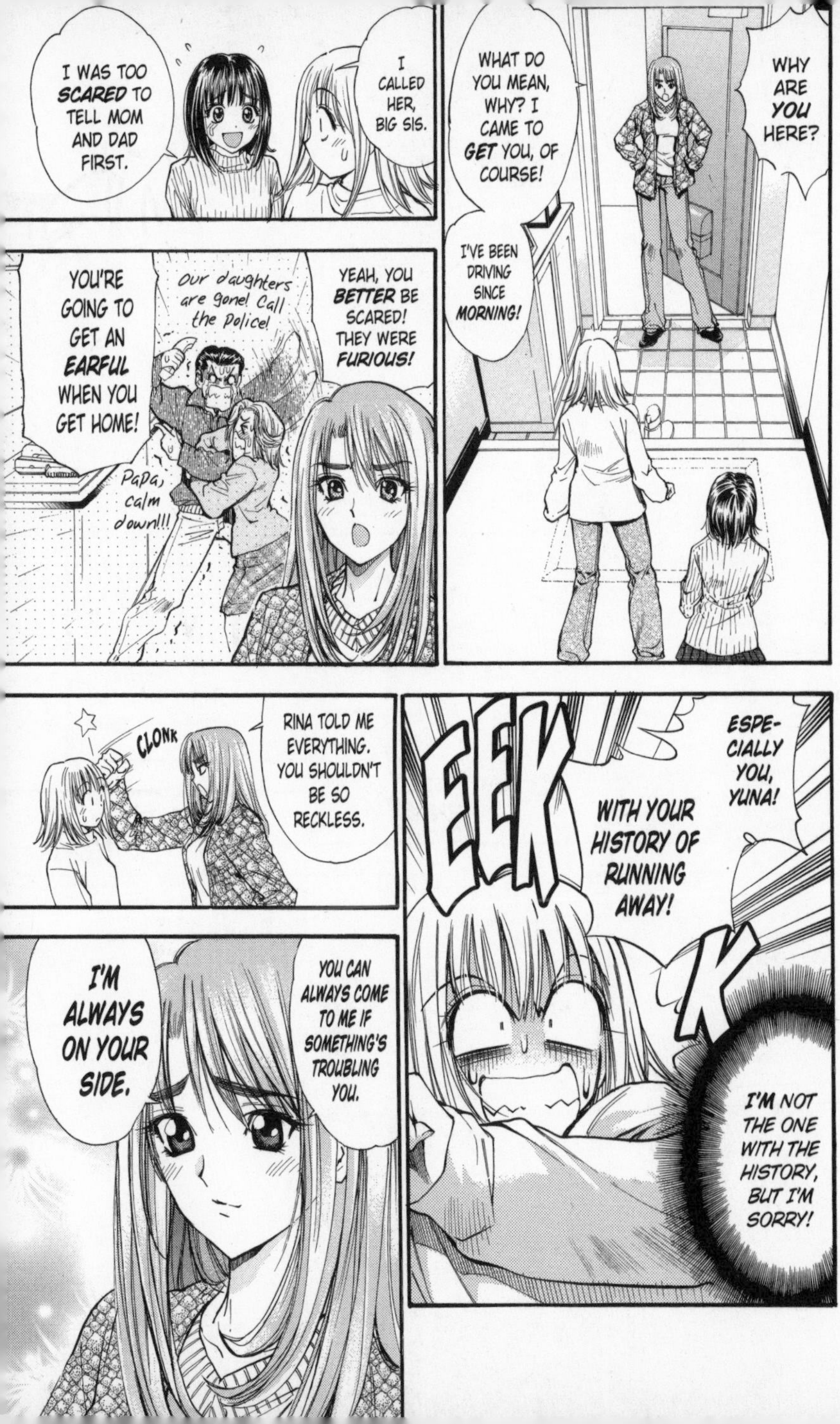

WHY ARE YOU HERE?
WHAT DO YOU MEAN, WHY? I CAME TO GET YOU, OF COURSE!
I'VE BEEN DRIVING SINCE MORNING!
I CALLED HER, BIG SIS.
I WAS TOO SCARED TO TELL MOM AND DAD FIRST.
YEAH, YOU BETTER BE SCARED! THEY WERE FURIOUS!
Our daughters are gone! Call the police!
YOU'RE GOING TO GET AN EARFUL WHEN YOU GET HOME!
Papa, calm down!!!
ESPE-CIALLY YOU, YUNA!
WITH YOUR HISTORY OF RUNNING AWAY!
EEK
K
I'M NOT THE ONE WITH THE HISTORY, BUT I'M SORRY!
RINA TOLD ME EVERYTHING. YOU SHOULDN'T BE SO RECKLESS.
CLONK
YOU CAN ALWAYS COME TO ME IF SOMETHING'S TROUBLING YOU.
I'M ALWAYS ON YOUR SIDE.

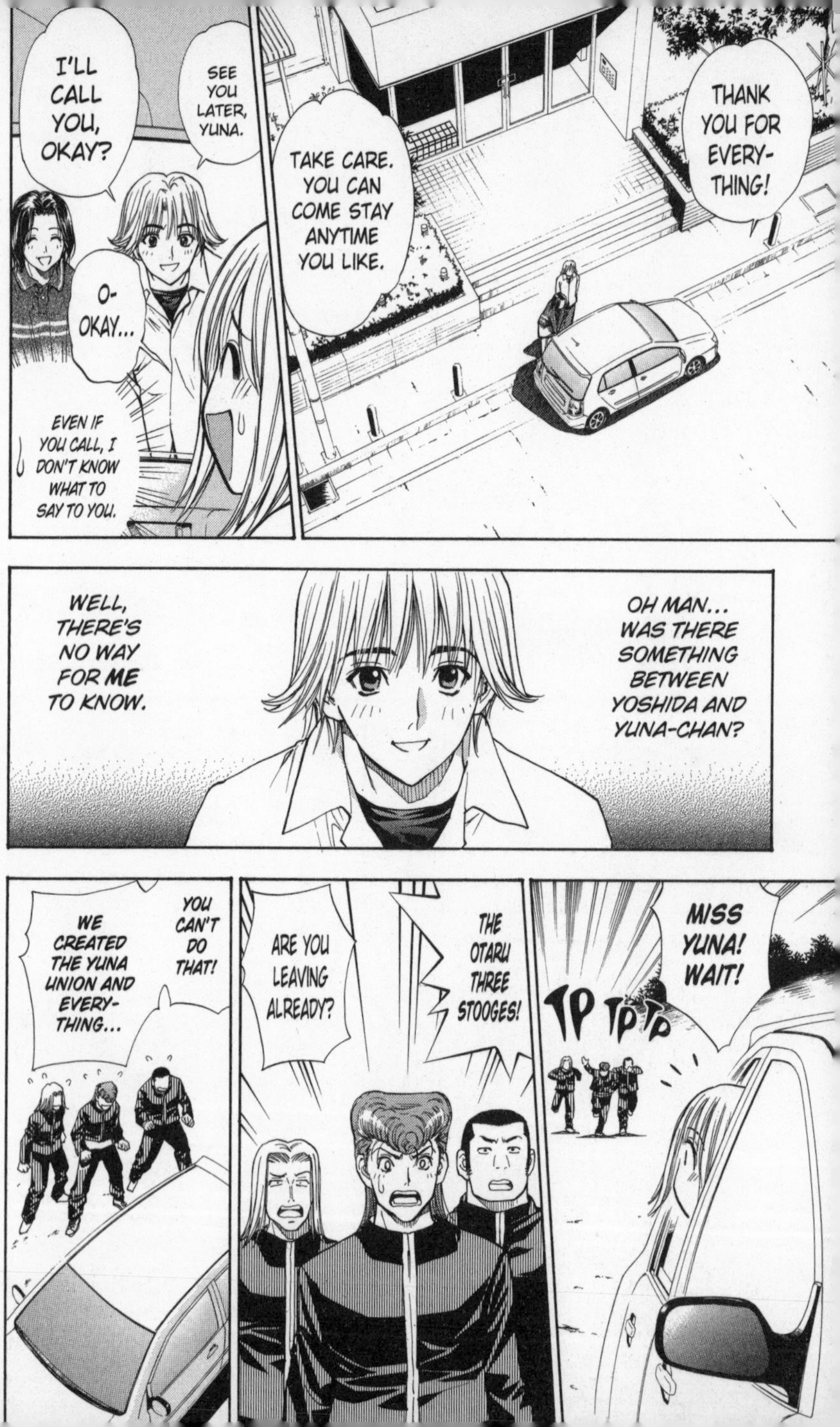
THANK YOU FOR EVERY-THING!
TAKE CARE. YOU CAN COME STAY ANYTIME YOU LIKE.
SEE YOU LATER, YUNA.
I'LL CALL YOU, OKAY?
O-OKAY...
EVEN IF YOU CALL, I DON'T KNOW WHAT TO SAY TO YOU.
OH MAN... WAS THERE SOMETHING BETWEEN YOSHIDA AND YUNA-CHAN?
WELL, THERE'S NO WAY FOR ME TO KNOW.
MISS YUNA! WAIT!
TP TP TP
THE OTARU THREE STOOGES!
ARE YOU LEAVING ALREADY?
YOU CAN'T DO THAT!
WE CREATED THE YUNA UNION AND EVERY-THING...

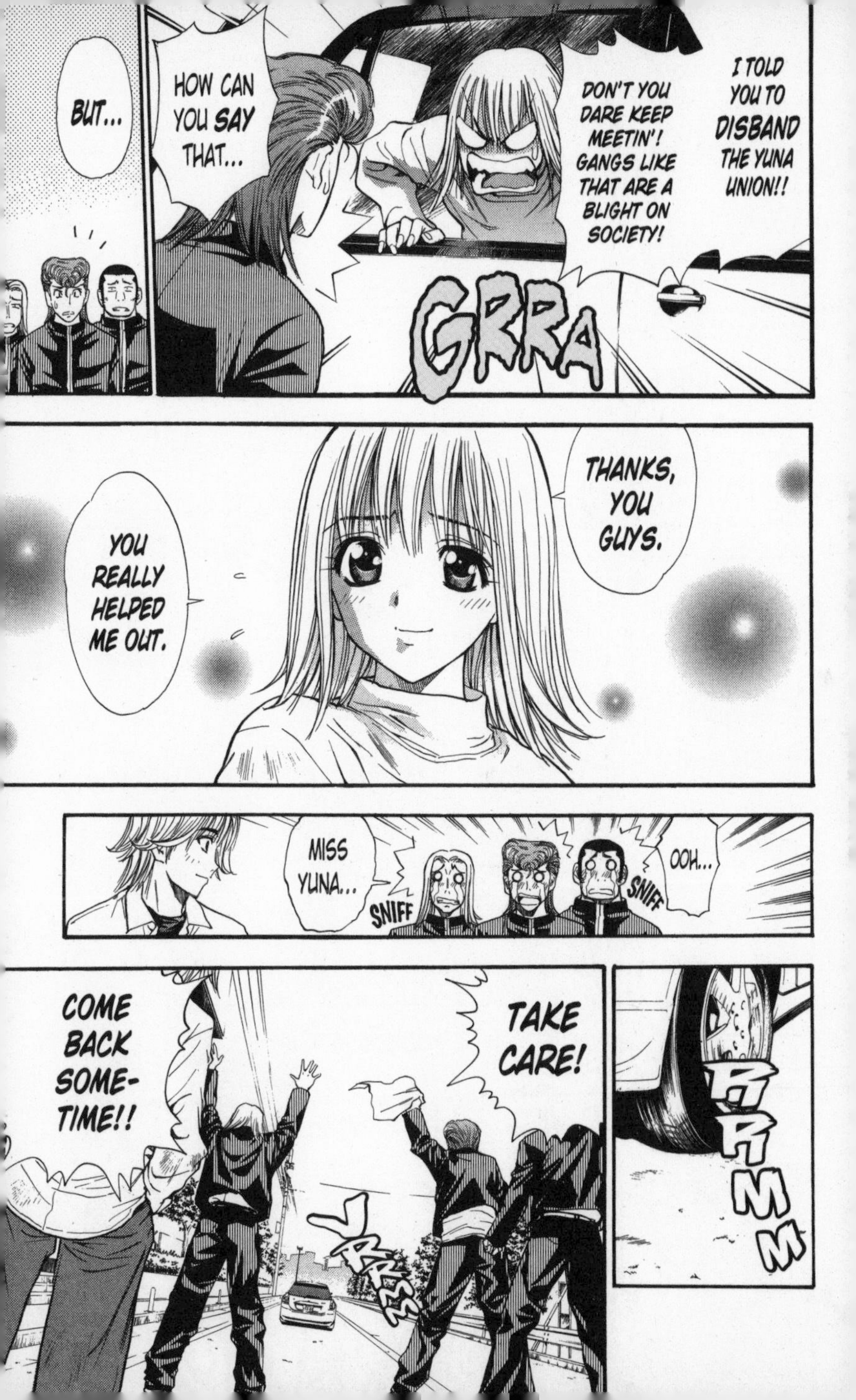
I TOLD YOU TO DISBAND THE YUNA UNION!!
DON'T YOU DARE KEEP MEETIN'! GANGS LIKE THAT ARE A BLIGHT ON SOCIETY!
GRRA
HOW CAN YOU SAY THAT...
BUT...
THANKS, YOU GUYS.
YOU REALLY HELPED ME OUT.
OOH...
SNIFF
SNIFF
MISS YUNA...
BRRMM
TAKE CARE!
COME BACK SOME-TIME!!

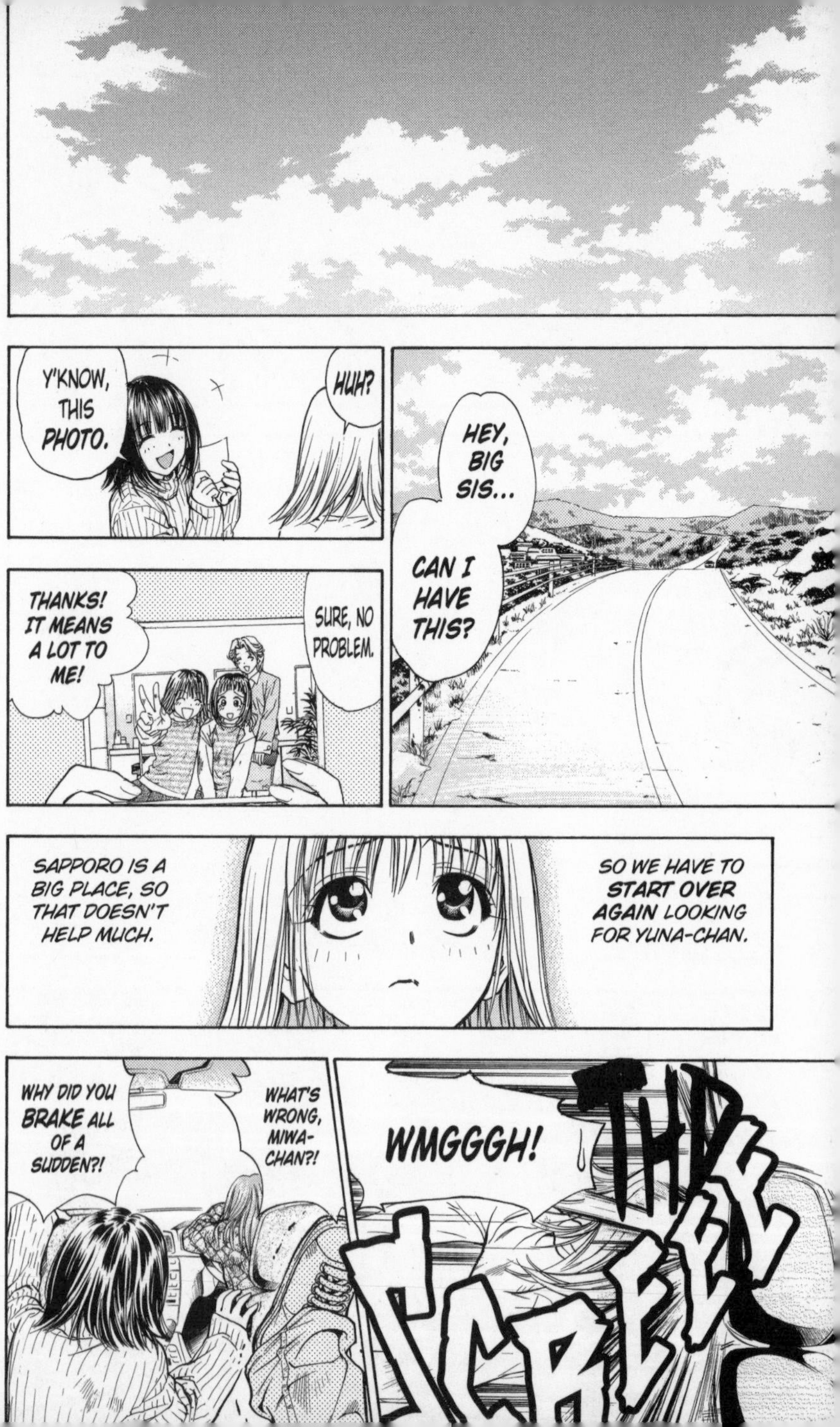
HEY, BIG SIS...
CAN I HAVE THIS?
HUH?
Y'KNOW, THIS PHOTO.
SURE, NO PROBLEM.
THANKS! IT MEANS A LOT TO ME!
SO WE HAVE TO START OVER AGAIN LOOKING FOR YUNA-CHAN.
SAPPORO IS A BIG PLACE, SO THAT DOESN'T HELP MUCH.
WMGGGH!
WHAT'S WRONG, MIWA-CHAN?!
WHY DID YOU BRAKE ALL OF A SUDDEN?!

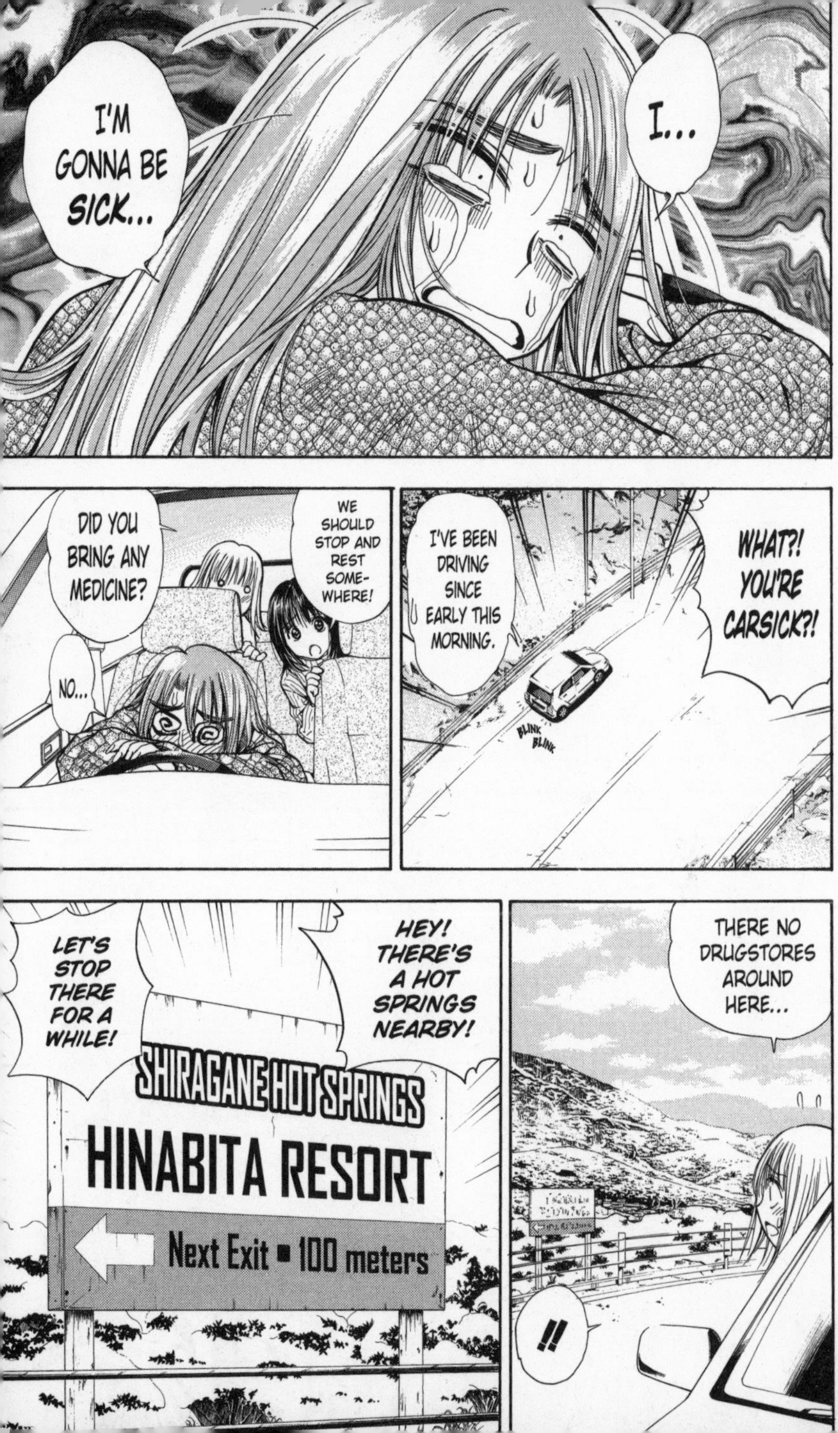
I...
I'M GONNA BE SICK...
WHAT?! YOU'RE CARSICK?!
I'VE BEEN DRIVING SINCE EARLY THIS MORNING.
BLINK BLINK
WE SHOULD STOP AND REST SOME-WHERE!
DID YOU BRING ANY MEDICINE?
NO...
THERE NO DRUGSTORES AROUND HERE...
!!
HEY! THERE'S A HOT SPRINGS NEARBY!
LET'S STOP THERE FOR A WHILE!
SHIRAGANE HOT SPRINGS
HINABITA RESORT
Next Exit ■ 100 meters

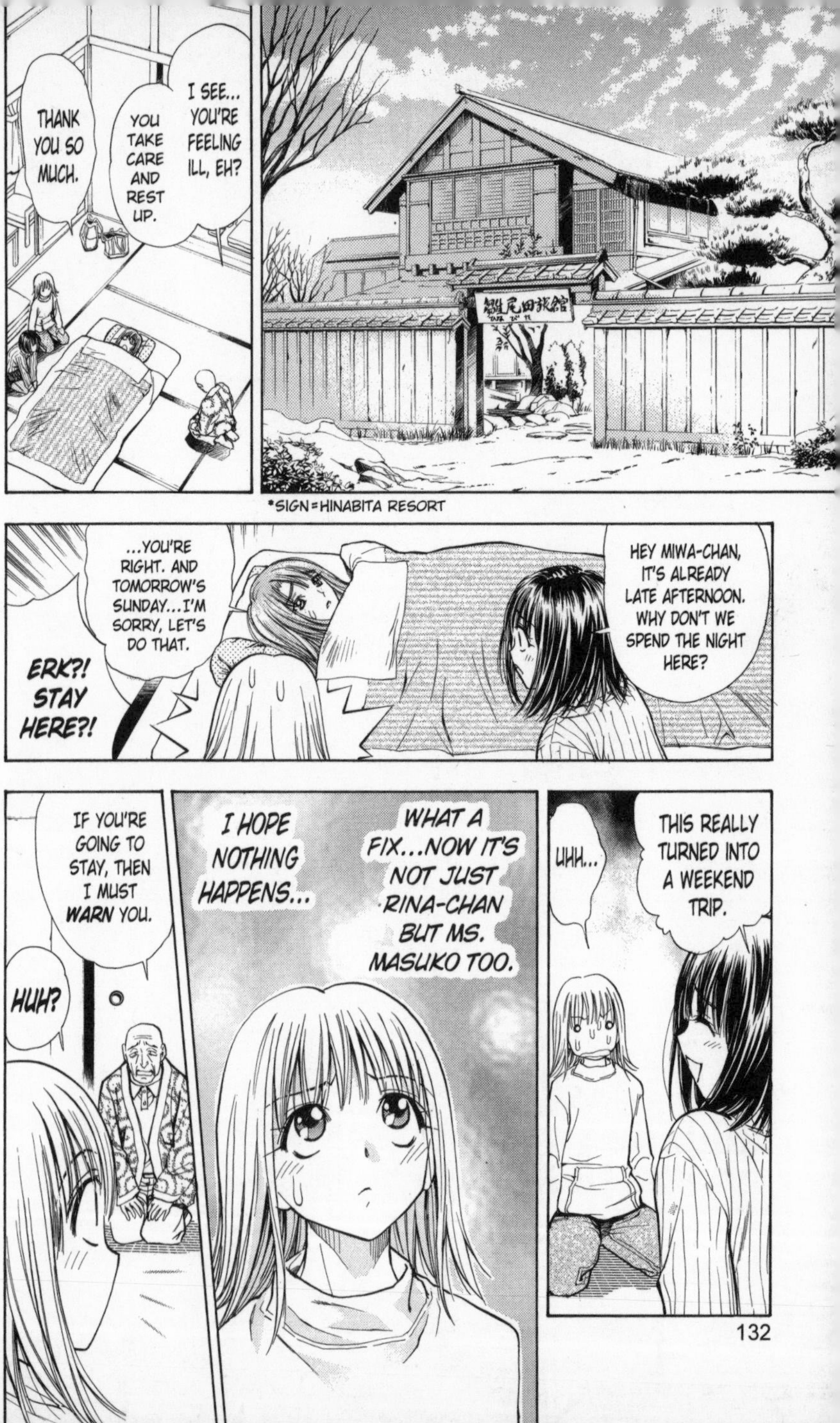
I SEE... YOU'RE FEELING ILL, EH?
YOU TAKE CARE AND REST UP.
THANK YOU SO MUCH.
*SIGN=HINABITA RESORT
HEY MIWA-CHAN, IT'S ALREADY LATE AFTERNOON. WHY DON'T WE SPEND THE NIGHT HERE?
...YOU'RE RIGHT. AND TOMORROW'S SUNDAY...I'M SORRY, LET'S DO THAT.
ERK?! STAY HERE?!
THIS REALLY TURNED INTO A WEEKEND TRIP.
UHH...
WHAT A FIX...NOW IT'S NOT JUST RINA-CHAN BUT MS. MASUKO TOO.
I HOPE NOTHING HAPPENS...
IF YOU'RE GOING TO STAY, THEN I MUST WARN YOU.
HUH?

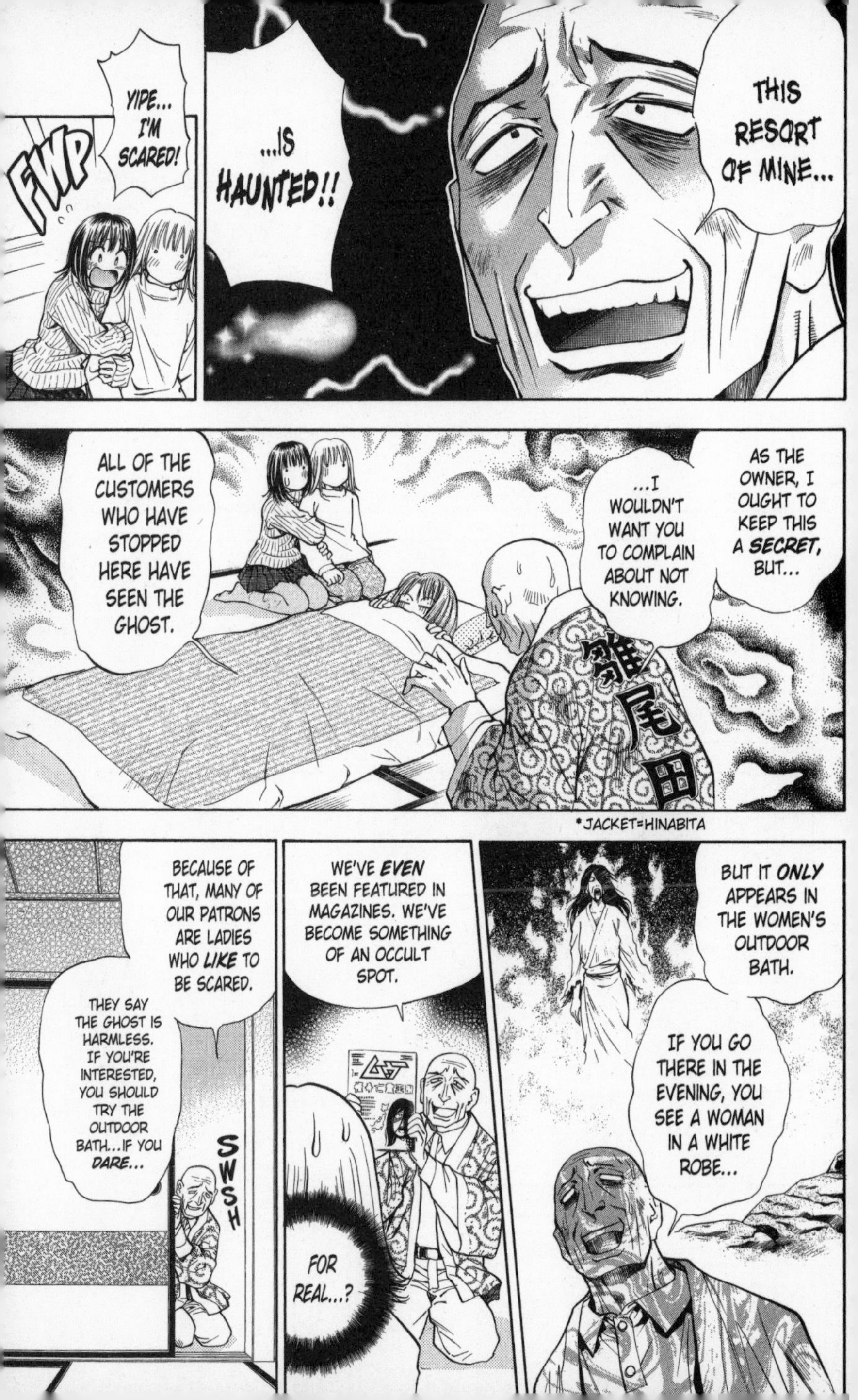
THIS RESORT OF MINE...
...IS HAUNTED!!
FWP
YIPE... I'M SCARED!
AS THE OWNER, I OUGHT TO KEEP THIS A ***SECRET***, BUT...
...I WOULDN'T WANT YOU TO COMPLAIN ABOUT NOT KNOWING.
ALL OF THE CUSTOMERS WHO HAVE STOPPED HERE HAVE SEEN THE GHOST.
雛尾田
BUT IT ***ONLY*** APPEARS IN THE WOMEN'S OUTDOOR BATH.
IF YOU GO THERE IN THE EVENING, YOU SEE A WOMAN IN A WHITE ROBE...
WE'VE ***EVEN*** BEEN FEATURED IN MAGAZINES. WE'VE BECOME SOMETHING OF AN OCCULT SPOT.
FOR REAL...?
BECAUSE OF THAT, MANY OF OUR PATRONS ARE LADIES WHO ***LIKE*** TO BE SCARED.
THEY SAY THE GHOST IS HARMLESS. IF YOU'RE INTERESTED, YOU SHOULD TRY THE OUTDOOR BATH...IF YOU ***DARE***...
SWSH

*JACKET=HINABITA

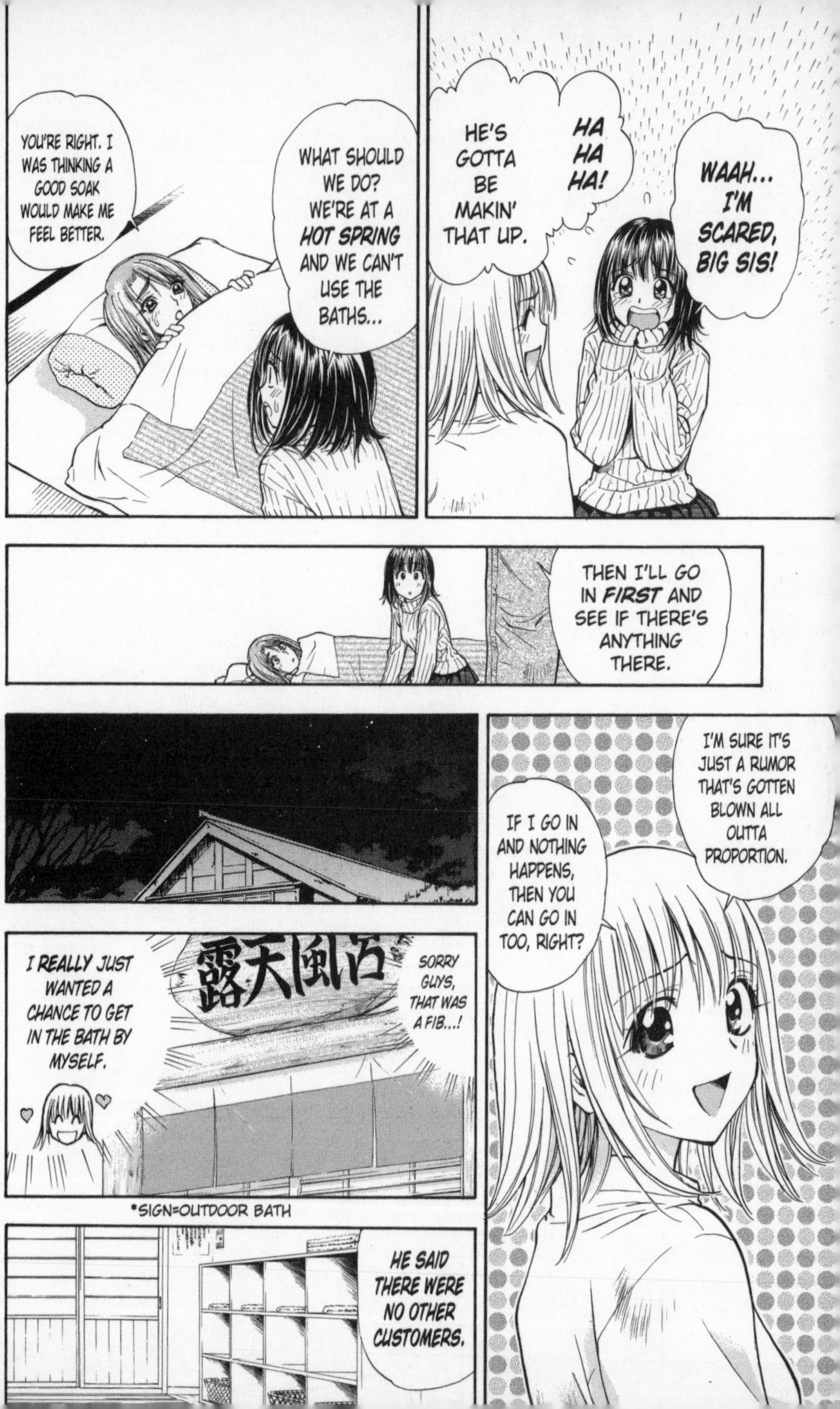
WAAH... I'M SCARED, BIG SIS!
HA HA HA!
HE'S GOTTA BE MAKIN' THAT UP.
WHAT SHOULD WE DO? WE'RE AT A HOT SPRING AND WE CAN'T USE THE BATHS...
YOU'RE RIGHT. I WAS THINKING A GOOD SOAK WOULD MAKE ME FEEL BETTER.
THEN I'LL GO IN FIRST AND SEE IF THERE'S ANYTHING THERE.
I'M SURE IT'S JUST A RUMOR THAT'S GOTTEN BLOWN ALL OUTTA PROPORTION.
IF I GO IN AND NOTHING HAPPENS, THEN YOU CAN GO IN TOO, RIGHT?
SORRY GUYS, THAT WAS A FIB...!
露天風呂
I REALLY JUST WANTED A CHANCE TO GET IN THE BATH BY MYSELF.
*SIGN=OUTDOOR BATH
HE SAID THERE WERE NO OTHER CUSTOMERS.

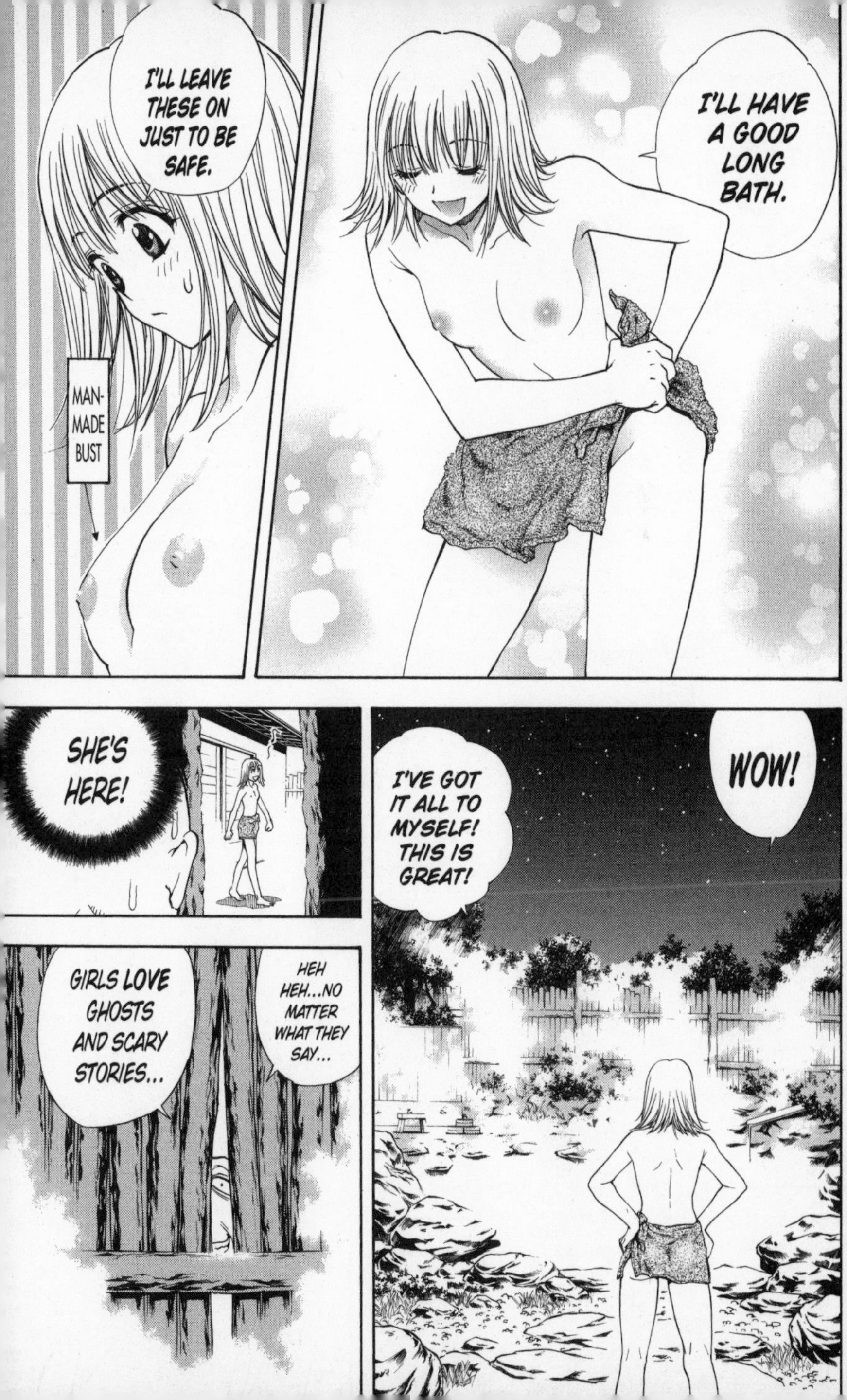
I'LL HAVE A GOOD LONG BATH.
I'LL LEAVE THESE ON JUST TO BE SAFE.
MAN-MADE BUST
WOW!
I'VE GOT IT ALL TO MYSELF! THIS IS GREAT!
SHE'S HERE!
HEH HEH...NO MATTER WHAT THEY SAY...
GIRLS LOVE GHOSTS AND SCARY STORIES...

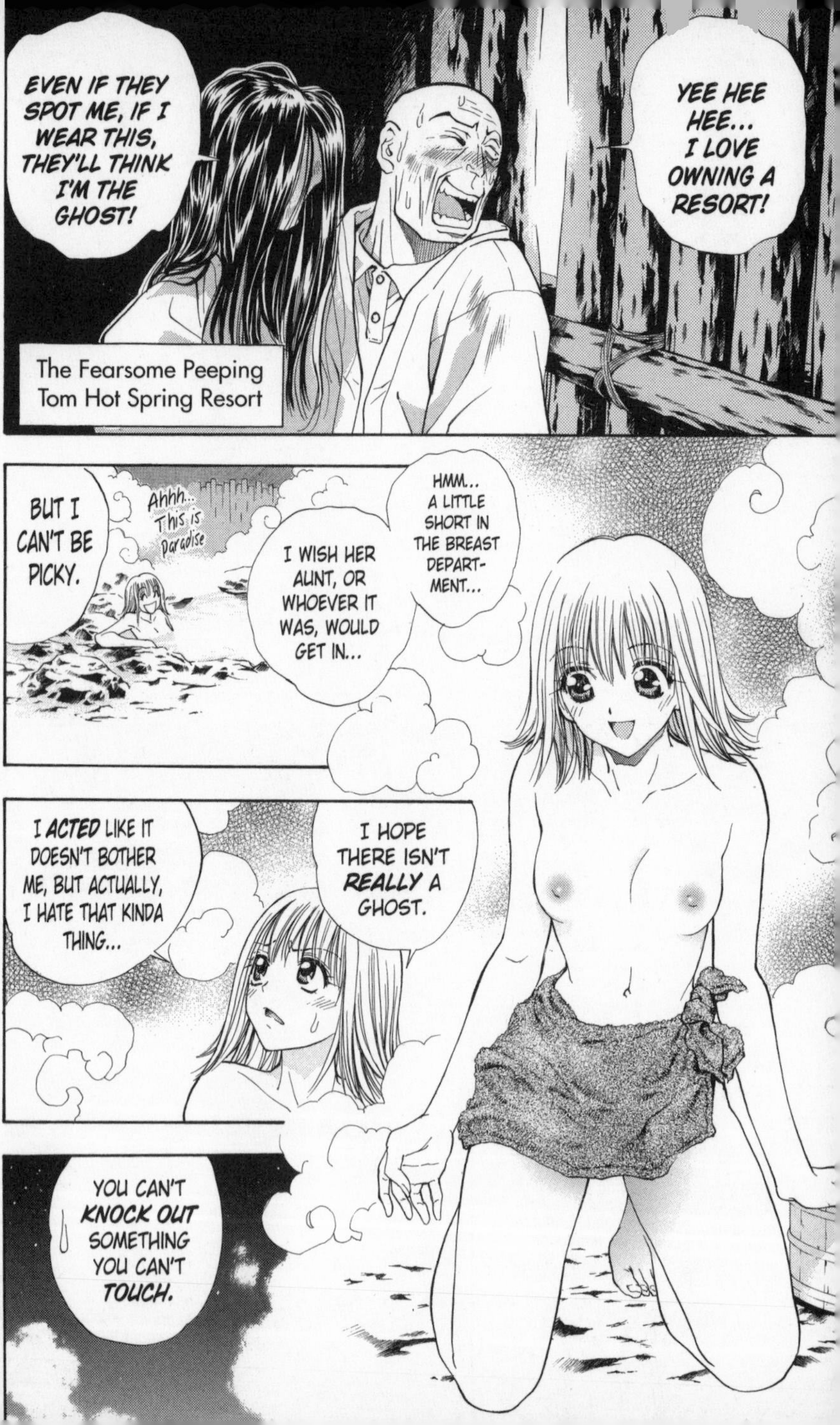
YEE HEE HEE... I LOVE OWNING A RESORT!
EVEN IF THEY SPOT ME, IF I WEAR THIS, THEY'LL THINK I'M THE GHOST!
The Fearsome Peeping Tom Hot Spring Resort
HMM... A LITTLE SHORT IN THE BREAST DEPARTMENT...
I WISH HER AUNT, OR WHOEVER IT WAS, WOULD GET IN...
Ahhh... This is Paradise
BUT I CAN'T BE PICKY.
I HOPE THERE ISN'T REALLY A GHOST.
I ACTED LIKE IT DOESN'T BOTHER ME, BUT ACTUALLY, I HATE THAT KINDA THING...
YOU CAN'T KNOCK OUT SOMETHING YOU CAN'T TOUCH.

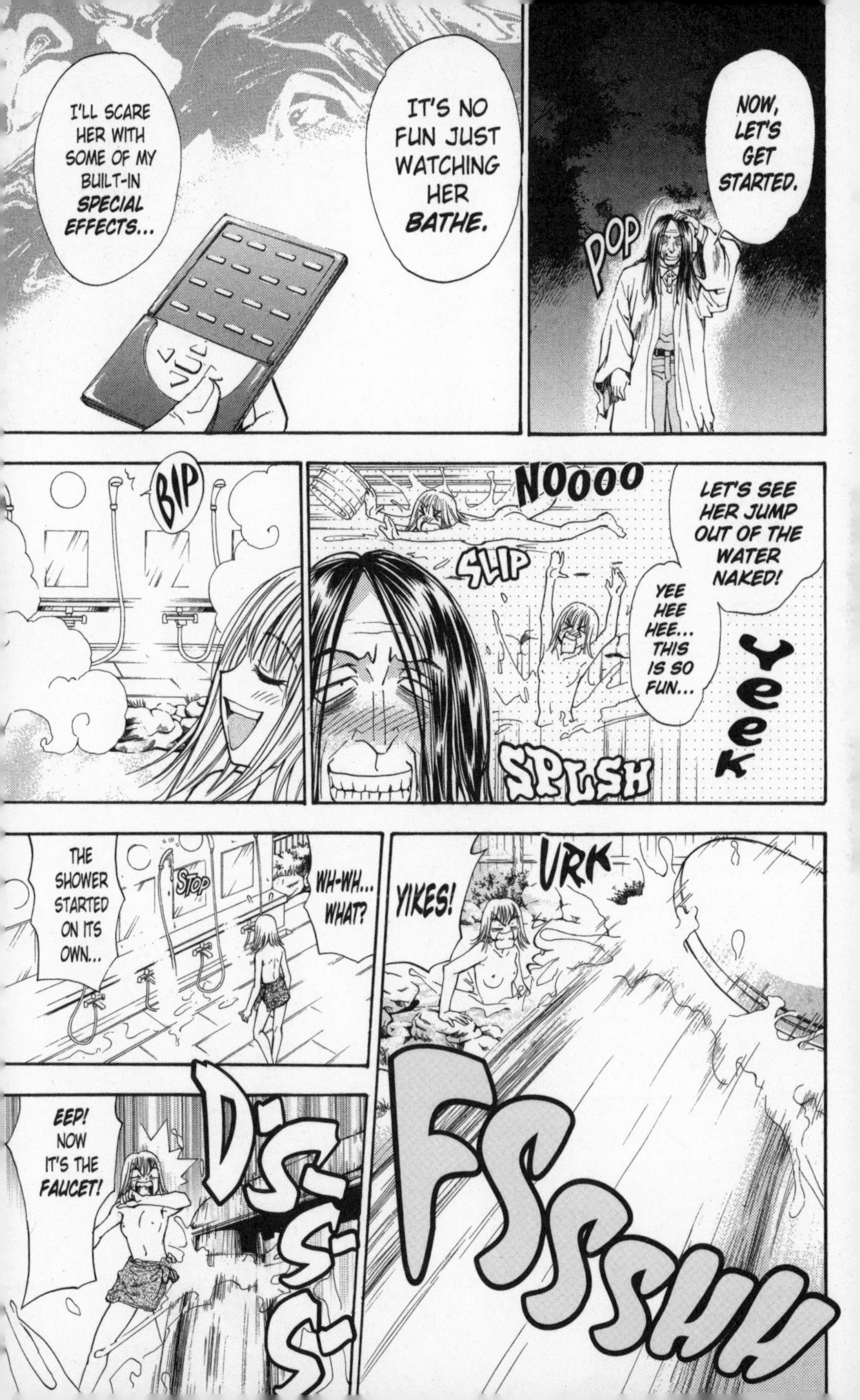
NOW, LET'S GET STARTED.
POP
IT'S NO FUN JUST WATCHING HER BATHE.
I'LL SCARE HER WITH SOME OF MY BUILT-IN SPECIAL EFFECTS...
LET'S SEE HER JUMP OUT OF THE WATER NAKED!
YEEK
NOOOO
SLIP
YEE HEE HEE... THIS IS SO FUN...
SPLSH
BIP
URK
YIKES!
WH-WH... WHAT?
STOP
THE SHOWER STARTED ON ITS OWN...
FSSSHH
DSSS
EEP! NOW IT'S THE FAUCET!

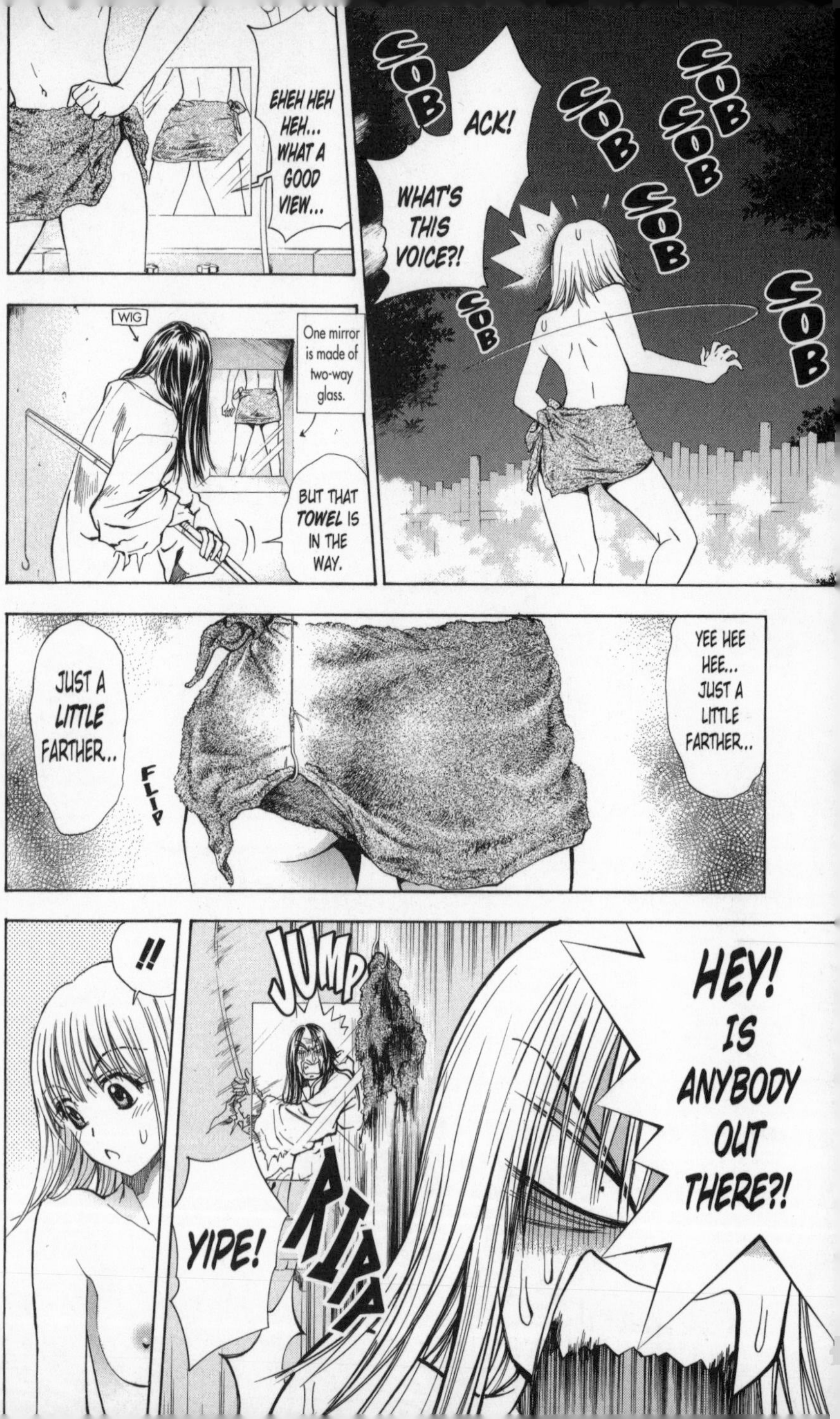
SOB SOB SOB SOB SOB
ACK!
WHAT'S THIS VOICE?!
SOB
SOB
SOB
EHEH HEH HEH... WHAT A GOOD VIEW...
WIG
One mirror is made of two-way glass.
BUT THAT TOWEL IS IN THE WAY.
YEE HEE HEE... JUST A LITTLE FARTHER..
FLIP
JUST A LITTLE FARTHER...
HEY! IS ANYBODY OUT THERE?!
JUMP
RIPP
YIPE!
!!

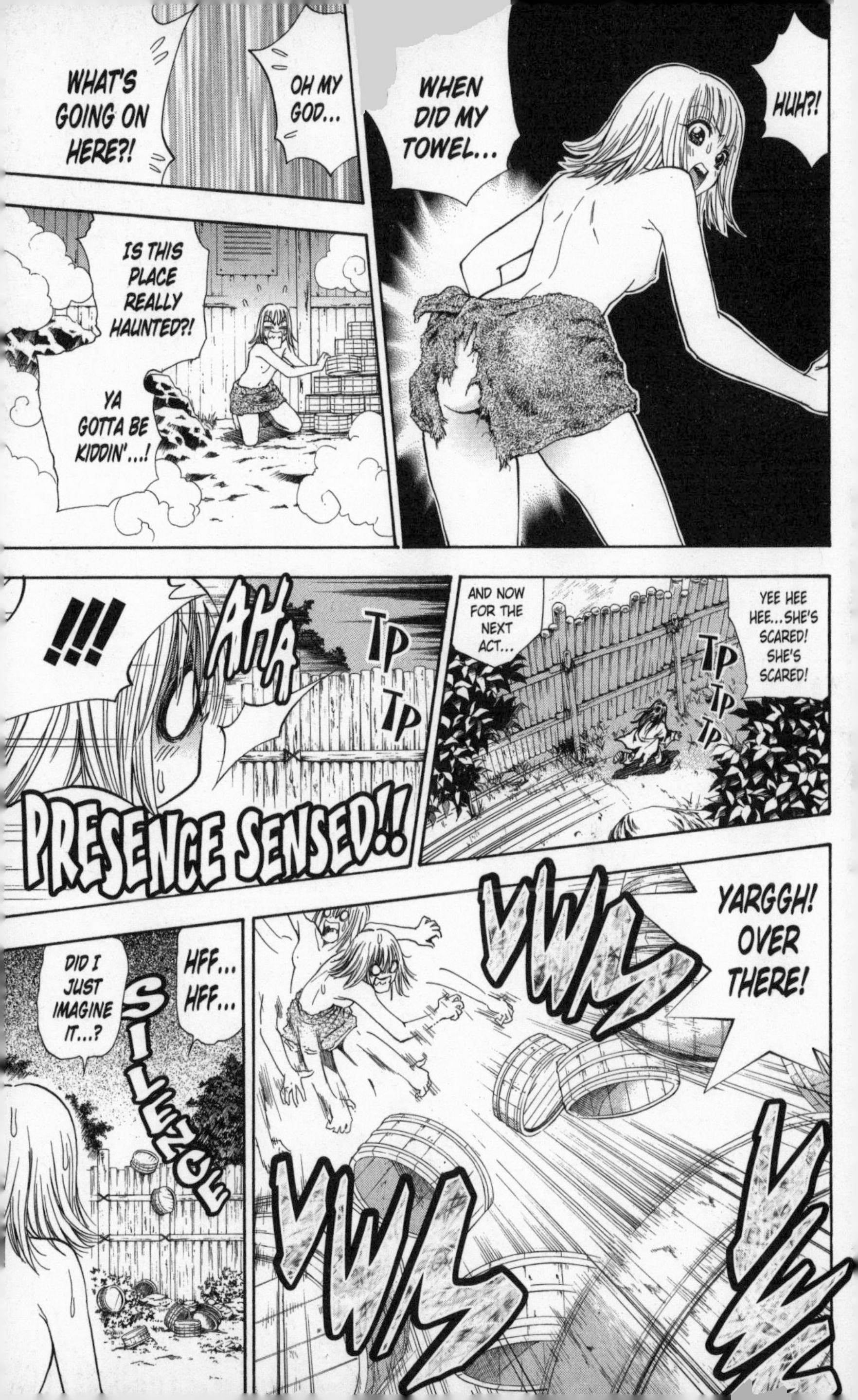
HUH?!
WHEN DID MY TOWEL...
OH MY GOD...
WHAT'S GOING ON HERE?!
IS THIS PLACE REALLY HAUNTED?!
YA GOTTA BE KIDDIN'...!
YEE HEE HEE...SHE'S SCARED! SHE'S SCARED!
TP TP TP
AND NOW FOR THE NEXT ACT...
TP TP
!!!
PRESENCE SENSED!!
YARGGH! OVER THERE!
HFF... HFF...
DID I JUST IMAGINE IT...?
SILENCE

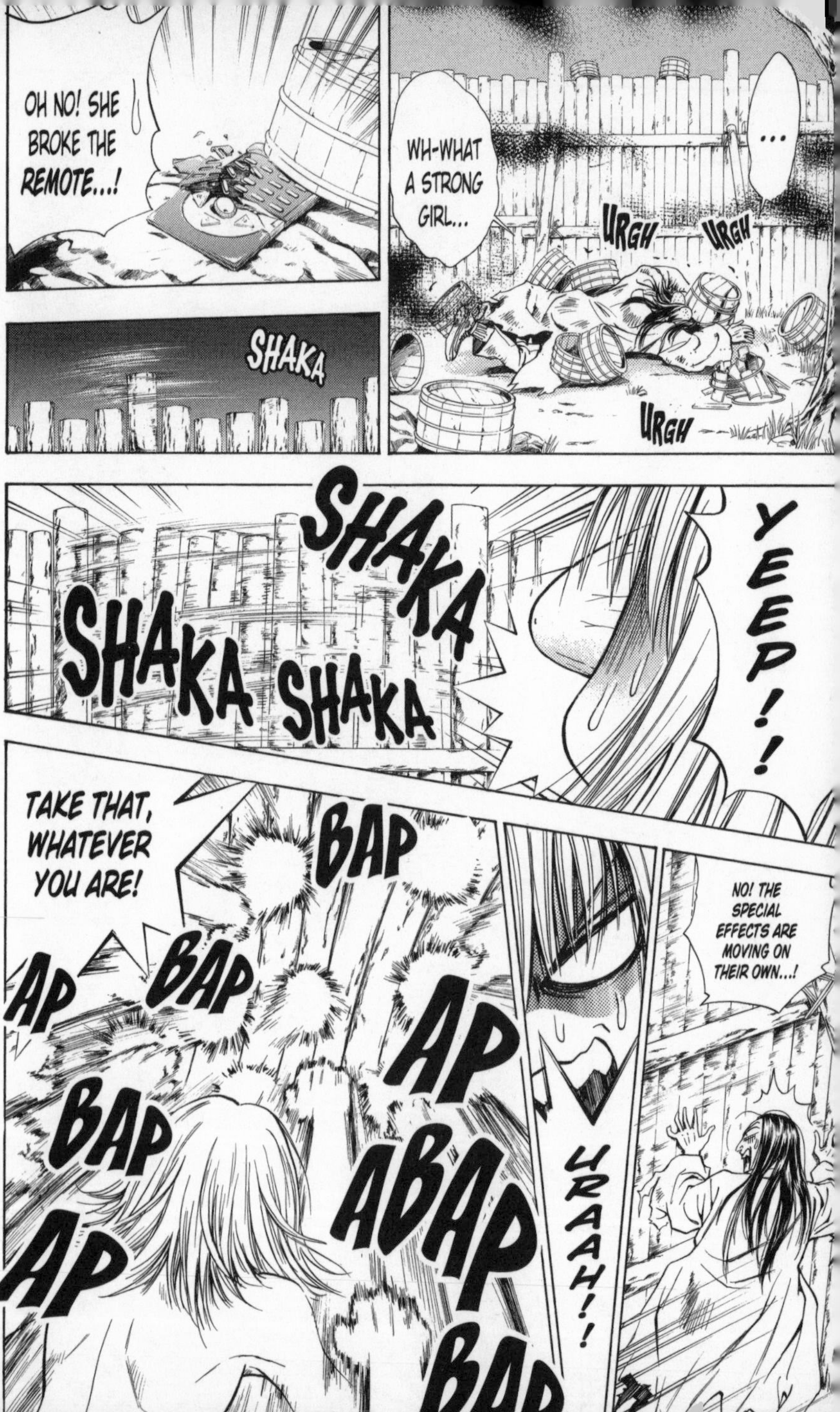
...
WH-WHAT A STRONG GIRL...
URGH
URGH
URGH
OH NO! SHE BROKE THE REMOTE...!
SHAKA
YEEP!!
SHAKA
SHAKA
SHAKA
NO! THE SPECIAL EFFECTS ARE MOVING ON THEIR OWN...!
URAAAH!!
TAKE THAT, WHATEVER YOU ARE!
BAP
AP
ABAP
BAP
BAP
AP
BAP
AP

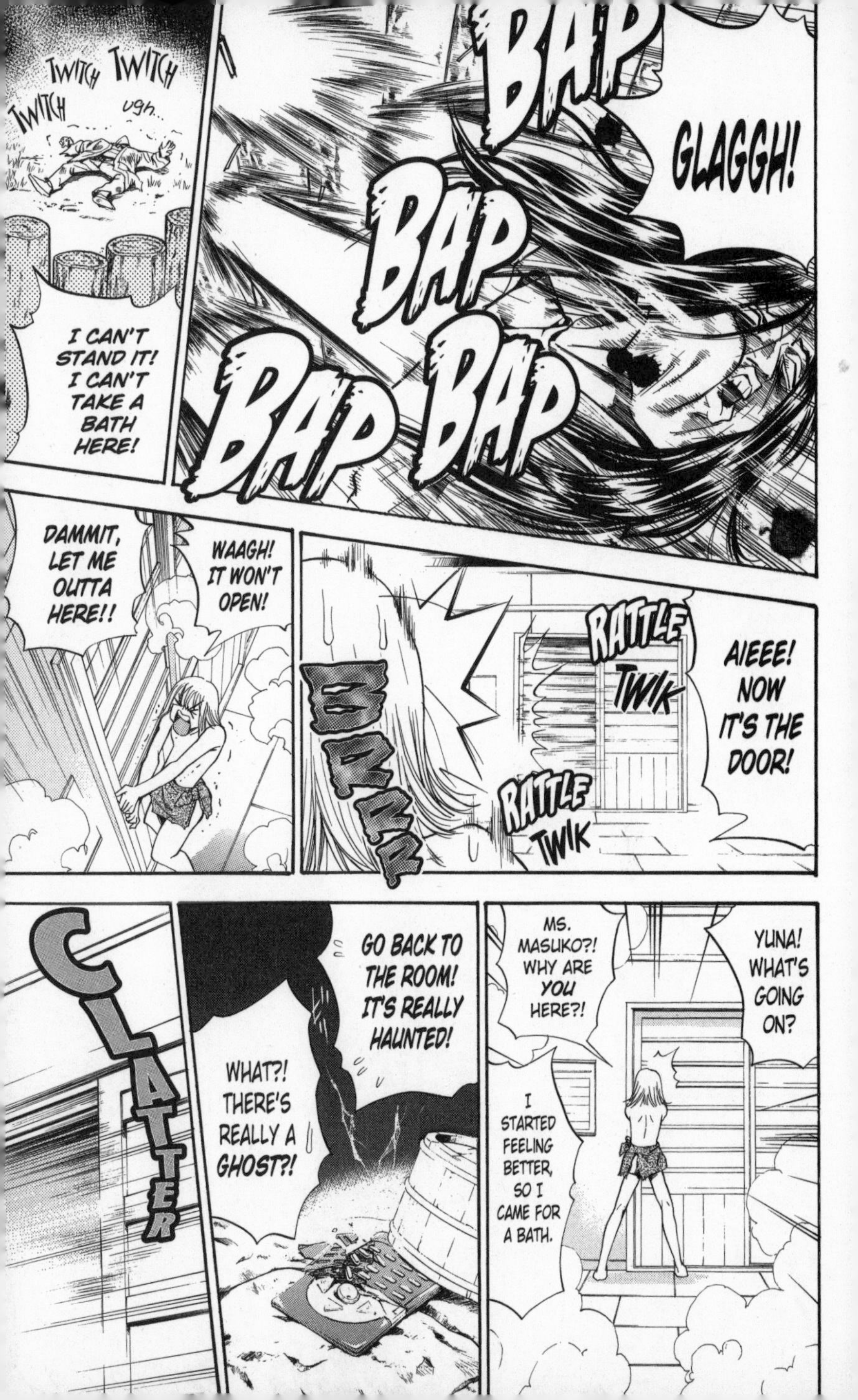
BAP
GLAGGH!
BAP
BAP
BAP
TWITCH TWITCH
TWITCH
ugh...
I CAN'T STAND IT! I CAN'T TAKE A BATH HERE!
RATTLE
TWIK
AIEEE! NOW IT'S THE DOOR!
RATTLE
TWIK
WAAGH! IT WON'T OPEN!
DAMMIT, LET ME OUTTA HERE!!
YUNA! WHAT'S GOING ON?
MS. MASUKO?! WHY ARE YOU HERE?!
I STARTED FEELING BETTER, SO I CAME FOR A BATH.
GO BACK TO THE ROOM! IT'S REALLY HAUNTED!
WHAT?! THERE'S REALLY A GHOST?!
CLATTER

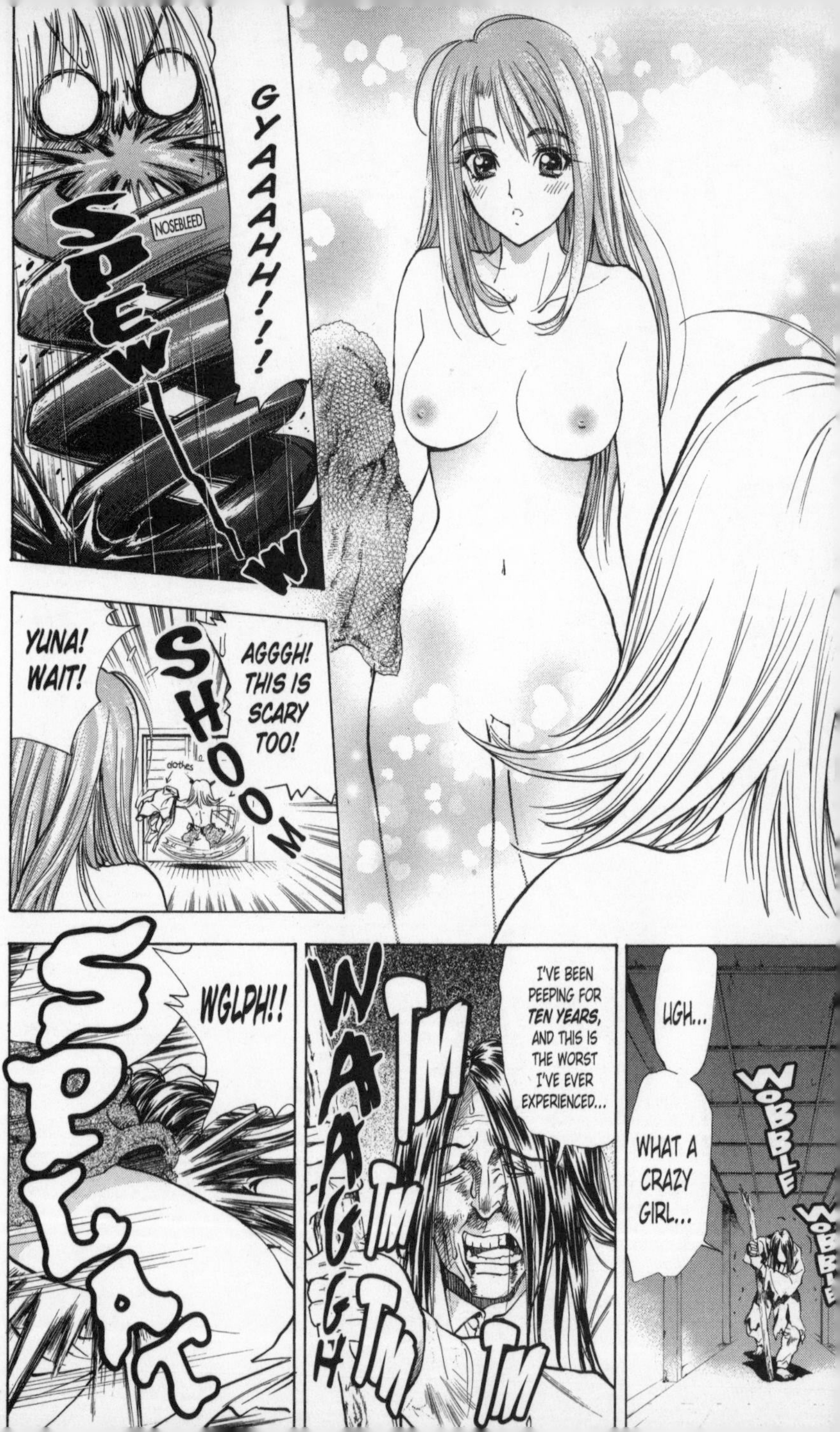
GYAAAAHH!!!
NOSEBLEED
SPEW
AGGGH! THIS IS SCARY TOO!
SHOOOOM
YUNA! WAIT!
clothes
UGH...
WHAT A CRAZY GIRL...
WOBBLE
WOBBLE
I'VE BEEN PEEPING FOR TEN YEARS, AND THIS IS THE WORST I'VE EVER EXPERIENCED...
TM
WAAAGH
TM
TM
TM
TM
WGLPH!!
SPLAT

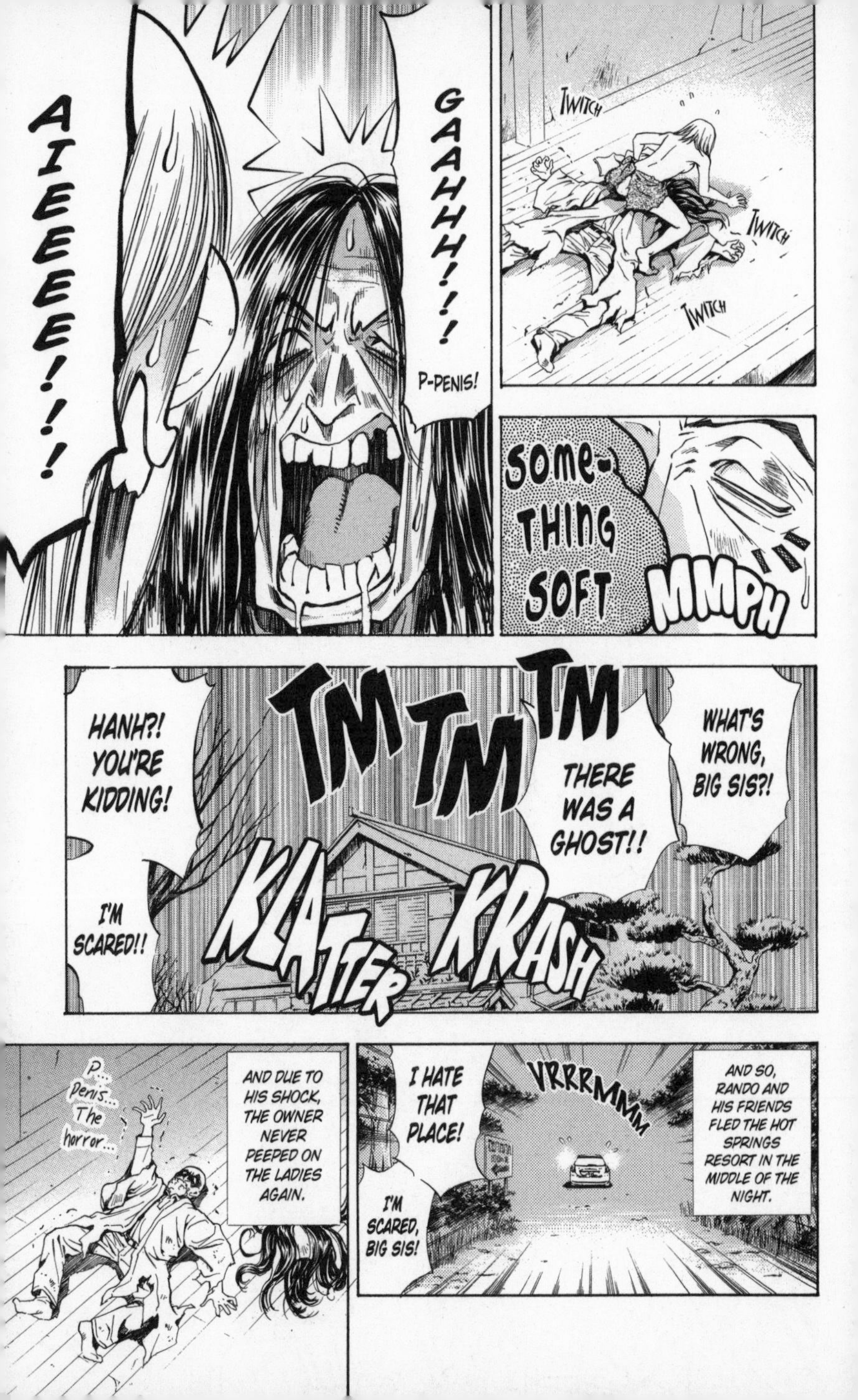
TWITCH
TWITCH
TWITCH
SOME-THING SOFT
MMPH
GAAHHH!!!
P-PENIS!
AIEEEEEE!!!
WHAT'S WRONG, BIG SIS?!
TM TM TM
THERE WAS A GHOST!!
KRASH
KLATTER
HANH?! YOU'RE KIDDING!
I'M SCARED!!
AND SO, RANDO AND HIS FRIENDS FLED THE HOT SPRINGS RESORT IN THE MIDDLE OF THE NIGHT.
VRRRMMM
I HATE THAT PLACE!
I'M SCARED, BIG SIS!
AND DUE TO HIS SHOCK, THE OWNER NEVER PEEPED ON THE LADIES AGAIN.
P... Penis... The horror...

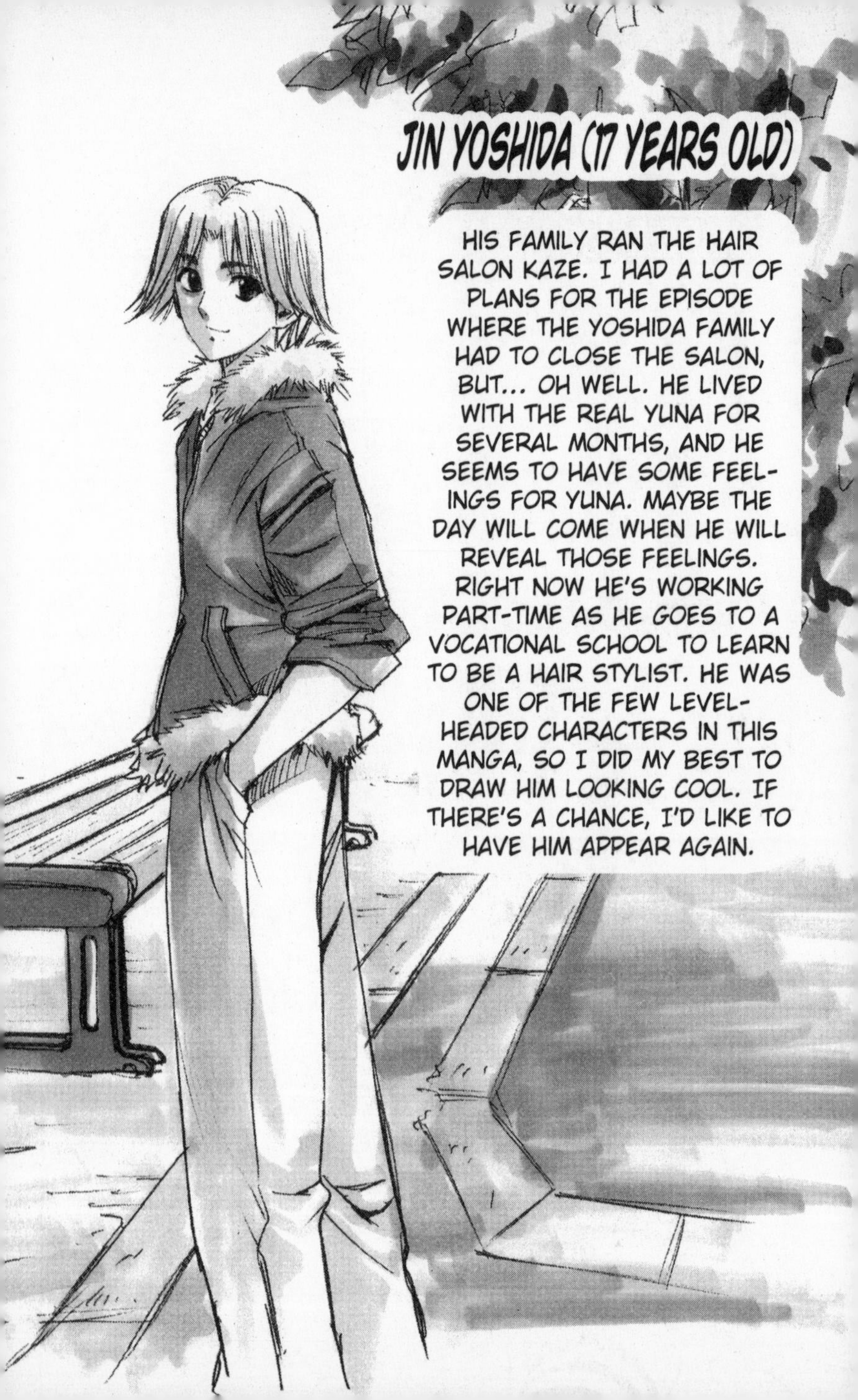

JIN YOSHIDA (17 YEARS OLD)

HIS FAMILY RAN THE HAIR SALON KAZE. I HAD A LOT OF PLANS FOR THE EPISODE WHERE THE YOSHIDA FAMILY HAD TO CLOSE THE SALON, BUT... OH WELL. HE LIVED WITH THE REAL YUNA FOR SEVERAL MONTHS, AND HE SEEMS TO HAVE SOME FEELINGS FOR YUNA. MAYBE THE DAY WILL COME WHEN HE WILL REVEAL THOSE FEELINGS. RIGHT NOW HE'S WORKING PART-TIME AS HE GOES TO A VOCATIONAL SCHOOL TO LEARN TO BE A HAIR STYLIST. HE WAS ONE OF THE FEW LEVEL-HEADED CHARACTERS IN THIS MANGA, SO I DID MY BEST TO DRAW HIM LOOKING COOL. IF THERE'S A CHANCE, I'D LIKE TO HAVE HIM APPEAR AGAIN.

Chapter 35: False Memories = Big Trouble

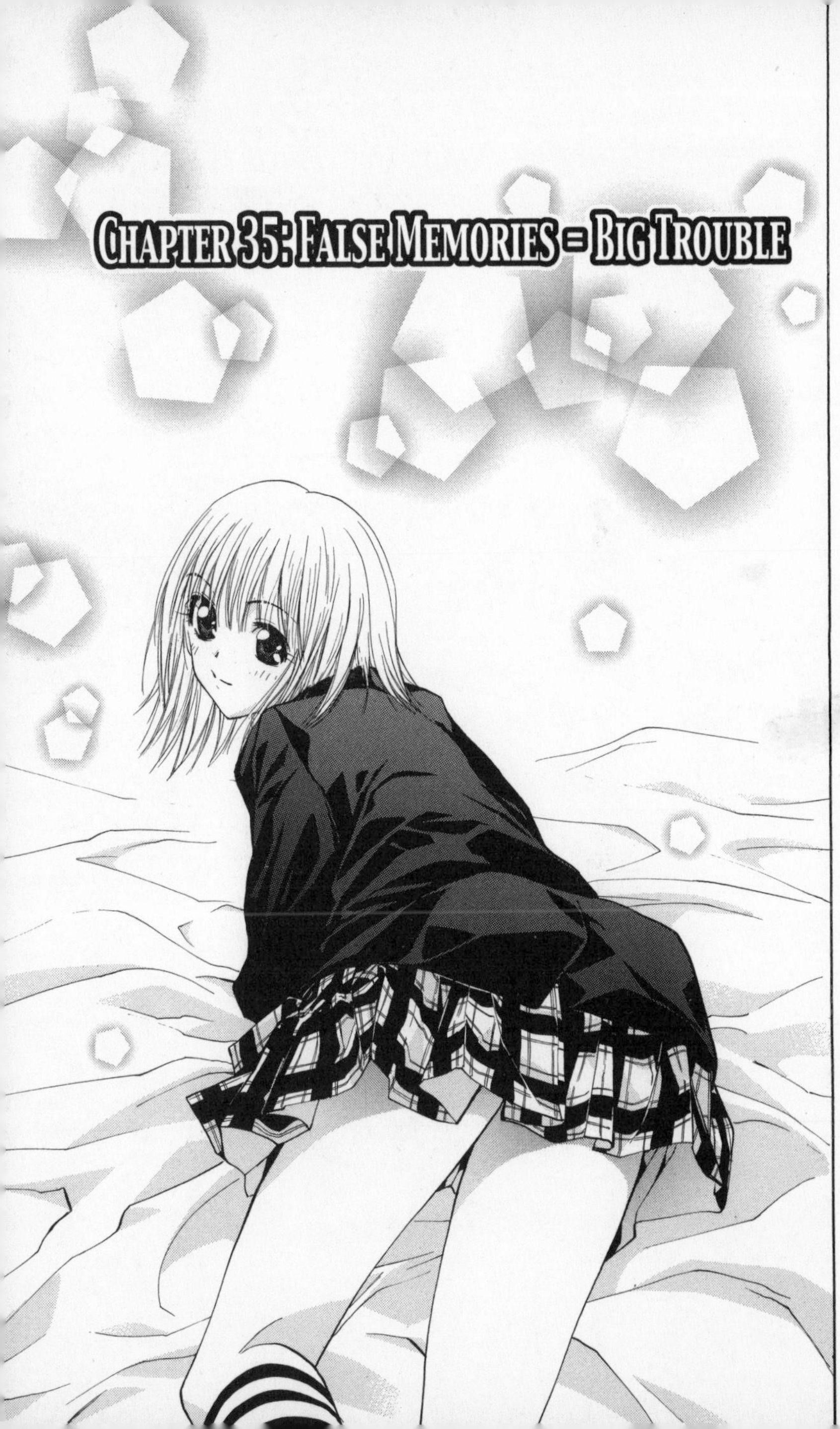

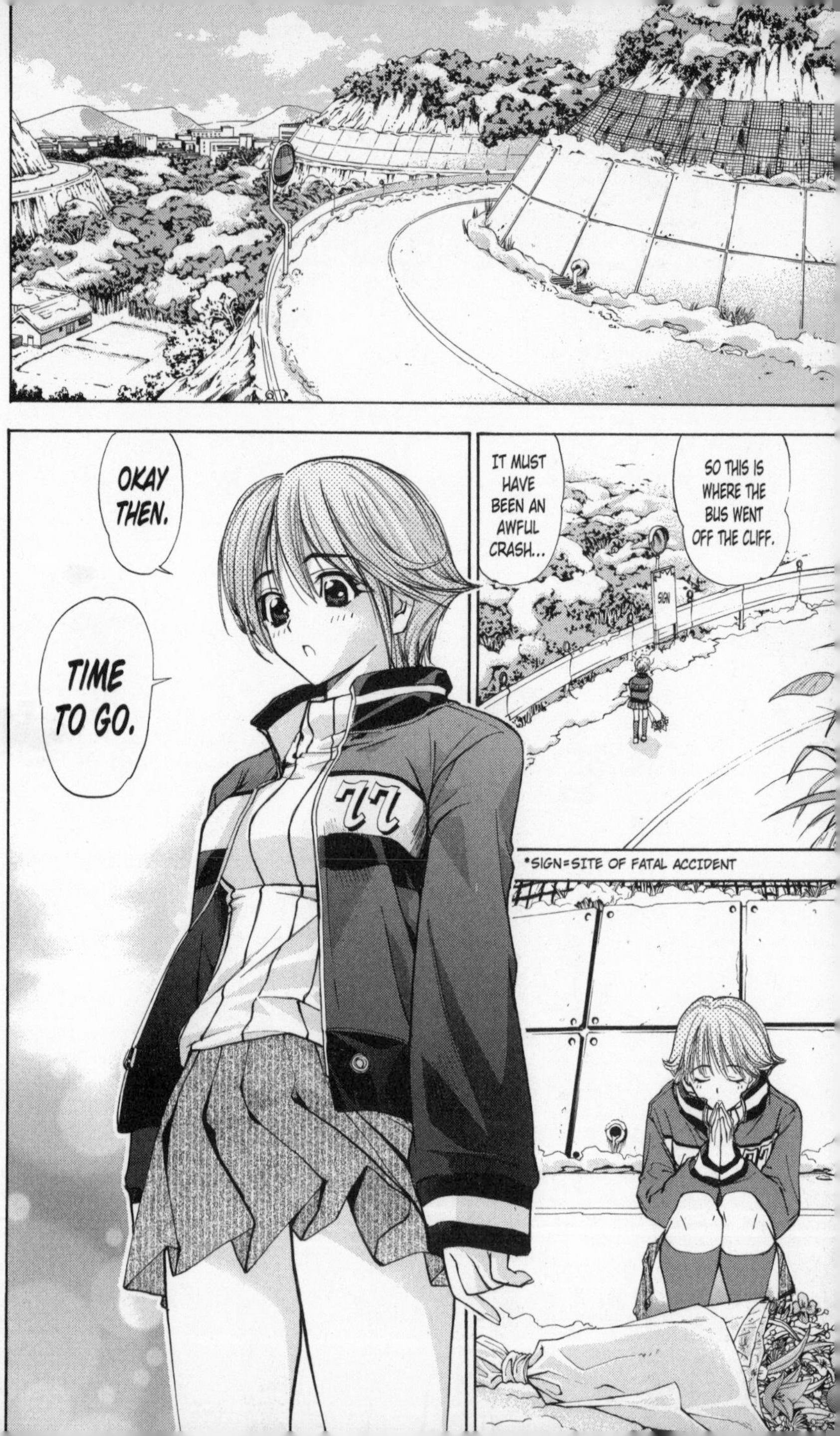
SO THIS IS WHERE THE BUS WENT OFF THE CLIFF.
IT MUST HAVE BEEN AN AWFUL CRASH...
SIGN
*SIGN=SITE OF FATAL ACCIDENT
OKAY THEN.
TIME TO GO.

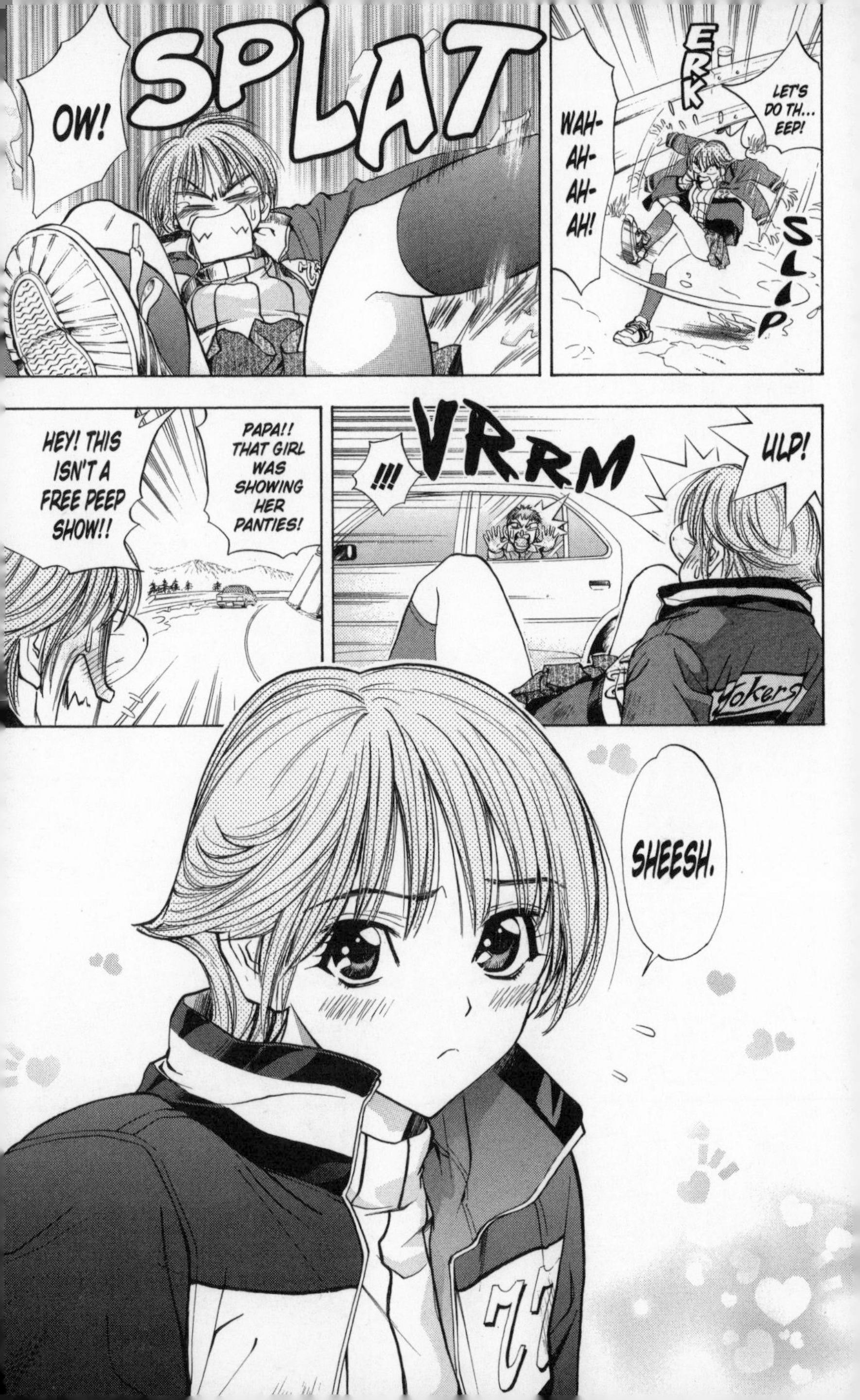
LET'S DO TH... EEP!
ERK
WAH-AH-AH-AH!
SLIP
SPLAT
OW!
ULP!
VRRM
!!!
PAPA!! THAT GIRL WAS SHOWING HER PANTIES!
HEY! THIS ISN'T A FREE PEEP SHOW!!
SHEESH.

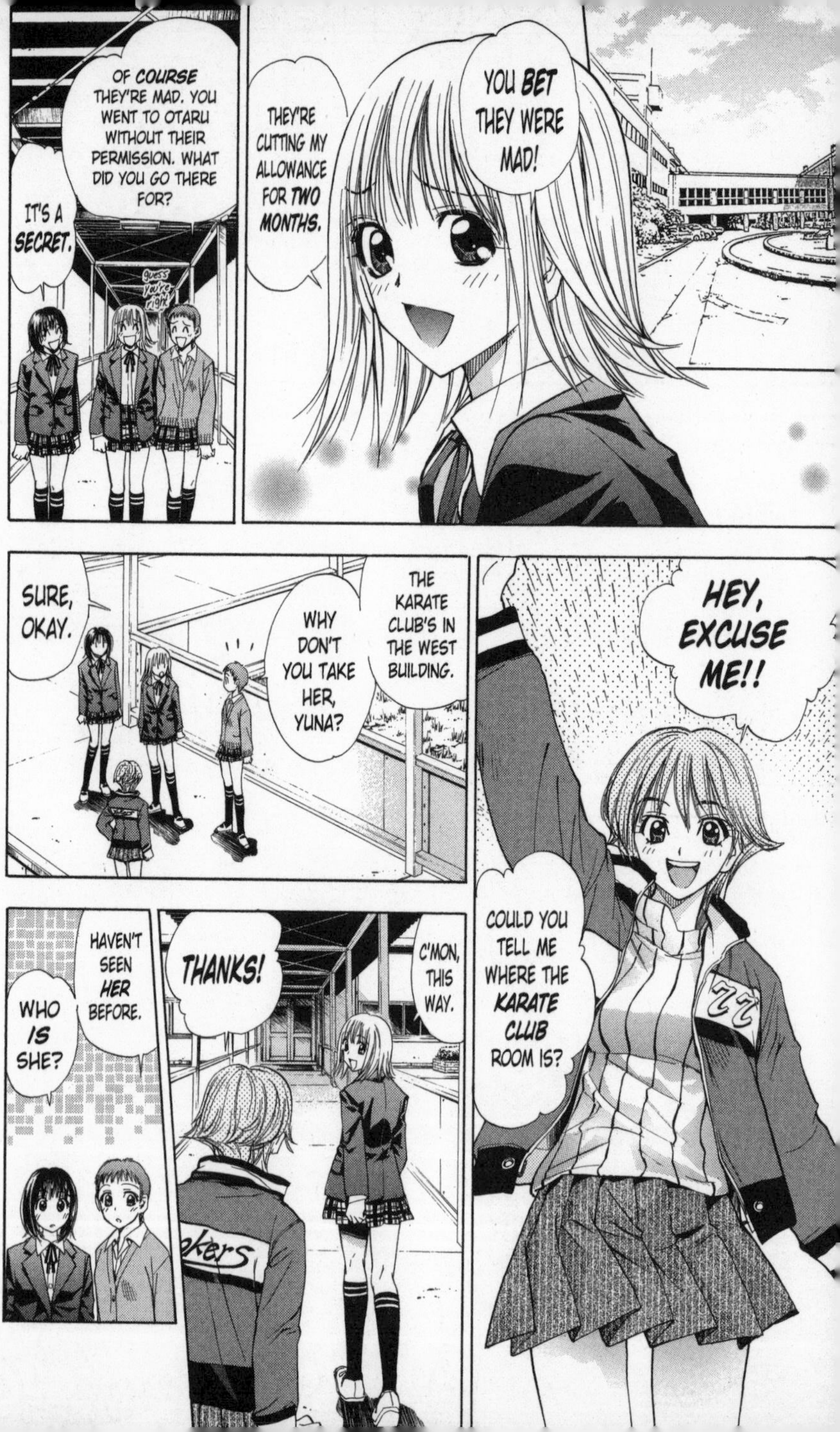

YOU BET THEY WERE MAD!
THEY'RE CUTTING MY ALLOWANCE FOR TWO MONTHS.
OF COURSE THEY'RE MAD. YOU WENT TO OTARU WITHOUT THEIR PERMISSION. WHAT DID YOU GO THERE FOR?
IT'S A SECRET.
guess you're right
HEY, EXCUSE ME!!
COULD YOU TELL ME WHERE THE KARATE CLUB ROOM IS?
THE KARATE CLUB'S IN THE WEST BUILDING.
WHY DON'T YOU TAKE HER, YUNA?
SURE, OKAY.
C'MON, THIS WAY.
THANKS!
HAVEN'T SEEN HER BEFORE.
WHO IS SHE?

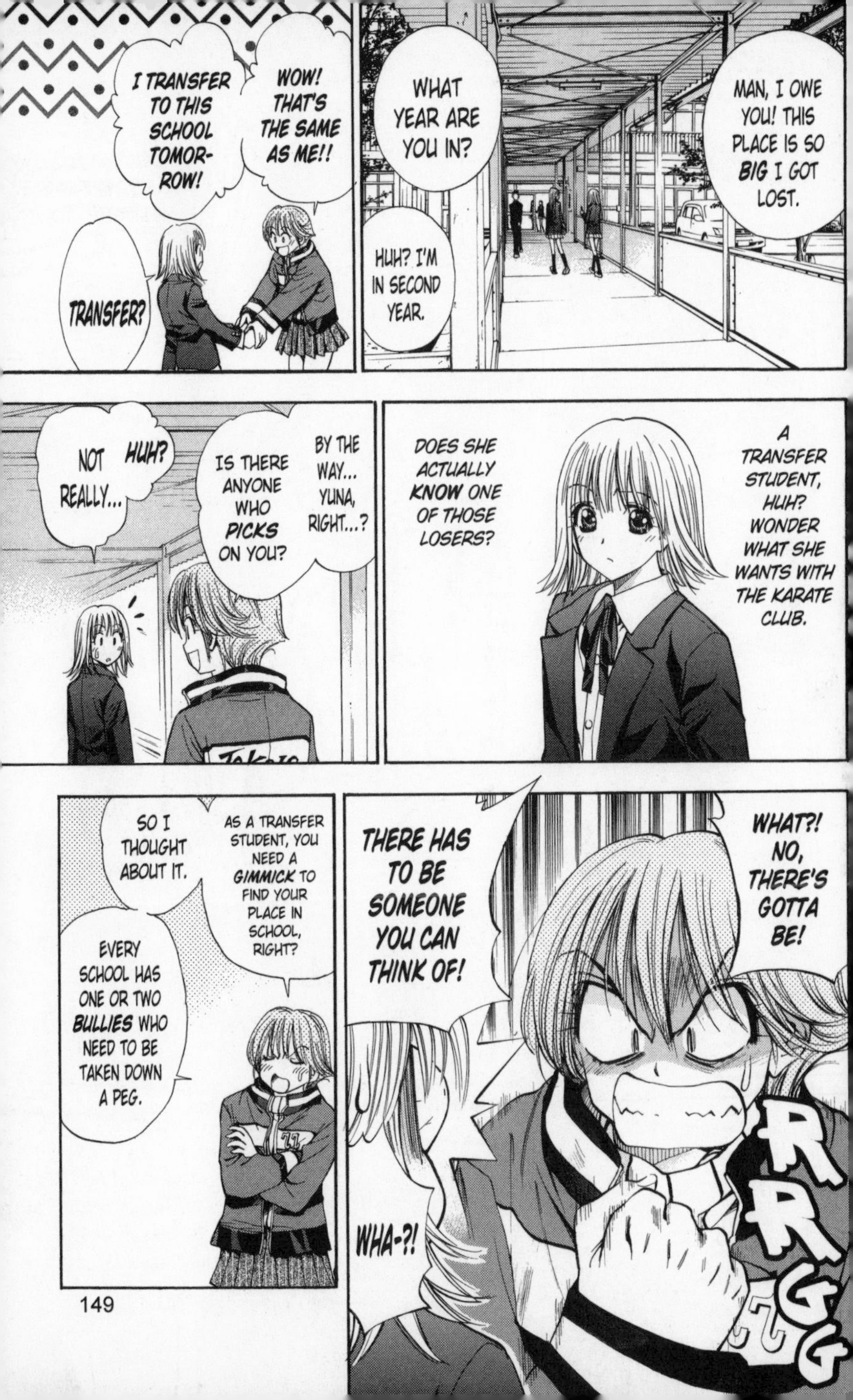
MAN, I OWE YOU! THIS PLACE IS SO BIG I GOT LOST.
WHAT YEAR ARE YOU IN?
HUH? I'M IN SECOND YEAR.
WOW! THAT'S THE SAME AS ME!!
I TRANSFER TO THIS SCHOOL TOMORROW!
TRANSFER?
A TRANSFER STUDENT, HUH? WONDER WHAT SHE WANTS WITH THE KARATE CLUB.
DOES SHE ACTUALLY KNOW ONE OF THOSE LOSERS?
BY THE WAY... YUNA, RIGHT...?
IS THERE ANYONE WHO PICKS ON YOU?
HUH?
NOT REALLY...
WHAT?! NO, THERE'S GOTTA BE!
THERE HAS TO BE SOMEONE YOU CAN THINK OF!
WHA-?!
RRGG
AS A TRANSFER STUDENT, YOU NEED A GIMMICK TO FIND YOUR PLACE IN SCHOOL, RIGHT?
SO I THOUGHT ABOUT IT.
EVERY SCHOOL HAS ONE OR TWO BULLIES WHO NEED TO BE TAKEN DOWN A PEG.

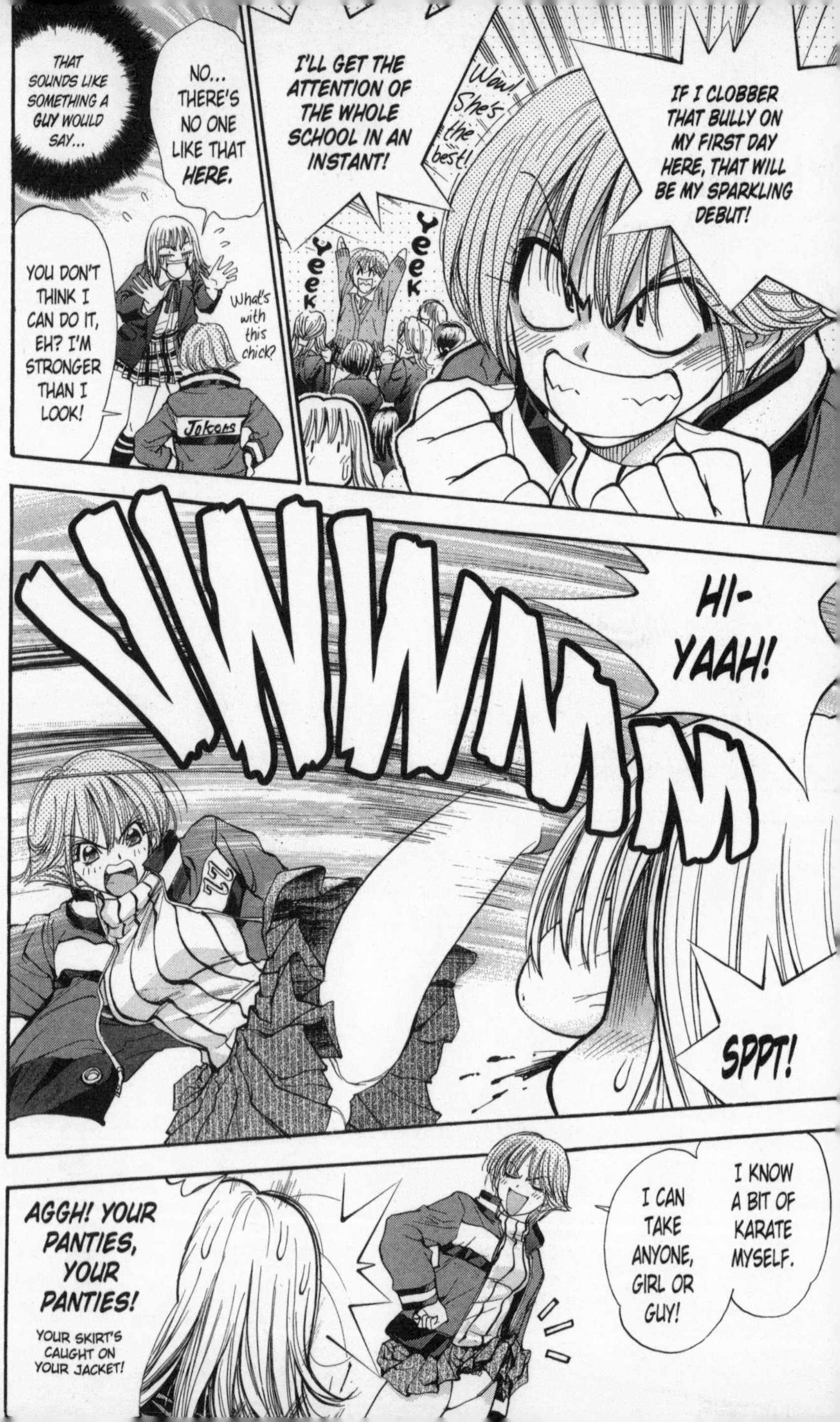
IF I CLOBBER THAT BULLY ON MY FIRST DAY HERE, THAT WILL BE MY SPARKLING DEBUT!
Wow! She's the best!
I'LL GET THE ATTENTION OF THE WHOLE SCHOOL IN AN INSTANT!
Yeek Yeek
NO... THERE'S NO ONE LIKE THAT HERE.
THAT SOUNDS LIKE SOMETHING A GUY WOULD SAY...
YOU DON'T THINK I CAN DO IT, EH? I'M STRONGER THAN I LOOK!
What's with this chick?
Jokers
HI-YAAH!
VWWMMM
SPPT!
I KNOW A BIT OF KARATE MYSELF.
I CAN TAKE ANYONE, GIRL OR GUY!
AGGH! YOUR PANTIES, YOUR PANTIES!
YOUR SKIRT'S CAUGHT ON YOUR JACKET!

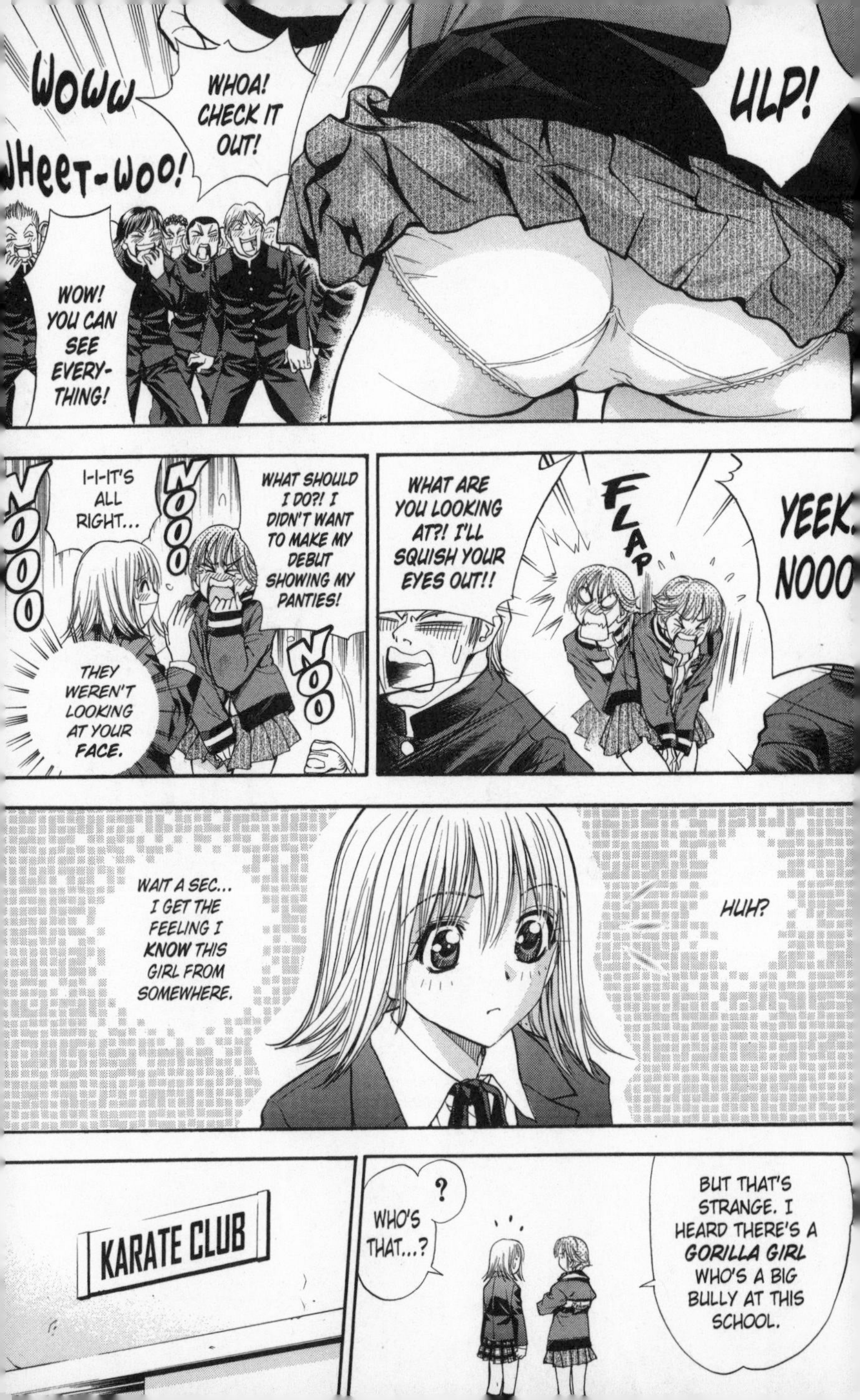
ULP!
WHOA! CHECK IT OUT!
WOWW
HEET-WOO!
WOW! YOU CAN SEE EVERY-THING!
YEEK. NOOO
FLAP
WHAT ARE YOU LOOKING AT?! I'LL SQUISH YOUR EYES OUT!!
WHAT SHOULD I DO?! I DIDN'T WANT TO MAKE MY DEBUT SHOWING MY PANTIES!
NOOO
I-I-IT'S ALL RIGHT...
NOOOO
NOO
THEY WEREN'T LOOKING AT YOUR FACE.
HUH?
WAIT A SEC... I GET THE FEELING I KNOW THIS GIRL FROM SOMEWHERE.
BUT THAT'S STRANGE. I HEARD THERE'S A GORILLA GIRL WHO'S A BIG BULLY AT THIS SCHOOL.
?
WHO'S THAT...?
KARATE CLUB

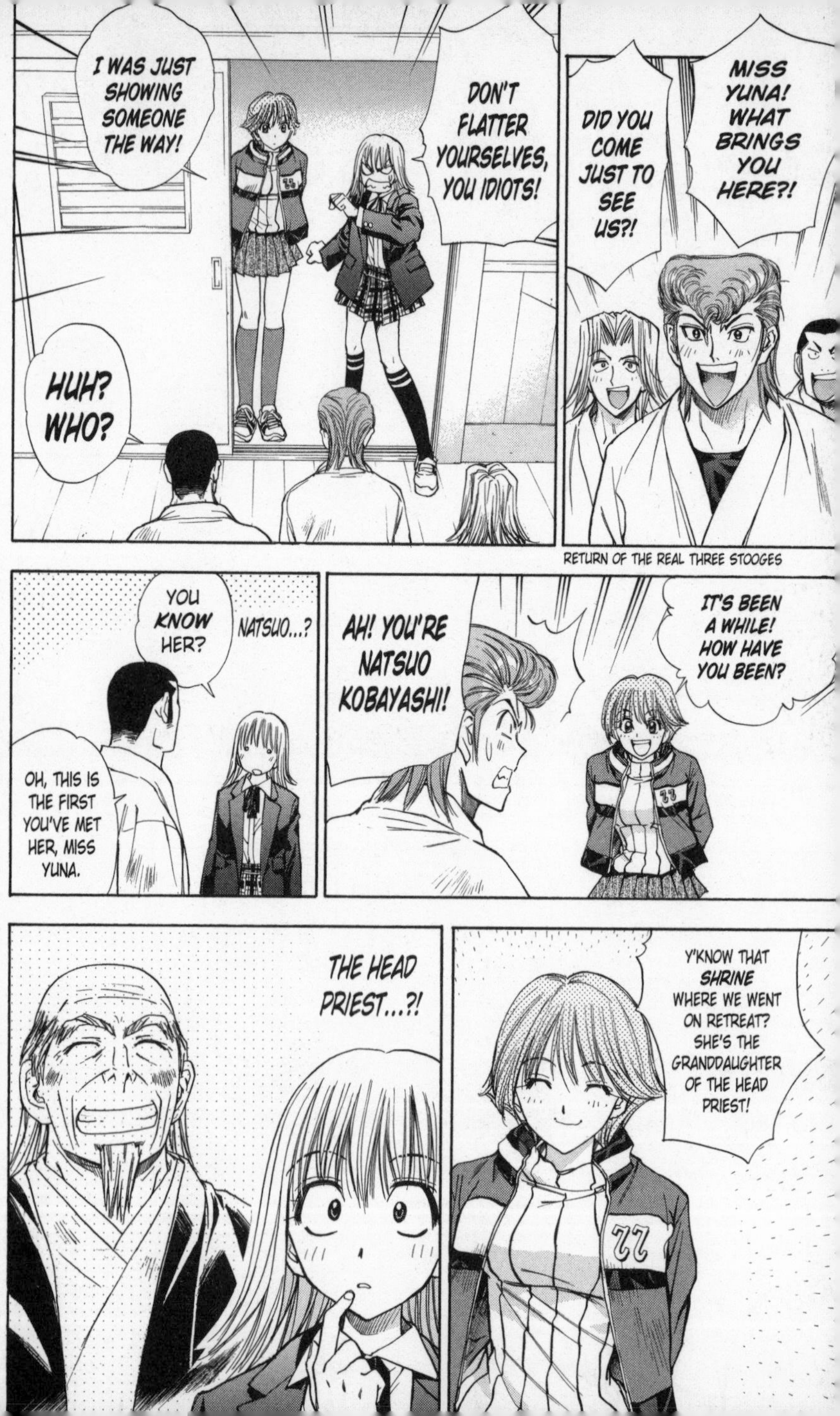
MISS YUNA! WHAT BRINGS YOU HERE?!
DID YOU COME JUST TO SEE US?!
DON'T FLATTER YOURSELVES, YOU IDIOTS!
I WAS JUST SHOWING SOMEONE THE WAY!
HUH? WHO?
RETURN OF THE REAL THREE STOOGES
IT'S BEEN A WHILE! HOW HAVE YOU BEEN?
AH! YOU'RE NATSUO KOBAYASHI!
NATSUO...?
YOU KNOW HER?
OH, THIS IS THE FIRST YOU'VE MET HER, MISS YUNA.
Y'KNOW THAT SHRINE WHERE WE WENT ON RETREAT? SHE'S THE GRANDDAUGHTER OF THE HEAD PRIEST!
THE HEAD PRIEST...?!

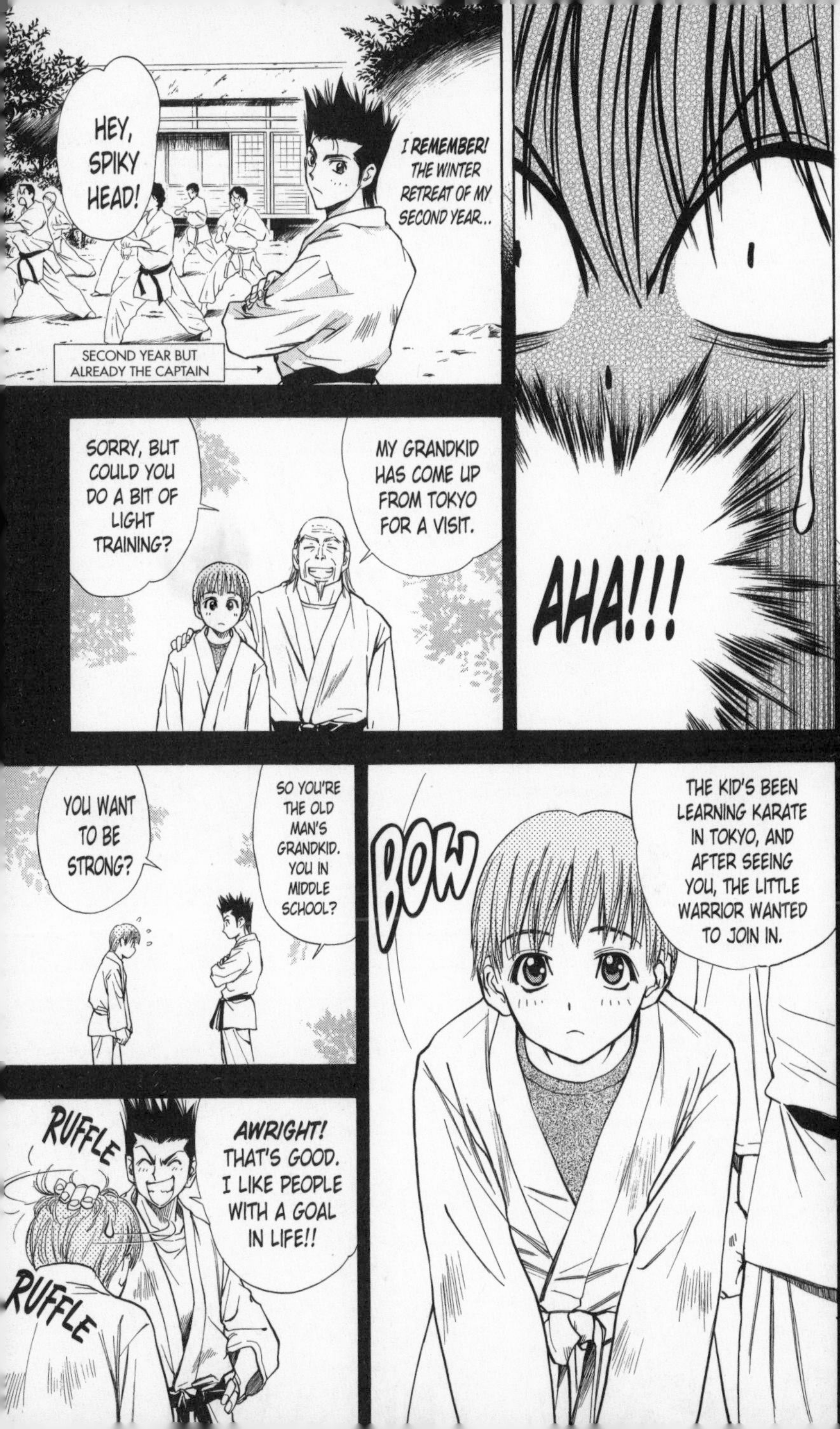
AHA!!!
I REMEMBER! THE WINTER RETREAT OF MY SECOND YEAR...
HEY, SPIKY HEAD!
SECOND YEAR BUT ALREADY THE CAPTAIN
MY GRANDKID HAS COME UP FROM TOKYO FOR A VISIT.
SORRY, BUT COULD YOU DO A BIT OF LIGHT TRAINING?
THE KID'S BEEN LEARNING KARATE IN TOKYO, AND AFTER SEEING YOU, THE LITTLE WARRIOR WANTED TO JOIN IN.
BOW
SO YOU'RE THE OLD MAN'S GRANDKID. YOU IN MIDDLE SCHOOL?
YOU WANT TO BE STRONG?
AWRIGHT! THAT'S GOOD. I LIKE PEOPLE WITH A GOAL IN LIFE!!
RUFFLE
RUFFLE

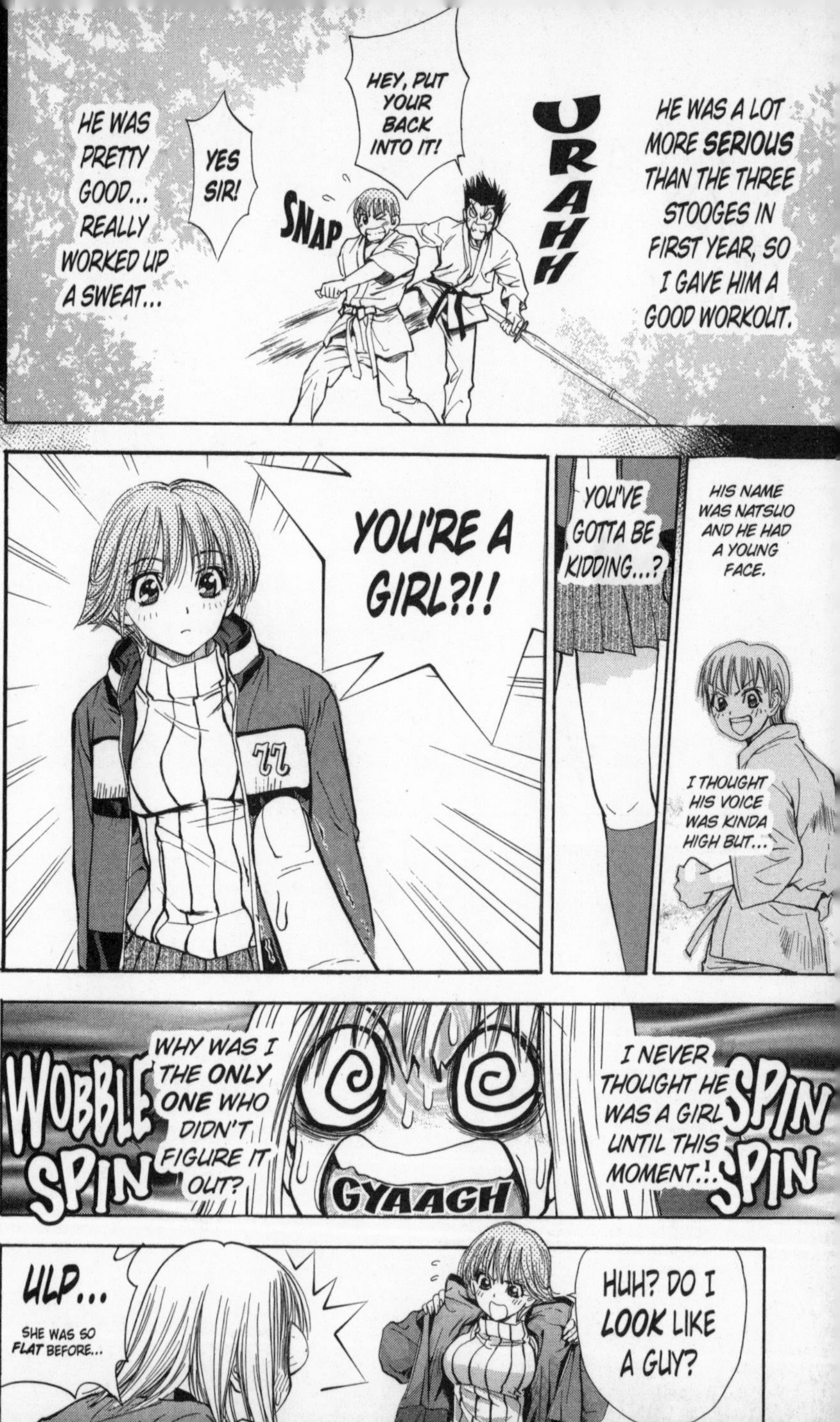
HE WAS A LOT MORE SERIOUS THAN THE THREE STOOGES IN FIRST YEAR, SO I GAVE HIM A GOOD WORKOUT.
URAHH
HEY, PUT YOUR BACK INTO IT!
YES SIR!
SNAP
HE WAS PRETTY GOOD... REALLY WORKED UP A SWEAT...
HIS NAME WAS NATSUO AND HE HAD A YOUNG FACE.
I THOUGHT HIS VOICE WAS KINDA HIGH BUT...
YOU'VE GOTTA BE KIDDING...?
YOU'RE A GIRL?!!
SPIN SPIN
I NEVER THOUGHT HE WAS A GIRL UNTIL THIS MOMENT...
GYAAGH
WHY WAS I THE ONLY ONE WHO DIDN'T FIGURE IT OUT?
WOBBLE SPIN
HUH? DO I LOOK LIKE A GUY?
ULP...
SHE WAS SO FLAT BEFORE...

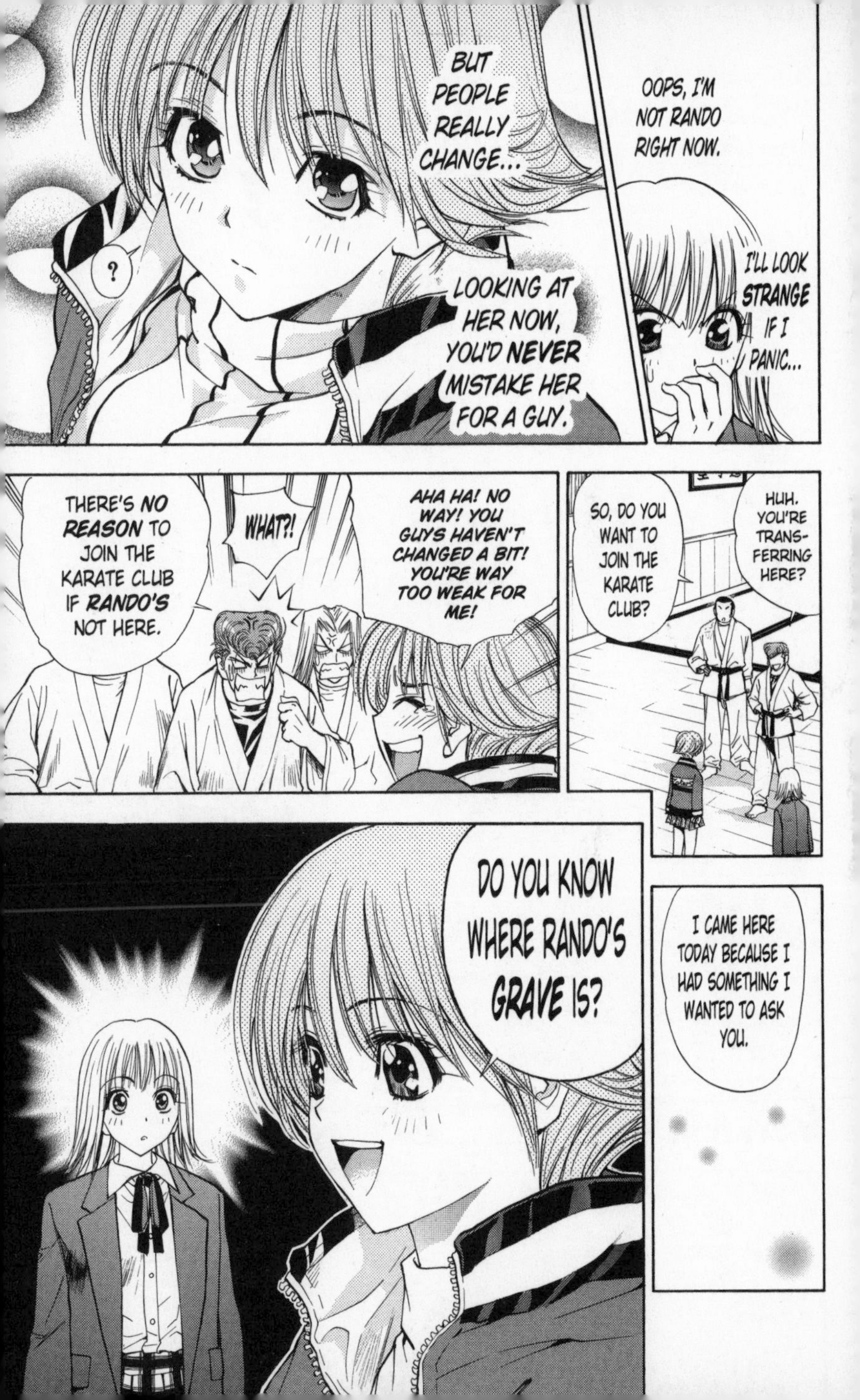
OOPS, I'M NOT RANDO RIGHT NOW.
I'LL LOOK STRANGE IF I PANIC...
BUT PEOPLE REALLY CHANGE...
?
LOOKING AT HER NOW, YOU'D NEVER MISTAKE HER FOR A GUY.
HUH. YOU'RE TRANS-FERRING HERE?
SO, DO YOU WANT TO JOIN THE KARATE CLUB?
AHA HA! NO WAY! YOU GUYS HAVEN'T CHANGED A BIT! YOU'RE WAY TOO WEAK FOR ME!
WHAT?!
THERE'S NO REASON TO JOIN THE KARATE CLUB IF RANDO'S NOT HERE.
I CAME HERE TODAY BECAUSE I HAD SOMETHING I WANTED TO ASK YOU.
DO YOU KNOW WHERE RANDO'S GRAVE IS?

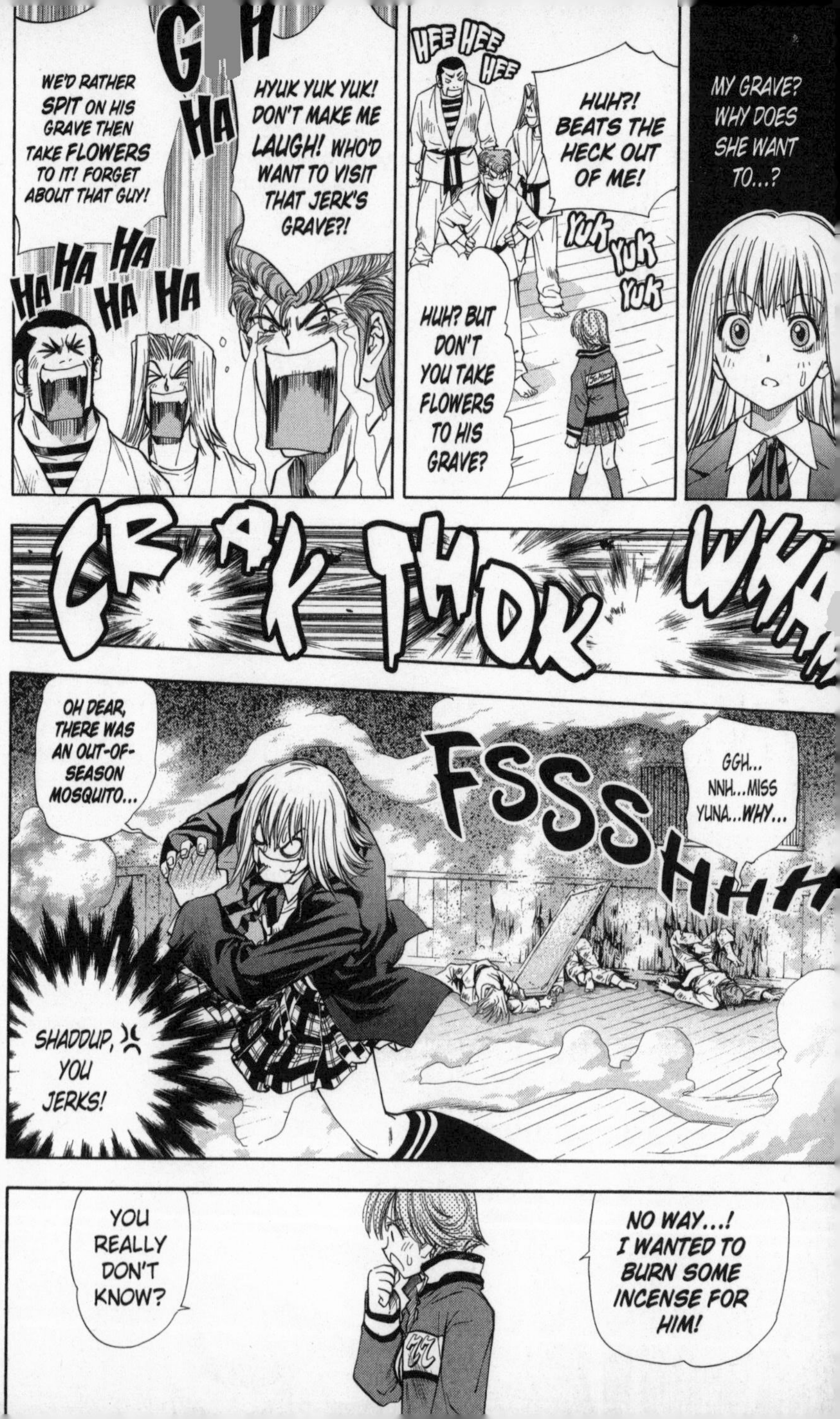
MY GRAVE? WHY DOES SHE WANT TO...?
HUH?! BEATS THE HECK OUT OF ME!
HEE HEE HEE
YUK YUK YUK
HUH? BUT DON'T YOU TAKE FLOWERS TO HIS GRAVE?
HYUK YUK YUK! DON'T MAKE ME LAUGH! WHO'D WANT TO VISIT THAT JERK'S GRAVE?!
HA
WE'D RATHER SPIT ON HIS GRAVE THEN TAKE FLOWERS TO IT! FORGET ABOUT THAT GUY!
HA HA HA HA HA HA
WHA
THOK
CRAK
GGH... NNH...MISS YUNA...WHY...
FSSSHHH
OH DEAR, THERE WAS AN OUT-OF-SEASON MOSQUITO...
SHADDUP, YOU JERKS!
NO WAY...! I WANTED TO BURN SOME INCENSE FOR HIM!
YOU REALLY DON'T KNOW?

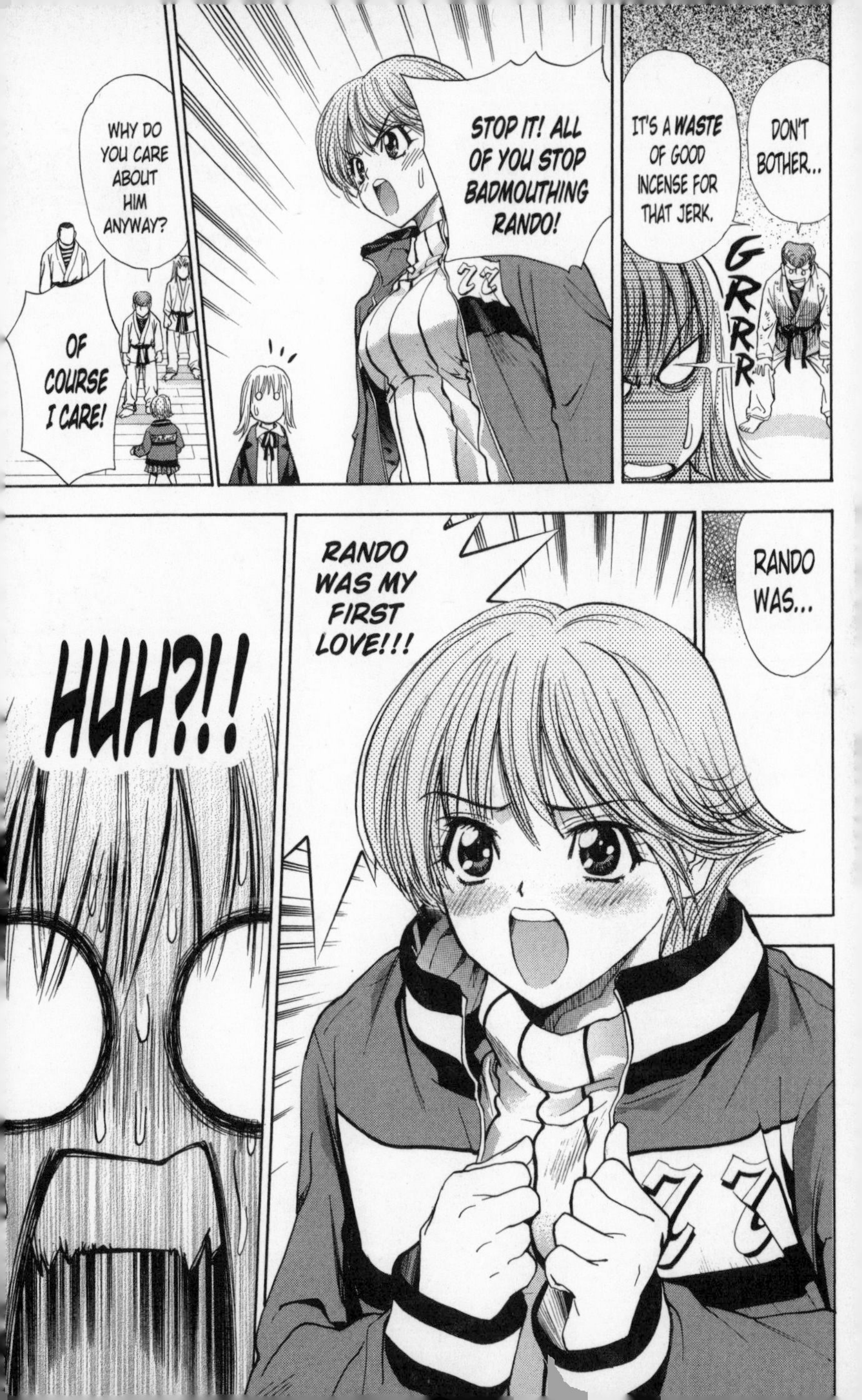
DON'T BOTHER...
IT'S A WASTE OF GOOD INCENSE FOR THAT JERK.
GRRR
STOP IT! ALL OF YOU STOP BADMOUTHING RANDO!
WHY DO YOU CARE ABOUT HIM ANYWAY?
OF COURSE I CARE!
RANDO WAS...
RANDO WAS MY FIRST LOVE!!!
HUH?!!

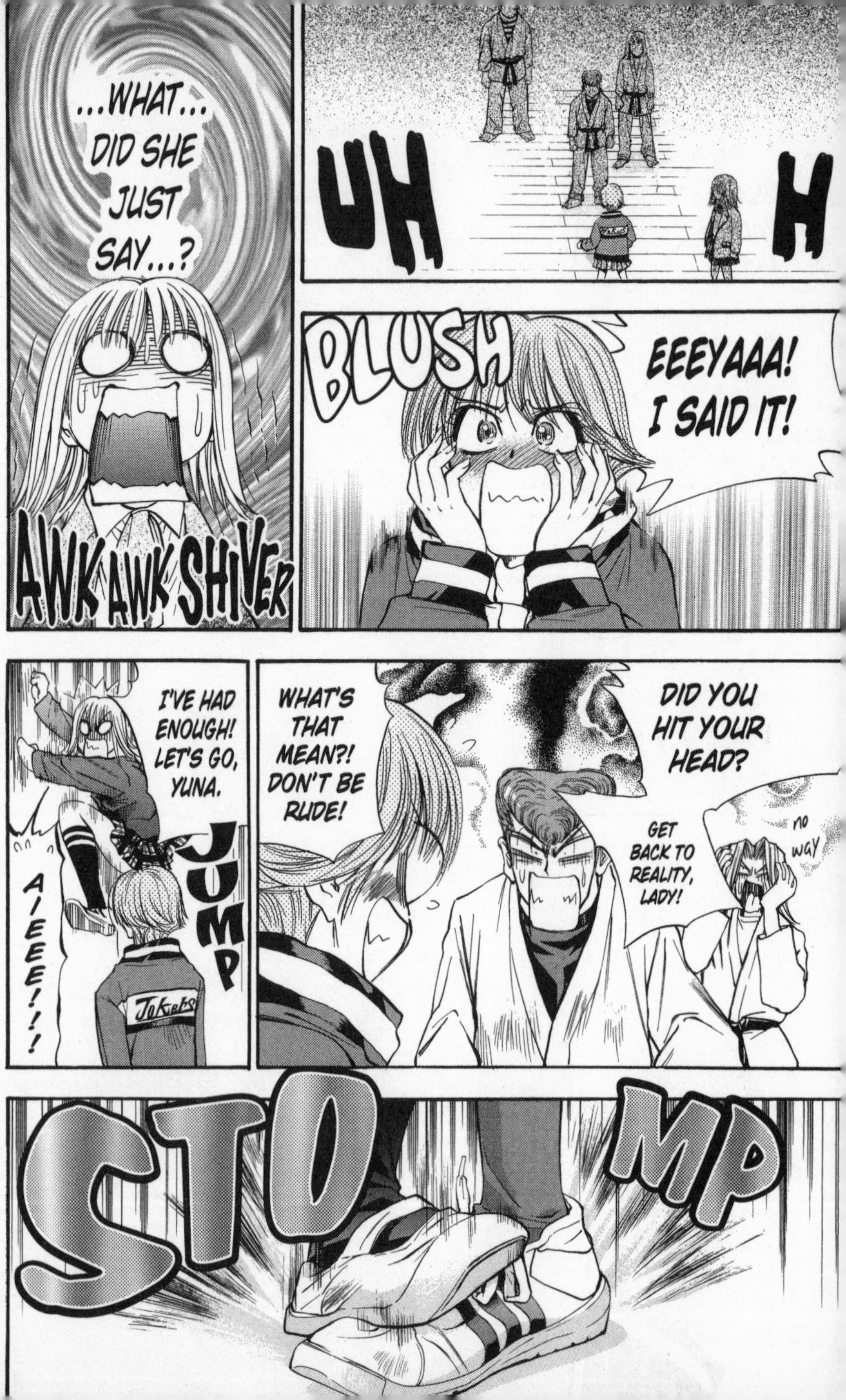
UH
H
BLUSH
EEEYAAA! I SAID IT!
...WHAT... DID SHE JUST SAY...?
AWK AWK SHIVER
DID YOU HIT YOUR HEAD?
no way
GET BACK TO REALITY, LADY!
WHAT'S THAT MEAN?! DON'T BE RUDE!
I'VE HAD ENOUGH! LET'S GO, YUNA.
JUMP
AIEEE!!!
STOMP

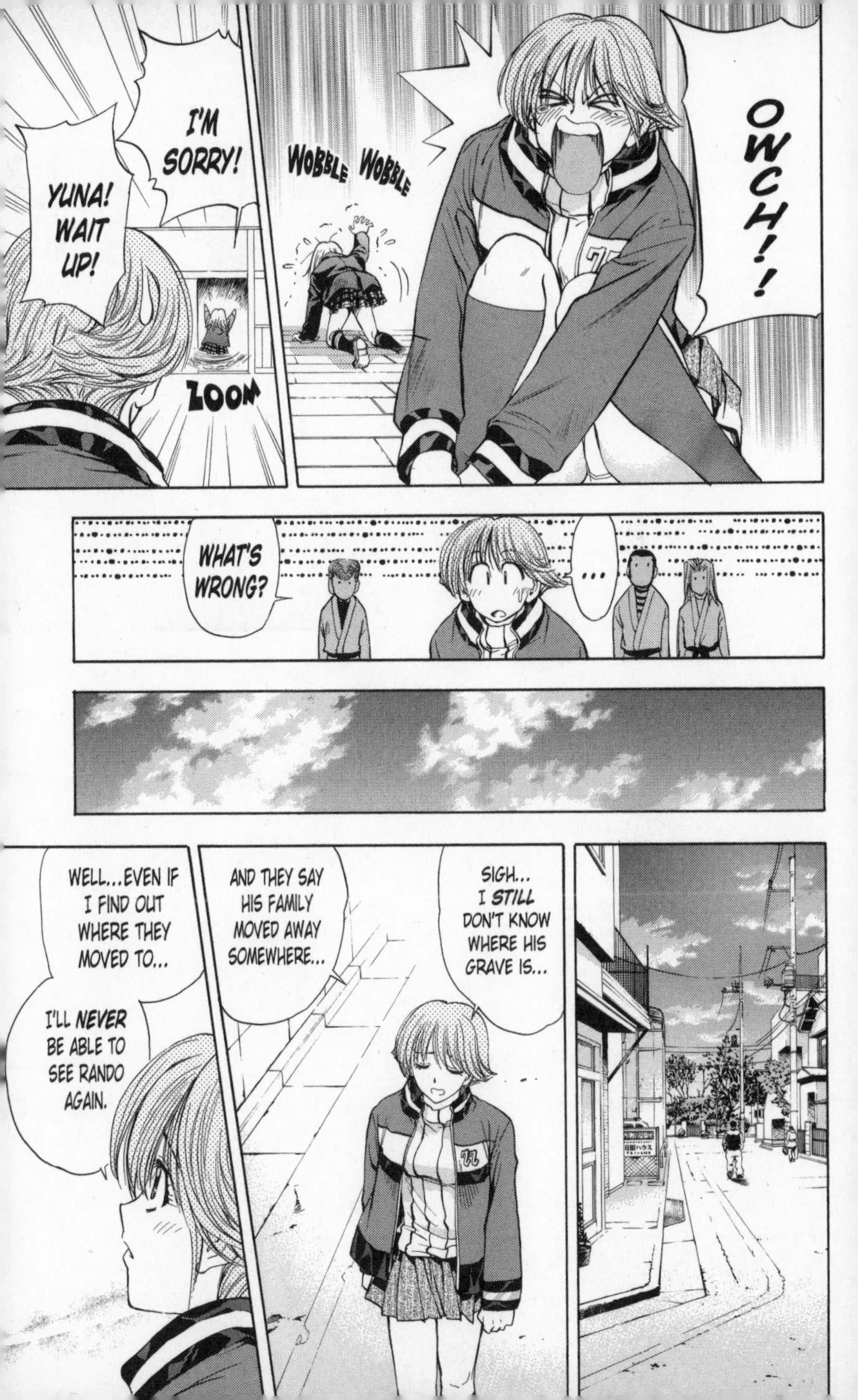
OWCH!!
WOBBLE WOBBLE
I'M SORRY!
YUNA! WAIT UP!
ZOOM
...
WHAT'S WRONG?
SIGH... I *STILL* DON'T KNOW WHERE HIS GRAVE IS...
AND THEY SAY HIS FAMILY MOVED AWAY SOMEWHERE...
WELL...EVEN IF I FIND OUT WHERE THEY MOVED TO...
I'LL *NEVER* BE ABLE TO SEE RANDO AGAIN.

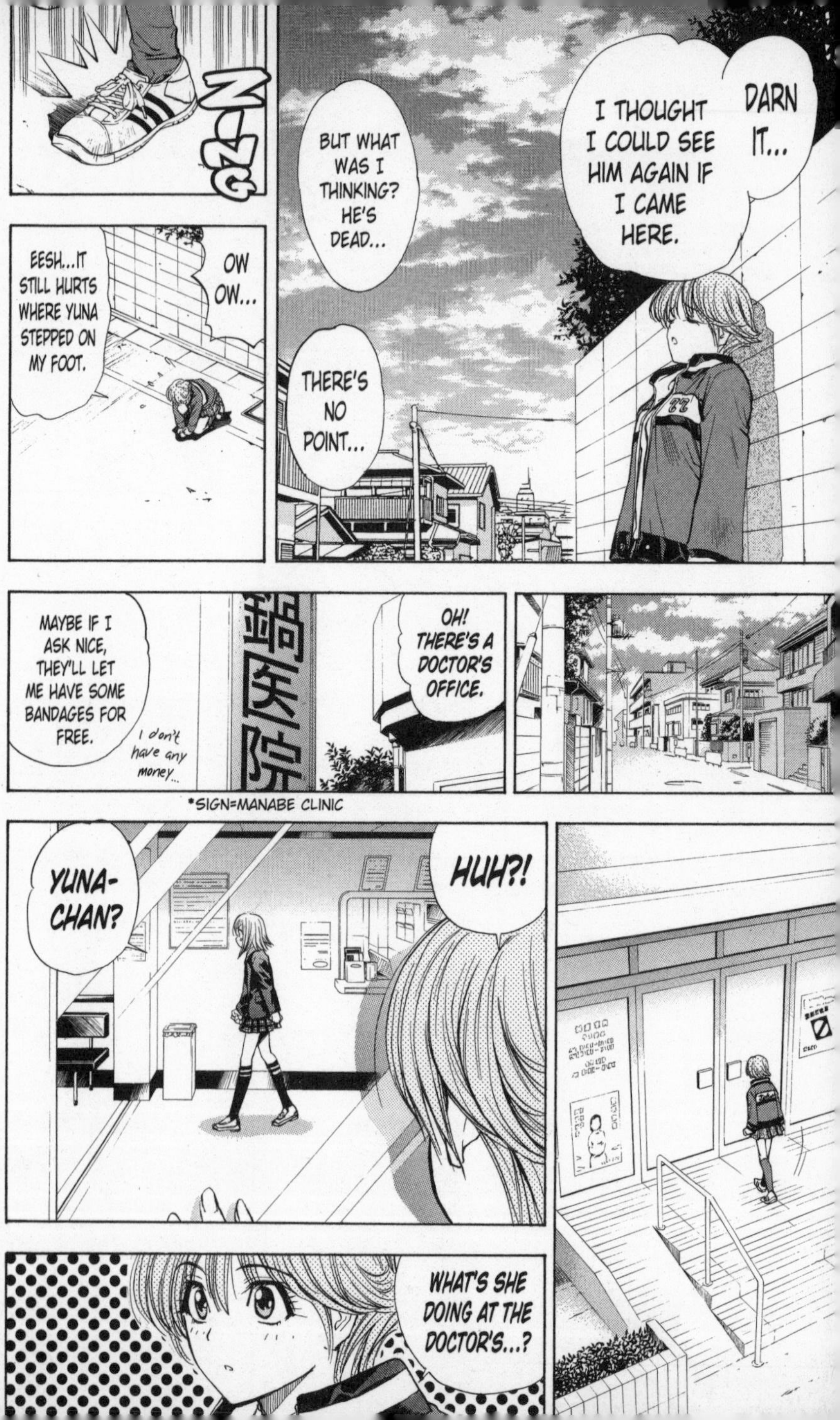
DARN IT...
I THOUGHT I COULD SEE HIM AGAIN IF I CAME HERE.
BUT WHAT WAS I THINKING? HE'S DEAD...
THERE'S NO POINT...
ZING
OW OW...
EESH...IT STILL HURTS WHERE YUNA STEPPED ON MY FOOT.
OH! THERE'S A DOCTOR'S OFFICE.
鍋医院
MAYBE IF I ASK NICE, THEY'LL LET ME HAVE SOME BANDAGES FOR FREE.
I don't have any money...
HUH?!
YUNA-CHAN?
WHAT'S SHE DOING AT THE DOCTOR'S...?
*SIGN=MANABE CLINIC

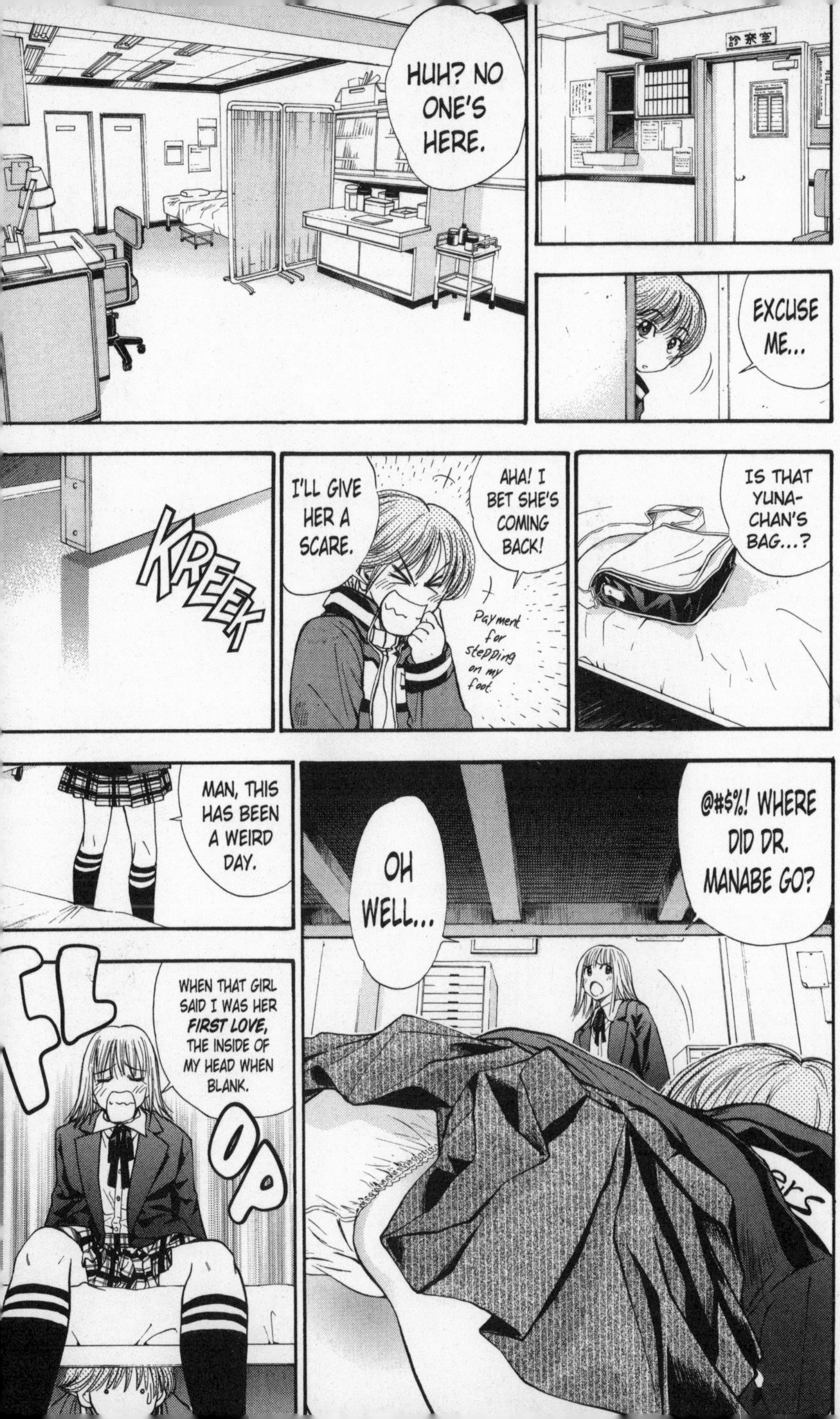
EXCUSE ME...
HUH? NO ONE'S HERE.
IS THAT YUNA-CHAN'S BAG...?
AHA! I BET SHE'S COMING BACK!
I'LL GIVE HER A SCARE.
Payment for stepping on my foot.
KREEK
@#$%! WHERE DID DR. MANABE GO?
OH WELL...
MAN, THIS HAS BEEN A WEIRD DAY.
WHEN THAT GIRL SAID I WAS HER **FIRST LOVE,** THE INSIDE OF MY HEAD WHEN BLANK.
FLOP

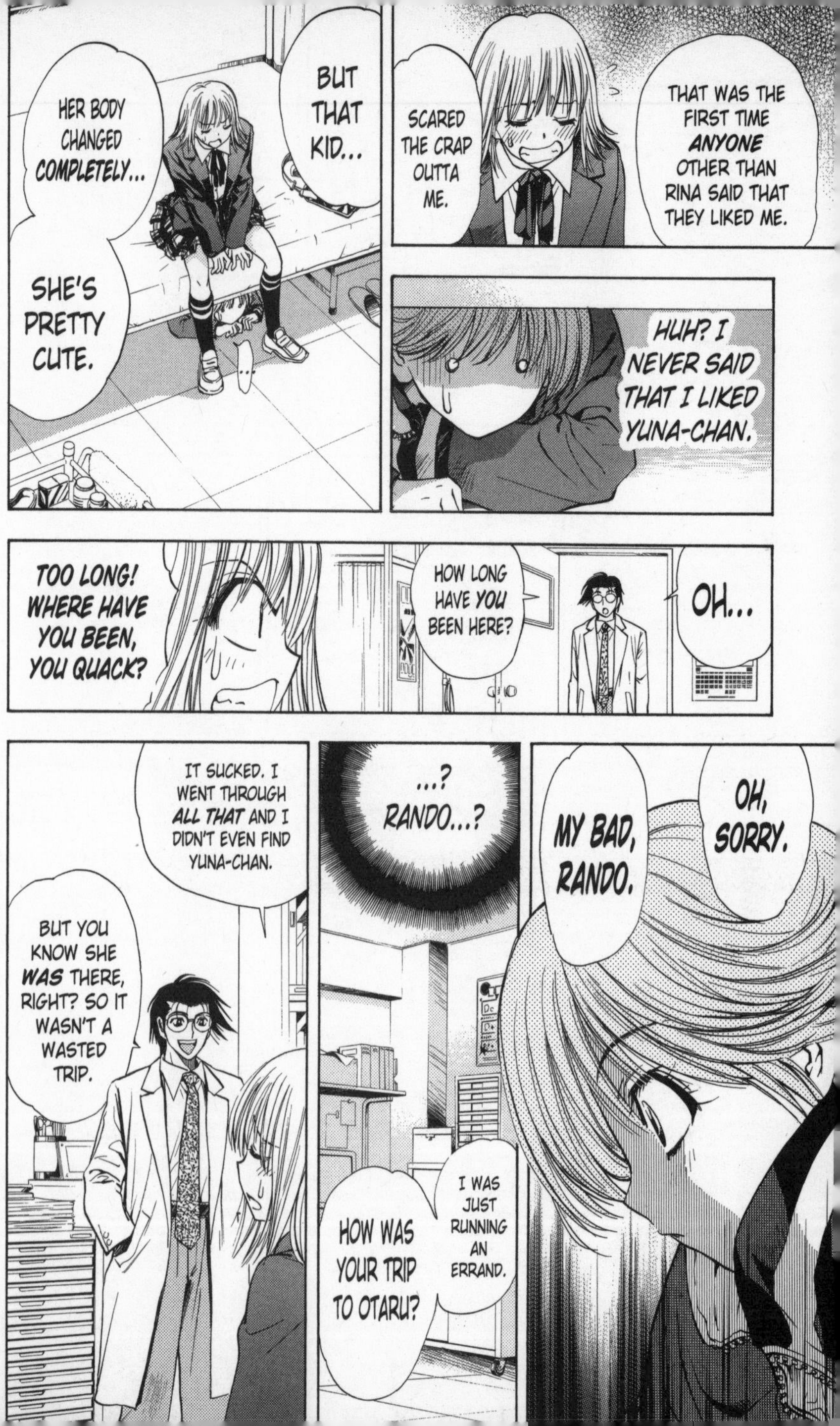
THAT WAS THE FIRST TIME ANYONE OTHER THAN RINA SAID THAT THEY LIKED ME.
SCARED THE CRAP OUTTA ME.
HUH? I NEVER SAID THAT I LIKED YUNA-CHAN.
BUT THAT KID...
HER BODY CHANGED COMPLETELY...
SHE'S PRETTY CUTE.
...
OH...
HOW LONG HAVE YOU BEEN HERE?
TOO LONG! WHERE HAVE YOU BEEN, YOU QUACK?
OH, SORRY.
MY BAD, RANDO.
...? RANDO...?
I WAS JUST RUNNING AN ERRAND.
HOW WAS YOUR TRIP TO OTARU?
IT SUCKED. I WENT THROUGH ALL THAT AND I DIDN'T EVEN FIND YUNA-CHAN.
BUT YOU KNOW SHE WAS THERE, RIGHT? SO IT WASN'T A WASTED TRIP.

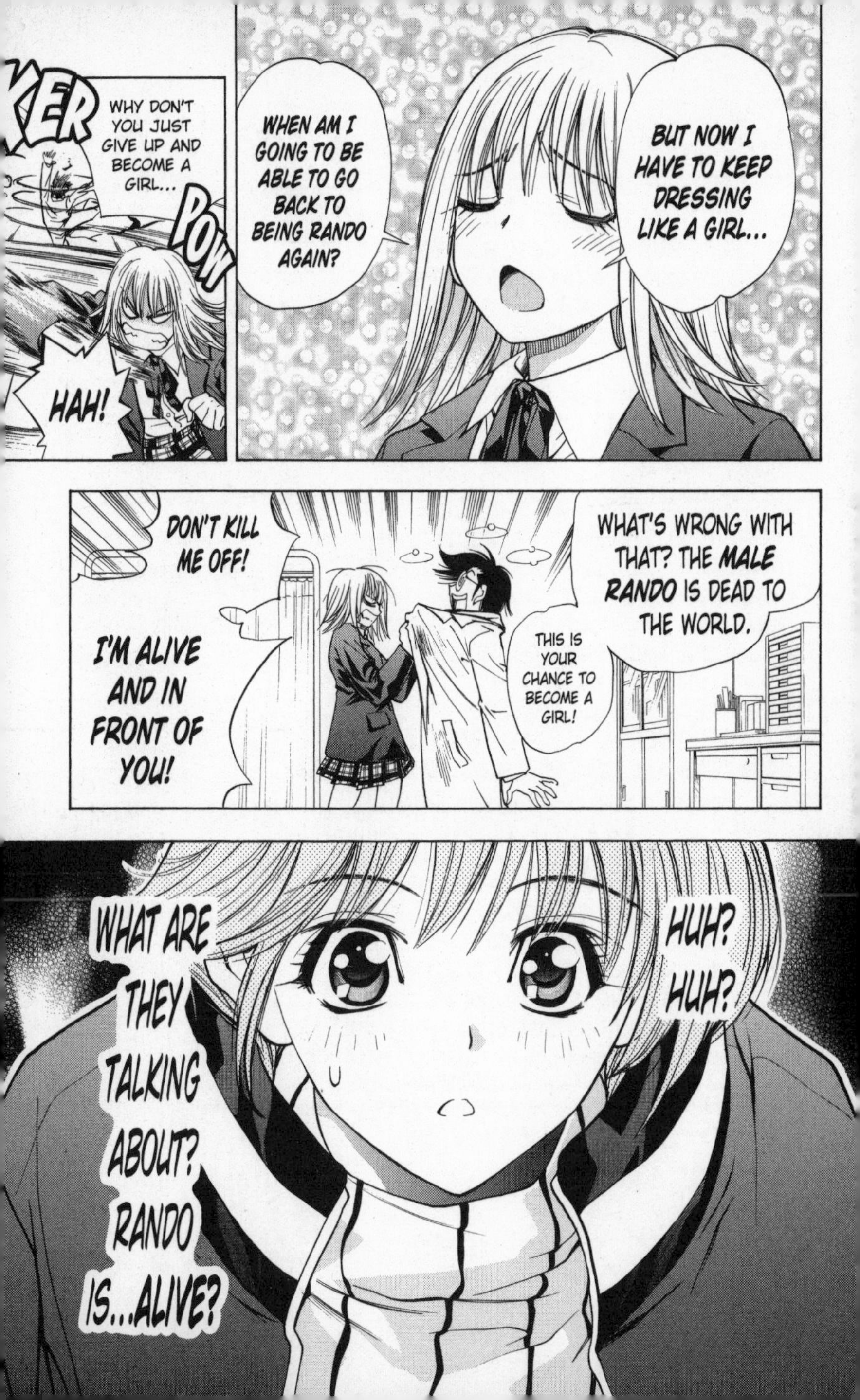
BUT NOW I HAVE TO KEEP DRESSING LIKE A GIRL...
WHEN AM I GOING TO BE ABLE TO GO BACK TO BEING RANDO AGAIN?
KER
WHY DON'T YOU JUST GIVE UP AND BECOME A GIRL...
POW
HAH!
WHAT'S WRONG WITH THAT? THE MALE RANDO IS DEAD TO THE WORLD.
THIS IS YOUR CHANCE TO BECOME A GIRL!
DON'T KILL ME OFF!
I'M ALIVE AND IN FRONT OF YOU!
HUH? HUH?
WHAT ARE THEY TALKING ABOUT? RANDO IS...ALIVE?

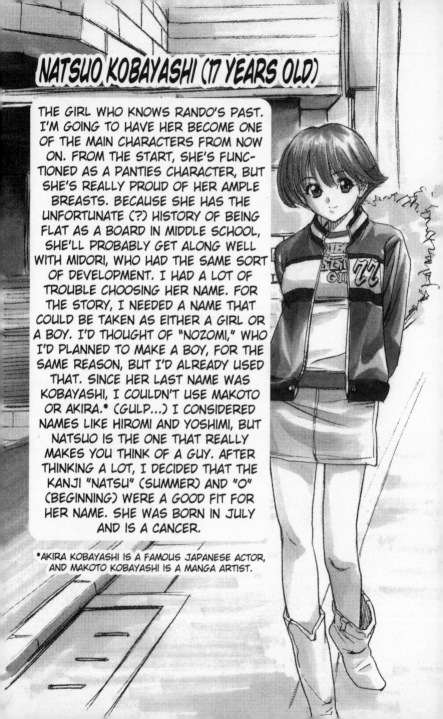

NATSUO KOBAYASHI (17 YEARS OLD)

THE GIRL WHO KNOWS RANDO'S PAST. I'M GOING TO HAVE HER BECOME ONE OF THE MAIN CHARACTERS FROM NOW ON. FROM THE START, SHE'S FUNCTIONED AS A PANTIES CHARACTER, BUT SHE'S REALLY PROUD OF HER AMPLE BREASTS. BECAUSE SHE HAS THE UNFORTUNATE (?) HISTORY OF BEING FLAT AS A BOARD IN MIDDLE SCHOOL, SHE'LL PROBABLY GET ALONG WELL WITH MIDORI, WHO HAD THE SAME SORT OF DEVELOPMENT. I HAD A LOT OF TROUBLE CHOOSING HER NAME. FOR THE STORY, I NEEDED A NAME THAT COULD BE TAKEN AS EITHER A GIRL OR A BOY. I'D THOUGHT OF "NOZOMI," WHO I'D PLANNED TO MAKE A BOY, FOR THE SAME REASON, BUT I'D ALREADY USED THAT. SINCE HER LAST NAME WAS KOBAYASHI, I COULDN'T USE MAKOTO OR AKIRA.* (GULP...) I CONSIDERED NAMES LIKE HIROMI AND YOSHIMI, BUT NATSUO IS THE ONE THAT REALLY MAKES YOU THINK OF A GUY. AFTER THINKING A LOT, I DECIDED THAT THE KANJI "NATSU" (SUMMER) AND "O" (BEGINNING) WERE A GOOD FIT FOR HER NAME. SHE WAS BORN IN JULY AND IS A CANCER.

*AKIRA KOBAYASHI IS A FAMOUS JAPANESE ACTOR, AND MAKOTO KOBAYASHI IS A MANGA ARTIST.

Chapter 36: Natsuo Overdrive!

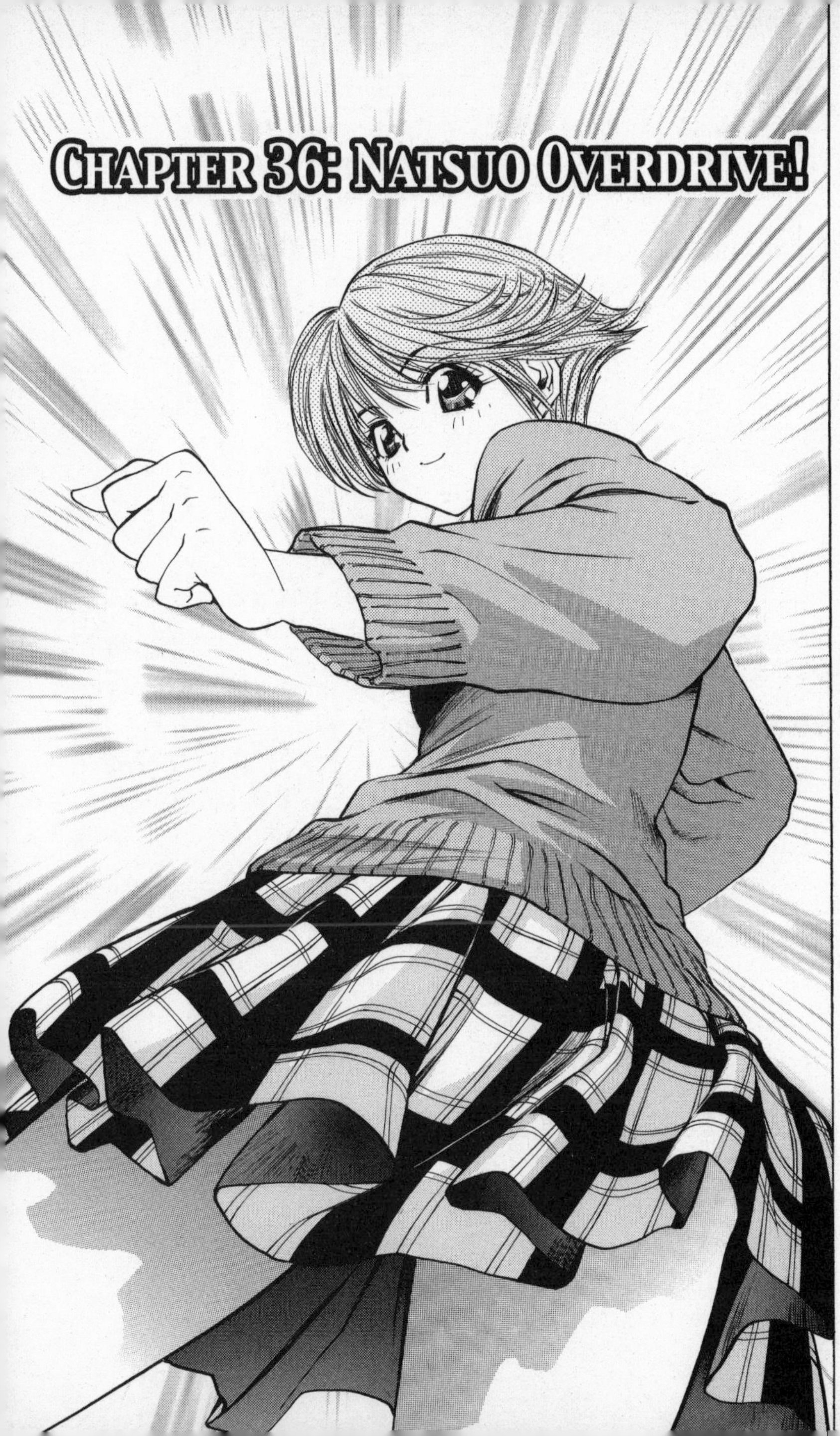

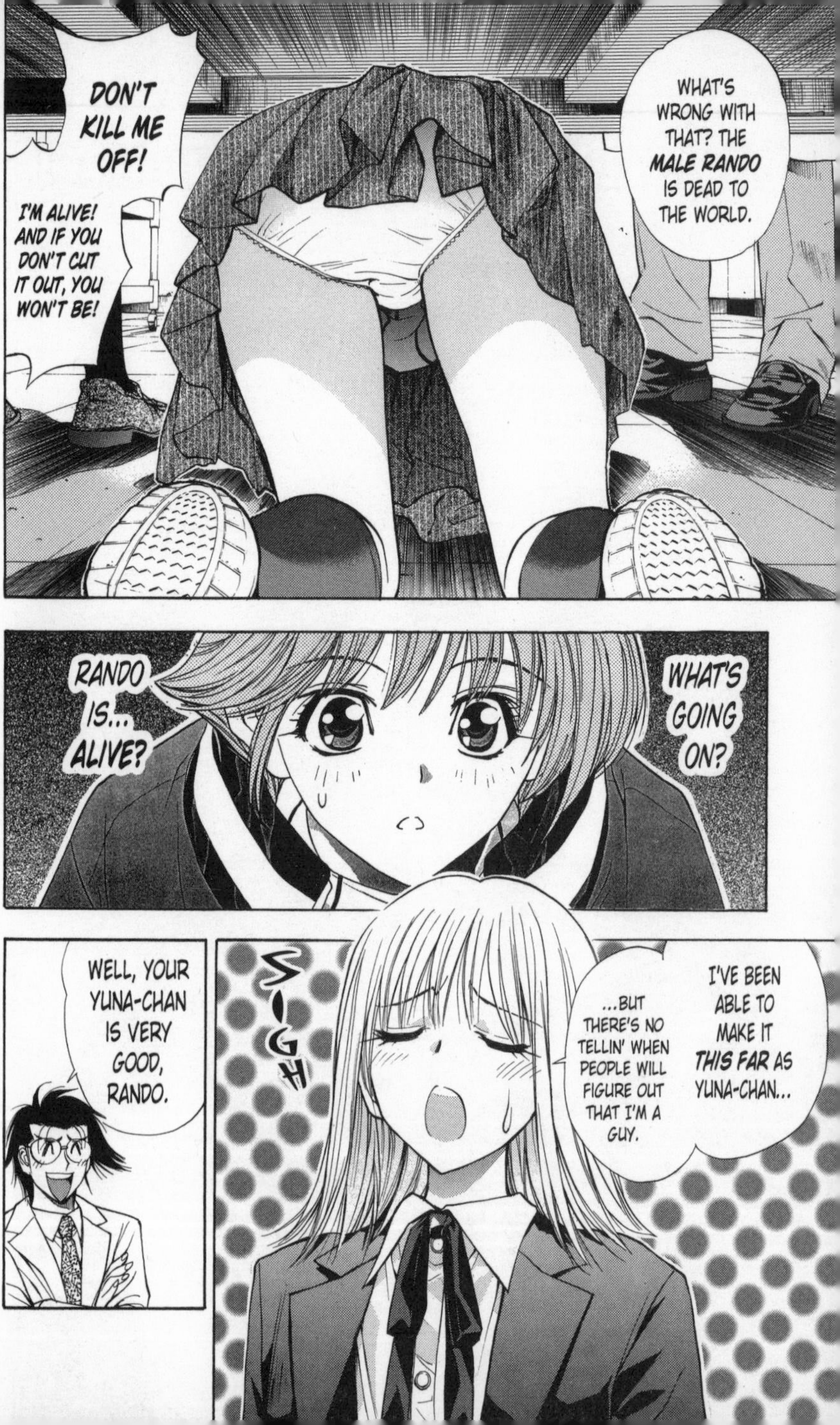
WHAT'S WRONG WITH THAT? THE MALE RANDO IS DEAD TO THE WORLD.
DON'T KILL ME OFF!
I'M ALIVE! AND IF YOU DON'T CUT IT OUT, YOU WON'T BE!
WHAT'S GOING ON?
RANDO IS... ALIVE?
I'VE BEEN ABLE TO MAKE IT THIS FAR AS YUNA-CHAN...
...BUT THERE'S NO TELLIN' WHEN PEOPLE WILL FIGURE OUT THAT I'M A GUY.
SIGH
WELL, YOUR YUNA-CHAN IS VERY GOOD, RANDO.

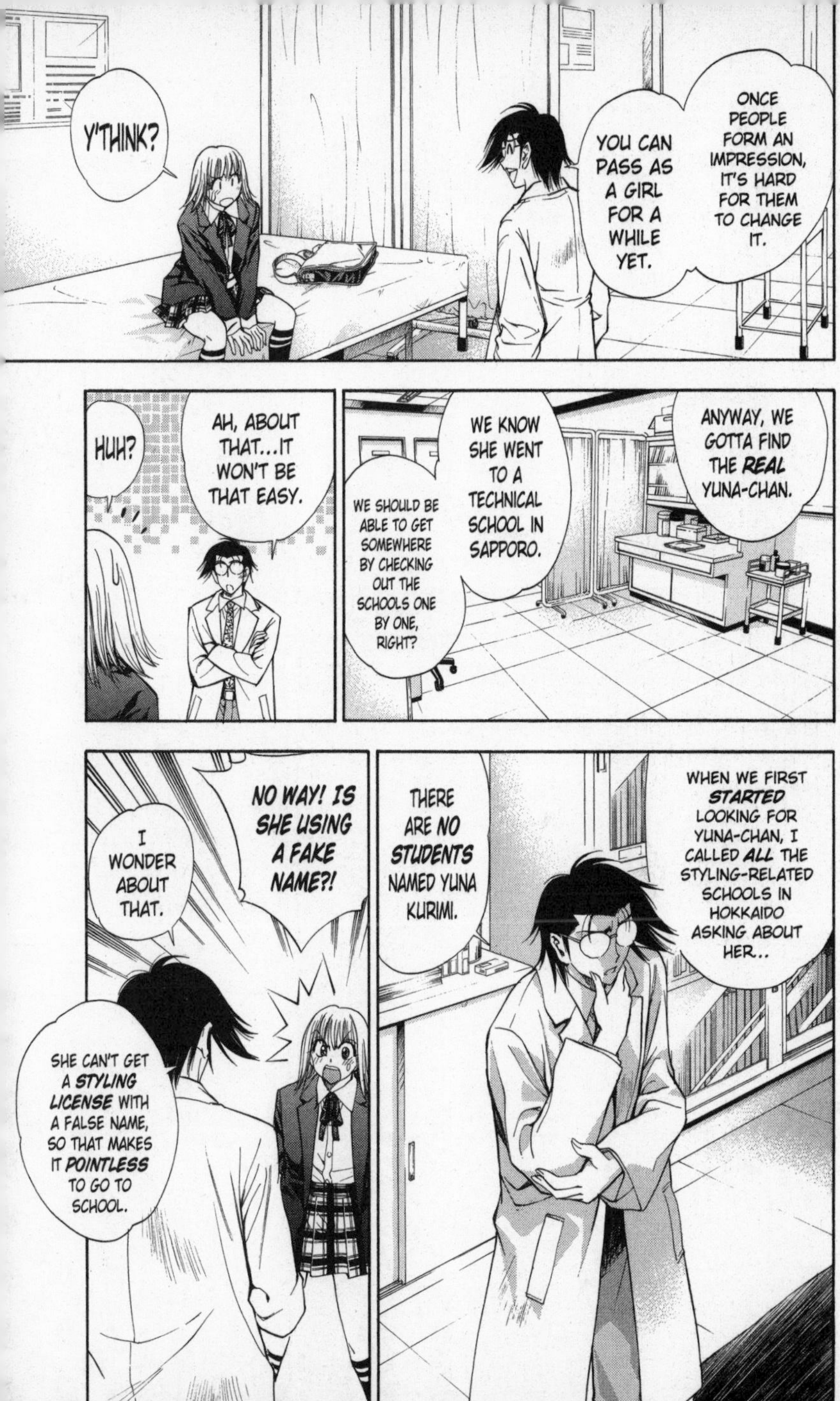
ONCE PEOPLE FORM AN IMPRESSION, IT'S HARD FOR THEM TO CHANGE IT.
YOU CAN PASS AS A GIRL FOR A WHILE YET.
Y'THINK?
ANYWAY, WE GOTTA FIND THE **REAL** YUNA-CHAN.
WE KNOW SHE WENT TO A TECHNICAL SCHOOL IN SAPPORO.
WE SHOULD BE ABLE TO GET SOMEWHERE BY CHECKING OUT THE SCHOOLS ONE BY ONE, RIGHT?
AH, ABOUT THAT...IT WON'T BE THAT EASY.
HUH?
WHEN WE FIRST **STARTED** LOOKING FOR YUNA-CHAN, I CALLED **ALL** THE STYLING-RELATED SCHOOLS IN HOKKAIDO ASKING ABOUT HER...
THERE ARE **NO STUDENTS** NAMED YUNA KURIMI.
NO WAY! IS SHE USING A FAKE NAME?!
I WONDER ABOUT THAT.
SHE CAN'T GET A **STYLING LICENSE** WITH A FALSE NAME, SO THAT MAKES IT **POINTLESS** TO GO TO SCHOOL.

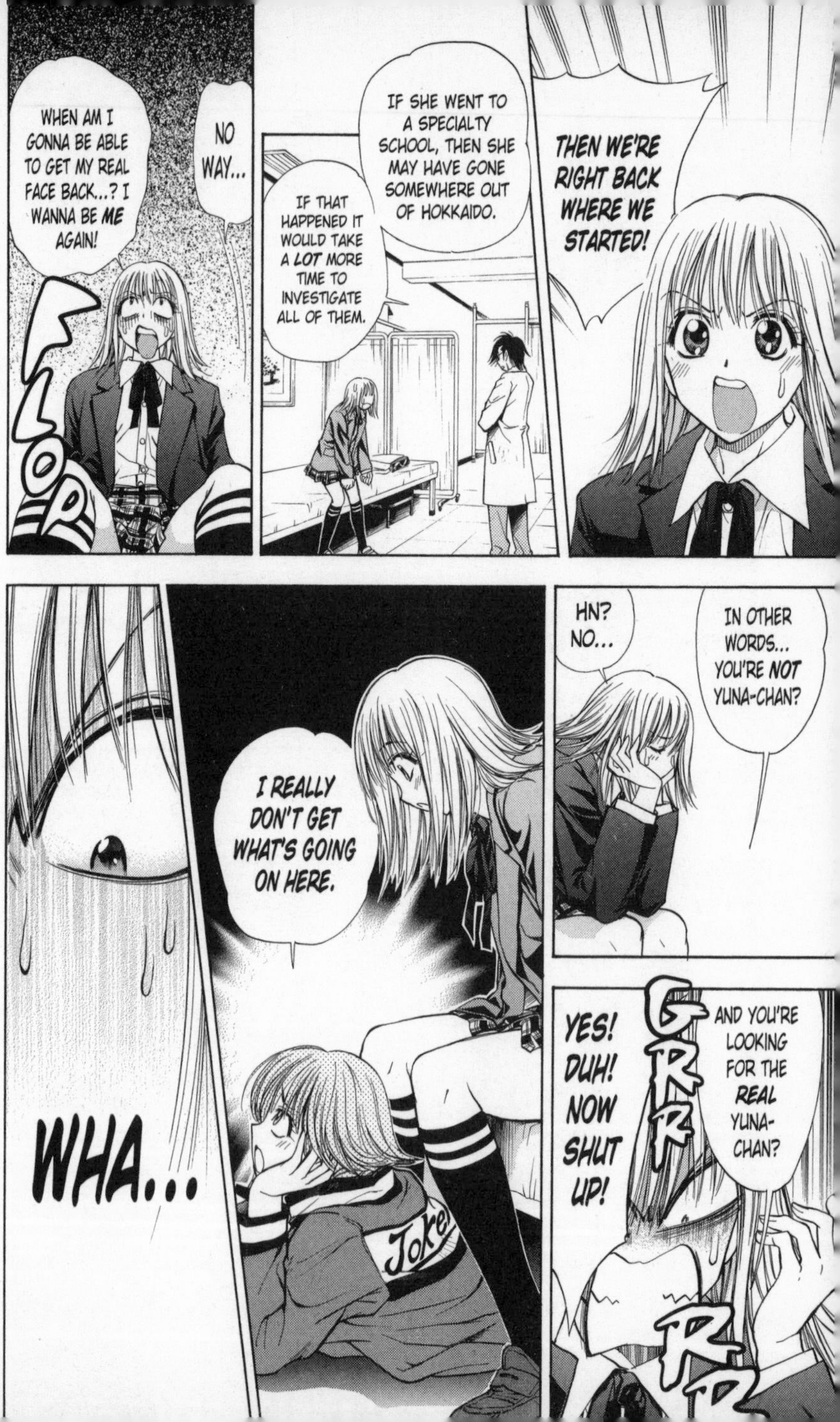
THEN WE'RE RIGHT BACK WHERE WE STARTED!
IF SHE WENT TO A SPECIALTY SCHOOL, THEN SHE MAY HAVE GONE SOMEWHERE OUT OF HOKKAIDO.
IF THAT HAPPENED IT WOULD TAKE A *LOT* MORE TIME TO INVESTIGATE ALL OF THEM.
NO WAY...
WHEN AM I GONNA BE ABLE TO GET MY REAL FACE BACK...? I WANNA BE *ME* AGAIN!
FLOP
IN OTHER WORDS... YOU'RE *NOT* YUNA-CHAN?
HN? NO...
AND YOU'RE LOOKING FOR THE *REAL* YUNA-CHAN?
GRR
YES! DUH! NOW SHUT UP!
RRR
I REALLY DON'T GET WHAT'S GOING ON HERE.
Joker
WHA...

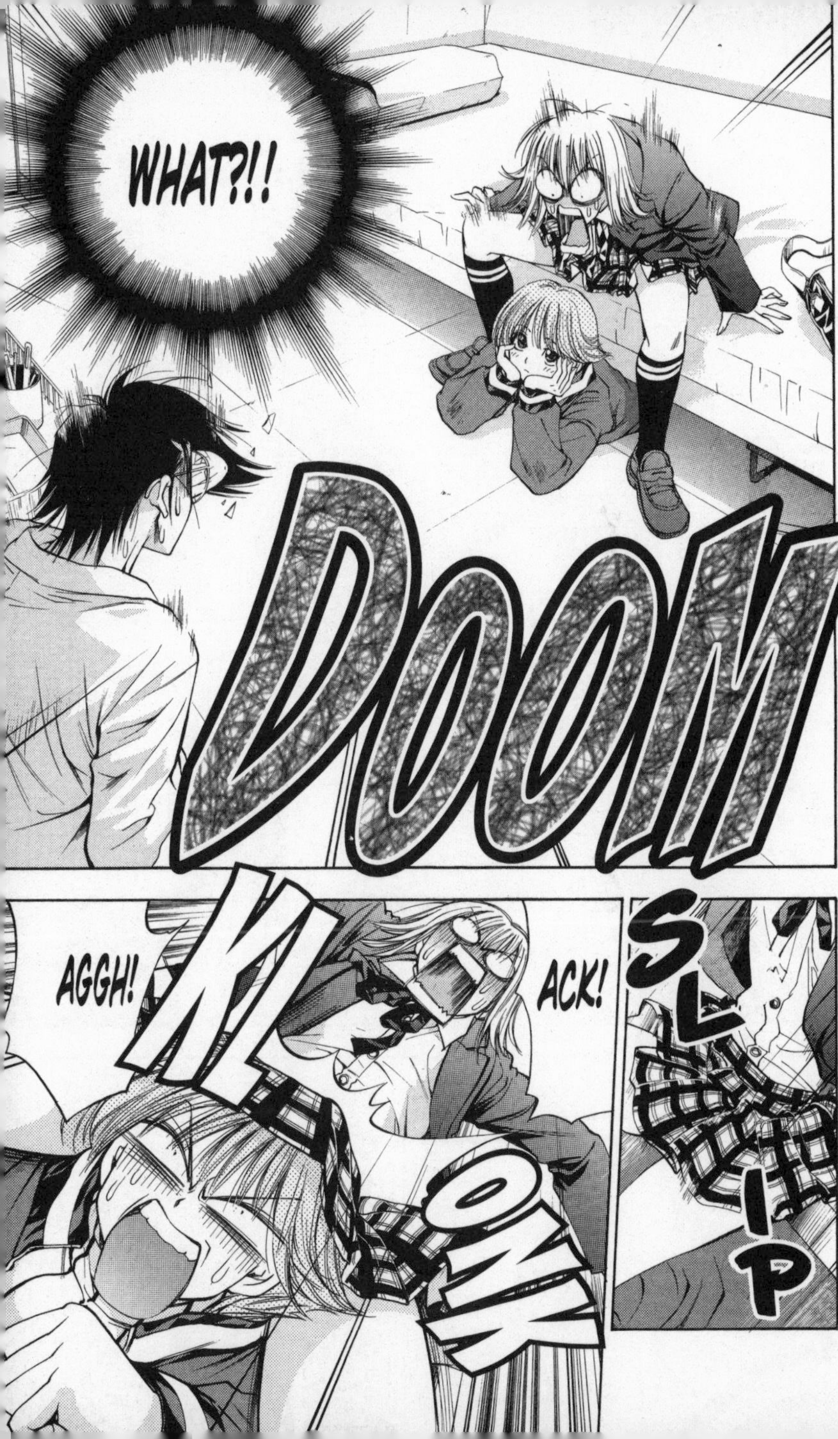
WHAT?!!
DOOM
SLIP
ACK!
WONK
AGGH!

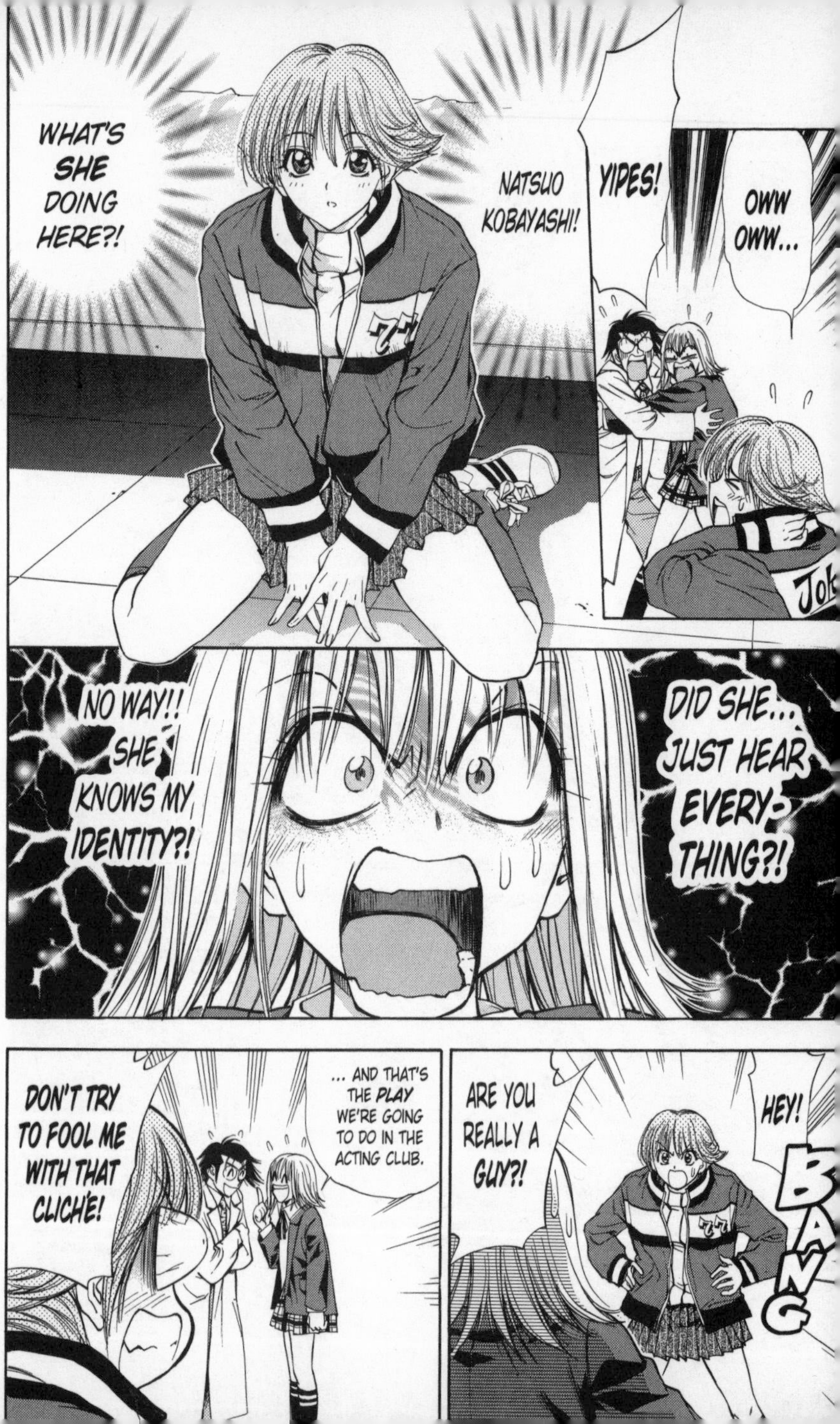
OWW OWW...
YIPES!
NATSUO KOBAYASHI!
WHAT'S SHE DOING HERE?!
DID SHE... JUST HEAR EVERY-THING?!
NO WAY!! SHE KNOWS MY IDENTITY?!
HEY!
BANG
ARE YOU REALLY A GUY?!
... AND THAT'S THE PLAY WE'RE GOING TO DO IN THE ACTING CLUB.
DON'T TRY TO FOOL ME WITH THAT CLICHÉ!

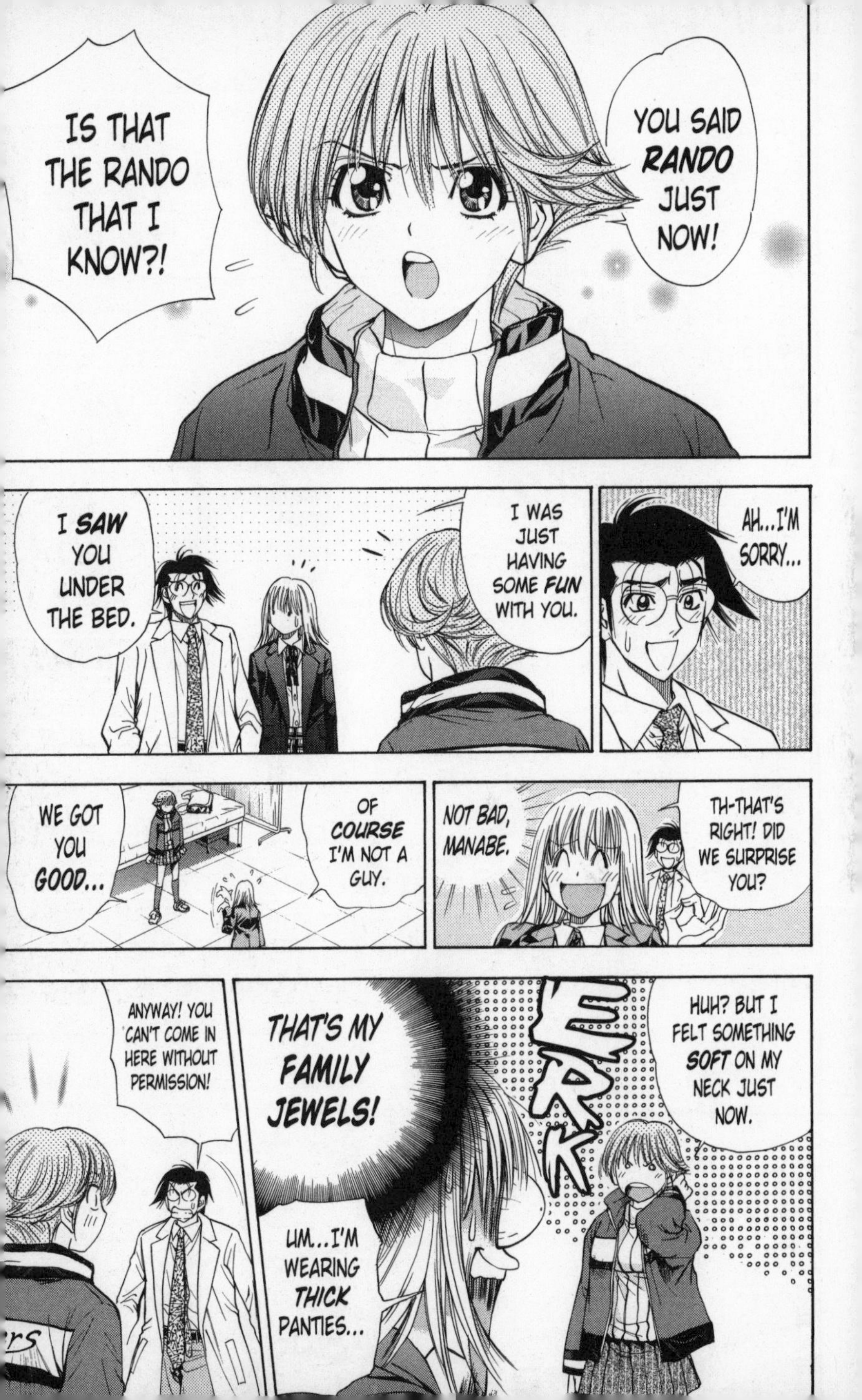
YOU SAID RANDO JUST NOW!
IS THAT THE RANDO THAT I KNOW?!
AH...I'M SORRY...
I WAS JUST HAVING SOME FUN WITH YOU.
I SAW YOU UNDER THE BED.
TH-THAT'S RIGHT! DID WE SURPRISE YOU?
NOT BAD, MANABE.
OF COURSE I'M NOT A GUY.
WE GOT YOU GOOD...
HUH? BUT I FELT SOMETHING SOFT ON MY NECK JUST NOW.
ERK
THAT'S MY FAMILY JEWELS!
UM...I'M WEARING THICK PANTIES...
ANYWAY! YOU CAN'T COME IN HERE WITHOUT PERMISSION!

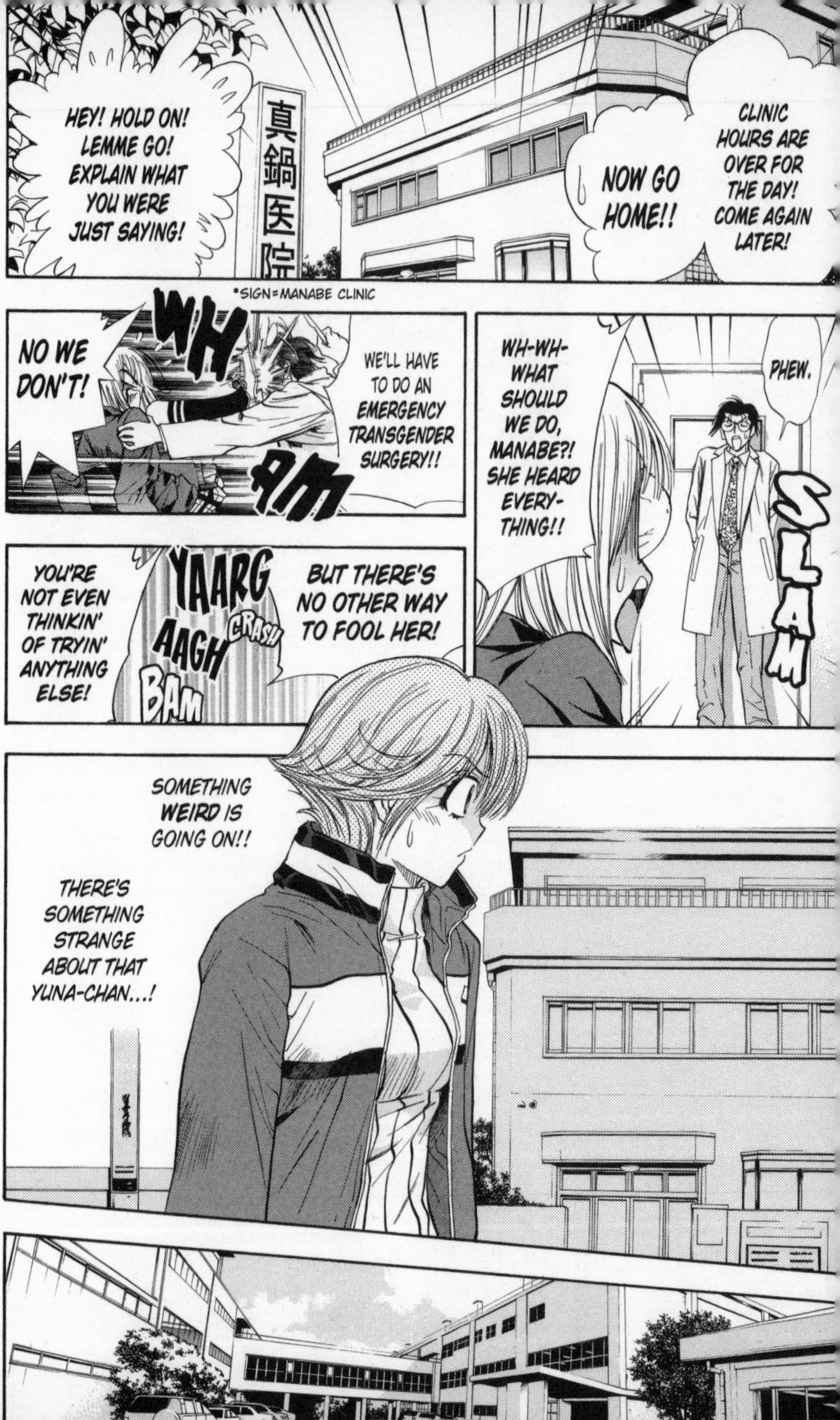

CLINIC HOURS ARE OVER FOR THE DAY! COME AGAIN LATER!
NOW GO HOME!!
HEY! HOLD ON! LEMME GO! EXPLAIN WHAT YOU WERE JUST SAYING!
真鍋医院
*SIGN=MANABE CLINIC
PHEW.
SLAM
WH-WH-WHAT SHOULD WE DO, MANABE?! SHE HEARD EVERY-THING!!
WE'LL HAVE TO DO AN EMERGENCY TRANSGENDER SURGERY!!
WHAM
NO WE DON'T!
BUT THERE'S NO OTHER WAY TO FOOL HER!
YAARG
AAGH
CRASH
BAM
YOU'RE NOT EVEN THINKIN' OF TRYIN' ANYTHING ELSE!
SOMETHING WEIRD IS GOING ON!!
THERE'S SOMETHING STRANGE ABOUT THAT YUNA-CHAN...!

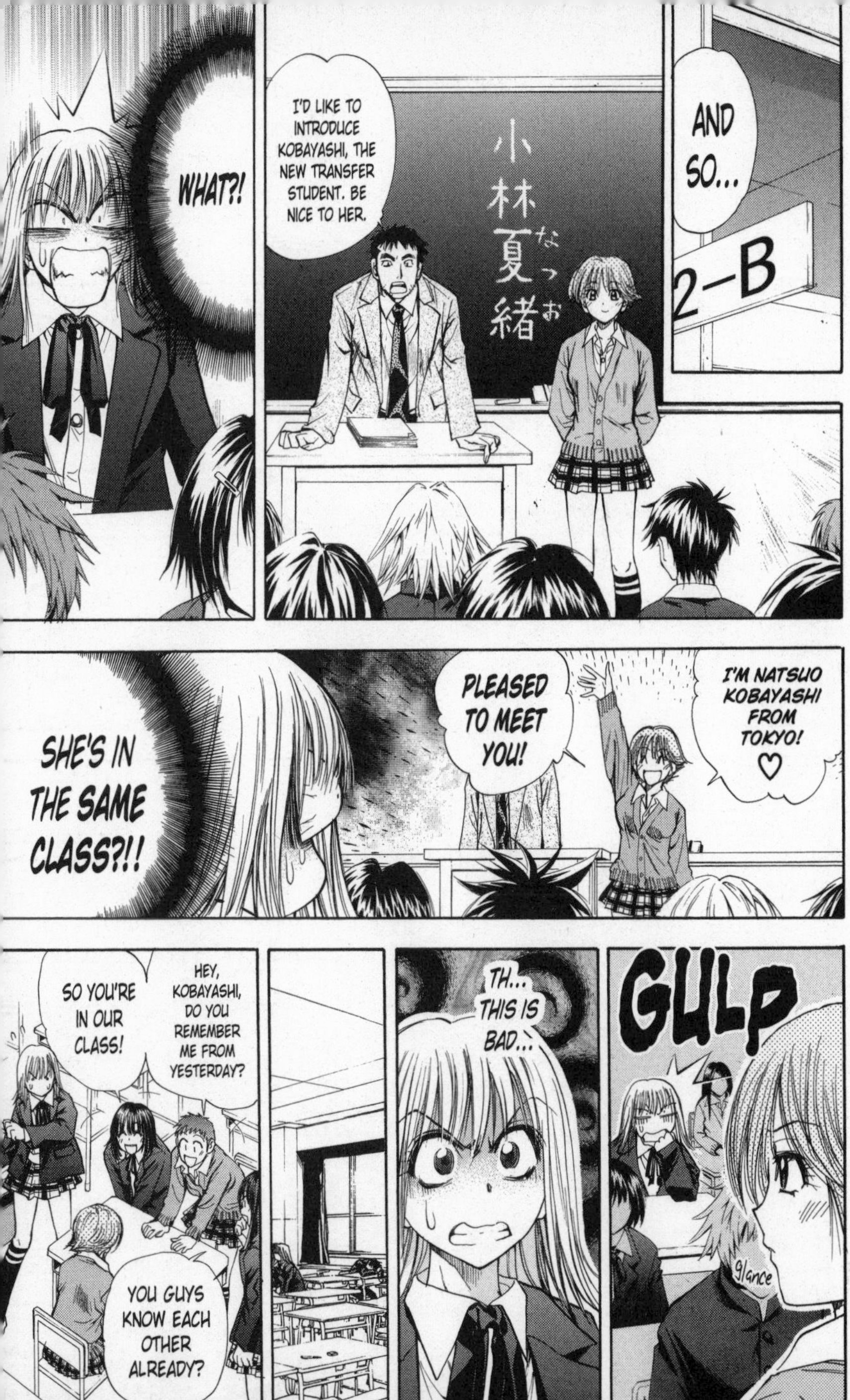
AND SO...
2-B
I'D LIKE TO INTRODUCE KOBAYASHI, THE NEW TRANSFER STUDENT. BE NICE TO HER.
小林夏緒
なつお
WHAT?!
I'M NATSUO KOBAYASHI FROM TOKYO! ♡
PLEASED TO MEET YOU!
SHE'S IN THE SAME CLASS?!!
GULP
glance
TH... THIS IS BAD...
HEY, KOBAYASHI, DO YOU REMEMBER ME FROM YESTERDAY?
SO YOU'RE IN OUR CLASS!
YOU GUYS KNOW EACH OTHER ALREADY?

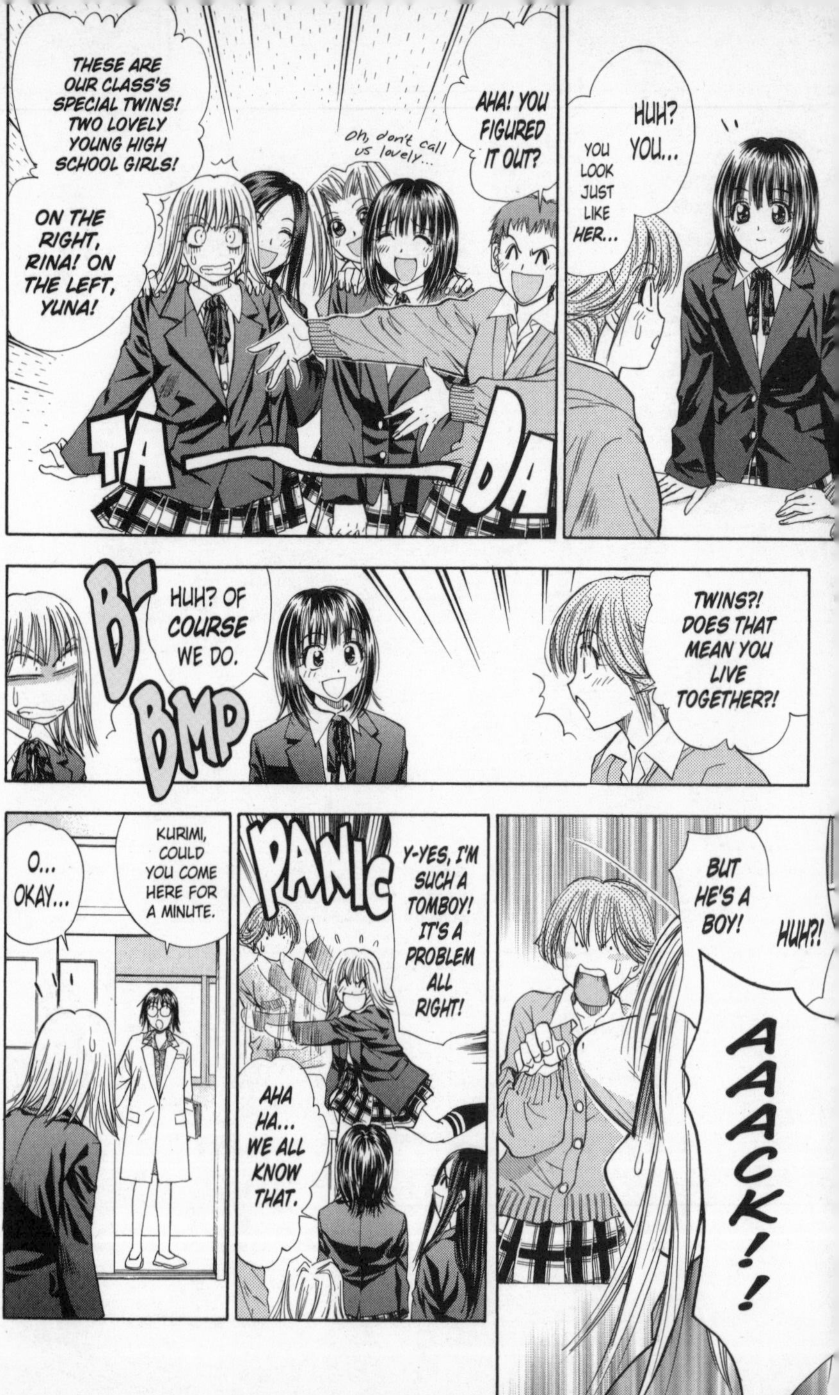
HUH? YOU...
YOU LOOK JUST LIKE HER...
AHA! YOU FIGURED IT OUT?
Oh, don't call us lovely...
THESE ARE OUR CLASS'S SPECIAL TWINS! TWO LOVELY YOUNG HIGH SCHOOL GIRLS!
ON THE RIGHT, RINA! ON THE LEFT, YUNA!
TA—DA
TWINS?! DOES THAT MEAN YOU LIVE TOGETHER?!
HUH? OF COURSE WE DO.
B-BMP
BUT HE'S A BOY!
HUH?!
AAACK!!
Y-YES, I'M SUCH A TOMBOY! IT'S A PROBLEM ALL RIGHT!
PANIC
AHA HA... WE ALL KNOW THAT.
KURIMI, COULD YOU COME HERE FOR A MINUTE.
O... OKAY...

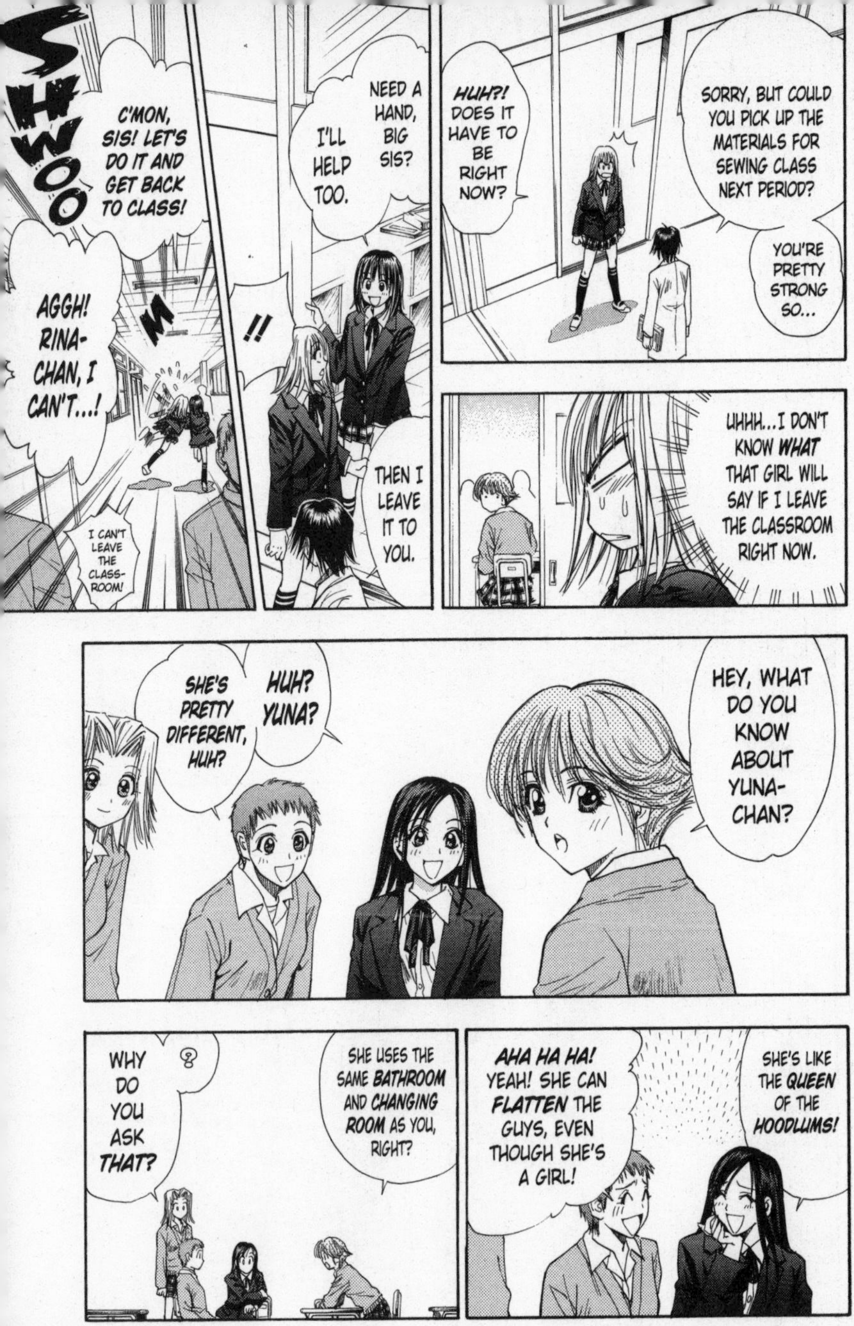
SORRY, BUT COULD YOU PICK UP THE MATERIALS FOR SEWING CLASS NEXT PERIOD?
YOU'RE PRETTY STRONG SO...
HUH?! DOES IT HAVE TO BE RIGHT NOW?
UHHH...I DON'T KNOW WHAT THAT GIRL WILL SAY IF I LEAVE THE CLASSROOM RIGHT NOW.
NEED A HAND, BIG SIS?
I'LL HELP TOO.
!!
THEN I LEAVE IT TO YOU.
SHWOO
C'MON, SIS! LET'S DO IT AND GET BACK TO CLASS!
M
AGGH! RINA-CHAN, I CAN'T...!
I CAN'T LEAVE THE CLASSROOM!
HEY, WHAT DO YOU KNOW ABOUT YUNA-CHAN?
HUH? YUNA?
SHE'S PRETTY DIFFERENT, HUH?
SHE'S LIKE THE QUEEN OF THE HOODLUMS!
AHA HA HA! YEAH! SHE CAN FLATTEN THE GUYS, EVEN THOUGH SHE'S A GIRL!
SHE USES THE SAME BATHROOM AND CHANGING ROOM AS YOU, RIGHT?
?
WHY DO YOU ASK THAT?

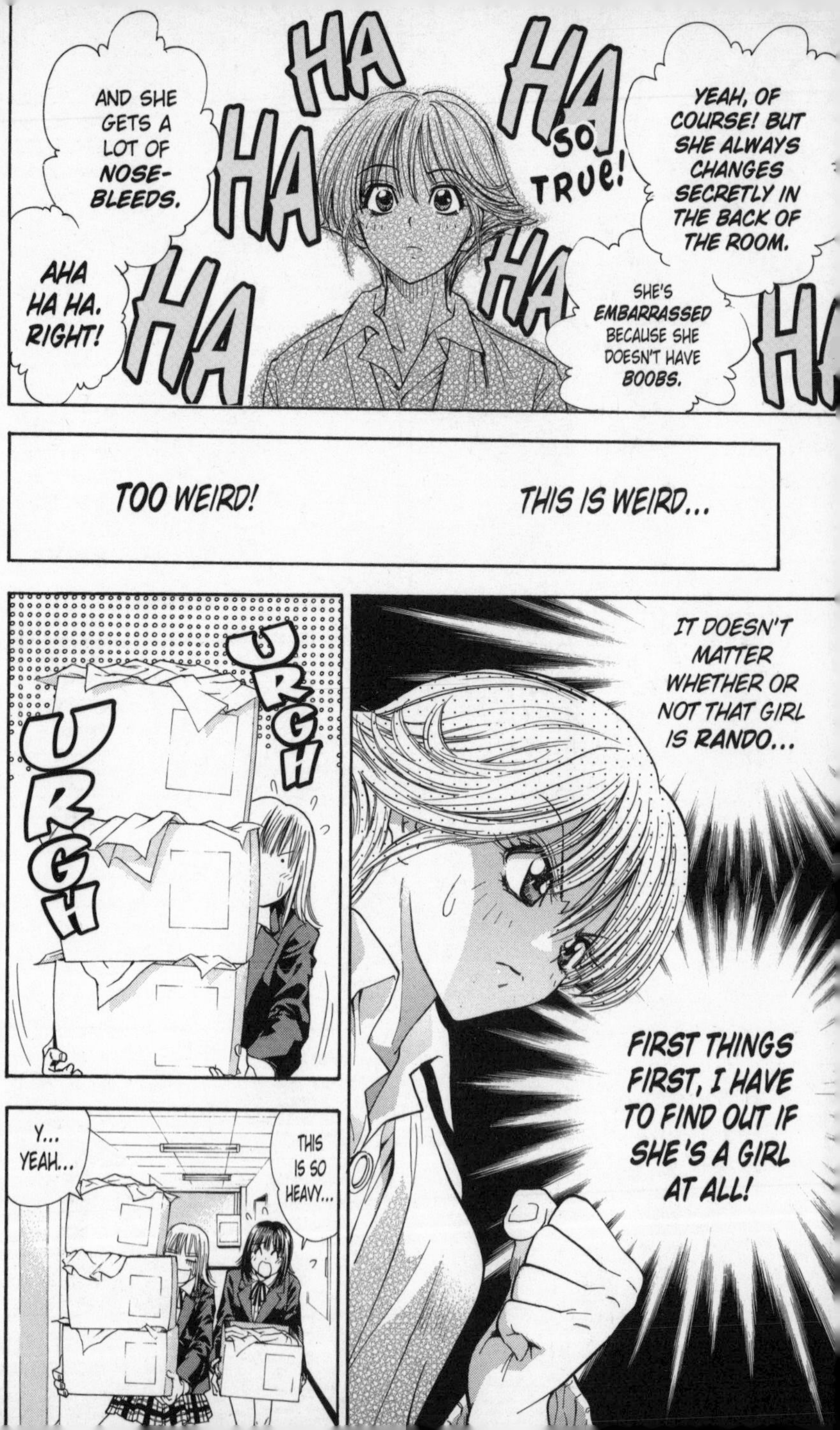
YEAH, OF COURSE! BUT SHE ALWAYS CHANGES SECRETLY IN THE BACK OF THE ROOM.
SO TRUE!
HA HA HA
SHE'S EMBARRASSED BECAUSE SHE DOESN'T HAVE BOOBS.
HA HA HA
AND SHE GETS A LOT OF NOSE-BLEEDS.
AHA HA HA. RIGHT!
THIS IS WEIRD...
TOO WEIRD!
IT DOESN'T MATTER WHETHER OR NOT THAT GIRL IS RANDO...
FIRST THINGS FIRST, I HAVE TO FIND OUT IF SHE'S A GIRL AT ALL!
URGH
URGH
THIS IS SO HEAVY...
Y... YEAH...

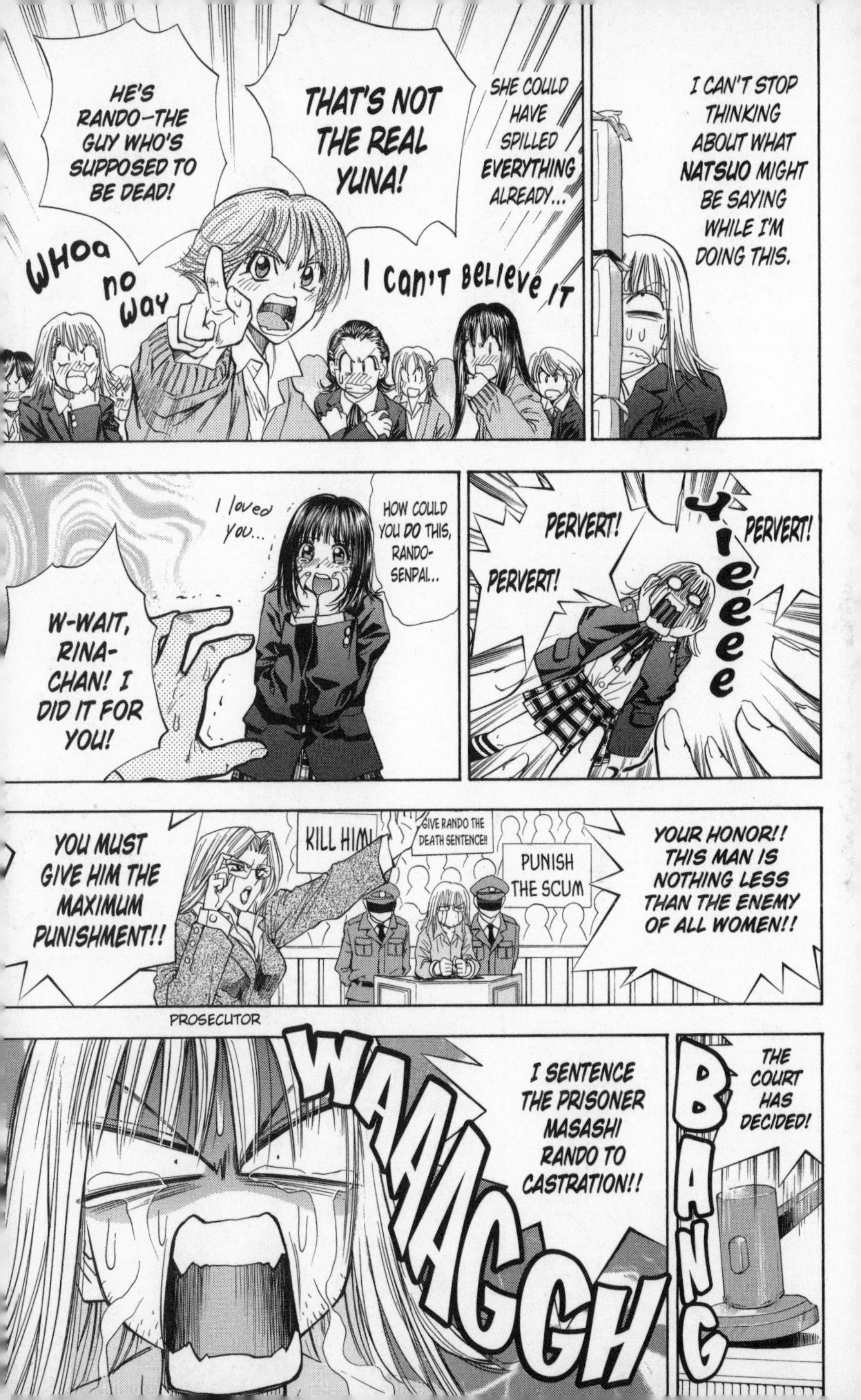
I CAN'T STOP THINKING ABOUT WHAT NATSUO MIGHT BE SAYING WHILE I'M DOING THIS.
SHE COULD HAVE SPILLED EVERYTHING ALREADY...
THAT'S NOT THE REAL YUNA!
HE'S RANDO—THE GUY WHO'S SUPPOSED TO BE DEAD!
I can't believe it
WHOa no way
PERVERT!
Yieeeee
PERVERT!
PERVERT!
HOW COULD YOU DO THIS, RANDO-SENPAI...
I loved you...
W-WAIT, RINA-CHAN! I DID IT FOR YOU!
YOUR HONOR!! THIS MAN IS NOTHING LESS THAN THE ENEMY OF ALL WOMEN!!
PUNISH THE SCUM
GIVE RANDO THE DEATH SENTENCE!!
KILL HIM!
YOU MUST GIVE HIM THE MAXIMUM PUNISHMENT!!
PROSECUTOR
THE COURT HAS DECIDED!
BANG
I SENTENCE THE PRISONER MASASHI RANDO TO CASTRATION!!
WAAAAGGH

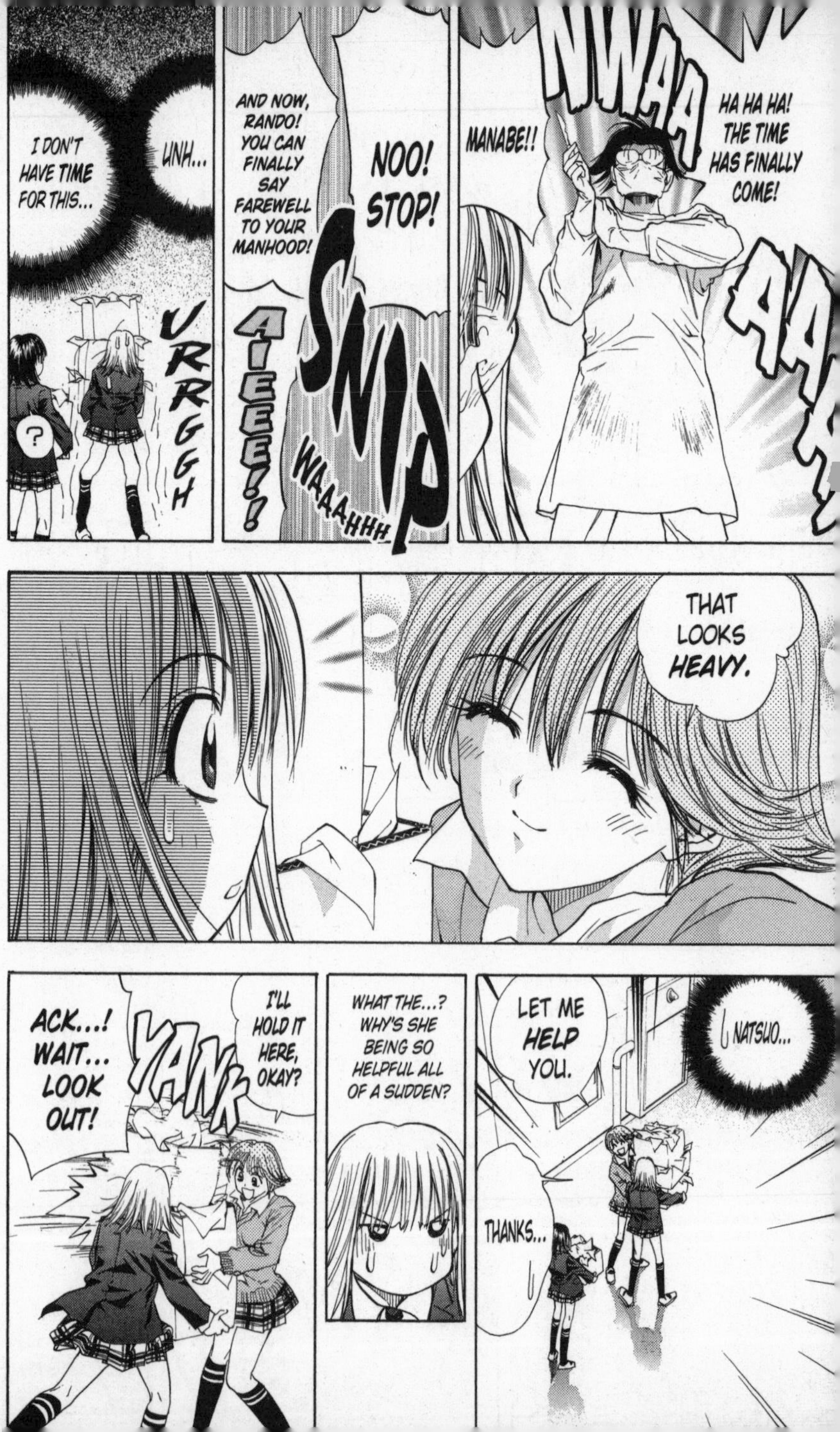
NWAA
HA HA HA! THE TIME HAS FINALLY COME!
AA
MANABE!!
NOO! STOP!
AND NOW, RANDO! YOU CAN FINALLY SAY FAREWELL TO YOUR MANHOOD!
SNIP
AIEEEE!!
WAAAAHHH
UNH...
I DON'T HAVE TIME FOR THIS...
URRGGH
?
THAT LOOKS HEAVY.
NATSUO...
LET ME HELP YOU.
THANKS...
WHAT THE...? WHY'S SHE BEING SO HELPFUL ALL OF A SUDDEN?
I'LL HOLD IT HERE, OKAY?
YANK
ACK...! WAIT... LOOK OUT!

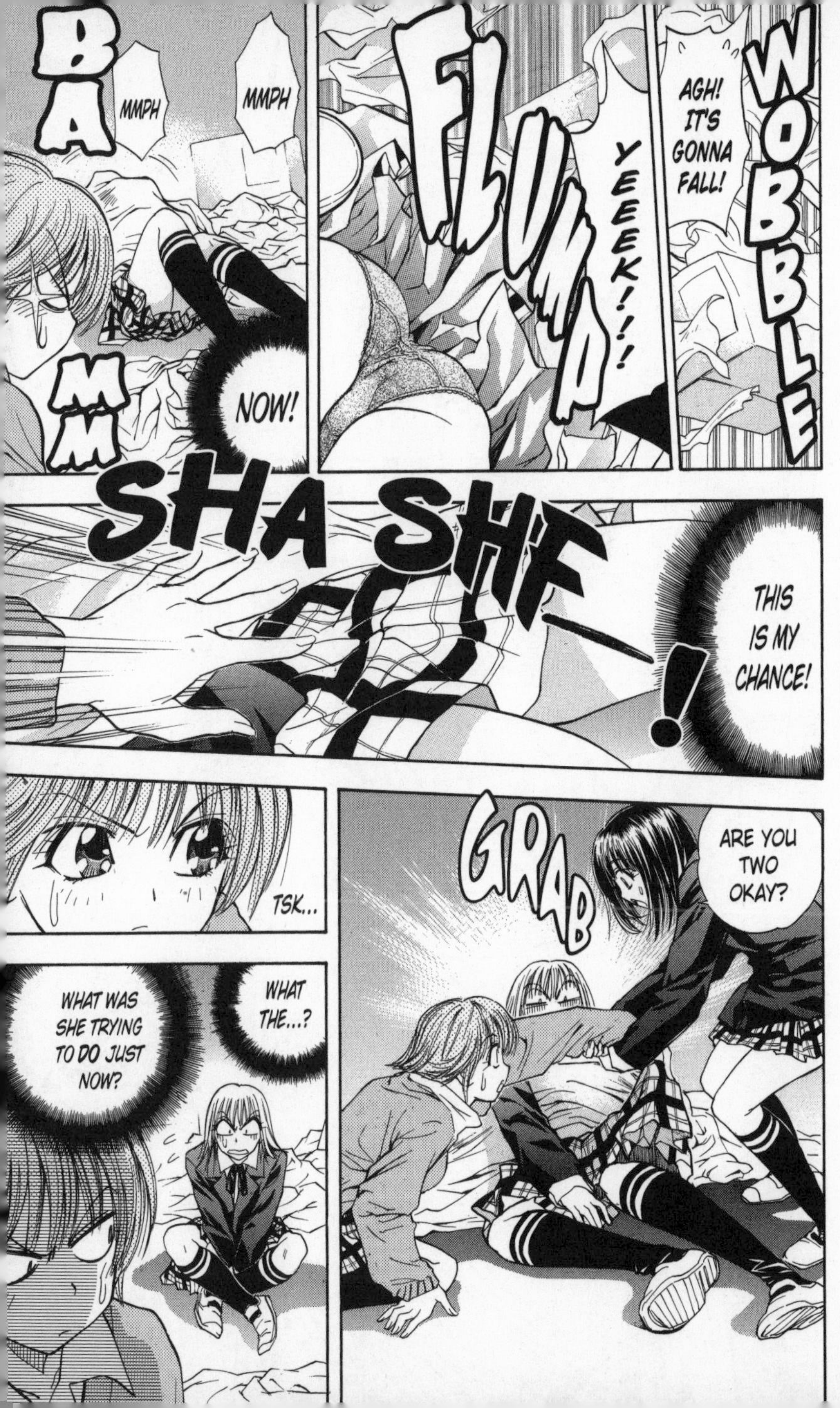
WOBBLE
AGH! IT'S GONNA FALL!
FLUMP
YEEEK!!!
MMPH
MMPH
BA
NOW!
MMM
THIS IS MY CHANCE!
SHA SHF
!
ARE YOU TWO OKAY?
GRAB
TSK...
WHAT THE...?
WHAT WAS SHE TRYING TO DO JUST NOW?

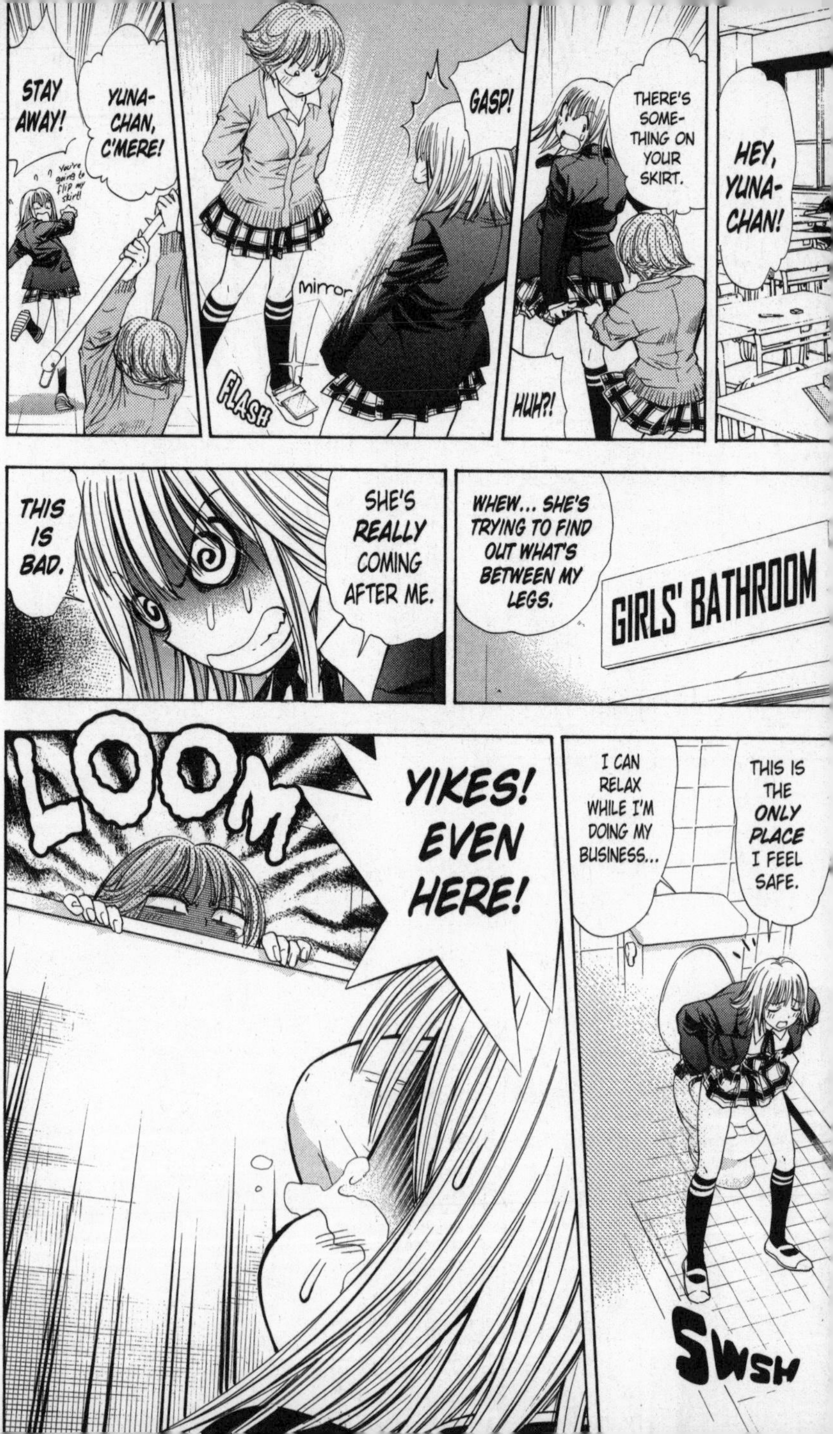
HEY, YUNA-CHAN!
THERE'S SOME-THING ON YOUR SKIRT.
HUH?!
GASP!
mirror
FLASH
YUNA-CHAN, C'MERE!
STAY AWAY!
You're going to flip my skirt!
WHEW... SHE'S TRYING TO FIND OUT WHAT'S BETWEEN MY LEGS.
GIRLS' BATHROOM
SHE'S REALLY COMING AFTER ME.
THIS IS BAD.
THIS IS THE ONLY PLACE I FEEL SAFE.
I CAN RELAX WHILE I'M DOING MY BUSINESS...
SWSH
YIKES! EVEN HERE!
LOOM

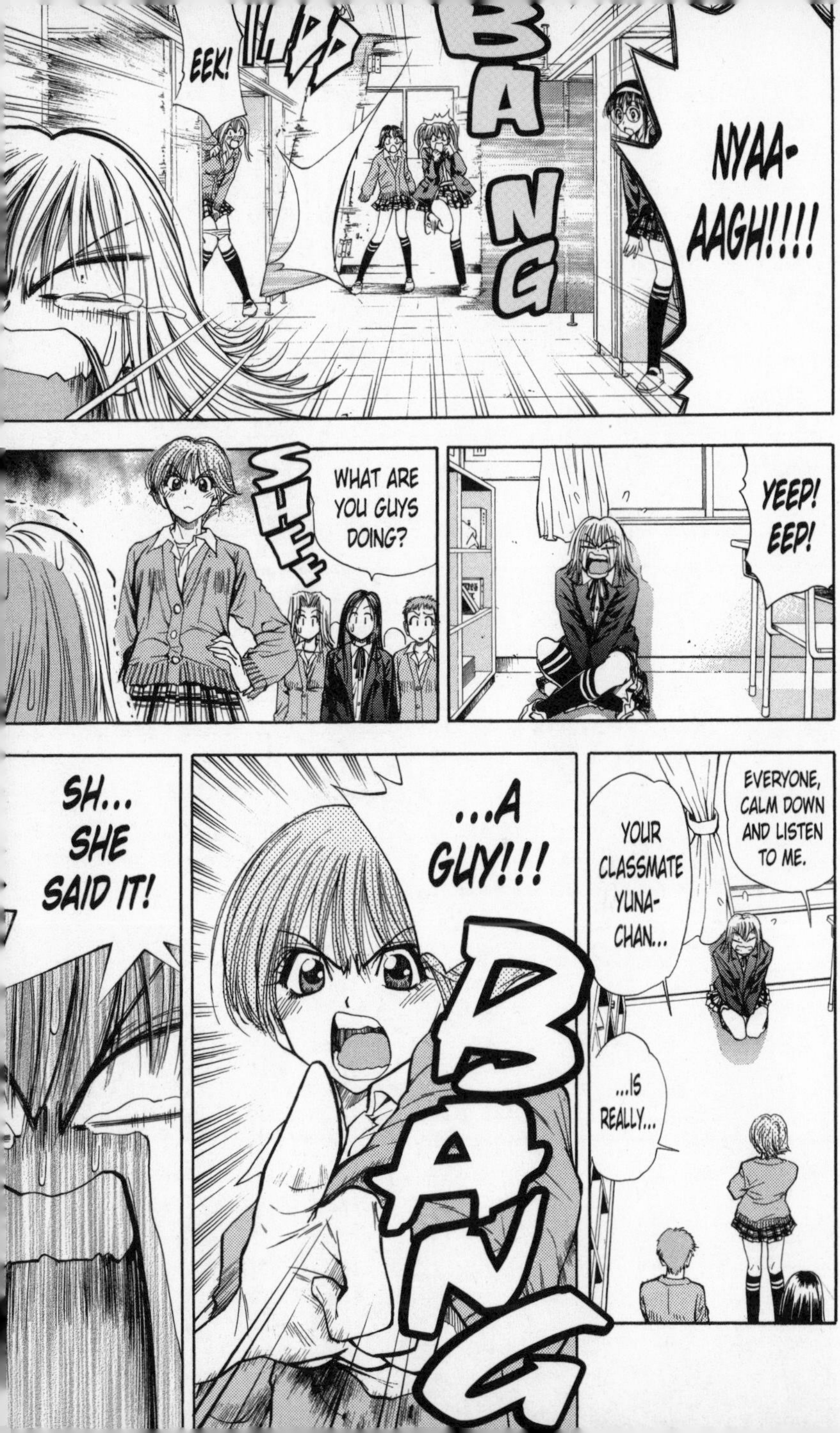
NYAA-AAGH!!!!
BANG
EEK!
YEEP! EEP!
WHAT ARE YOU GUYS DOING?
EVERYONE, CALM DOWN AND LISTEN TO ME.
YOUR CLASSMATE YUNA-CHAN...
...IS REALLY...
...A GUY!!!
BANG
SH... SHE SAID IT!

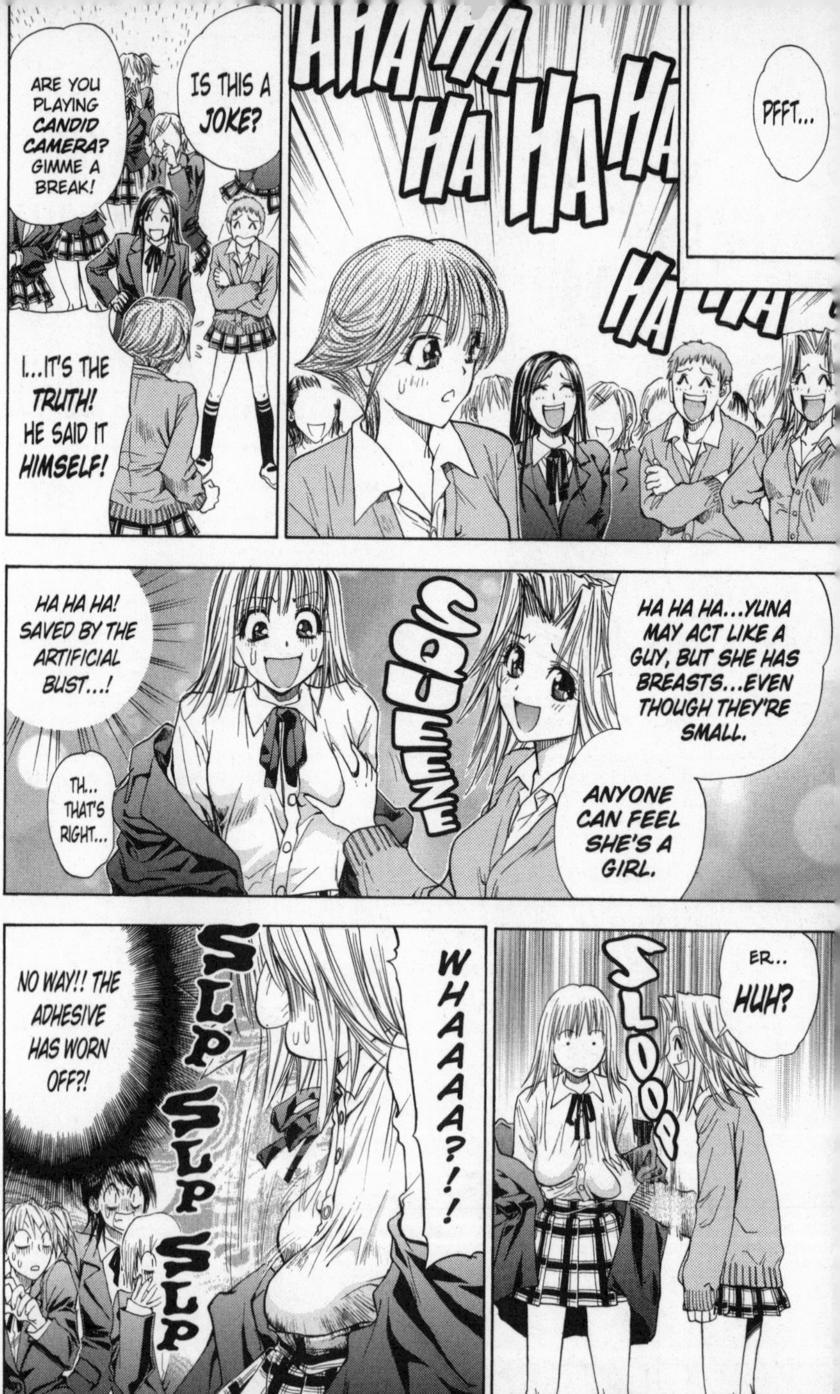
PFFT...
HA HA HA HA HA HA HA
HA HA
IS THIS A JOKE?
ARE YOU PLAYING CANDID CAMERA? GIMME A BREAK!
I...IT'S THE TRUTH! HE SAID IT HIMSELF!
HA HA HA...YUNA MAY ACT LIKE A GUY, BUT SHE HAS BREASTS...EVEN THOUGH THEY'RE SMALL.
ANYONE CAN FEEL SHE'S A GIRL.
SQUEEZE
HA HA HA! SAVED BY THE ARTIFICIAL BUST...!
TH... THAT'S RIGHT...
ER.. HUH?
SLOOP
WHAAAAA?!!
SLP SLP SLP SLP
NO WAY!! THE ADHESIVE HAS WORN OFF?!

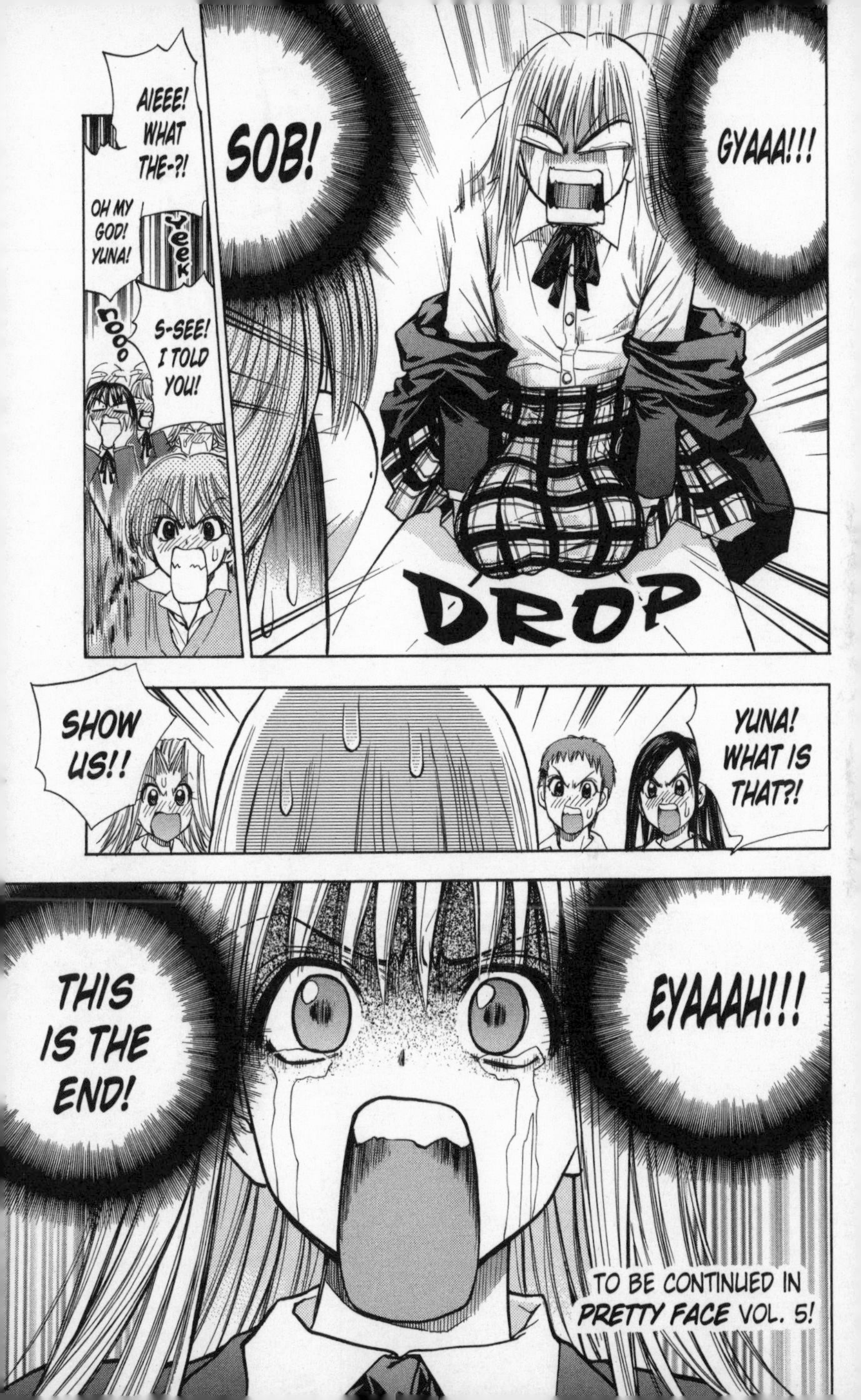
GYAAA!!!
SOB!
DROP
AIEEE! WHAT THE-?!
Yeek
OH MY GOD! YUNA!
S-SEE! I TOLD YOU!
nooo
YUNA! WHAT IS THAT?!
SHOW US!!
EYAAAH!!!
THIS IS THE END!
TO BE CONTINUED IN PRETTY FACE VOL. 5!

IN THE NEXT VOLUME...

It's over! Or is it? How can Rando's charade possibly
continue when his fake breasts fall off in front of the
entire class? What about when his pants are pulled
down? Don't believe us? Join us in two months for
Pretty Face Vol. 5: The Prison Years or, possibly, an even
weirder, more shocking plot twist!

COMING APRIL 2008!

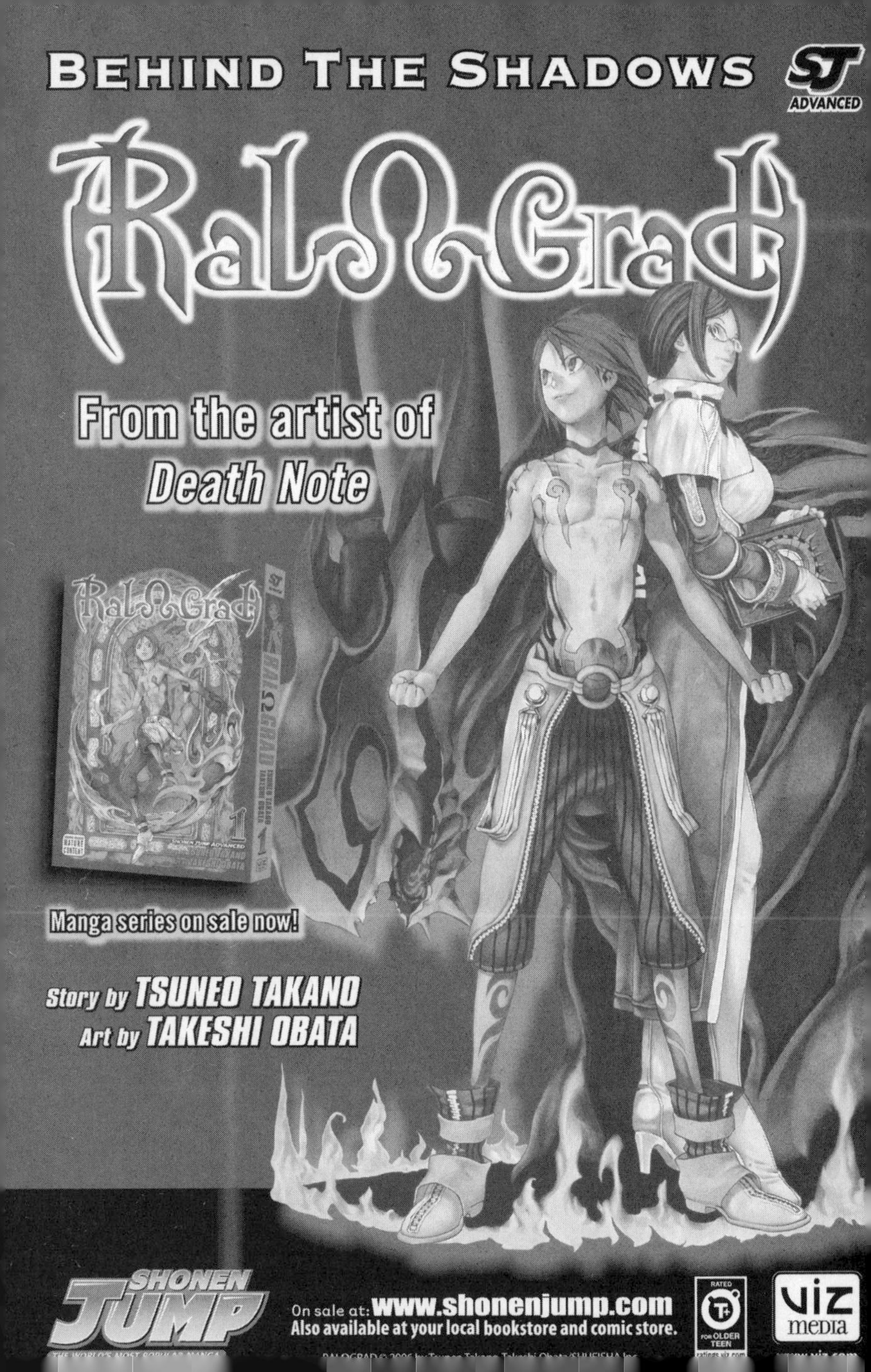
BEHIND THE SHADOWS
SJ ADVANCED
RaLΩGrad
From the artist of
Death Note
Manga series on sale now!
Story by TSUNEO TAKANO
Art by TAKESHI OBATA
SHONEN JUMP
On sale at: www.shonenjump.com
Also available at your local bookstore and comic store.
RATED T+ FOR OLDER TEEN
viz media

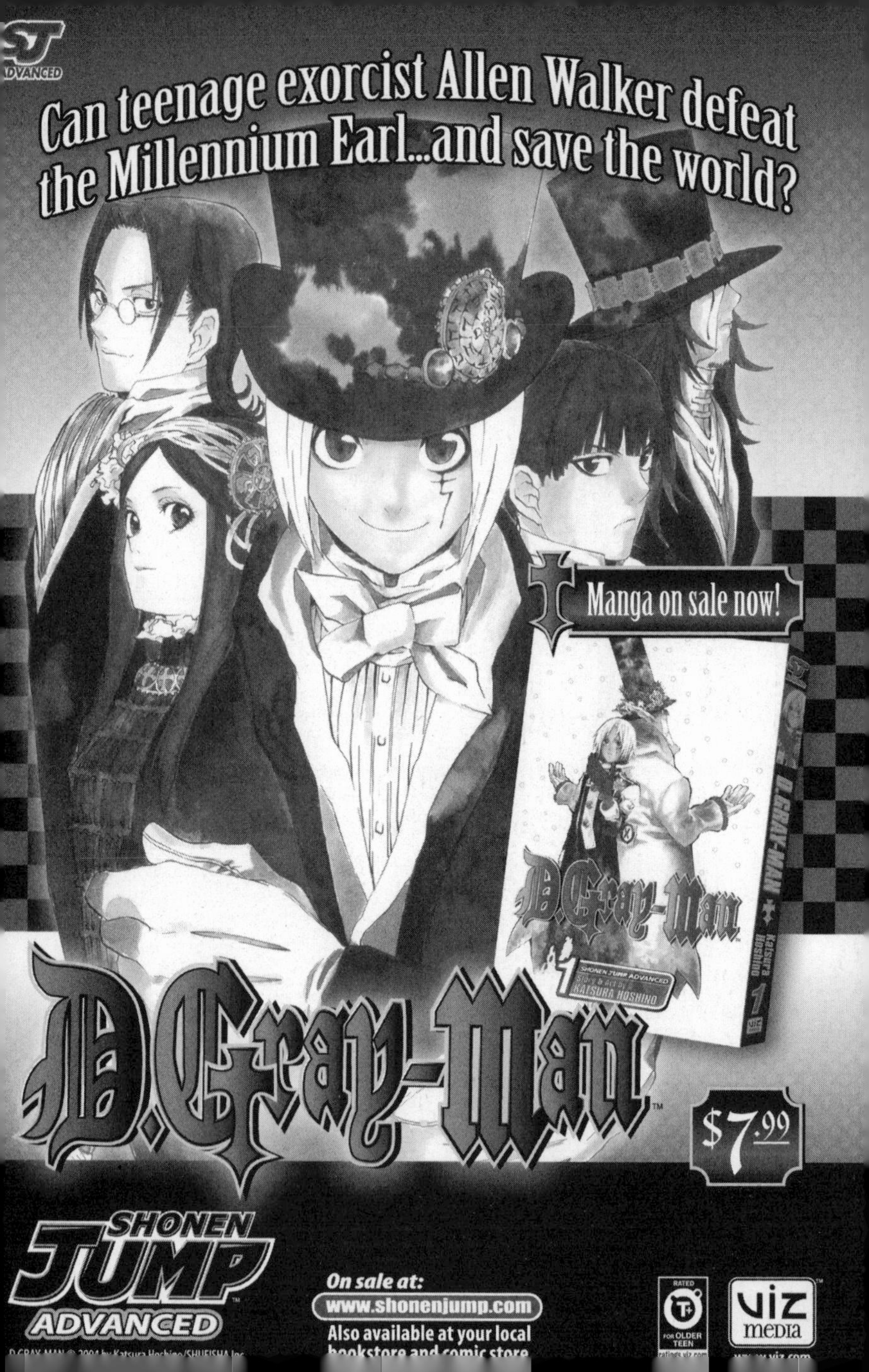

Can teenage exorcist Allen Walker defeat the Millennium Earl...and save the world?
Manga on sale now!
D.Gray-man
SHONEN JUMP ADVANCED
Story & Art by KATSURA HOSHINO
D.GRAY-MAN
Katsura Hoshino
1
D.Gray-man™
$7.99
SHONEN JUMP ADVANCED
On sale at:
www.shonenjump.com
Also available at your local bookstore and comic store
RATED T+ FOR OLDER TEEN
viz media
D.GRAY-MAN © 2004 by Katsura Hoshino/SHUEISHA Inc.

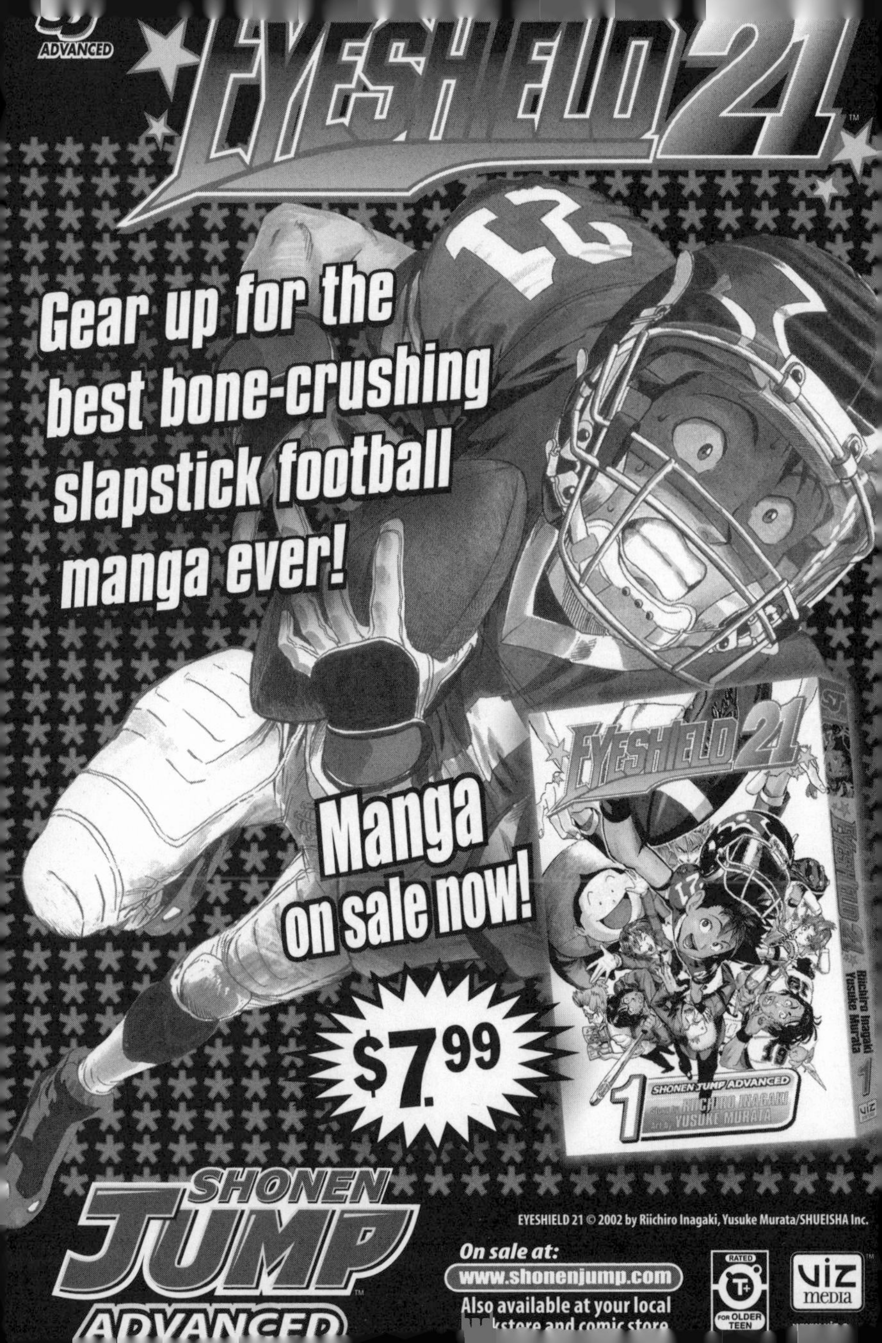
SJ ADVANCED
EYESHIELD 21™
Gear up for the best bone-crushing slapstick football manga ever!
Manga on sale now!
$7.99
EYESHIELD 21
SHONEN JUMP ADVANCED
1
SHONEN JUMP ADVANCED™
EYESHIELD 21 © 2002 by Riichiro Inagaki, Yusuke Murata/SHUEISHA Inc.
On sale at:
www.shonenjump.com
Also available at your local
RATED T+ FOR OLDER TEEN
VIZ media™

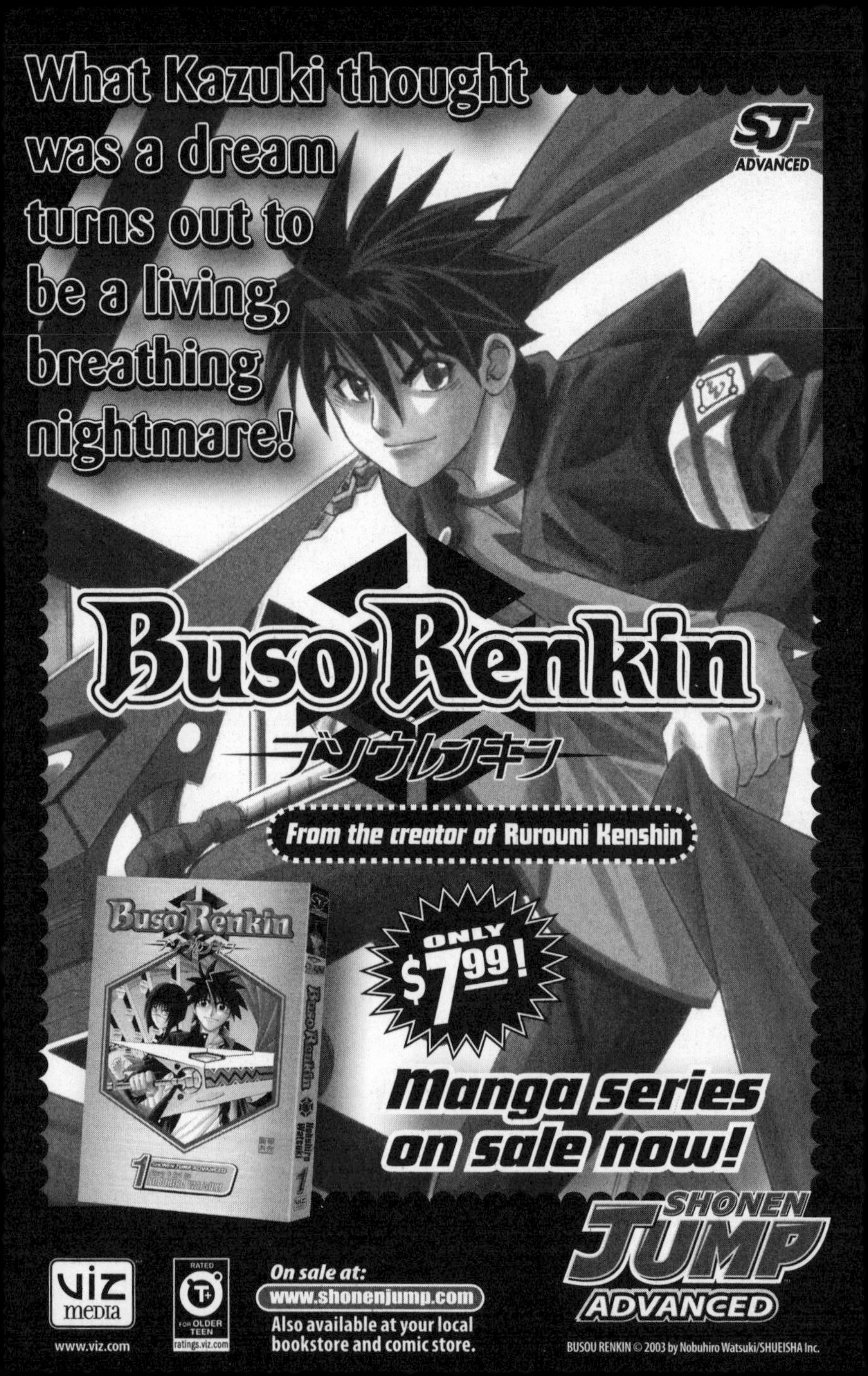

DEATH NOTE 13
デスノート
HOW TO READ

"A god of death has no obligation to completely explain how to use the note or rules which will apply to the human who owns it."

BUT FOR FANS, WE'VE CREATED *DEATH NOTE*
HOW TO READ 13—AN ULTIMATE ENCYCLOPEDIA THAT EXPLAINS IT ALL WITH:

PLUS, A BONUS MANGA CHAPTER OF NEVER-BEFORE-TRANSLATED MATERIAL!
•COMPLETE CHARACTER BIOGRAPHIES •DETAILED STORYLINE SUMMARIES •PRODUCTION NOTES •BEHIND-THE-SCENES
COMMENTARIES •EXCLUSIVE INTERVIEWS WITH CREATORS TSUGUMI OHBA AND TAKESHI OBATA

GET THE COMPLETE *DEATH NOTE* COLLECTION—BUY THE MANGA, FICTION AND ANIME TODAY!

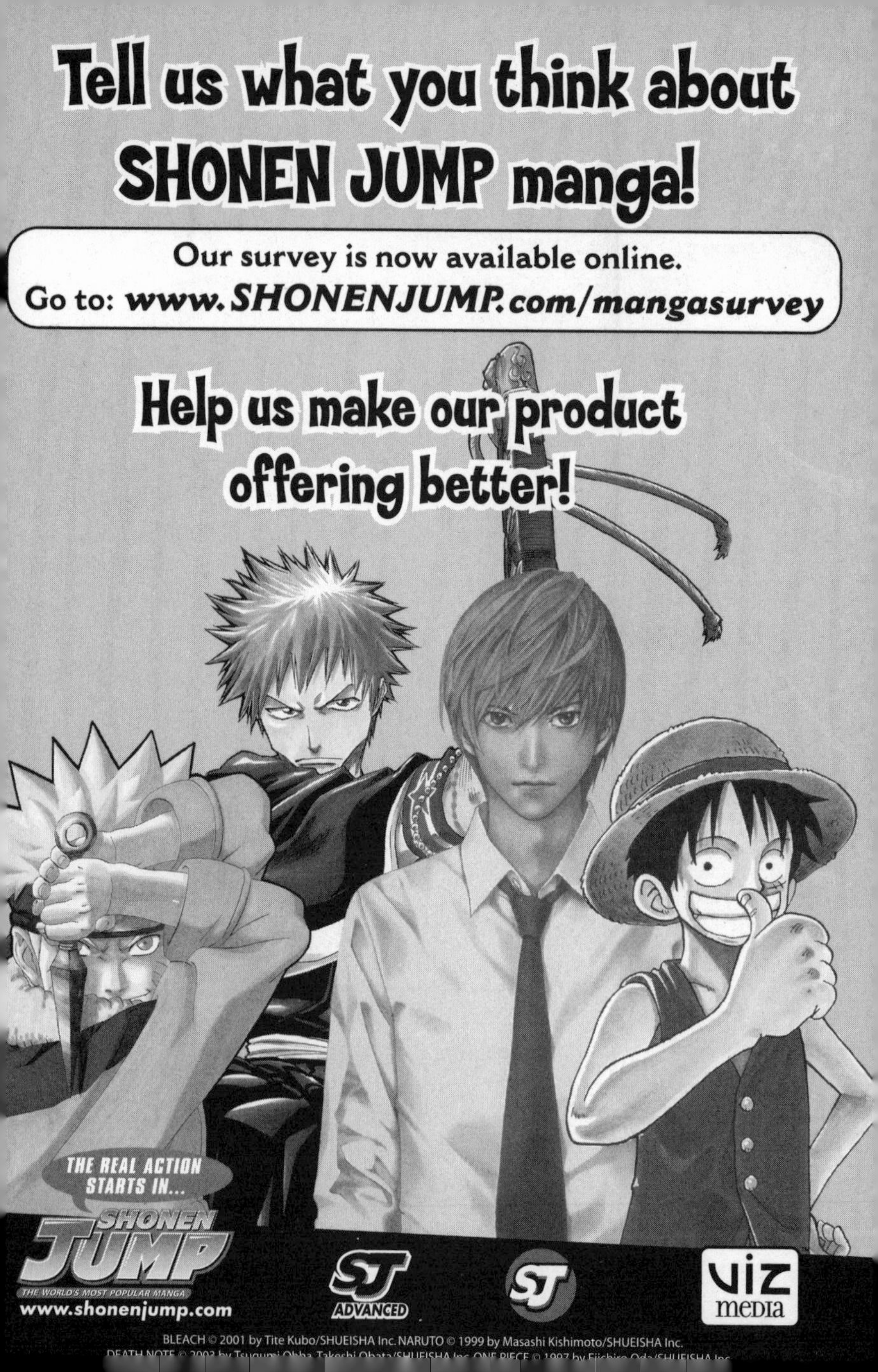
Tell us what you think about SHONEN JUMP manga!
Our survey is now available online.
Go to: www.SHONENJUMP.com/mangasurvey
Help us make our product offering better!
THE REAL ACTION STARTS IN...
SHONEN JUMP
THE WORLD'S MOST POPULAR MANGA
www.shonenjump.com
SJ ADVANCED
SJ
VIZ MEDIA
BLEACH © 2001 by Tite Kubo/SHUEISHA Inc. NARUTO © 1999 by Masashi Kishimoto/SHUEISHA Inc.
DEATH NOTE © 2003 by Tsugumi Ohba, Takeshi Obata/SHUEISHA Inc. ONE PIECE © 1997 by Eiichiro Oda/SHUEISHA Inc.